KANDIS WILLIAMS: A SURFACE

EDITED BY
TAYLOR
JASPER

WALKER
ART
CENTER

WITH CONTRIBUTIONS BY

DENISE FERREIRA DA SILVA

CHERYL I. HARRIS

MIREILLE MILLER-YOUNG

DENISE RYNER

MLONDOLOZI ZONDI

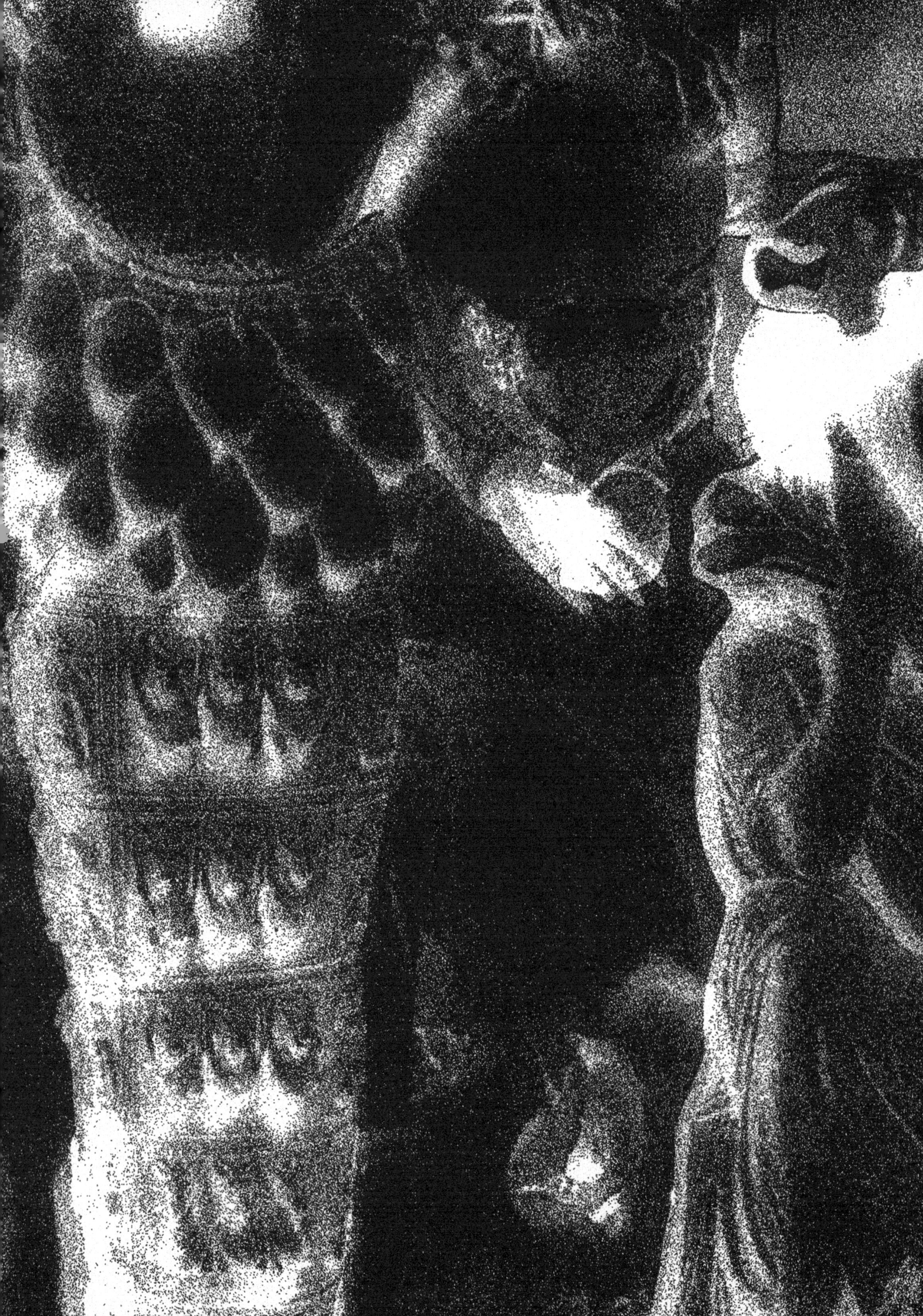

CONTENTS

FOREWORD

The Walker Art Center is extremely proud to present *Kandis Williams: A Surface*, the Berlin-based American artist's first survey exhibition in the United States, and to produce this accompanying catalogue. Williams's multidisciplinary approach engages deeply with themes of race, gender, power, and the body. At a time when questions of identity and social justice are at the forefront of public discourse, Williams challenges us to actively question the images we consume, the narratives we accept, and the structures of power that shape our personal and collective realities. Her work is a potent reminder that art can be a tool for both reflection and action—a means of confronting uncomfortable truths and imagining new possibilities.

Kandis Williams: A Surface was organized by Taylor Jasper, Susan and Rob White Assistant Curator, Visual Arts, in close dialogue with the artist, and expertly supported by Laurel Rand-Lewis, curatorial fellow, visual arts. I applaud Taylor for her visionary approach in shaping the exhibition, skillfully weaving together the artist's bold interrogations within a curatorial framework that invites deep reflection and engagement, as well as for her astute contribution to this book. We are grateful to the institutions and individuals who generously lent works to the exhibition, listed on page 282, and to Williams's galleries, Galerie Hubert Winter, Vienna, and Heidi, Berlin. Our deep appreciation goes to the exhibition's patrons, including the Edward R. Bazinet Charitable Foundation for its long-standing support of early career artist projects; Charlie Pohlad and the Pohlad Family for their early commitment to this project; and Rosina Lee Yue for her support of the production of this publication. I also want to acknowledge the Andrew W. Mellon Foundation for its support of Walker publications.

I thank the Walker's Board of Trustees, listed on page 284, who are central in buttressing the vision of our institution. I also am grateful for the guidance of the Walker's senior leadership team: Aslı Altay, head of design, content, and communications; Kim Hollingsworth Taylor, chief financial officer; Henriette Huldisch, chief curator and director of curatorial affairs; Amanda Hunt, head of public engagement, learning, and impact; Jaidyn Martin, director of human resources; Felice Clark, director of business development; Keith Parker, director of operations; and Christopher Stevens, chief of advancement. I join Taylor in thanking those listed in her acknowledgments, which follow, and the many dedicated staff members at the Walker who have made this exhibition and publication possible.

I extend our warmest thanks to Kandis Williams for her steadfast commitment to the exhibition. We are immensely grateful for her deep engagement in the curatorial process, her dedication, and her generosity.

Mary Ceruti
Executive Director

ACKNOWLEDGMENTS

First and foremost, I extend my deepest gratitude to Kandis Williams, whose rigorous, boundary-pushing, and profoundly generative practice is the subject of this exhibition and catalogue.

I have been engaged with her practice since first encountering her exhibition *A Field* at the Institute for Contemporary Art at Virginia Commonwealth University in 2020. The site-responsive installation explored the entrenched narratives of agricultural labor, horticulture, and Blackness. In a display of collage, video, and sculpture that entangled plant life and Black bodies, the artist identified the similarities of subjugation and control between incarcerated people on Virginia prison farms and the crops they cultivated. I was immediately captivated by the potency of Williams's meticulously compiled collages and the rigor of her research-based practice. In 2021, while part of the curatorial team at the Momentary in Bentonville, Arkansas, I invited Williams for a weeklong research visit, during which we spent time together in regional archives and special collections, poring over images and historical records of anti-Black violence. Participating in and bearing witness to Williams's research process was transformative. It introduced me to the acute sensitivities and nuances of the complex relationships between contemporary art and its enabling institutions, and encouraged me to boldly engage with issues of care, authorship, conflict, and reconciliation within the context of the work I do with museums, galleries, and artist-driven spaces.

Upon my arrival at the Walker Art Center in January 2023, I proposed Williams as an artist of interest, and the exhibition began to develop into a midcareer survey. *Kandis Williams: A Surface* presents a decade of Williams's practice, showcasing both acclaimed and lesser-known works. Her multidisciplinary approach—spanning video, collage, installation, and publishing—reminds us of the interconnectedness of our bodies, our histories, and the broader structures that shape our existence, while creating new avenues and counternarratives that imagine how we might live differently. I am grateful to Kandis for her trust, generosity, and diligence throughout the process of bringing *A Surface* to fruition.

In the realization of this project, I am thankful for the partnership and assistance of the artist's gallerists: Pauline Seguin, owner, Heidi, Berlin; and Natascha Burger, senior director, Galerie Hubert Winter, Vienna. I join our executive director, Mary Ceruti, in expressing appreciation to the lenders to the exhibition and to the funders who made the exhibition and this publication possible.

At the Walker Art Center, I extend my heartfelt thanks to the many talented and passionate individuals who have contributed to this endeavor. My appreciation goes to Mary Ceruti for her steadfast leadership and for believing in this project. To my colleagues in the visual arts department—Henriette Huldisch, chief curator and director of curatorial affairs; Siri Engberg, senior curator and director, visual arts; Pavel Pyś, curator of visual arts and collection strategy; and Rosario Güiraldes, curator, visual arts—thank you for your thoughtful insights, guidance, and collaborative spirit throughout the development and realization of this exhibition. I am indebted to and grateful for the unwavering support of curatorial fellow Laurel Rand-Lewis, who brought great attentiveness and diligence to this project. A special thank-you to the exhibition's registrar, Kayla Nordlund, and head technician, Jonathan Karen, who oversaw the show's implementation with precision and care. I am indebted to the Walker's stellar exhibition installation team—Doc Czypinski, Kirk McCall, Peter Murphy, Joel Schwarz, and Jeffrey Sherman, among many others—whose unparalleled attention to detail and commitment to every artist we work with make the Walker's exhibitions so special. I am also thankful for the guidance of Joe King, director of collections and exhibition management, and Sarah Lampen, associate director of learning and accessibility, for ensuring that our visitors can safely and meaningfully engage with the exhibition.

It is an honor to bring about this first comprehensive publication on Williams's work, which was so thoughtfully designed by the Walker's senior designer, Nazlı Ercan. Her dedication to making every page speak to the artist's vision is deeply appreciated. I am indebted to Denise Ryner, Andrea B. Laporte Curator at the Institute of Contemporary Art, Philadelphia, whose essay in this volume expands upon and complicates the discussions that Williams's work provokes. Her intellectual generosity elevates this publication and contributes to the broader conversations that this exhibition hopes to inspire. Complementing the essays in this book are reprinted texts by Denise Ferreira da Silva, Cheryl I. Harris, Mireille Miller-Young, and Mlondolozi Zondi that provide insightful theoretical frameworks. The publication benefited from the crucial feedback of editor Michelle Piranio; the guidance of the Walker's director of design, Mark Owens; and the tenacity of the Walker's publications manager, Jake Yuzna, who kept us on track toward a timely completion. I am also deeply grateful to the artists, scholars, and cultural workers who contributed their time and knowledge to this project, either directly or through their wider impact on Williams's work.

Our exhibitions are realized because of the diligence and management of every detail, including contracts, travel arrangements, and the organization of opening-day activities, under the watchful eye of Erin McNeil, manager of curatorial affairs; Hania Imdad, department coordinator, curatorial affairs; and Lena Menefee-Cook, department coordinator, visual arts. I am grateful to Christopher Stevens, chief of advancement, and Marla Stack, director of major giving and institutional relations, for their tireless efforts, as well as to Janine DeFeo, manager of interpretation, for partnering with us on developing interpretation for this exhibition. My appreciation goes to Aslı Altay, head of design, content, and communications, and Rachel Joyce, assistant director of public relations, for sharing the exhibition with audiences in the Twin Cities as well as nationally and internationally.

Finally, I extend my deep gratitude to a number of individuals whose influence and encouragement have profoundly shaped my personal and professional journey. To Julie Noyes, my elementary school art teacher, whose classroom first ignited my passion for art and instilled an enduring love for creative exploration. To Jacquelyn Y. McLendon, professor emerita of English and Africana studies and director emerita of Black studies at the College of William & Mary, for nurturing my writing and growth as a thinker. Thank you to my brother, Justin, my lifelong friend and the Batman to my Robin, for always having my back. To my parents, Amy and Keith Jasper, for their relentless dedication to fostering my creative pursuits and inclinations, and giving me the confidence to believe I could do anything. And to my wife, Alexis, whose steadfast support has been a constant source of strength and inspiration. Her belief in me and this work has made all the difference, and for that I am endlessly grateful.

Taylor Jasper
Susan and Rob White
Assistant Curator, Visual Arts

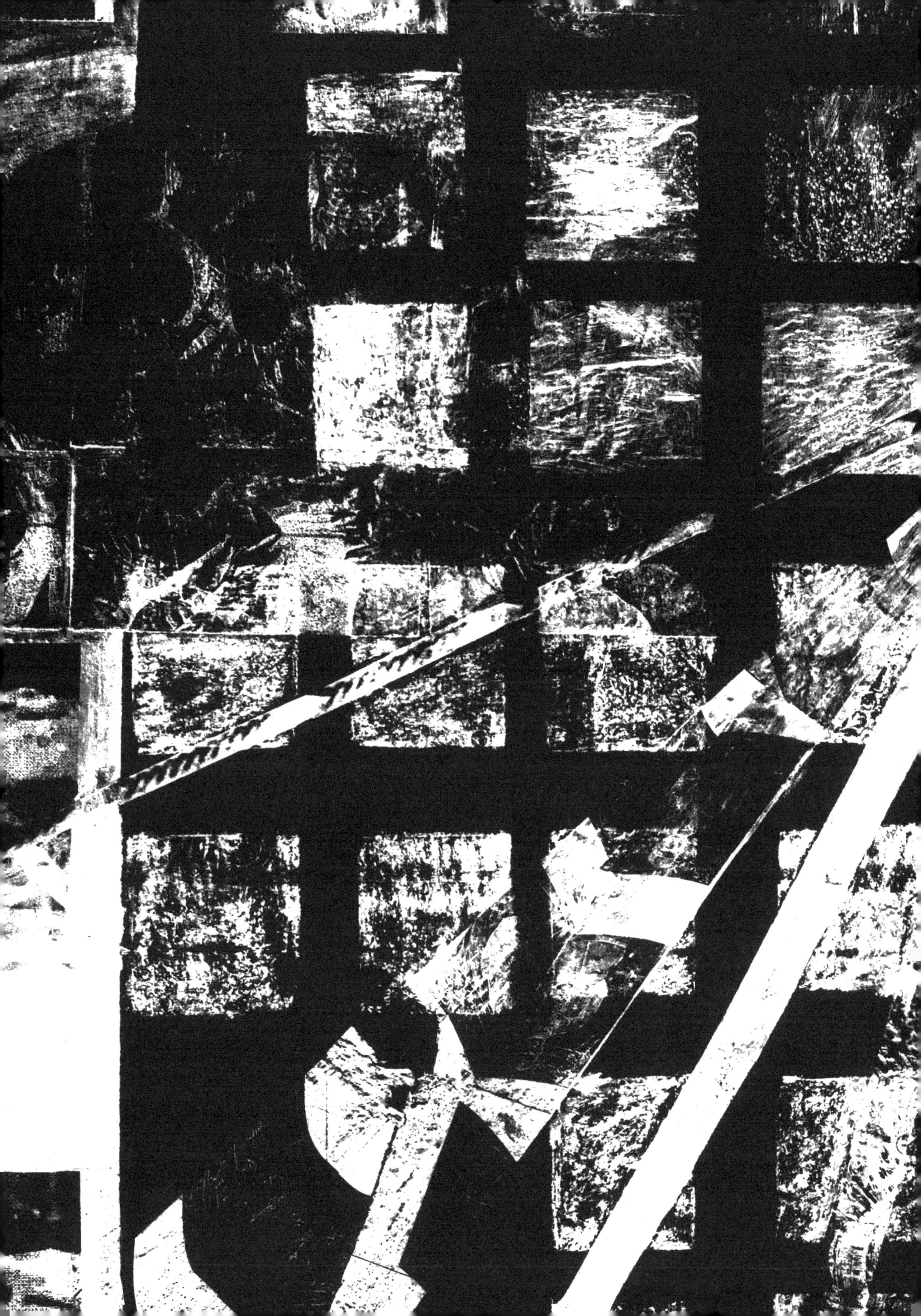

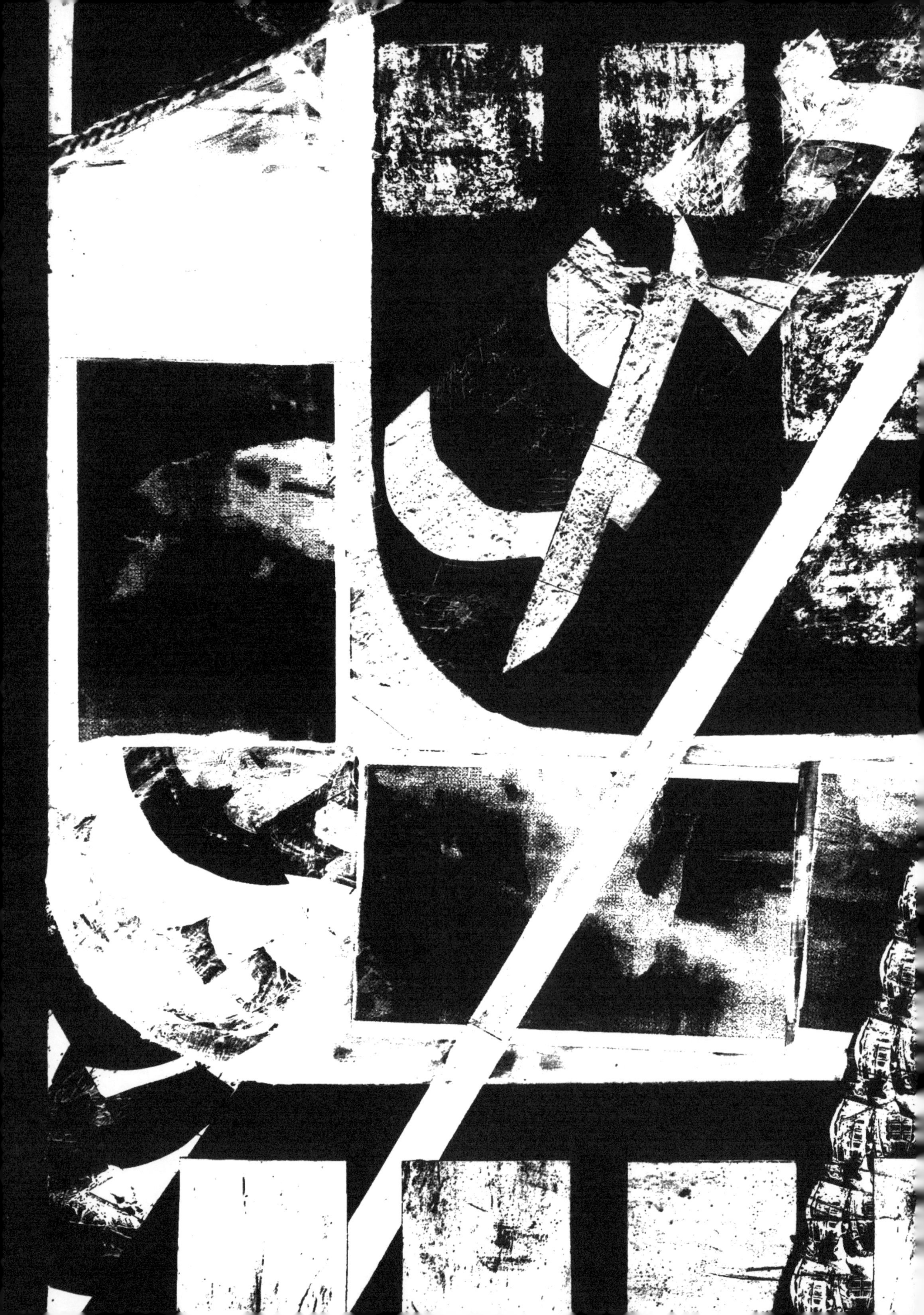

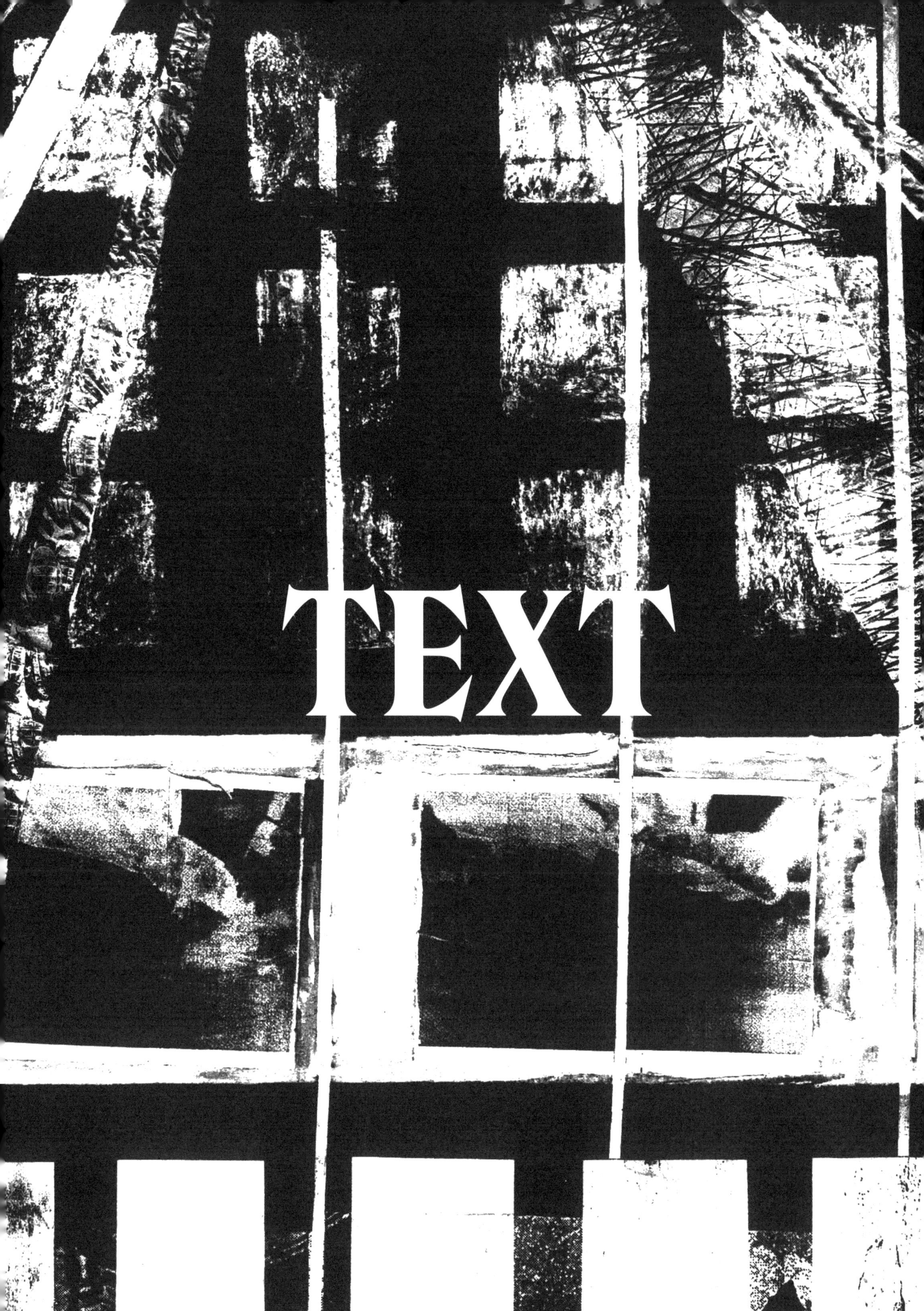
TEXT

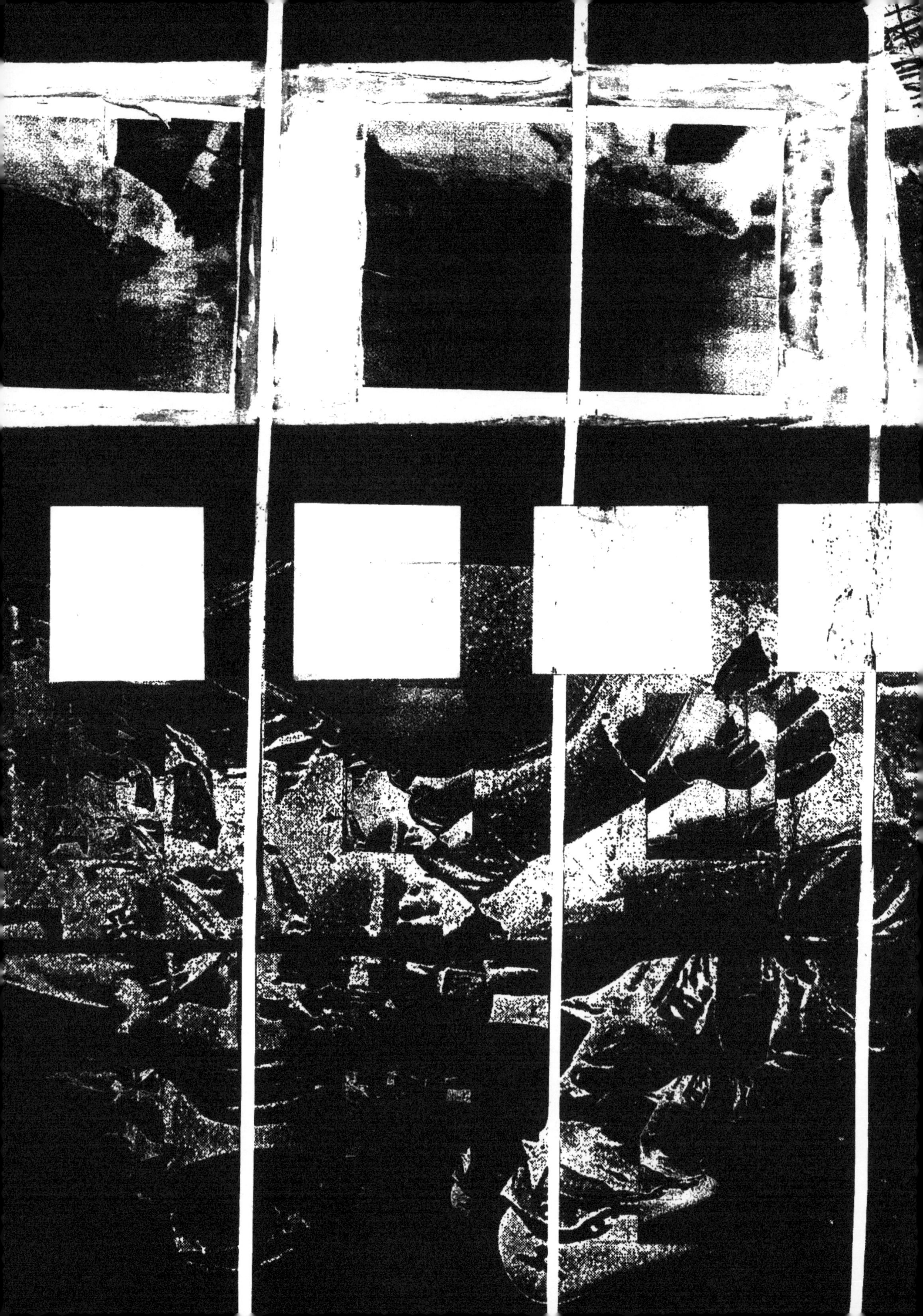

A METHOD

TAYLOR JASPER

A METHOD
by Taylor Jasper

Over the last decade, Kandis Williams's multidisciplinary practice has been marked by a persistent engagement with the politics of representation, labor, and the body. Her work challenges us to consider and reconsider the ways in which Black bodies have been dispossessed, displaced, disciplined, and commodified throughout history, while also offering visual counternarratives that reclaim agency and autonomy. Across video, film, sculpture, installation, and works on paper, Williams interrogates the power dynamics that shape our perceptions of race and identity. Her distinct collage method challenges monolithic visual culture to reconcile histories of erasure, oppression, and colonization.

Collage is the conceptual connective tissue throughout Williams's oeuvre, functioning as both technique and method. In her works, the surface—as a physical and a conceptual space—acts as a site for unraveling systems of dominance, subordination, oppression, and disenfranchisement. Engaging with the surface as more than just a plane for imagery, she uses collage to layer, disrupt, and fragment, visually representing the dismantling of oppressive structures. The acts of cutting, pasting, and reassembling become symbolic of dissecting entrenched ideologies and power dynamics, revealing the hidden mechanisms that sustain them. In this way, the surface becomes a charged space of critique, where the complexities of social hierarchies are exposed, questioned, and reframed. By reframing the visual archive as both a tool and a site of resistance, collage reveals the dynamic interplay between storytelling, history, and pedagogy to demonstrate how meaningful ruptures to a uniform visual code are also crucial opportunities for innovation, transformation, and even revolution.

Williams's collages examine the power and privilege that art history, mass media, the archive, and constructions of identity hold, and counternarrative is a useful lens to understand the types of critiques they engender. Arising from the vantage point of those who have been historically marginalized, counternarratives serve to critique dominant knowledge and linear temporality to instead visualize other models for recounting history outside of both temporal and spatial norms. In doing so, counternarratives become a way of displacing and moving aside what has been deemed the ideological "center," such as the Western canon of art history. Questioning and reconstructing these popular notions, counternarratives shift this "center" as a form of resistance against traditional modes of domination to situate radical imaginings in their histories. They fill a need for stories that match one's own experiences of self, particularly those that are at odds with socially constrained dominant narratives.[1]

Collage challenges qualities of aesthetic realism through the fragmentation, layering, and juxtaposition of disparate images and mediums, and thus the reading of a collage requires an expansive perspective that understands the artwork to be, fundamentally, a dialogue. Because the materials of a collage are often distinct and diverse, this multidisciplinary approach introduces new forms of engagement with images, ideas, and objects that have been included or contextualized within the art historical canon. Collage therefore introduces a whole new array of material and conceptual considerations both within and outside of the context of art. In the case of Williams's practice, psychological, sociological, and political perspectives informed by critical theory, postcolonial theory, and intersectional Black feminist theory are foundational, speaking to a similarly fragmented and nonlinear understanding of identity and relations that collage has the demonstrated capacity to illustrate.

Though collage has a continuous history from the early twentieth century on, Williams is drawn to generative moments when the medium was used to disrupt linear narratives, fragment dominant ideologies, and articulate new political or social possibilities. From the Eurocentric perspective that has largely dominated the history of collage, Cubism, Dadaism, and Surrealism are acknowledged as the three modernist movements that challenged the status quo of art making. Artists such as Georges

1 Farah Godrej, "Spaces for Counter-Narratives: The Phenomenology of Reclamation," *Frontiers: A Journal of Women Studies* 32, no. 3 (2011): 111–133.

Braque and Pablo Picasso in Paris at the dawn of the twentieth century and Hannah Höch and Raoul Hausmann in Germany in the 1920s used collage and photomontage to address social conditions as subject matter. These movements continue to be regarded as vital forces in contemporary culture that helped catalyze modernist tendencies, opening up new ways of seeing and understanding contemporary life from the early twentieth century onward. At the same time in North America, artists throughout the Harlem Renaissance adopted the form and sensibilities of collage to articulate national Black cultural identity and international modernism. Through this, they demonstrated how analogies, juxtapositions, and other aesthetic frictions have historical and political implications.[2] By merging African traditions with Western modernist techniques, these artists used collage to visually assert Black identity and agency in the face of systemic racism and exclusion. The layered, fragmented nature of collage allowed them to break from traditional linear modes of representation, creating a space for multiple narratives to coexist and to challenge dominant ideologies. Figures like Romare Bearden, Aaron Douglas, and Faith Ringgold deployed collage's disjunctive elements to symbolize the complexities of Black life, weaving together cultural memory, diasporic heritage, and contemporary experience. In doing so, they engaged in a form of visual activism, reimagining Black histories and futures in ways that contested racialized narratives and situated Black art within the broader currents of global modernism. The medium became not only a formal innovation but also a vital tool in the fight for cultural and political recognition.

With two world wars and an ongoing civil rights fight for freedom, the impulse that drove the creation of collage as a combinatory technique arrived through multiple points of entry into a hybrid and multiracial world. Over the course of the twentieth century, artists turned to collage for its capacity to address personal, social, and political experiences and critiques at once. In this context, collage offered new opportunities for uncovering relationships, oppositions, transitions, and intersections of social

2 Rachel Farebrother, *The Collage Aesthetic in the Harlem Renaissance* (Abingdon, Oxon: Routledge, 2016).

reality, using tangible materials of that reality as the instruments for critique.

Williams's engagement with collage as a critical practice reflects her deep interest in how fragmented images and texts can disassemble entrenched power structures, especially those related to race, gender, and representation. For her, collage is not merely a technique but a radical form of reassembly—a way to present complex, layered truths that challenge the viewer's perception of reality. Her work often incorporates found images, historical references, and the body itself to create densely layered compositions that evoke histories of oppression while simultaneously imagining liberatory futures. In doing so, she taps into the medium's capacity for resistance and renewal, making it a powerful means for examining the present through the lens of past disruptions and future potentials.

As a pedagogical tool and a strategy of resistance, collage is unprecedented as a medium. It is directly informed by the very politics and oppressive social structures that underlie many of the most popular distributions of media on a widespread scale. The radical act of cutting up these material objects and the ideas they represent reinstates the artist with a degree of agency over cultural narratives, creating the space for critique and setting the record "straight" through purposeful juxtaposition. By employing and updating methodologies presented by Dada, Surrealist, Cubist, and Harlem Renaissance artists and others, Williams builds on an ever-expanding definition of collage that goes beyond critique and instead folds in the radical implications of counternarratives to restructure cultural narratives, challenge the inherent supremacy of the archive, and mend perceived gaps in cultural knowledge.

Williams's practice is intricately woven with critical theories of race, gender, and power, drawing from a range of intellectual traditions, particularly the writings of Michel Foucault, Hortense J. Spillers, Sylvia Wynter, Cheryl I. Harris, and Denise Ferreira da Silva. Foucault's concept of biopolitics—the idea that

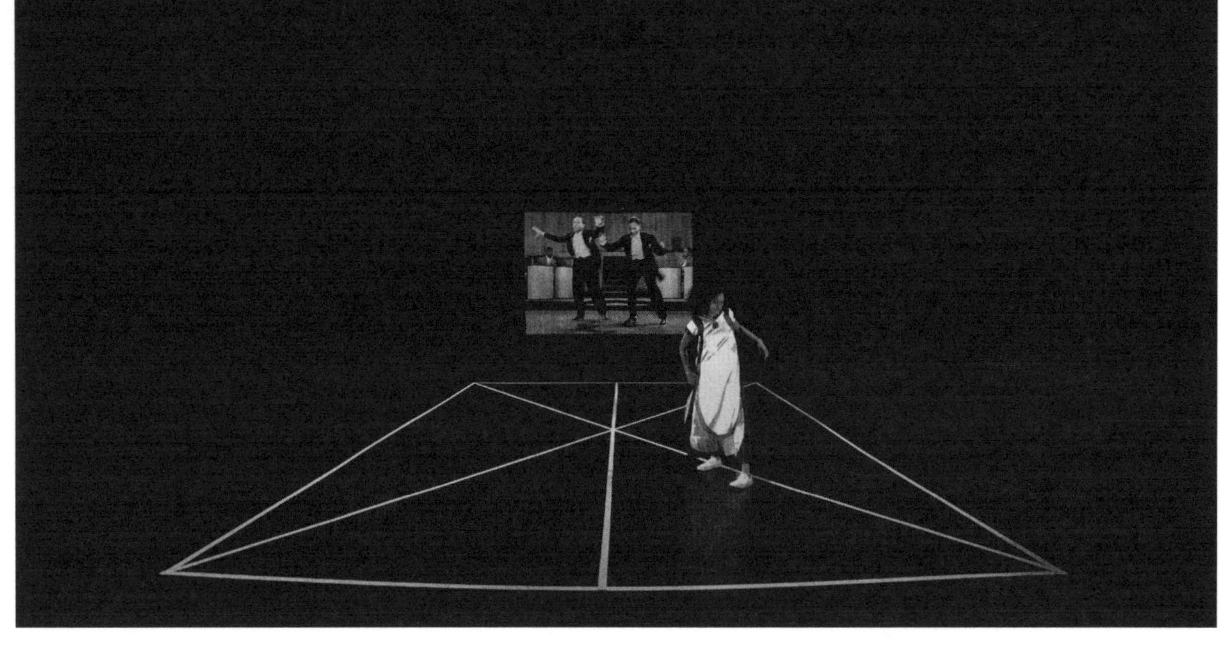

Fig. 1 Kandis Williams, *Triadic Ballet*, 2021 (video still) (pages 156–161)

power extends into the control of bodies and populations—is a crucial framework for understanding Williams's exploration of how Black bodies have been regulated, policed, and surveilled throughout history.[3] She directly engages with the ways in which state violence and systemic racism manifest in the lived experiences of Black individuals, confronting the viewer with the realities of carceral logic, surveillance, and the commodification of labor. *Triadic Ballet* (2021), for example, delves into the intersections of choreography, power, and systemic control, drawing an analogy between the structuring of bodies in dance and the physical discipline found in systems of political oppression, such as prisons and military institutions (fig. 1). Though Williams's work references Oskar Schlemmer's iconic 1922 dance piece of the same name, she does not attempt to replicate it. Instead, she recontextualizes the original within a contemporary framework that critiques how Black bodies, in particular, have been subjected to regimentation and exploitation throughout history. In this work, Williams interrogates how choreography mirrors societal methods of organizing and controlling bodies, even in spaces that appear to celebrate self-expression, such as dance.

3 Michel Foucault, *The Birth of Biopolitics: Lectures at the Collège de France, 1978–1979*, ed. Michel Senellart, trans. Graham Burchell (New York: Palgrave Macmillan, 2008).

Triadic Ballet features a single woman dancing atop a black floor marked with a white square segmented into six triangles, which both guide and restrict her movements. The geometry of the floor, with its strict divisions, serves on the one hand as a formal device through which Williams explores the tensions between freedom and constraint in movement and on the other hand as a metaphor for the external forces—societal, racial, and institutional—that seek to confine and shape Black bodies. Acting as both choreographer and visual artist, Williams constructed the visual space and dictated the dancer's movements through the imposed structure of geometric shapes. This juxtaposition between the rigid precision of the geometric environment and the expressive potential of dance not only reflects a deeper tension between autonomy and control but also underscores how Black performers, historically subjected to the scrutiny of audiences and institutions, evoke broader histories of surveillance, racialized violence, and systemic oppression, whereby Black bodies have been policed and regulated in both public and private spaces alike. Yet, even within these constraints, the dancer's movements carry a potential for resistance and liberation. Williams complicates the narrative of subjugation, illustrating how, within repressive structures, Black bodies can carve out spaces for survival, self-expression, and resilience, challenging viewers to consider how these dynamics of control persist across various contexts.

In creating *Triadic Ballet* and its accompanying collages, Williams worked intimately with Black dancers in her studio to develop a choreography that interrogated the intersections of form, body, and identity. Bringing the dancers into a collaborative space, Williams initiated conversations around the shapes and forms their bodies naturally assumed, as well as the dance techniques in which they were versed. These discussions revealed the complex dynamics Black dancers often face within the dance world, where certain phenotypic traits are seen as predisposing them to specific roles or positions. Together, they explored how these dancers' bodies navigate particular attitudes and techniques, considering how each movement felt to them physically and the implications of embodying these forms.[4] Williams was intentional in choreographing movements that challenged stereotypical notions about the Black body while also celebrating its versatility and strength. She constructed sequences in which each dancer's movements were a precise, deliberate set of actions that began, transformed, and concluded in a smooth arc. Her choreography drew from a wide array of vernacular dance styles, blending forms such as elements of the Native American Buffalo Dance with jazz motifs and yoga's tree pose. Drawing on the Martha Graham training of her lead dancer, Natasha Diamond-Walker, Williams created a hybrid choreography that is both concise and layered, collapsing historical and contemporary dance traditions. In this way, Williams not only highlighted the specificity and adaptability of Black dancers but also offered a commentary on the broader conversations within dance about race, body politics, and movement as a form of resistance.

Behind the dancer, a screen displays a series of contrasting clips, including footage of the Nicholas Brothers' energetic tap dancing from the 1940s, a military parade, Janet Jackson's iconic "Rhythm Nation" video of 1989, and the notorious 1991 footage of Los Angeles police officers beating Rodney King. Williams's juxtaposition of these visuals suggests that dancing bodies—particularly those of Black performers—are subject to the same controlling forces as bodies in other repressive contexts. Choreography, like other systems of control, dictates how and where dancers move, rendering their movements subject to external forces, even as they appear fluid and free in the final performance.

The collages related to *Triadic Ballet* further develop Williams's critique, illustrating how choreography and discipline are intertwined in visual form. In *A Lift and a Kick conflated* (2021; page 177), cutouts of dancers from magazines, dance books, and her own studio photography are arranged to create clusters that overlap yet remain carefully orchestrated. *There Are Two Sides to*

4 Siddhartha Mitter and Siobhan Burke, "Kandis Williams Envisions Dancing Bodies without Borders," *New York Times*, October 28, 2021, https://www.nytimes.com/2021/10/28/arts/design/kandis-williams-ebony-haynes-52-walker.html.

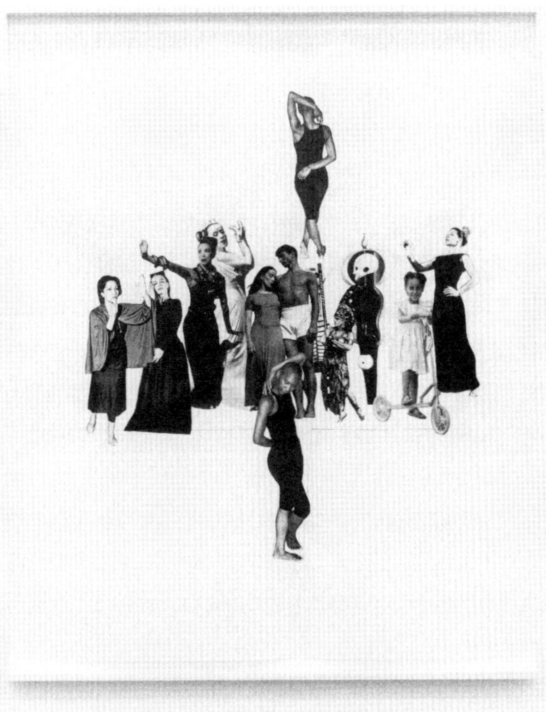

Fig. 2 Kandis Williams, *There are Two Sides to Every Line*, 2021, installation view, *Notes on Dance*, Galerie Hubert Winter, Vienna, 2024

Every Line (2021) features images of Martha Graham, the modern dance pioneer known for appropriating movements from Black dance traditions (fig. 2). By including Graham in this context, Williams highlights the long history of cultural appropriation within dance, suggesting that the extraction of creativity from marginalized bodies is another form of exploitation. Graham's incorporation of Black dance gestures becomes, in Williams's work, a metaphor for how Black culture, born from suffering and oppression, is often absorbed and commodified by the culture industry, much like the Nicholas Brothers' performances were repackaged in Hollywood or how the militaristic drills of "Rhythm Nation" found a home in mainstream media.

Racial and gendered representation is also a focus of Williams's critique, central to which are the writings of Spillers and Wynter, both of whom examine how Black bodies are rendered through colonial and patriarchal systems of power. Spillers's seminal essay "Mama's Baby, Papa's Maybe: An American

Grammar Book" (1987) introduced the concept of "ungendering," a key theoretical underpinning in Williams's exploration of how Black femininity is both hypervisible and erased within cultural production.[5] Spillers argues that the violent history of slavery fundamentally disrupted the gendered categories imposed on Black people, specifically Black women, rendering their bodies sites of objectification and control outside traditional gendered frameworks. Williams's work engages directly with this idea by creating collages that destabilize the viewer's understanding of gender, race, and power. For example, *Esophagus Pin-Up* (2016) uses disjointed images of bodies, focusing specifically on the esophagus and throat, areas symbolically tied to voice, consumption, and control(fig. 3). The throat, as a vulnerable part of the body, becomes a metaphor for how women's voices and persons have been historically silenced, manipulated, and consumed by dominant cultural forces. In drawing attention to this part of the body, Williams highlights the ways in which women have had to navigate systems of power that seek to control their voices and their bodies, while also resisting and reclaiming space for their own agency.

The term *pin-up* in the title evokes the hypersexualized, commodified image of women, yet Williams subverts this by presenting fragmented, unsettling imagery that resists the smooth, desirable surfaces of traditional pin-up iconography and the mirrored plexiglass on which the work is situated. Instead of glamour or seduction, there is a sense of distortion and dread in the work, which underscores the violence inherent in the

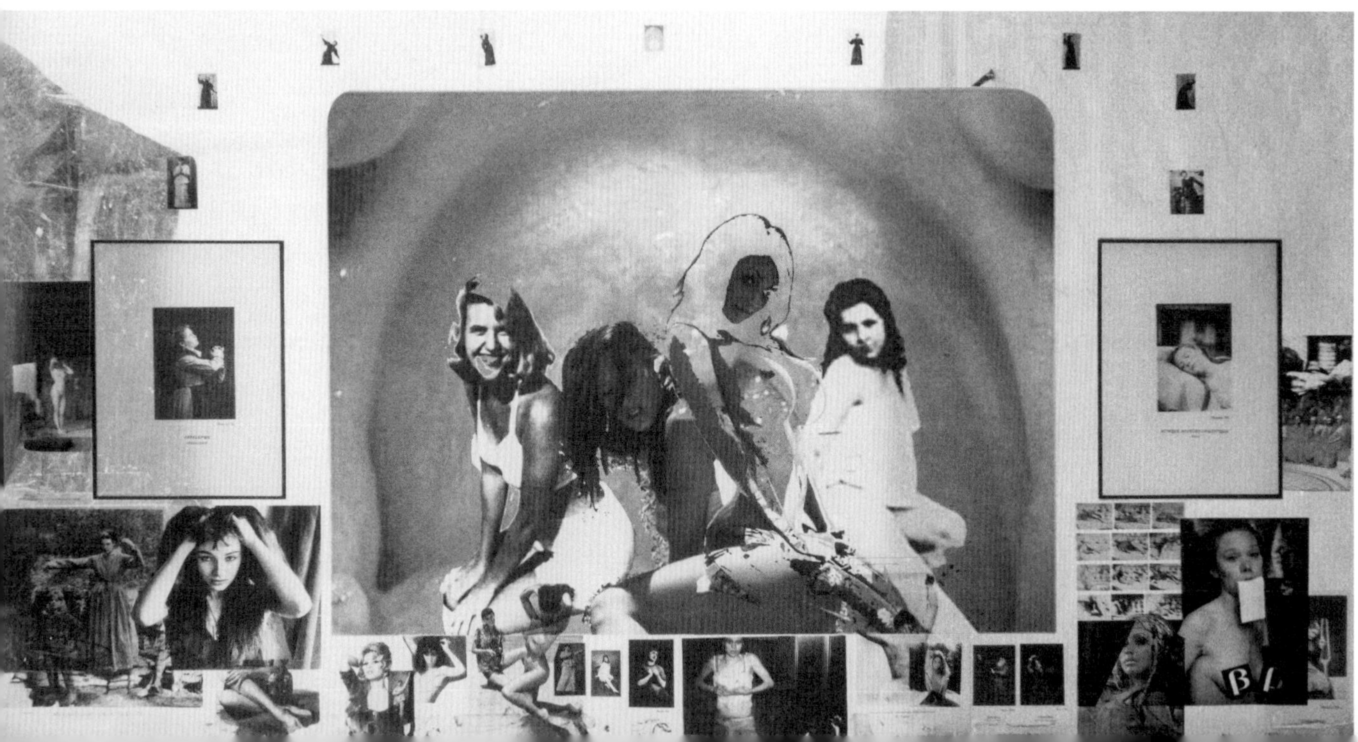

Fig. 3 Kandis Williams, *Esophagus Pin-Up*, 2016 (pages 90–91)

historical objectification of women. By juxtaposing imagery of the female form with anatomical elements, Williams explores the body not only as a site of desire but also as a locus of trauma, control, and rebellion.

The fragmentation in Williams's work is not merely aesthetic but speaks to the historical fragmentation of identity itself, particularly within Black experiences. Wynter's challenge to Western conceptions of "Man" as a universal subject, most notably articulated in her 2003 essay "Unsettling the Coloniality of Being/Power/Truth/Freedom: Towards the Human, After Man, Its Overrepresentation," resonates throughout Williams's oeuvre.[6] Wynter critiques the ways in which Enlightenment-era humanism constructed a normative, white male subject, relegating Black and Indigenous peoples to the margins of humanity. Williams disrupts this narrative by presenting alternative histories and counternarratives that make visible the lives and bodies erased by colonial and Eurocentric histories. Because most colonial and institutional archives are created by (and serve the purposes and biases of) white people in power, it becomes crucial to expand the possibilities of what an archive can be and seek alternative representations that rewrite or expand on the dominant narrative of history. As a passageway to understanding the past, the archival process has a distinct social and political impact that must be reclaimed, diversified, and decolonized to reflect cultural, rather than institutional, values and hold space for untold stories and counternarratives. Collage provides an opportunity to produce and manipulate cultural or domestic archives that are community-bound and exist in conscious opposition to traditional hierarchies embedded in institutional archives. Williams's work not only critiques these dominant narratives but also reclaims agency, suggesting that Black bodies are not simply subjects of violence but also exist as sites of resistance and resilience.

Harris's theory of whiteness as property and Ferreira da Silva's critique of global raciality further contextualize Williams's

5 Hortense J. Spillers, "Mama's Baby, Papa's Maybe: An American Grammar Book," *Diacritics* 17, no. 2 (Summer 1987): 65–81.

6 Sylvia Wynter, "Unsettling the Coloniality of Being/Power/Truth/Freedom: Towards the Human, After Man, Its Overrepresentation," *CR: The New Centennial Review* 3, no. 3 (2003): 257–337.

interrogation of labor, value, and the circulation of racialized images. Harris argues that the legal and social construction of whiteness operates as a form of property, conferring power and privilege that are protected and maintained through systemic racism.[7] Williams's *Atomic Karen* (2021) is a visual exploration of the mechanisms that maintain inequality, layered with the artist's signature cultural critique(fig. 4). The collage explores the fraught history of white female entitlement, epitomized by the "Karen" stereotype—shorthand for women who use their privilege to police or control marginalized groups, often in public spaces. The title itself fuses two powerful forces: the "Karen" archetype and the atomic bomb, symbolizing destructive, unchecked power. Williams assembles fragments of images—portraits, historical references, and abstract forms—into a disorienting yet coherent whole, creating a sense of dissonance. Through this juxtaposition, she critiques how systemic structures of whiteness can act as an overwhelming force, often unseen but omnipresent, with far-reaching consequences. *Atomic Karen* invites viewers to confront their own complicity in societal hierarchies, encouraging critical reflection on the roles individuals play within broader systems of power.

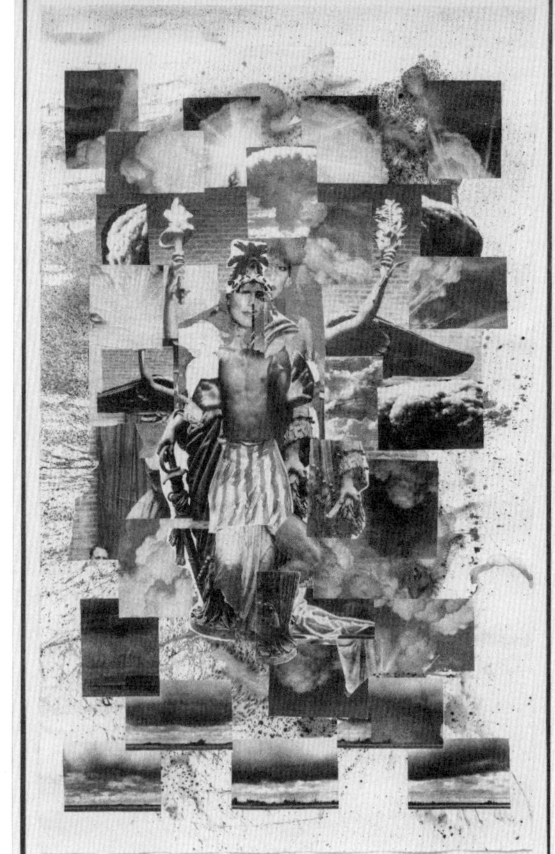

Fig. 4 Kandis Williams, *Atomic Karen*, 2021 (page 155)

This framework is also evident in Williams's critique of labor, notably in works like *A Field* (2020; page 41), where she investigates the legacy of plantation capitalism and how it continues to shape modern structures of labor and production, particularly for Black and marginalized communities. The exploitation of Black labor is not just historical but remains deeply embedded in contemporary systems of capital, an idea that Williams unpacks by highlighting the ways in which Black labor is commodified,

7 Cheryl I. Harris, "Whiteness as Property," *Harvard Law Review* 106, no. 8 (1993): 1707–1791; see also Harris, "Reflections on 'Whiteness as Property,'" reprinted in the present volume, pages 231–240.

surveilled, and devalued in a capitalist society. Ferreira da Silva's focus on how raciality shapes global power dynamics is similarly crucial to understanding Williams's broader critique of systemic racism. Particularly in *Toward a Global Idea of Race* (2007), Ferreira da Silva examines how racial distinctions underpin the global order, perpetuating inequality and exclusion on a structural level.[8] Williams engages with these ideas by questioning the global circulation of images of Blackness and the ways in which these images reinforce racial hierarchies and control. While critiquing these power structures she also offers a space for reimagining alternative futures, where Black bodies are no longer confined to the margins of representation but are central to the creation of new narratives and histories. Her work is a powerful assertion that another world is possible, one in which the histories of oppression and erasure are reconciled.

Our contemporary moment is defined by irony, fragmentation, and an increasing awareness that late capitalism is doomed and many of the things deemed valuable must be reoriented toward another future. Such a recognition may be traced back to the idea that parts of the world were so senselessly severed at the seams four hundred years ago with the Atlantic slave trade and the colonial conquests of domination by figures such as Christopher Columbus. This unforgettable history—and foundation—of violence must never be forgotten as the present moves forward. And yet these histories have been rewritten, specifically in the Western world, and force-fed as their own propaganda. The resulting entrenched racism and heteronormativity have been unraveled and rewritten by scholars and activists over the past few decades. The physical "cut" of collage is representative of a larger condition of rupture that is deeply rooted in intersectional Black feminist practices of dismantling patriarchal index and authority within the history of social movements. This opens up an entirely new network of engagement with visual culture at large, but specifically with recent developments such as the spread of alternative information. This way of thinking is akin to the process of collage as a method that is accessible by virtue of all that it encompasses.

8 Denise Ferreira da Silva, *Toward a Global Idea of Race* (Minneapolis: University of Minnesota Press, 2007).

Geared toward impulses to retell history, reframe identity, or otherwise reorient perspectives on the present and future, Williams's practice involves plumbing the flood of images and cultural objects found in Western culture to question the narratives they come to represent. Creating something new out of these images that have been shaped by a multitude of forces and structures becomes profoundly political in the matter of cut and paste, as the artist takes back agency over how she would like to assemble and represent reality, often in ways that are antithetical to the original intent. Williams's visual explorations document contemporary experience through cultural materials such as magazines, photographs, newspapers, maps, and other objects representative of Western sociopolitical zeitgeists. Working among different temporal moments, the artist likens the method of collage to archival work, collecting images from print and digital media that develop counternarratives to an overwhelmingly white and colonial archive.

Venus is a Sacrificial Form (2016) reimagines the figure of Venus, traditionally depicted as a symbol of idealized beauty and femininity in Western art, by confronting the violent history of objectification and exploitation embedded within such portrayals (fig. 5). The title evokes both reverence and subjugation, positioning the goddess as not merely a symbol of beauty but also a figure sacrificed to the societal ideals she has come to represent. The work weaves together a provocative array of images: the prehistoric Venus of Willendorf, iconic American sex symbol Marilyn Monroe, a young Blue Ivy Carter, and pop idol Britney Spears. By juxtaposing these figures, Williams critiques how female bodies, across history and cultures, are objectified, fetishized, and manipulated by societal forces. The Venus of Willendorf, an ancient fertility figure, represents idealized femininity tied to nature and reproduction, while Marilyn Monroe symbolizes the twentieth-century commodification of the female form, her image perpetually consumed by the male gaze. By inserting Blue Ivy Carter—a young Black girl often subjected to the public's gaze—into this lineage of female icons, Williams highlights the ways in which even the bodies of Black children are scrutinized, policed, and commodified by a racialized media. The inclusion of Britney Spears at her most vulnerable moment, bald and in the throes of a public mental health crisis, underscores ongoing attacks on women's autonomy when they reject or fail to conform to prescribed roles of beauty, desirability, or submissiveness. This mashup of figures, spanning from prehistory to contemporary pop culture, creates a layered critique of the ways in which female bodies are exploited, dissected, and controlled across time, drawing attention to how cultural myths of femininity and womanhood serve to uphold broader structures of power. By fragmenting and reassembling the body, Williams disrupts the traditional gaze that has long confined women, especially Black women, to limiting and often harmful narratives.

As both a refraction and a critique of the print industry and the social structures that define it, collage for Williams is a distinct space where characters and elements from different places of origin can gather in the timelessness of the present. In this manner, the method of collage reorients how historical time and archival practices operate to complicate and critique what an archive can represent. Importantly, the production of a counternarrative makes way for the development of counter-archives. Looking both within a colonial archive and outside of it, Williams unearths representations of Blackness while holding space for the irony and tensions of being conspicuously unseen by art history and dominant media outside of appropriation and tokenization. Such strategic readings of the archive produce counternarratives that readjust the understanding of the colonial past as unrepresentative of the oppressed and unarchived, and carve out a distinct space to acknowledge these histories on their own terms. Of Black archival practices, art writer Maandeeq Mohamed states, "We know

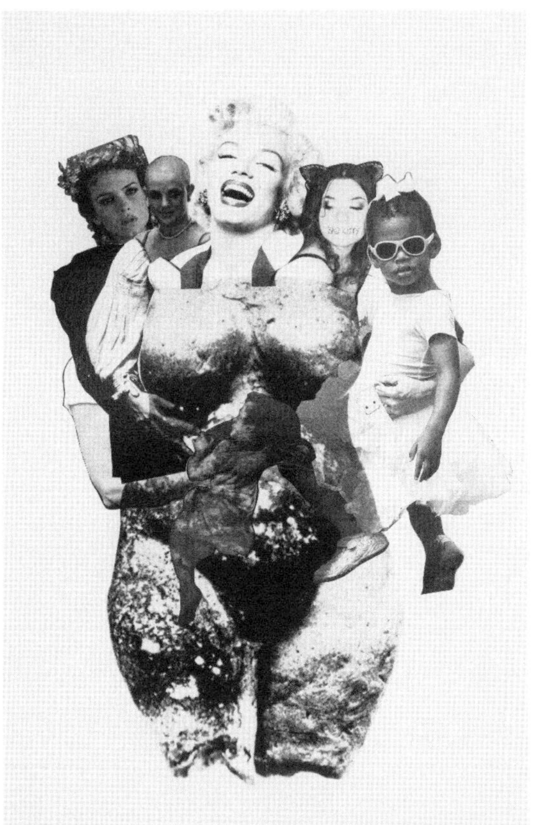

Fig. 5 Kandis Williams, *Venus is a Sacrificial Form*, 2016 (page 87)

that the archive will never be sufficient—if we are accounted for, it is via the violence of fact: scientific racism, and catalogues listing enslaved people as property.... Perhaps not knowing can be useful, insofar as it allows for a recognition of the fact that what is/isn't archived is but one of many fictions ... that constitute blackness in public life."[9] Williams creates connections, interpretations, and counternarratives that make sense of her worldview while paying homage to the sublime multiplicity and vast silences of the archive entangled with the unforgettable histories of racism and colonialism that inform the material culture left behind for future generations.

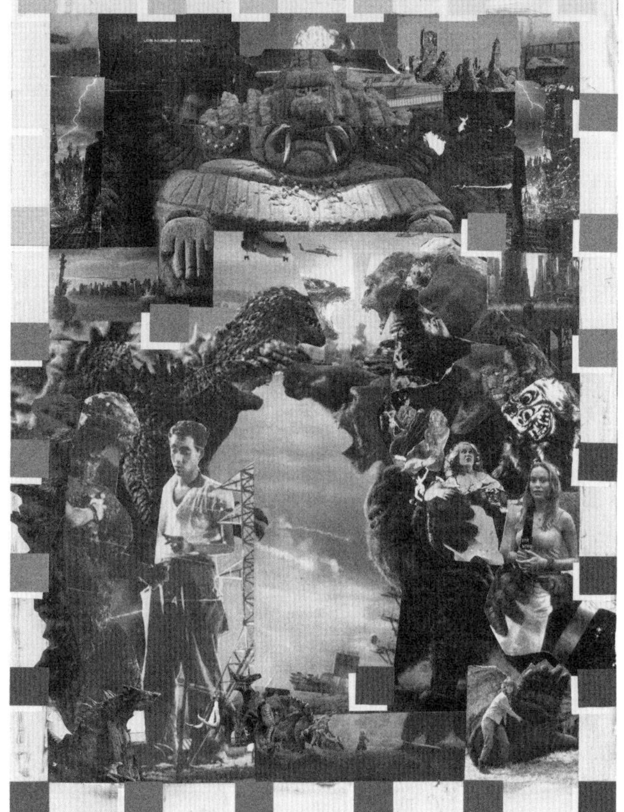

Fig. 6 Kandis Williams, *BEAST: "I am become Death, the destroyer of worlds. Oh no, it wasn't the airplanes. It was Beauty killed the Beast." "When Kong is put in chains and displayed in New York, the film evokes an unmistakable echo of the slave trade. Kong, in his brute strength and childlike emotions, is a cinematic symbol of the fear and fascination that black men elicited in white America. [...]" from gods and monsters that white people make up to kill us all*, 2024 (page 212)

The theoretical anchors for this analysis are deeply indebted to Black, feminist, Indigenous, and BIPOC discourse, scholarship, and embodied work that advocates for the disruption of hegemony to create space for artists and practices to speak out against violence, exclusion, and tokenism. There are many nuances, vulnerabilities, and possibilities in these perspectives that must be explored and nurtured with care and consideration for what remains left unsaid. These issues map onto Williams's work in ways that are informed by what motivates her to employ collage as a counternarrative and reparative device.

The fragmentation of experience illustrated in Williams's work is a direct result of the actions and decisions made by the wants of those who represent European colonialism, American hegemony, and Western capitalism, who have no consideration for the people whose lives are disproportionately affected by

9 Maandeeq Mohamed, "Somehow I Found You: On Black Archival Practices," *C Magazine*, no. 137 (Spring 2018), cmagazine.com/issues/137/somehow-i-found-you-on-black-archival-practices.

their destructive choices. It is not hyperbolic to state that capitalism and corporate greed have ravaged the natural environment to fragments while simultaneously trapping minds and lives in frustratingly repetitive spaces and cycles. Critical theorist Sara Ahmed offers compelling arguments for the notion of disorientation as a challenge to the underpinnings of white supremacy and heteronormativity entrenched in Western culture. As a tool in the construction of counternarratives, disorientation is a strategy that Ahmed reflects on, particularly in the context of the work of social philosopher and psychoanalyst Frantz Fanon, explaining, "From Fanon we learn about the experience of disorientation, as the experience of being an object among other objects, of being shattered, of being cut into pieces by the hostility of the white gaze."[10] Shifting how objects are gathered, this sense of disorientation speaks to the process of collage as a deliberate disturbance of a particular established order in pursuit of other relations. Elaborating on this, Ahmed posits a "queer phenomenology [that] would function as a disorientation device; it would not overcome the 'disalignment' of the horizontal and vertical axes, allowing the oblique to open up another angle on the world."[11] This choice not to overcome disorientation but to revel in the familiar as it becomes strange is a worthwhile point of consideration. The overlay of several narratives at once speaks to the inherent multiplicity of counternarratives, and the embrace of disorientation becomes a guiding light for visual analysis.

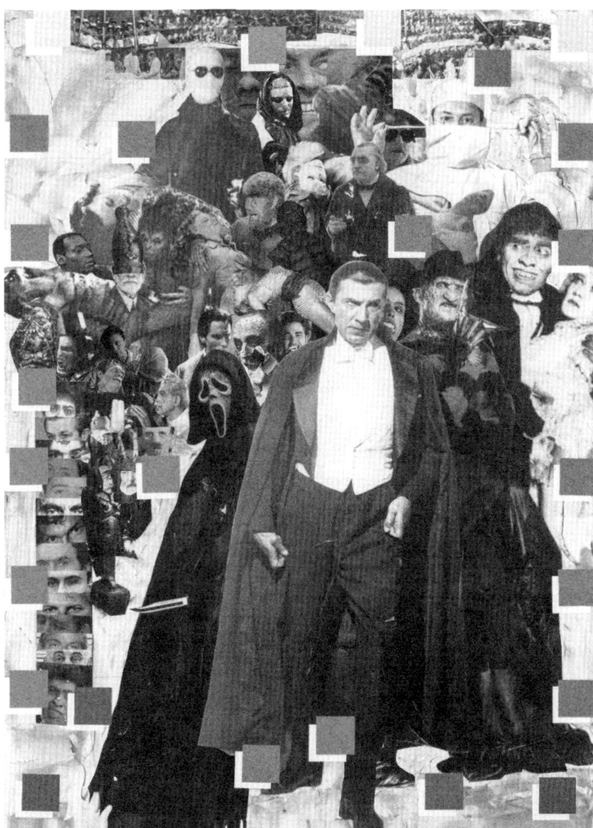

Fig. 7 Kandis Williams, VAMPIRE: *"I am Dracula. I bid you welcome. Listen to them. Children of the night. What music they make! The blood is the life, Mr. Renfield. I never drink ... wine. There are far worse things awaiting man than death."* [...], from *gods and monsters that white people make up to kill us all*, 2024 (page 205)

Reading memories and lineages in relation to one another, Williams's works create a space that welcomes the dedicated act of slow looking. The series *gods and monsters that white people make up to kill us all* (2024), for example, invites deep contemplation of its densely layered

10 Sara Ahmed, *Queer Phenomenology: Orientations, Objects, Others* (Durham, NC: Duke University Press, 2006), 160.
11 Ahmed, *Queer Phenomenology*, 172.

imagery (figs. 6, 7). The series draws from a wide array of archival, filmic, and pop cultural sources, weaving together fragments of history, myth, and media into complex visual narratives. Williams turns her gaze toward horror motifs—monsters, ghosts, and haunted figures—examining them as products of the white supremacist cultural imaginary. She posits that these creatures of horror are not merely fictional figures but manifestations of white anxieties and fears, serving as metaphors for the brutal realities of racial colonialism, violence, genocide, and class warfare. The series critiques how whiteness invents its own "monsters" to justify and perpetuate its dominance, all while inflicting real horrors upon racialized bodies and communities. The slow looking that Williams encourages reveals not only the deep-seated horrors embedded in these images but also the ways in which the cultural narratives of horror serve as coping mechanisms for white perpetrators of violence. As realities converge from fragments, Williams's collages unfold into masterful critiques of historical chronologies and contemporary pop culture at once.

The art of imagining beyond and toward other futures through the framework of narrative-based mythologies can be read as a resistance to a prevailing historical record that has been used as a tool to subjugate, erase, and control communities for centuries. Williams's two-channel film *Eurydice* (2017–2021) reimagines the Greek myth through a contemporary lens, focusing on themes of power, control, and the silencing of women (figs. 8, 9). In the original myth, Eurydice, wife of Orpheus, dies

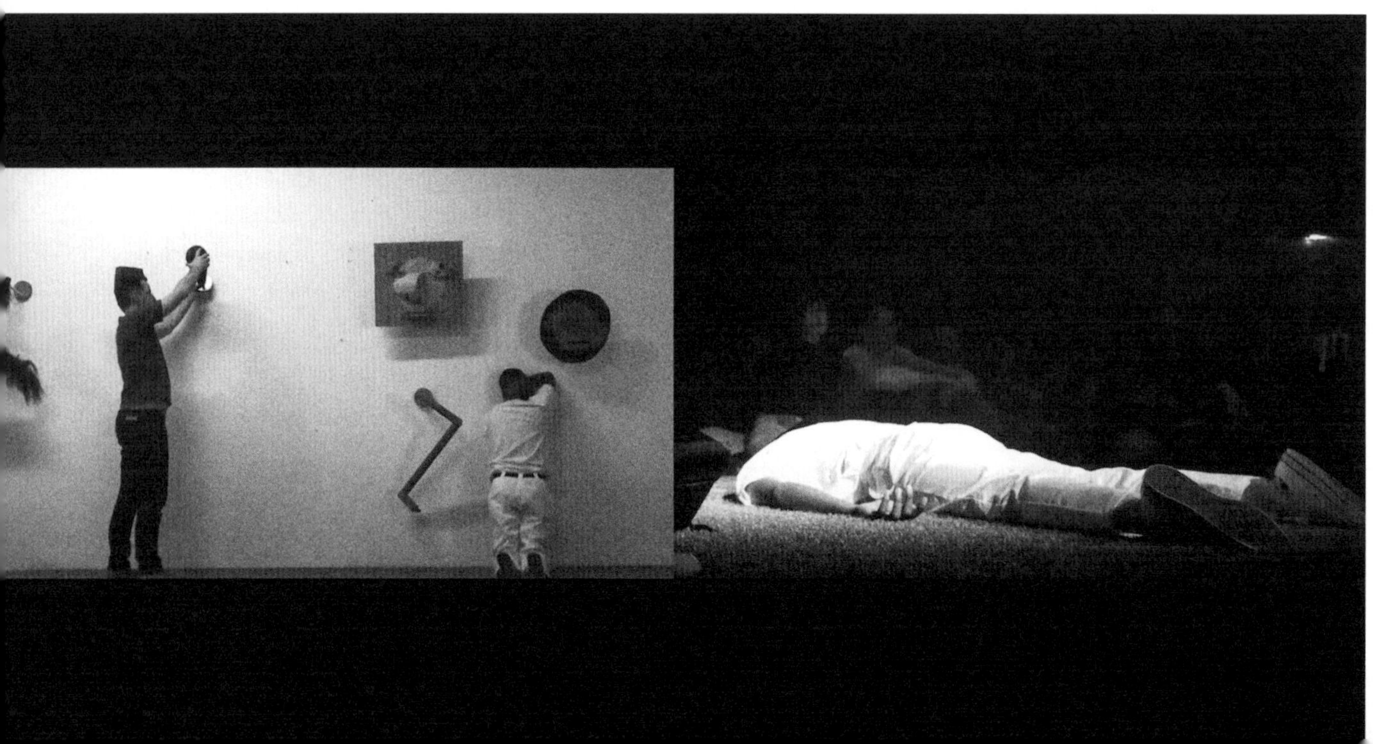

Fig. 8 Kandis Williams, *Eurydice*, 2017–2021 (video stills) (pages 92–99)

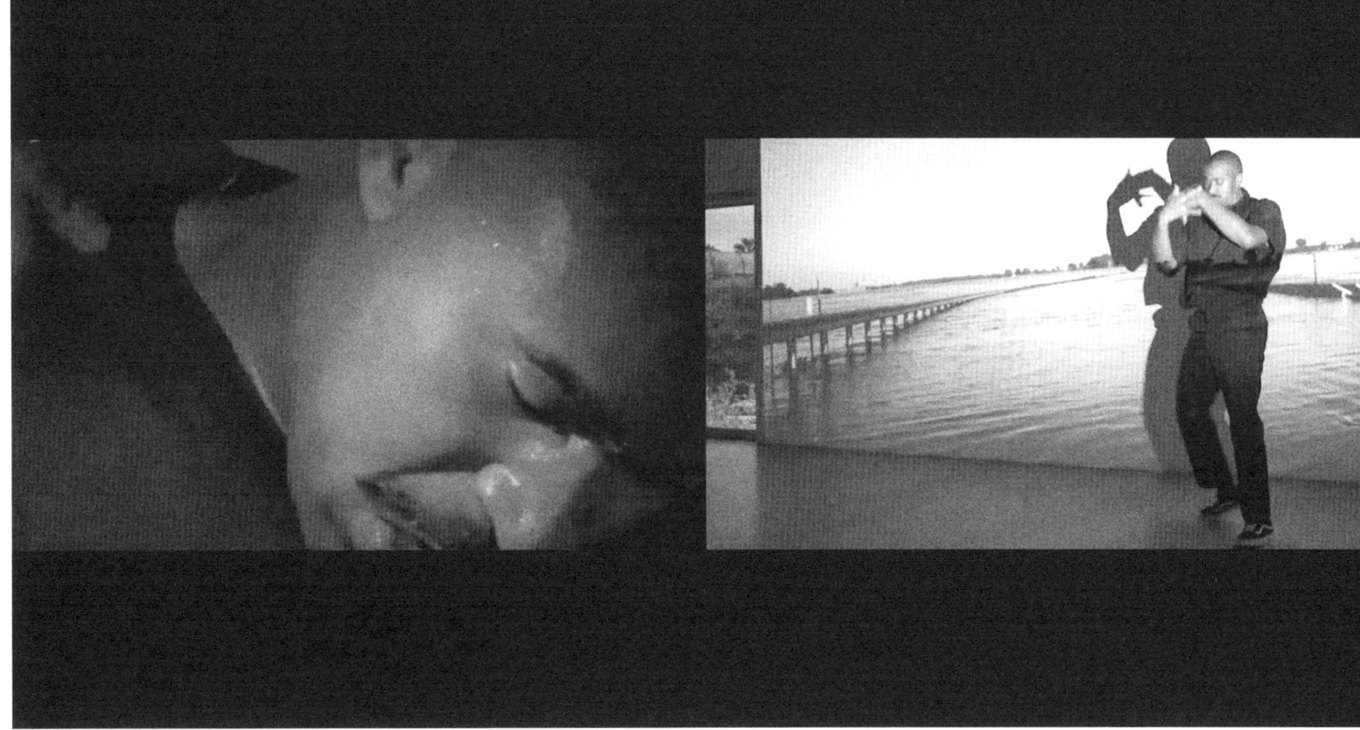

Fig. 9 Kandis Williams, *Eurydice*, 2017–2021 (video stills) (pages 92–99)

and is condemned to the underworld. Orpheus is granted permission to retrieve her on the condition that he not look back as she follows him out of Hades. He fails, condemning Eurydice to eternal damnation. Williams revisits this narrative, questioning the dynamics of male control and the objectification of women embedded within it. The film's dual-channel format mirrors the fragmented nature of the myth, juxtaposing imagery drawn from the ancient tale with modern-day visuals that evoke similar themes of constraint and erasure. One channel focuses on Eurydice as a figure trapped in a cycle of passivity and victimization, while the other provides a more fragmented, abstract perspective that disrupts her passive portrayal. By doing so, Williams creates a tension between the traditional narrative, which centers on Orpheus's experience, and a more nuanced exploration of Eurydice's plight as a woman whose fate is controlled by others. The film underscores the disempowerment inherent in Eurydice's story, while also offering a critique of the ways women's bodies and lives are controlled in broader cultural narratives. The split screen emphasizes the multiplicity of voices and experiences that have been obscured by patriarchal storytelling. The film destabilizes the conventional gaze, inviting the audience to consider Eurydice's story from her own perspective, one in which she is not simply a passive figure in Orpheus's tragedy but a woman grappling with the confines imposed on her. Bringing these mythologies into the present is therefore significant as a future-driven historical critique that lives on in many forms.

As both an act of intervention and an invitation for dialogue, the process of remixing, reframing, and reconceptualizing history through collage holds distinct epistemological power in this contemporary moment. By pushing up against hegemonic sociopolitical structures represented in visual culture by mass media, material processes of fragmentation and juxtaposition become emblems of a reality rethought. Necessarily deviant, the artist's act of cut and paste wields agency over objects of material culture, capturing a world made up of diverse and at times incommensurable pieces that are anything but neutral. With agency and innovation, collage re-presents material culture as profoundly personal, evocative, and able to be questioned—a gesture of freedom that has been consistent since its inception. It is clear that the structures of oppression that serve as the framework for Western settler culture cannot continue to go on as they do. Right now, the question of the future comes out of the uncertainty of our time: a sad, maddening, and just altogether bad moment. In such moments of bewildering temporality, there is an overwhelming gravitation toward other worlds, if only through a fragmented lens, that represent futures yet to fully come into view. A profound sense of hope for something better informs the ways in which material conditions of reality must be reimagined, not just conceptually but in the shifting of actual space and narratives.

Williams's practice is broadly geared toward impulses to retell history, reframe identity, or reorient perspectives. Resolutely turned toward history while simultaneously engaged profoundly with the present, her work with collage is demonstrative of the necessity for any attempt at reconciling with the past to be multifaceted; otherwise it takes on the character of propaganda. Williams's multidisciplinary works not only acknowledge but also resist and work against traditional political economic and social hierarchies that are deeply embedded in all our institutions. Through the questioning of such historiographic, photographic, artistic, and cultural records, Williams demonstrates how the manipulation, diversification, and decolonization of archives can shift the power they hold. As a process of retelling and recombining narratives from popular media and history, collage offers a creative way of thinking differently and beyond. Importantly, this serves as a crucial reminder of the ways that the past, present, and future are always in fluid conversation. A collage becomes a site of connection, distinctly grounded yet forged between places, and collaboration between both temporalities and mediums becomes an important motif. While the actual production of collage is often a long, laborious process of collecting and then rapidly condensing through purposeful juxtaposition, it sparks a dialogue that begins with the artist through the choices they make. This can involve the types of materials at their disposal as well as their own visual language. The dialogue is continued by the viewer bringing their own references and modes of connection to the work, and thus a chain of meaning is created. What I find beautiful about Williams's work is the fundamental destabilization of meaning, something that art history tends to hold very dear. Built into the very nature of a collage are plurality and expansive relationality—qualities that speak to the critical theories that inform Williams's attempt to unsettle and rebuild parts of history we were brought up to forget. While there will always be resistance to engaging with the dark sides of history, the attempt to understand and potentially reconcile where the gaps, fissures, and erasures exist is crucial to moving forward into a future that is equitable and makes space for many truths, histories, and mythologies to exist at once.

RETREAT AND RECLAIM

DENISE RYNER

RETREAT AND RECLAIM: KANDIS WILLIAMS'S VISIONS OF THE BLACK BODY AS A CONTESTED PLOT

by Denise Ryner

This body whose flesh carries the female and the male to the frontiers of survival bears in person the marks of a cultural text whose inside has been turned outside.

—Hortense J. Spillers, "Mama's Baby, Papa's Maybe: An American Grammar Book"[1]

For if the history of Caribbean society is that of a dual relation between plantation and plot, the two poles which originate in a single historical process, the ambivalence between the two has been and is the distinguishing characteristic of the Caribbean response. This ambivalence is at once the root cause of our alienation; and the possibility of our salvation.

—Sylvia Wynter, "Novel and History, Plot and Plantation"[2]

After that she was able to build a spiritual earth-works against her husband. His shells could no longer reach her. Amen.

—Zora Neale Hurston, "Sweat"[3]

1 Hortense J. Spillers, "Mama's Baby, Papa's Maybe: An American Grammar Book," *Diacritics* 17, no. 2 (Summer 1987): 67.

2 Sylvia Wynter, "Novel and History, Plot and Plantation" (1971), in *We Must Learn to Sit Down Together and Talk about a Little Culture: Decolonising Essays, 1967–1984*, ed. Demetrius L. Eudell (Leeds: Peepal Tree Press, 2022), 295.

3 Zora Neale Hurston, "Sweat" (1926), Biblioklept.org, January 21, 2013, https://biblioklept.org/2013/01/21/sweat-zora-neale-hurston/.

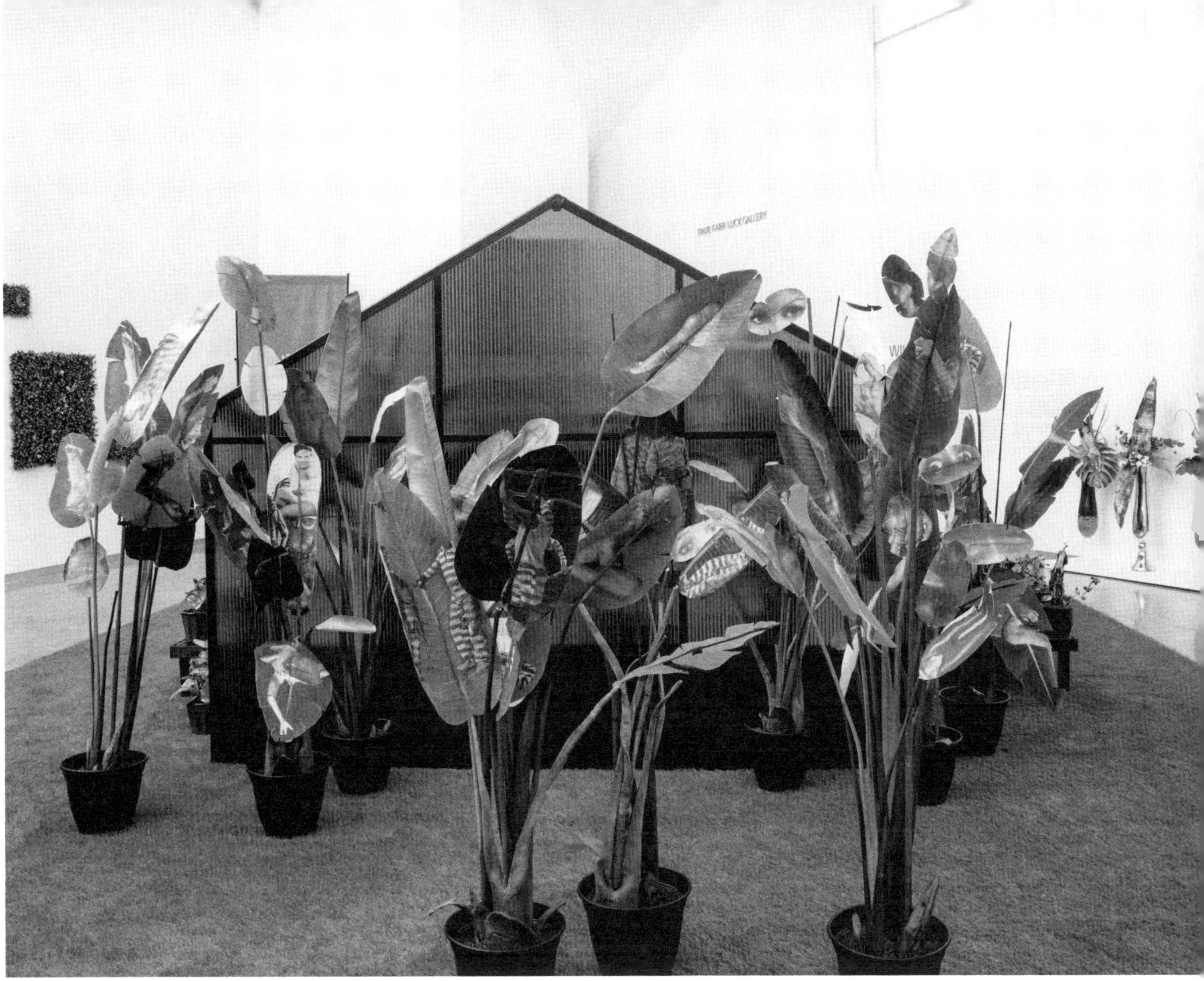

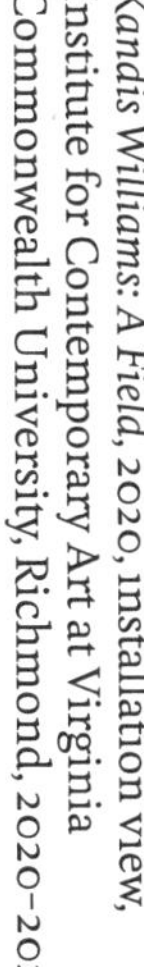

Fig. 1 *Kandis Williams: A Field*, 2020, installation view, Institute for Contemporary Art at Virginia Commonwealth University, Richmond, 2020–2021

ANNEXATION TANGO

The captivity and racial ordering of enslavement during the Middle Passage erased boundaries between Black laborers and the crops they produced. The indifference and menace of the captors, investors, and planter class dissolved captive workers' identities and traditional kinships, so they used indigenous memory to turn that loss of the boundary between laborer and field, the legal and social obscuring of their human-ness, and even the ever-present terror of death into sites of resistance to control and captivity. What Kandis Williams so effectively illustrates in her work is that this dynamic of erasure and resistance that flourished under racial capitalism continues to reproduce itself within each new field of wealth extraction, the commodity market, and the increasing peril of ecological catastrophe.

In Williams's 2020 series of works that make up the installation *A Field* (fig. 1), photographic collages of bodies are framed by representations of plant life, lawns, and fields.[4] Resting on a bed of artificial grass are sprouting, broad-leafed plant sculptures that carry on their leaves collaged images of the limbs and bodies of Black figures in midmotion related to dance, labor, and pornography. The lawn and commercially manufactured fake potted plants evoke a space of consumer leisure, sport, and surplus property. In the midst of this is a slick, industrial-looking greenhouse. A cutout turns the structure into a frame for viewing Williams's video *Annexation Tango* (figs. 7–10), based on her research into two former correctional facilities in Virginia, the Lorton Reformatory and the Virginia State Prison Farm, where both male and female inmates, many of whom were charged with transgressing vagrancy or vice laws, were made to do unpaid farm work.[5] *Annexation Tango* overlays footage of the institutions' agricultural fields with that of a Black dancer, and the instrumental tango soundtrack refers to that musical form's origins in the culture of enslaved African plantation workers transported to South America.

A Field draws together the relative leisure and comfort of American life for many and the stolen labor of transatlantic enslavement. That stolen labor was subsequently reproduced through the prison system and remains part of contemporary consumption under increasing wealth gaps, transnational empires, and global oppression, invoking cultural theorist Sylvia Wynter's observations that "plantation-societies," the primary example being enslaved field workers in the Caribbean, "came into being as adjuncts to the market system; their peoples came into being as an adjunct to the product, to the single crop commodity."[6] For Wynter, the flip side of this reduction of captive labor—indivisible from property and capital, bound to the industrialized plantation and the ordering of the owning class—is the plot: a place of sustenance and resistance where the laborers' folk

4 *A Field* was commissioned by the Institute for Contemporary Art at Virginia Commonwealth University, Richmond, where it was on view November 6, 2020, to September 12, 2021.

5 "In Discussion: Kandis Williams and Amber Esseiva," Institute for Contemporary Art at Virginia Commonwealth University, https://www.youtube.com/watch?v=RQAnBuDv61Q.

6 Wynter, "Novel and History, Plot and Plantation," 291.

culture, the score and choreography of their world-reordering, is cross-pollinated and takes root.[7]

COLD SWEAT

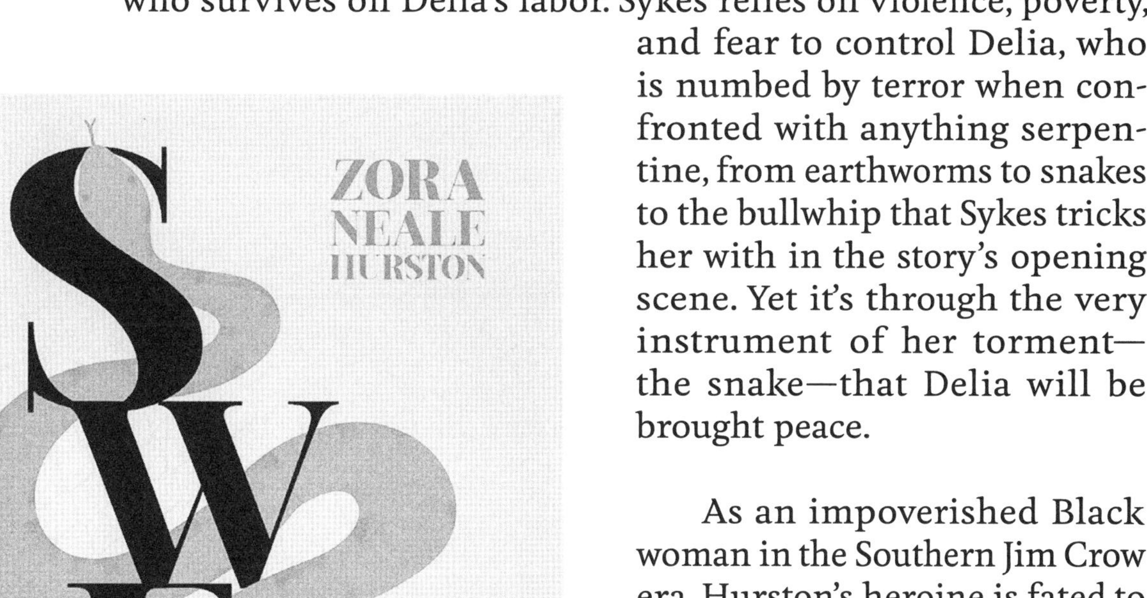

She squatted in the kitchen floor beside the great pile of clothes, sorting them into small heaps according to color, and humming a song in a mournful key, but wondering through it all where Sykes, her husband, had gone with her horse and buckboard.

Just then something long, round, limp and black fell upon her shoulders and slithered to the floor beside her. A great terror took hold of her. It softened her knees and dried her mouth so that it was a full minute before she could cry or move.[8]

About one average human lifespan after the signing of the Thirteenth Amendment to abolish slavery in the United States, Zora Neale Hurston published her 1926 short story "Sweat" (fig. 2), which centers on a series of events that lead to the empowerment of a Black Floridian washerwoman named Delia. She is abused, betrayed, and publicly humiliated by Sykes, the husband who survives on Delia's labor. Sykes relies on violence, poverty, and fear to control Delia, who is numbed by terror when confronted with anything serpentine, from earthworms to snakes to the bullwhip that Sykes tricks her with in the story's opening scene. Yet it's through the very instrument of her torment—the snake—that Delia will be brought peace.

As an impoverished Black woman in the Southern Jim Crow era, Hurston's heroine is fated to

Fig. 2 Cover of Zora Neale Hurston, *Sweat* (Read & Co. Classics, 2022)

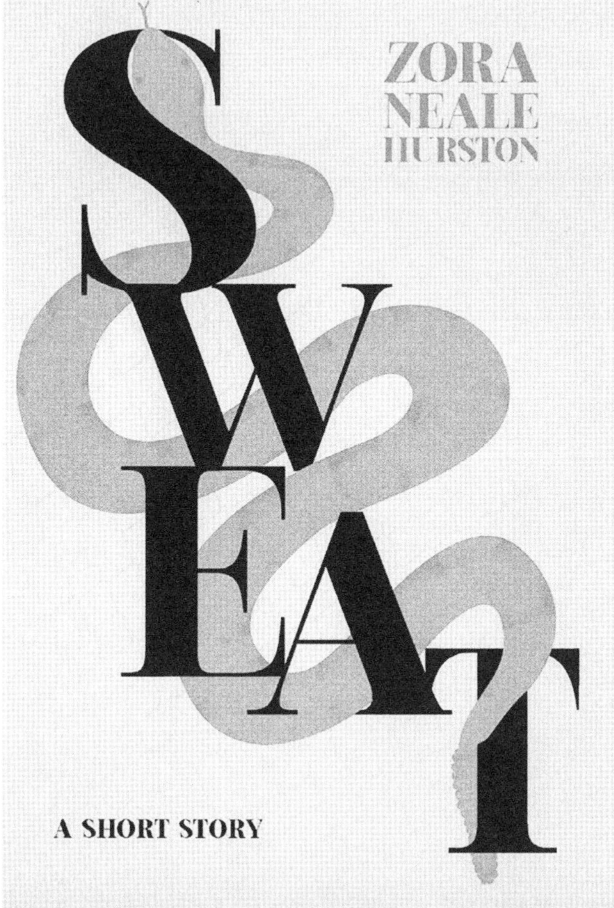

7 Wynter, 295.
8 Hurston, "Sweat."

sweat through the feminized, racialized labor of washing and delivering laundry for white households. She's also condemned to the cold sweat of fear. Delia is always described as squatting, stooped, carrying, and fetching, with barely any distinction made between her and the laundry that Sykes kicks and grinds into the ground. The legacy of life reordered after colonization and the Middle Passage is that mass industry, leisure, and markets have always been dependent on non-white women who, like Delia, are reduced to dust and expiration, their bodies dissolved until there's no more than the sweat on the surface of their skin.

SILENT SCREAM

The culture of racial capitalism's reordering, which withholds a binary female-ness as well as human-ness from bodies reformed by hard labor and remade as property, and which also idealizes female-ness as protected womanhood, leisurely, subdued, desirable, and available, is central to Williams's photomontages. Many of the film stills that make up *Pins and Needles* (2016) come from the golden age of the horror and B-movie genres (fig. 3). They're collaged with photo-documentation of women diagnosed with hysteria; at the center of it all is a retinal scan of an eyeball, subtly layered with and connected to similar medical imagery taken through hysteroscopy and esophagrams that are more prominent in Williams's other photomontages. The selected constellation of images emphasizes the history of medical and pop cultural imaging that stigmatizes women as oriented toward

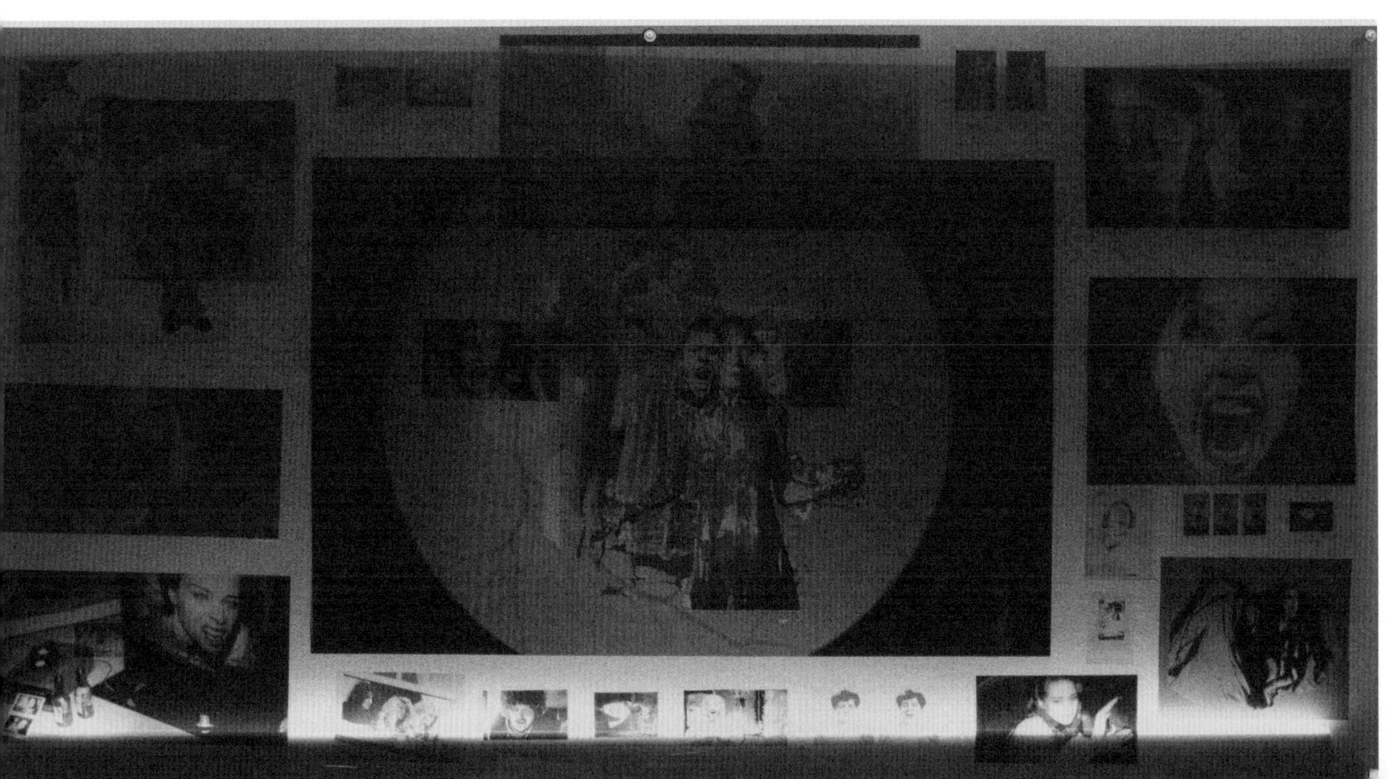

Fig. 3 Kandis Williams, *Pins and Needles*, 2016, vinyl adhesive on plexiglass, fluorescent light, 48 × 90 ¼ in. (121.9 × 229.2 cm), Los Angeles County Museum of Art, purchased with funds provided by Jen Rubio and Stewart Butterfield (M.2022.96a-b)

irrationality, whether expressed as fear, violence, or insanity. The work's title, *Pins and Needles*, evokes both medical intervention and emotional tension, and the repeated motif of the wide-open screaming mouth carries multiple meanings. In some images, the scream is that of being terrorized, the realization of impending danger and death at the hands of an unseen menace. In others, the scream is that of a terrorizing, vampiric fervor at the sight of the next victim. Both meanings, alongside the images of women in alleged fits of hysterics, also represent the margins of what is human. Their loss of control is associated with the absence of reason, civility, and restraint that defined the human in the wake of the European Enlightenment.

The photomontages that make up *Pins and Needles* are composed exclusively of images that read as white women, even if they are vampires and generally "othered." There is no visibility of Black women in these works, but they are not absent; in fact, the non-white woman is the frontier and measure of what is being limned as those pictured approach the border between the human and the invisible human. Despite the range of conditions, personalities, and eras depicted, these photomontages exhibit the enclosure of gender under racial capitalism.

In the photomontage *Esophagus Pin-Up* (2016; pages 90–91), we move past the open mouth and farther down the throat with medical-scope imaging of the inside of the human gullet. Each image features a woman posing either suggestively or dramatically. The central grouping of images features a quartet of women in various states of beckoning the viewer, separated from their original image context of advertising or pornography, offering themselves as part of a consumptive act. They are some of the most digestible images in terms of their unambiguity, compared to others featuring women in various states of undress or costumed performance that may derive from fashion or profile photography, photo-documentation of sex workers and psychiatric diagnosis, critical protests, or swoons of religious ecstasy. *Cervical Smile* (2016) follows suit with a similar layout around an internal endoscopic image, surrounded and overlaid with the smiles, with or without faces, of white women, evoking Hollywood publicity campaigns, cosmetic surgery, medical procedures, or torture (fig. 4).

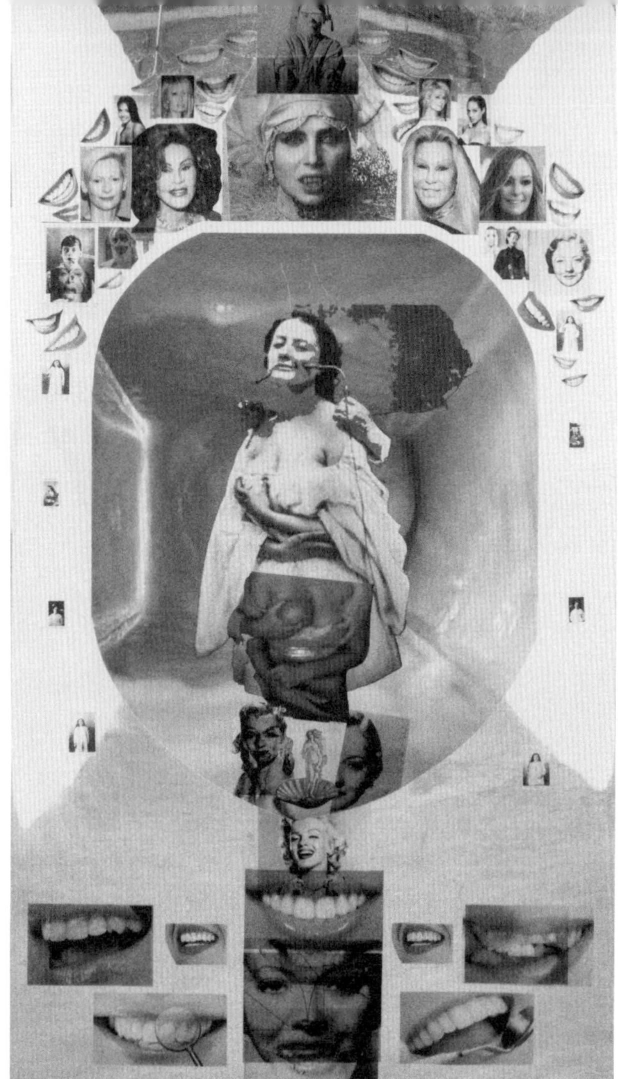

Fig. 4 Kandis Williams, *Cervical Smile*, 2016 (page 85)

Pins and Needles, *Esophagus Pin-Up*, and *Cervical Smile* were first shown in Williams's 2016 solo exhibition *Soft Colony* at Night Gallery in Los Angeles. The association of softness with leisure, protection, and fragility also traces out the racialized enclosure of new genders and classes of softness that was instrumentalized during the height of European colonial expansion to develop the cultural grammar that first excluded and then pressed Indigenous, African, and other non-white women into invisibility and forced labor through enslavement and indentured servitude, followed by sharecropping and continuing today through relegation to menial labor and otherwise precarious forms of employment.

PLOTTED RESISTANCES

Literary critic and scholar Hortense J. Spillers, writing about the "theft of the body" under the reordering of the Middle Passage, considers the disappearance of gender difference that accompanies the loss of agency and the territorialization of African and Indigenous bodies constricted in the holds of slave ships, subjected to punishing violence, and forced to labor under brutal conditions in the fields:

> That order, with its human sequence written in blood, *represents* for its African and indigenous peoples a scene of *actual* mutilation, dismemberment, and exile. First of all, their New-World, diasporic plight marked a *theft of the body*—a willful and violent (and unimaginable from this distance) severing of the captive body from its motive will, its active desire. Under these conditions, we lose at least *gender* difference *in the outcome*, and the female body and the male body become a territory of cultural and political maneuver, not at all gender-related, gender-specific.[9]

The *theft* that Spillers refers to is a rupture from Indigenous culture, place, and kin that continues to be experienced as a collectively dismembered and exiled body over which cultural and political maneuvers continue through state violence, stolen labor, and incarceration—all of which are part of the physical and psychological disfigurement of the Black body as no longer gendered and human. We see and experience this in Williams's sculptural montages and in *Annexation Tango*. The plantation haunts the bodies and the bodies haunt the plantation: disembodied Black limbs stretch across the waxy surface of leaves, and a dancer writhes in a void, superimposed over images of the prison and plantation, until grabbed and anchored by the work fields. Once the body has been lost and unmade through the violence of forced captivity, race, and commodification, refuge arrives not by making the body whole but rather by releasing the controlled and captive body, by dissolving the boundaries that enable the body to be desired and kept as territory. Hurston again: "After that she was able to build a spiritual earthworks." The body escapes capture and turns its mutilation, death, and exile into folklore, turns the violence of its territorialization into an indigenization by an irreversible rupture and haunting. The territorialized and exploited body turns poison into fits of rejuvenation.

Sykes lies dying from a rattlesnake bite as Delia rests and observes: "She crept over to the four-o'clocks and stretched herself

9 Spillers, "Mama's Baby, Papa's Maybe," 67. Italics in the original.

on the cool earth to recover."[10] Delia goes numb one more time as she loses control of her legs, not out of fear but from her long-awaited respite from torment. She shelters under the chinaberry tree, a plant with fruit known for toxicity rather than a fecund abundance that can be exploited. This type of death that Delia witnesses is also her refusal of the rational human will toward individualist productivity, a *Homo economicus*; instead, she resorts to *spiritual earthworks* of being unmade and remade as the less-than-human collective and the field.

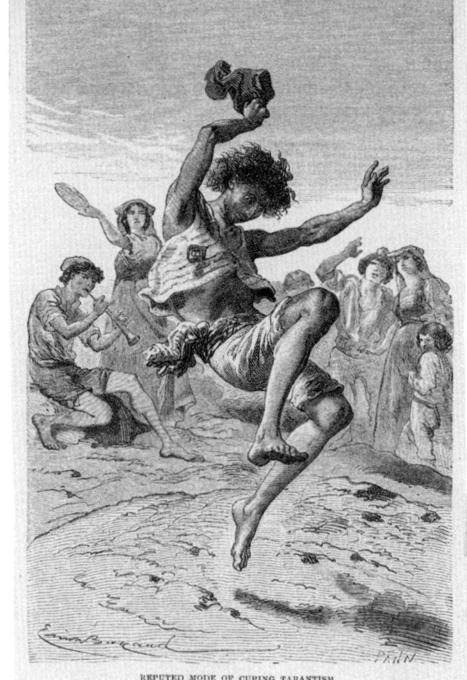

Fig. 5 Émile-Antoine Bayard, "Reputed Mode of Curing Tarantism," in *The Mediterranean Illustrated* (T. Nelson and Sons, 1880)

SEDUCED AND RECLAIMED

Returning to the mass-media and archival images of women in the grips of hysteria, reclassified at the edges of human and gender by medical and cultural institutions, brings us to Williams's interest in histories of mass psychogenic illness (MPI). She has researched accounts of collective hysteria expressed as compulsive actions, writhing, and dancing or similar behaviors, which in early instances were absorbed into regional folklore. The site of mass hysteria is often the space of the working classes, congregated in fields and later in factories. One of the earliest recorded instances of industrial MPI occurred in 1787 in a Lancashire cotton mill when a young girl who greatly feared mice and was confronted with one tossed at her by a coworker started an epidemic of mass convulsions among twenty-four workers.[11] But the most widely known historical case is tarantism (fig. 5), which emerged primarily among peasant women in the Apulia region of Italy in the fifteenth century and was attributed by "victims" to the bite of the tarantula:

10 Hurston, "Sweat."

11 Peter A. Boxer, "Occupational Mass Psychogenic Illness: History, Prevention, and Management," *Journal of Occupational Medicine* 27, no. 12 (December 1985): 868.

The afflicted, upon being bitten by the spider (which often was not seen), would run to the marketplace and begin dancing riotously. The behavior included animal-like squealing, obscene shouting, and a desire to be tipped over in the air. While the poison was said to remain in one's system for many years, the dancing mania occurred only at the height of summer. The afflicted might dance for days until exhausted, and the only cure was music, for which purpose the tarantella was written.[12]

Contemporary afflictions of MPI have followed low-status workers into the office cubicle, where collective headaches, dizziness, and nausea have replaced dancing and convulsions.[13] A 1985 study in the *Journal of Occupational Medicine* found that non-white women, especially those living and working in precarious circumstances, were overrepresented in instances of MPI.[14]

In Williams's *Annexation Tango*, not only does the dancer invoke the mass affliction of the field dancers but the video's title and soundtrack also index tango's origins in the gatherings of enslaved African workers in Argentina—a dance culture that emerged from the plot—and the transporting of the social ordering of African dancing societies that affirmed self-governance and Black culture(fig. 6).[15] Camera close-ups of the dancer in *Annexation Tango* reveal individual beads of sweat gathering in the contours of their skin, making their face, limbs, and palms shine like a perspiring screen. These visually tactile beads establish an additional surface to Williams's work that discourages trying to fix the body of the dancer within a defined space and time separate from the viewer's. Writer and film theorist Laura Marks

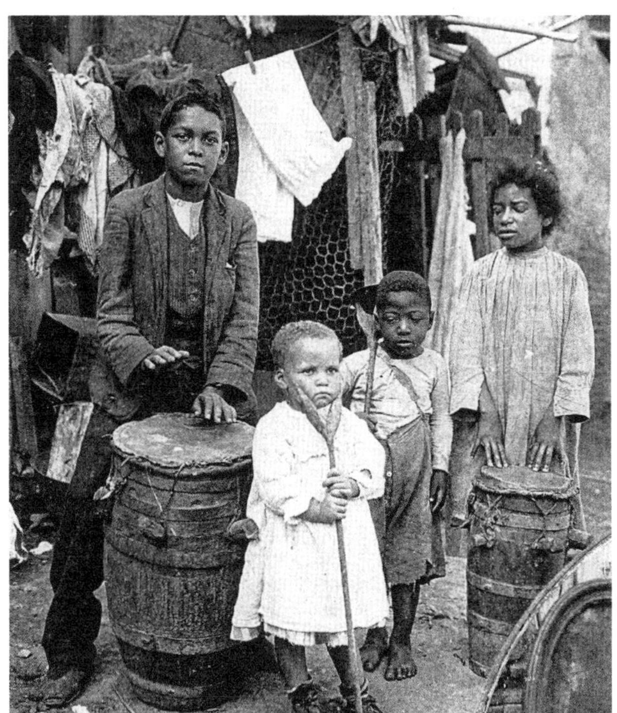

Fig. 6 Photographer unknown, "An Afro-Argentine Family of Buenos Aires," *Caras y Caretas*, March 28, 1908

12 Boxer, "Occupational Mass Psychogenic Illness," 868.
13 Boxer, 868.
14 Boxer, 870.
15 Elizabeth M. Seyler, "Review: Revealing the African Roots of Argentine Tango," *Dance Chronicle* 31, no. 1 (2008): 108.

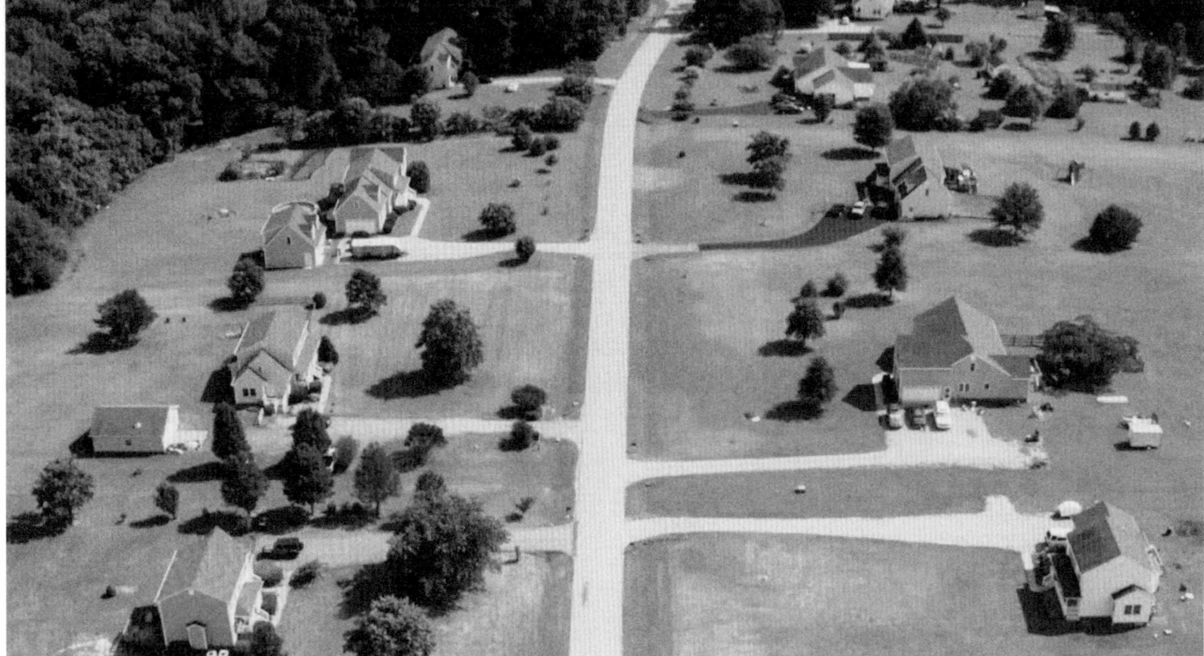

Fig. 7 Kandis Williams, *Annexation Tango*, 2020 (video still; detail) (pages 138–143)

notes that such experiences of haptic visuality, which involve the viewer's body in the process of seeing, combined with optical visuality, enact a shift and "a dialectical movement from far to near."[16] For Marks, "haptic looking tends to rest on the surface of its object rather than plunge into depth, tends not to distinguish form so much as discern texture. It is a labile, plastic sort of look, more inclined to move than to focus."[17] In this way, the subject of viewing is obscured and the viewer is encouraged to relinquish both the mastery and the separateness that are associated with optical viewing.[18]

OVERTURNED

The tidy grids of property, with houses framed by expanses of trimmed lawns, in the opening shots of *Annexation Tango* are at the other end of the spectrum to the catastrophic events in the closing scenes of the video(figs. 7–10). Though only the first scenes of settlement and property lines have been naturalized through settler-colonialism, both sequences represent the upending of worlds and devastating, planetary-level disruptions.[19] The dissolution of the division between human

16 Laura U. Marks, "Video Haptics and Erotics," *Screen* 39, no. 4 (Winter 1998): 332.
17 Marks, "Video Haptics and Erotics," 338.
18 Marks, 341.
19 *Annexation Tango*, Vimeo, uploaded by Morán Morán, October 4, 2022, https://vimeo.com/756994858.

and nonhuman, and the capture of land, the body, and its descendants as commodity through Europe's colonizing empires and racial capitalism call for no less than a second (or yet another) total overturning of worlds. This overturning, or undoing, requires an invocation of equally destructive forces, and perhaps is even already put into motion as the eventual outcome of the Anthropocene era's environmental devastation. As if to image this undoing, *Annexation Tango* features clips and image-reversals of fires and violently contracting and expanding storm (or smoke?) clouds, consuming, respectively, the ground from below and the heavens from above.

What this re-worlding and dehumanization looks like in Wynter's description is the forced agricultural labor in the "plantation area" of the Caribbean as "adjunct to the product," where not only are beings and bodies configured as twinned with commodity production but also lives and land are totally subsumed into and dominated by the needs and market value of the single-crop plantation. According to Wynter, such is the cultural legacy of the region's alienation, uninterrupted by abolition and independence in the postcolonial Caribbean, which is "without exception still 'enchanted,' imprisoned, deformed and schizophrenic in its bewitched reality," brought into existence through colonialism's

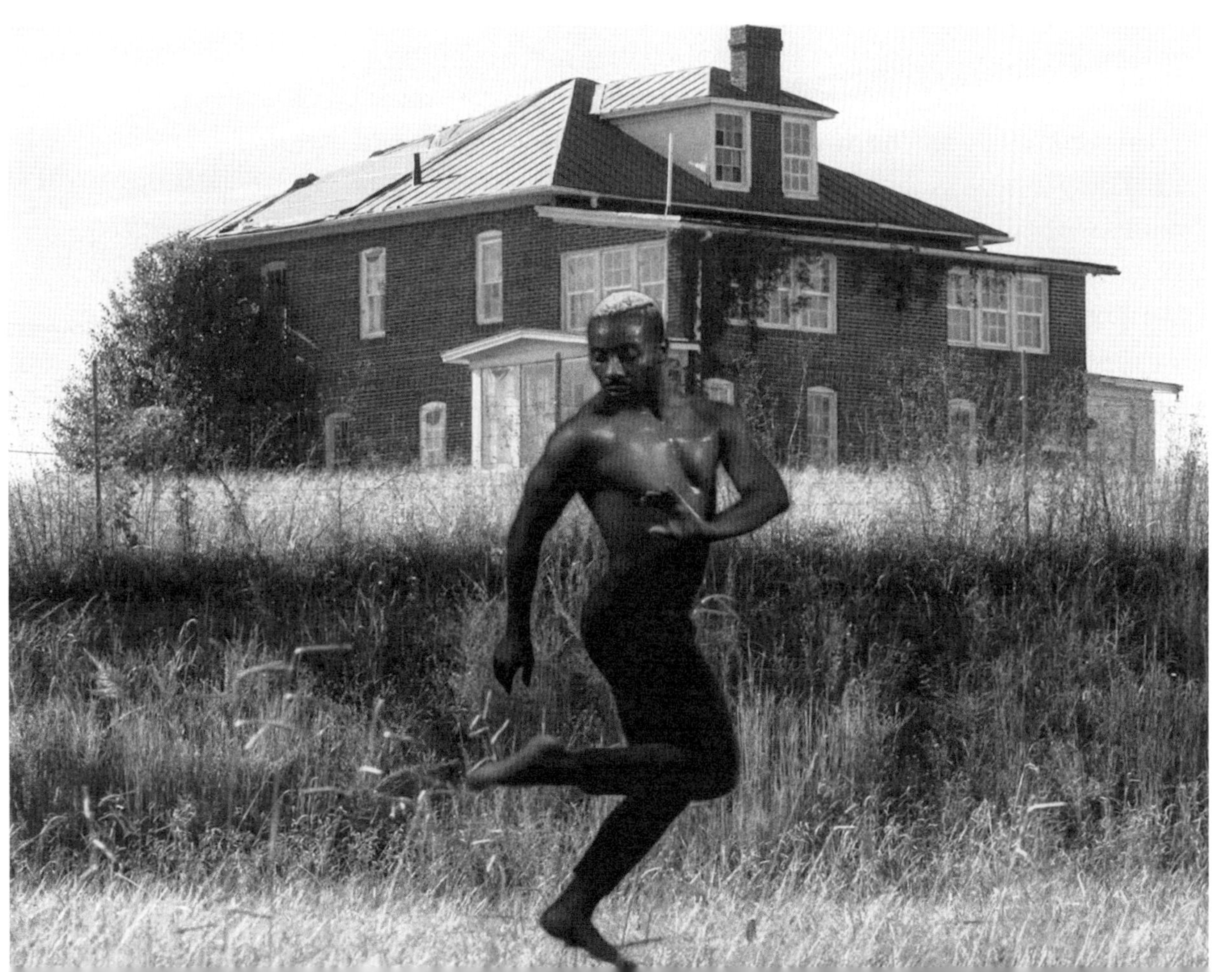

Fig. 8 Kandis Williams, *Annexation Tango*, 2020 (video still) (pages 138–143)

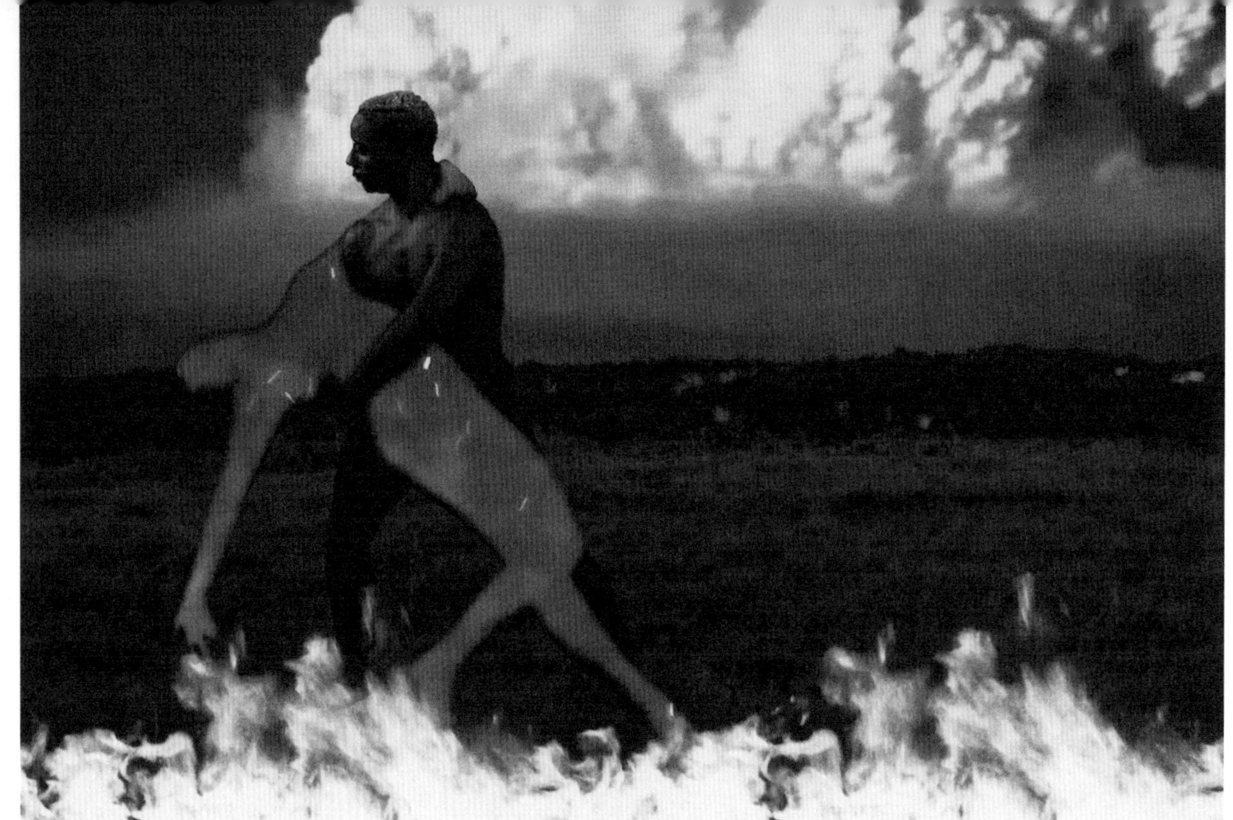

Figs. 9, 10 Kandis Williams, *Annexation Tango*, 2020 (video stills) (pages 138–143)

narrative arcs and fictions that reordered Indigenous, African, and beyond-human worlds into hierarchies of economic and human agency.[20]

The containers of extracted labor, sweat, and fear—the field and the factory—transform the body into an asset without agency. Necessary to surviving the plantation is the plot, a space for underclass subsistence, dominated by crops as use-value for sustenance.[21] It is through exhaustion, toxicity, and breakdown that the hopeless and brutalized find the capacity to begin the process of turning both body and plantation, or the captive and the territory, into reclaimed social and cultural spaces for the rooting of identity and kinship lost through exile.

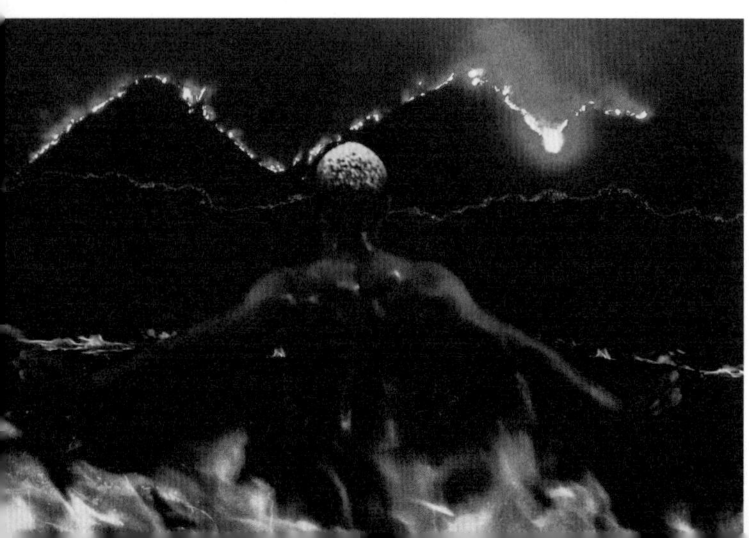

20 Wynter, "Novel and History, Plot and Plantation," 291.
21 Wynter, 291.

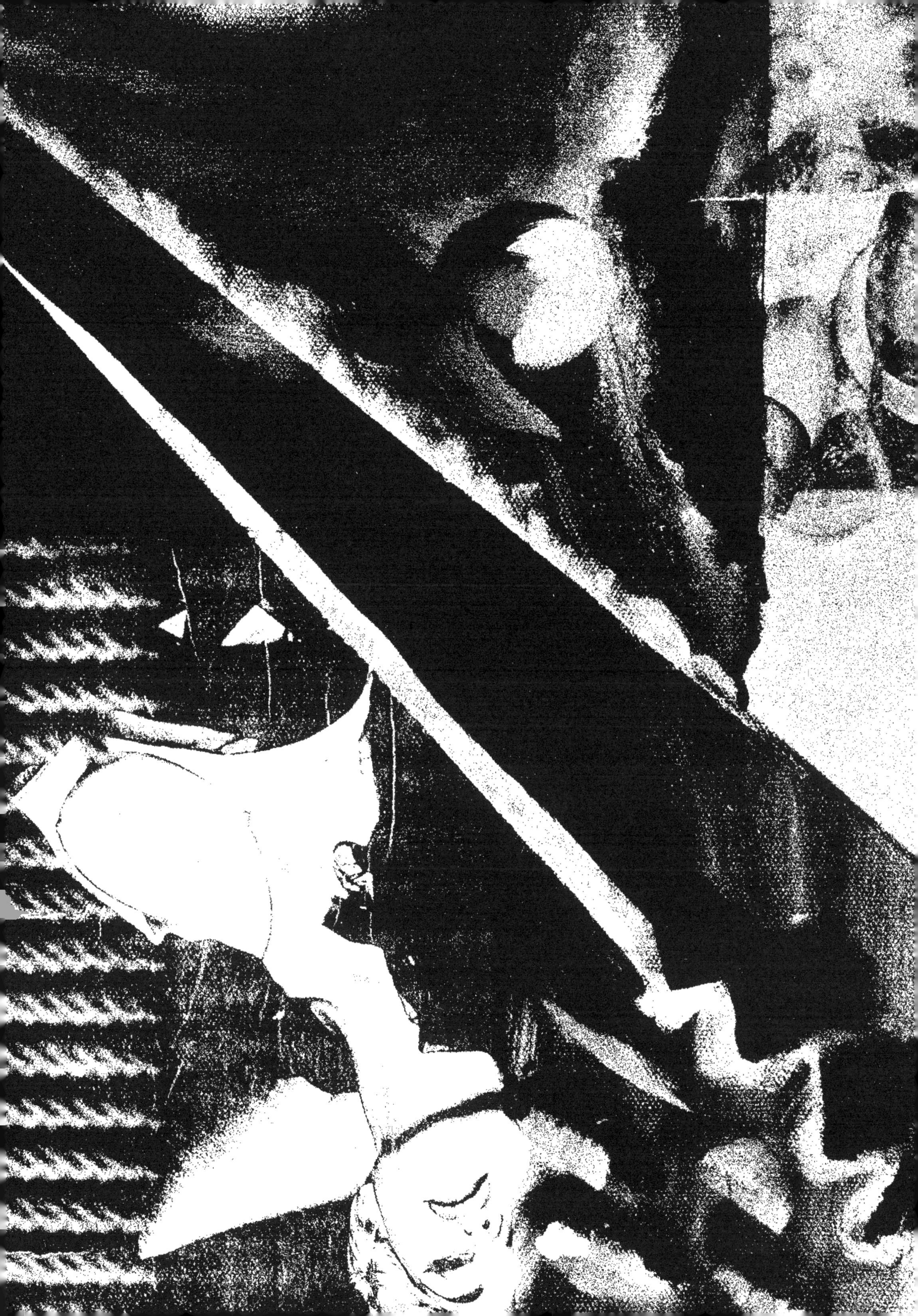

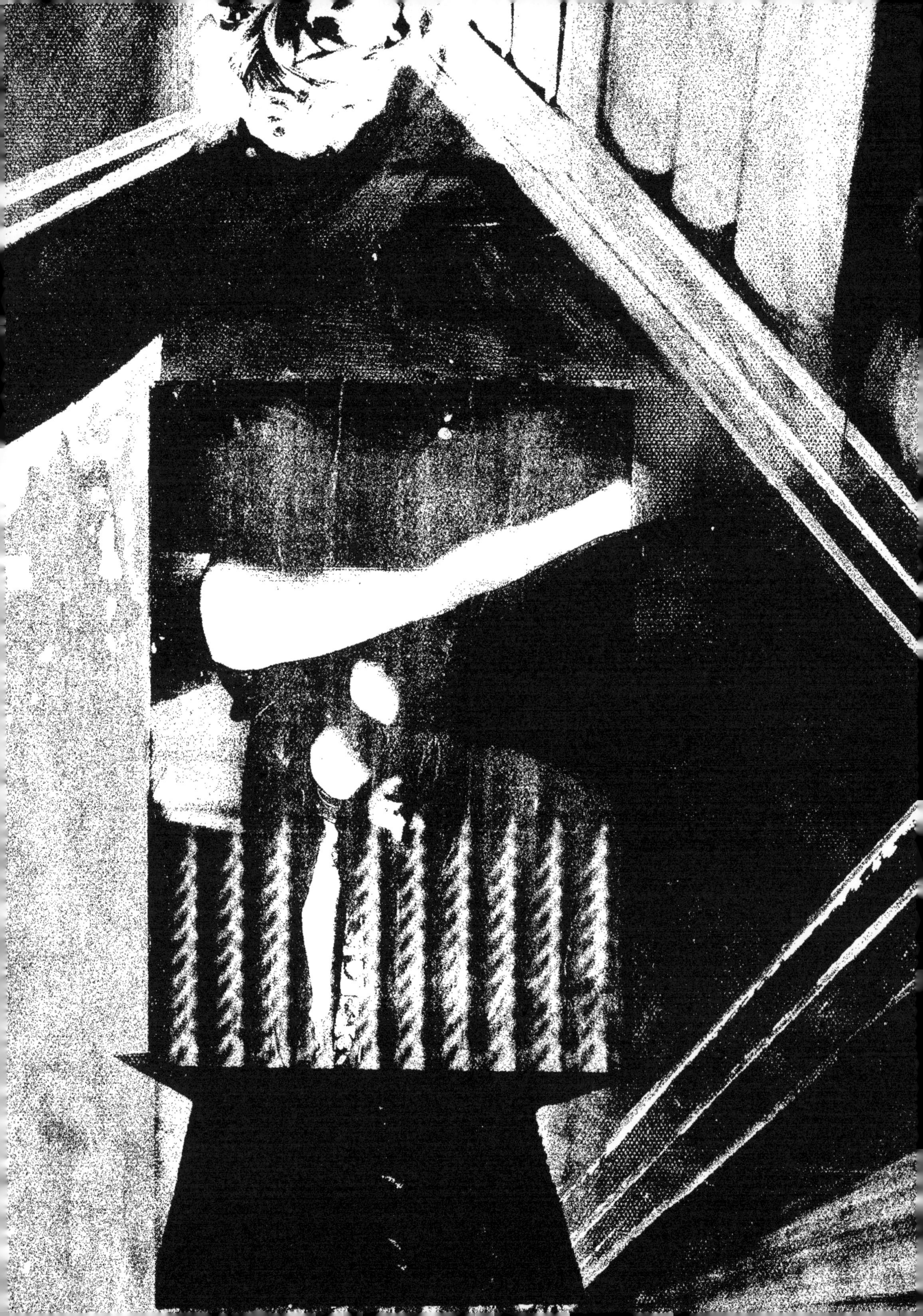

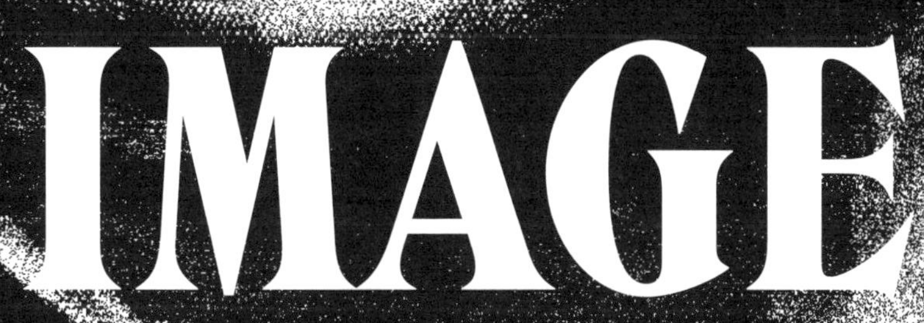
IMAGE

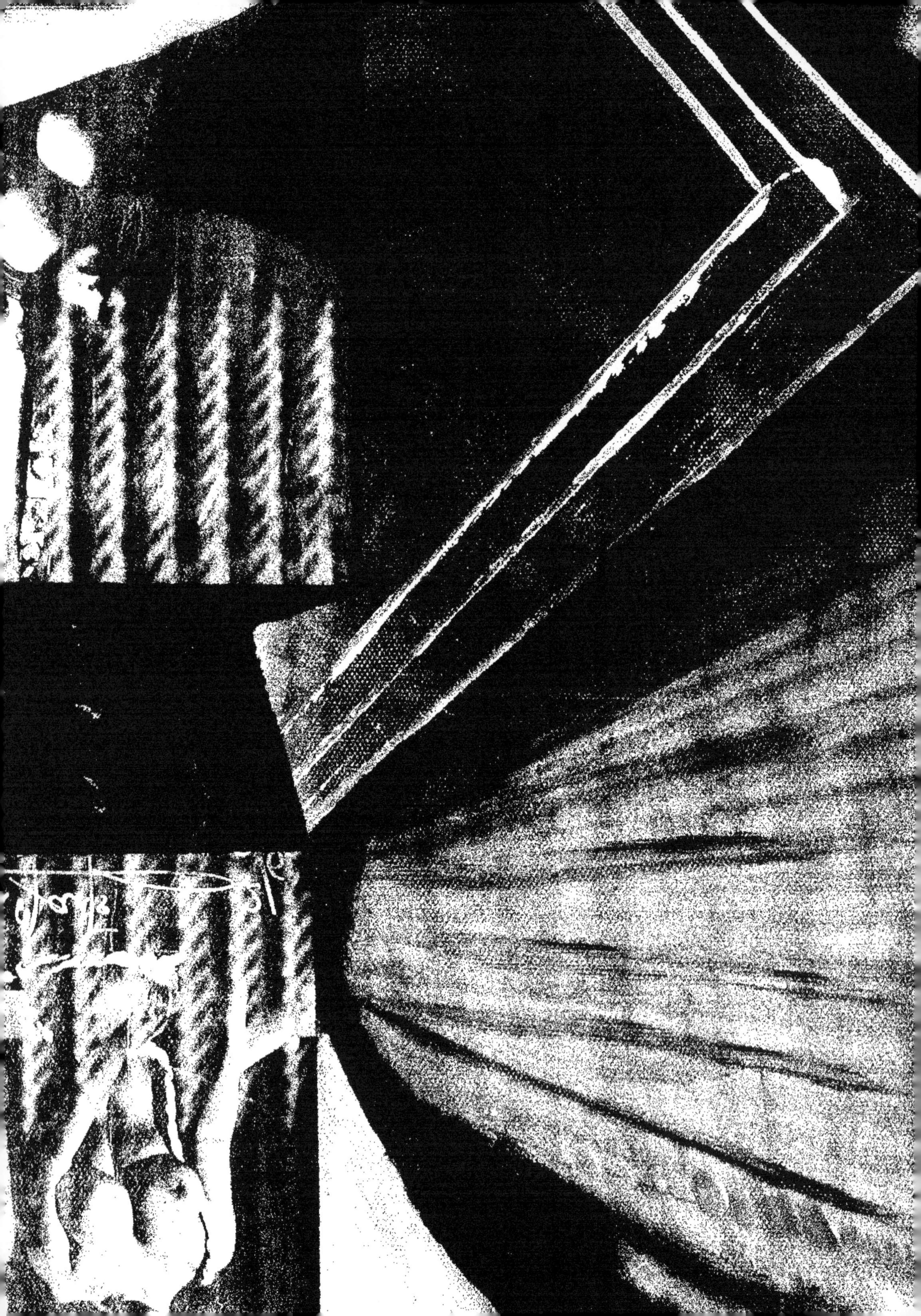

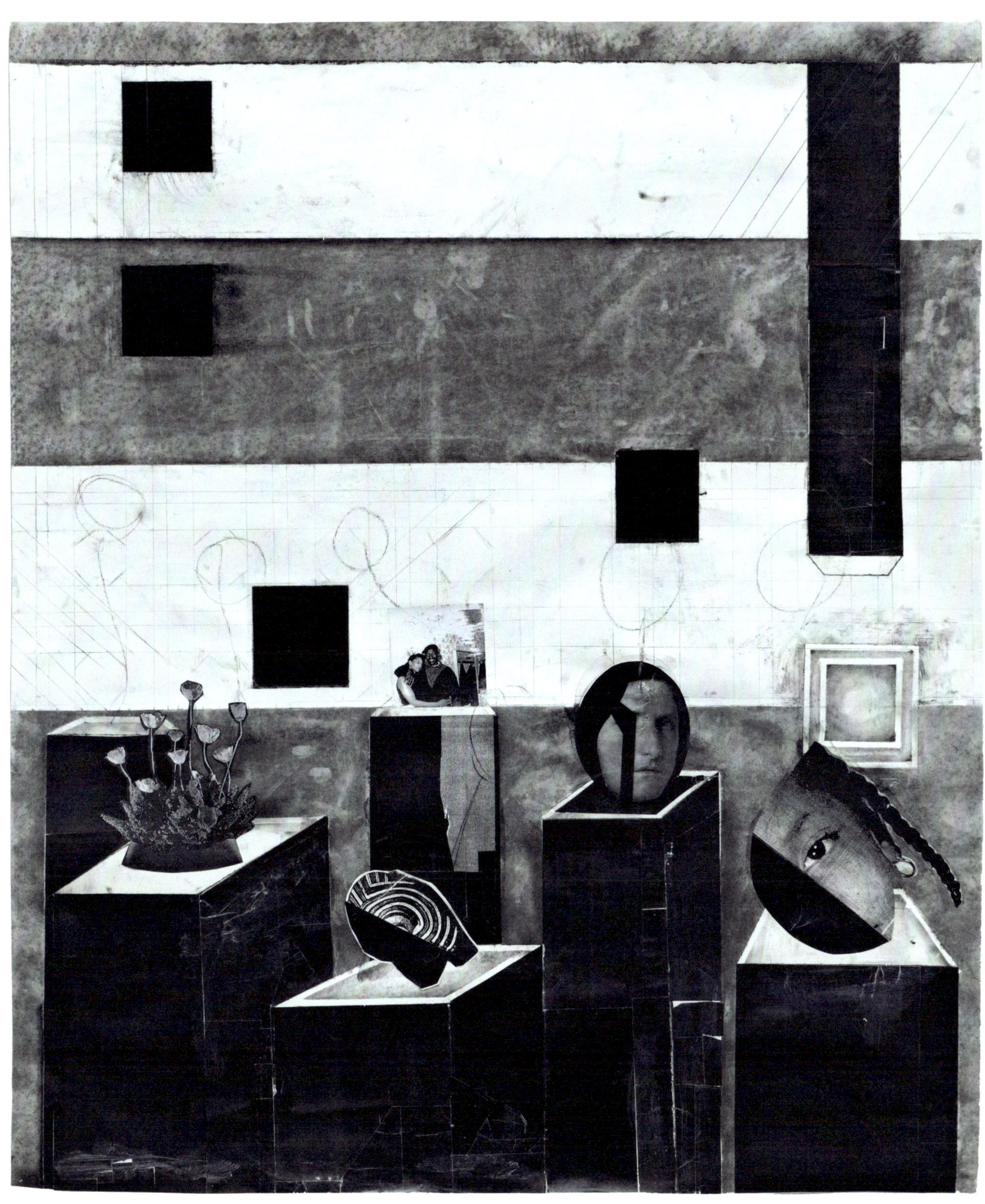

Pedestal, 2013, collage print on paper

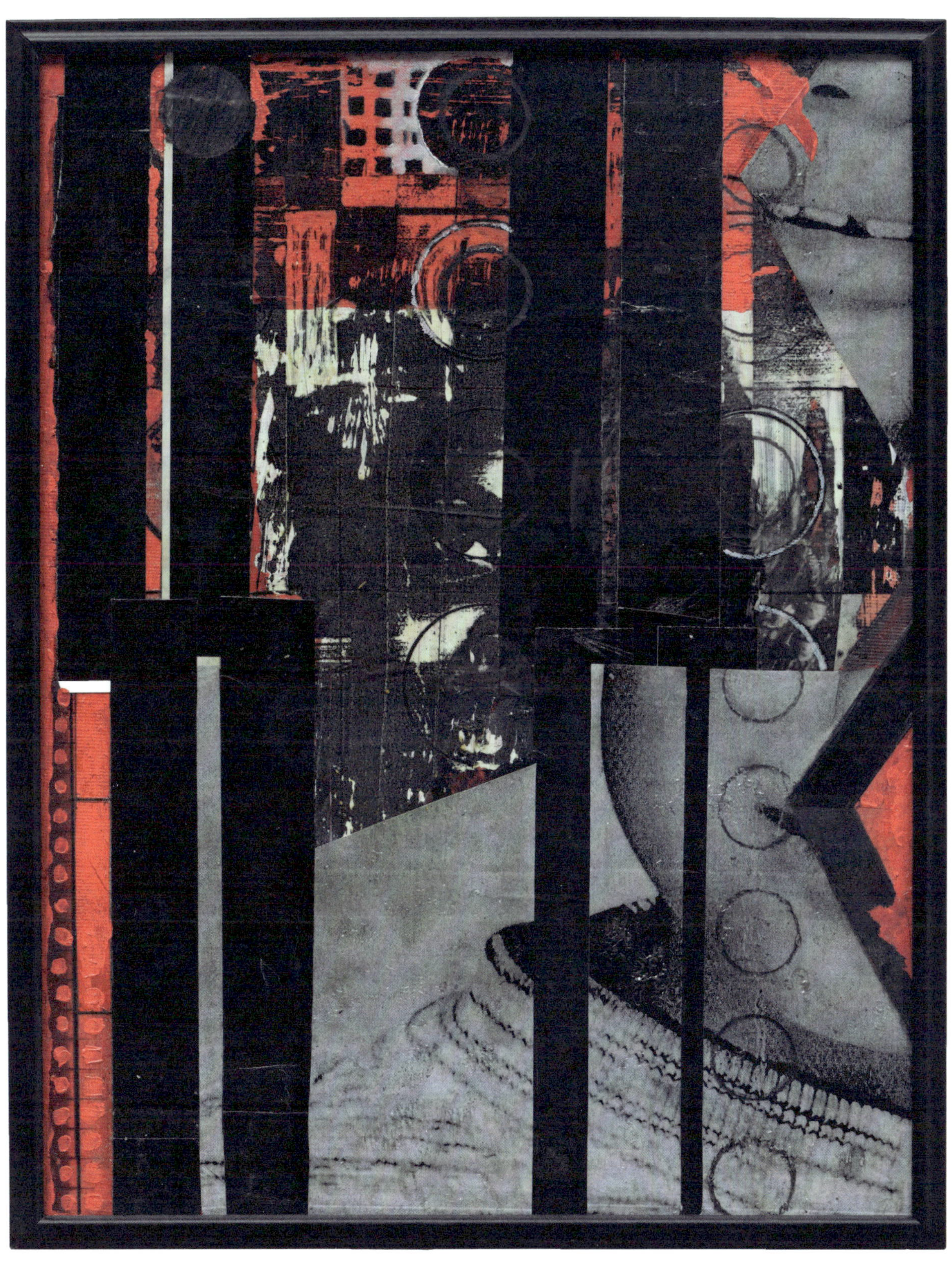

Child M/other 3, 2013, acrylic paint and collage on canvas

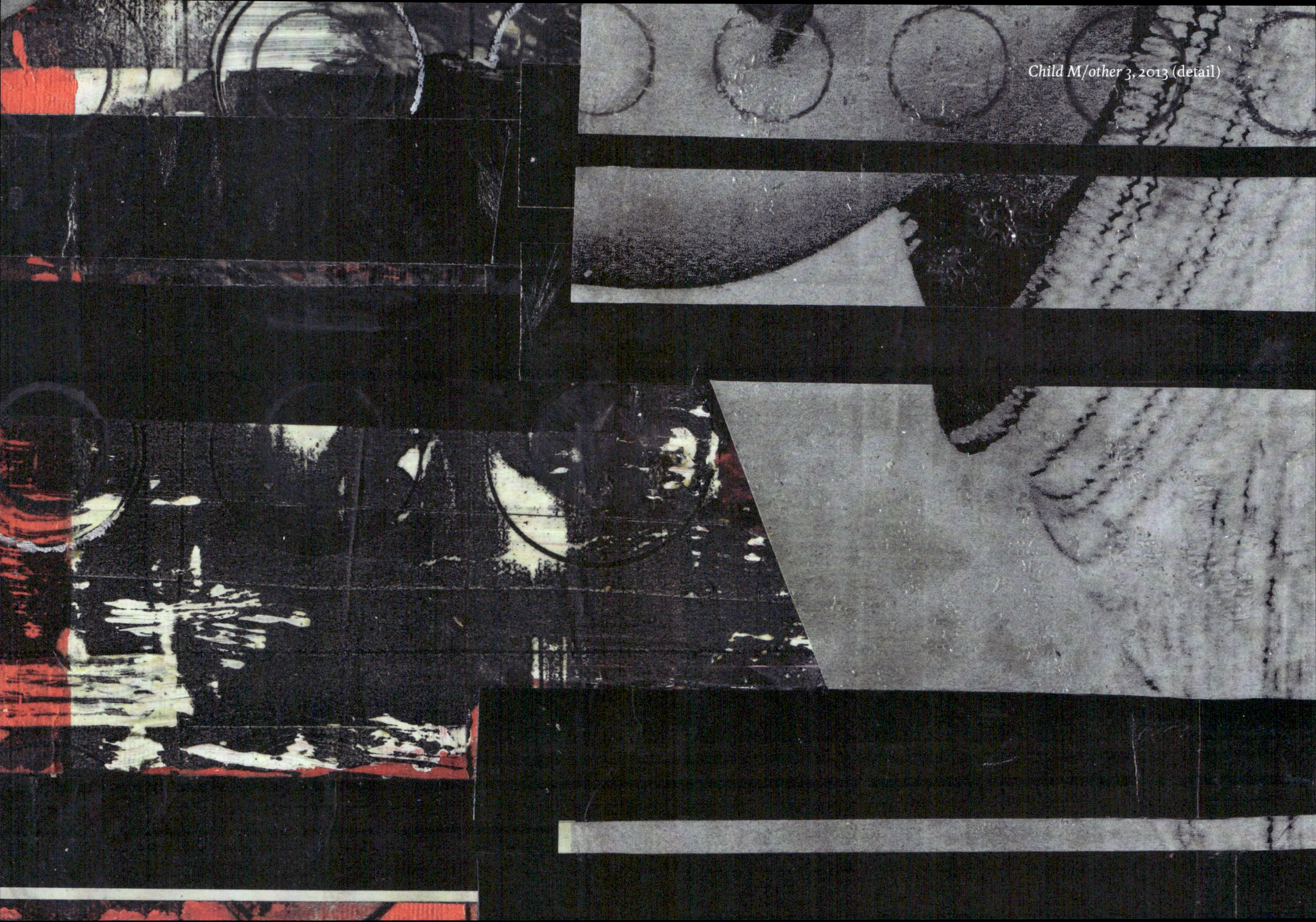

Child M/other 3, 2013 (detail)

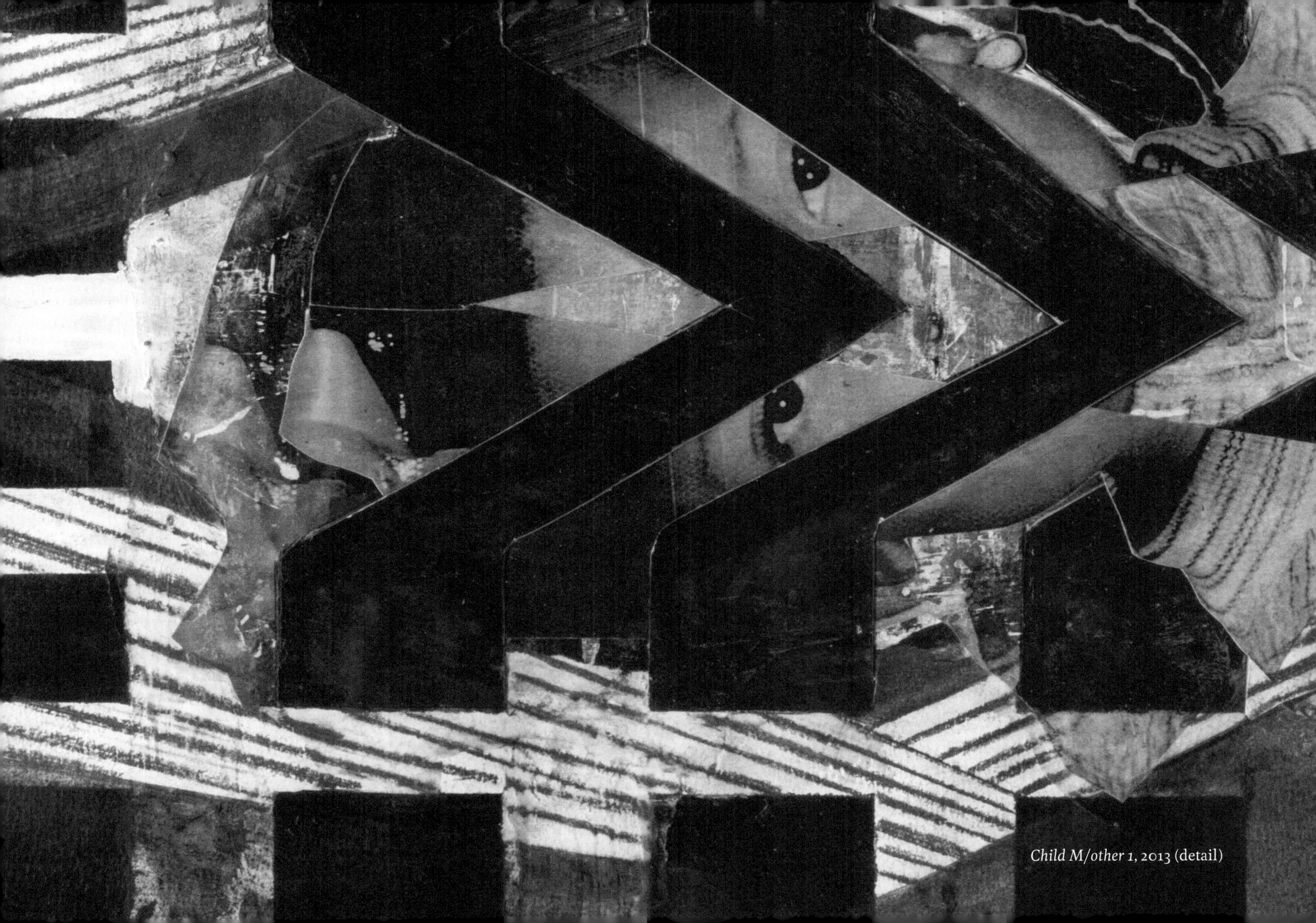

Child M/other 1, 2013 (detail)

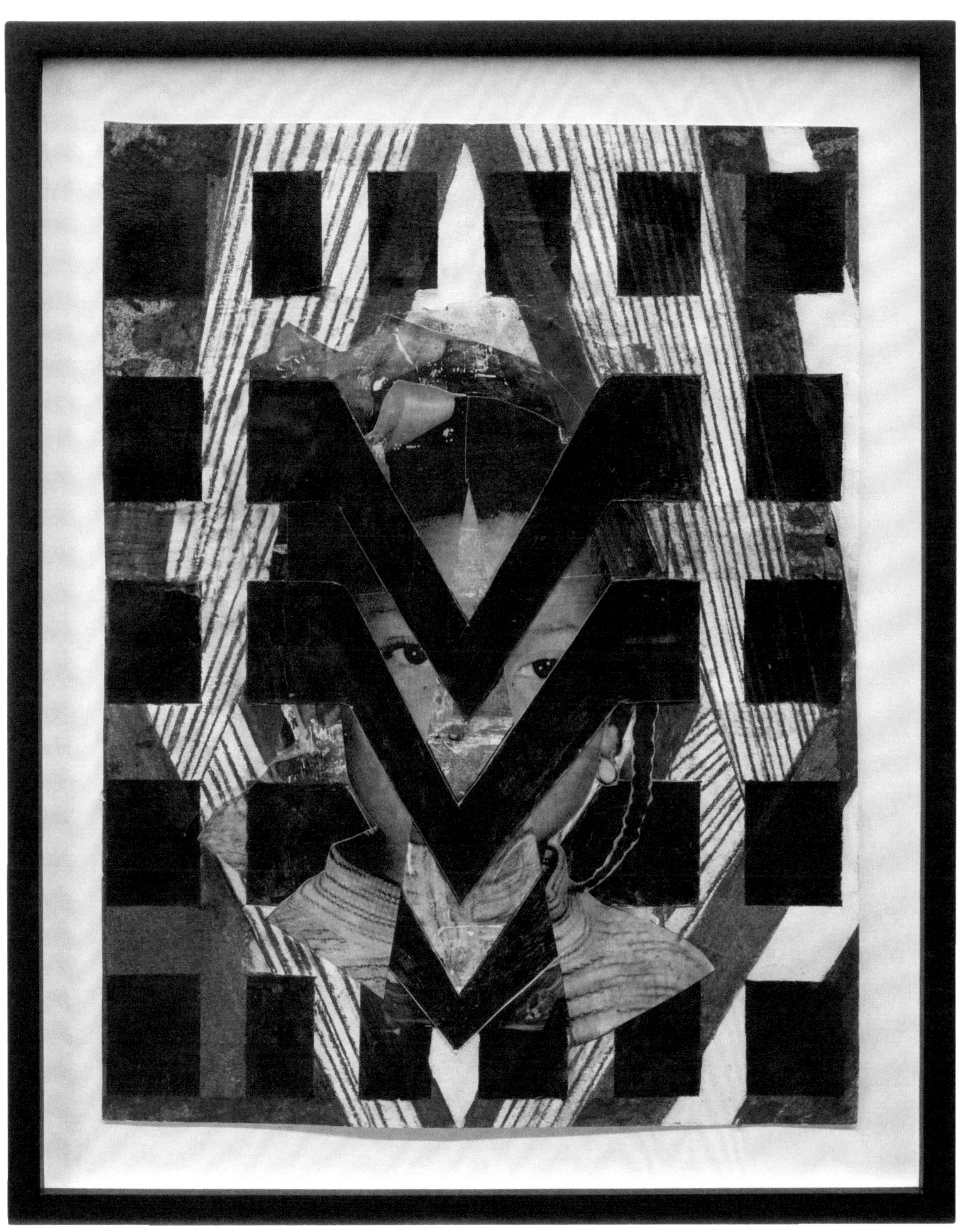

Child M/other 1, 2013, acrylic paint and collage on canvas

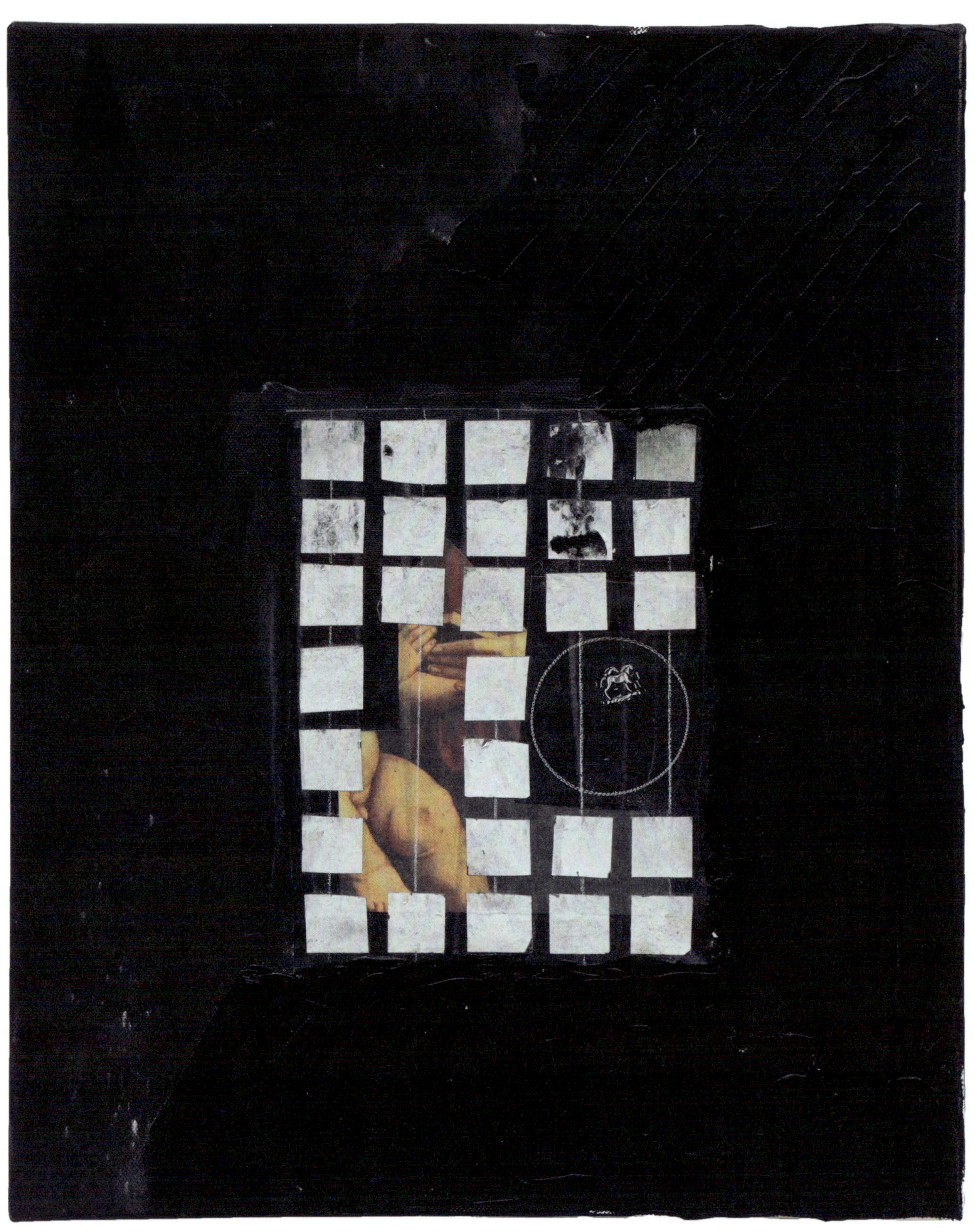

to be gazed at endlessly by the mother is a primary narcissistic demand, 2013, acrylic paint and collage on canvas

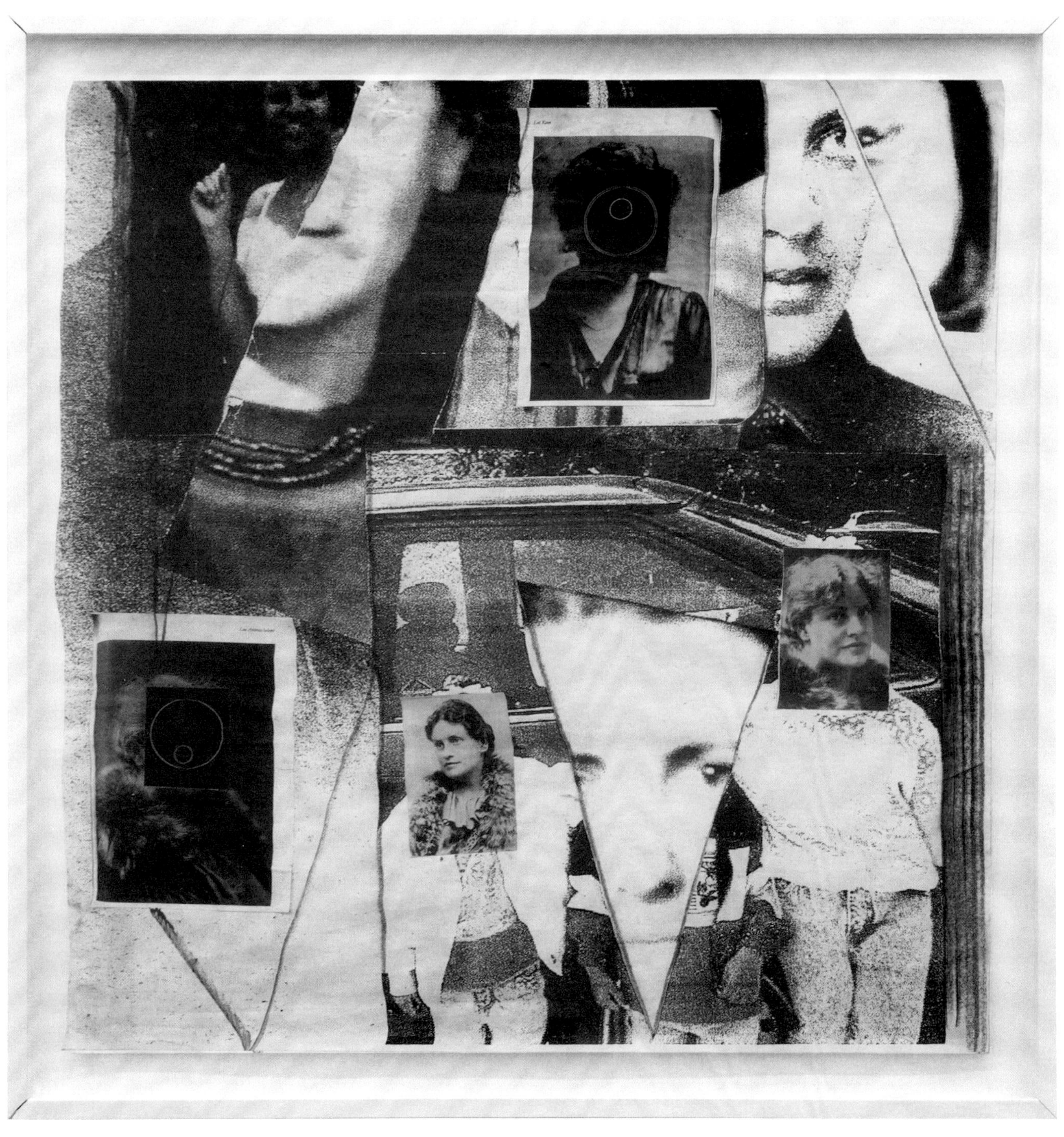

The Endless Gaze, 2014, mixed media on paper

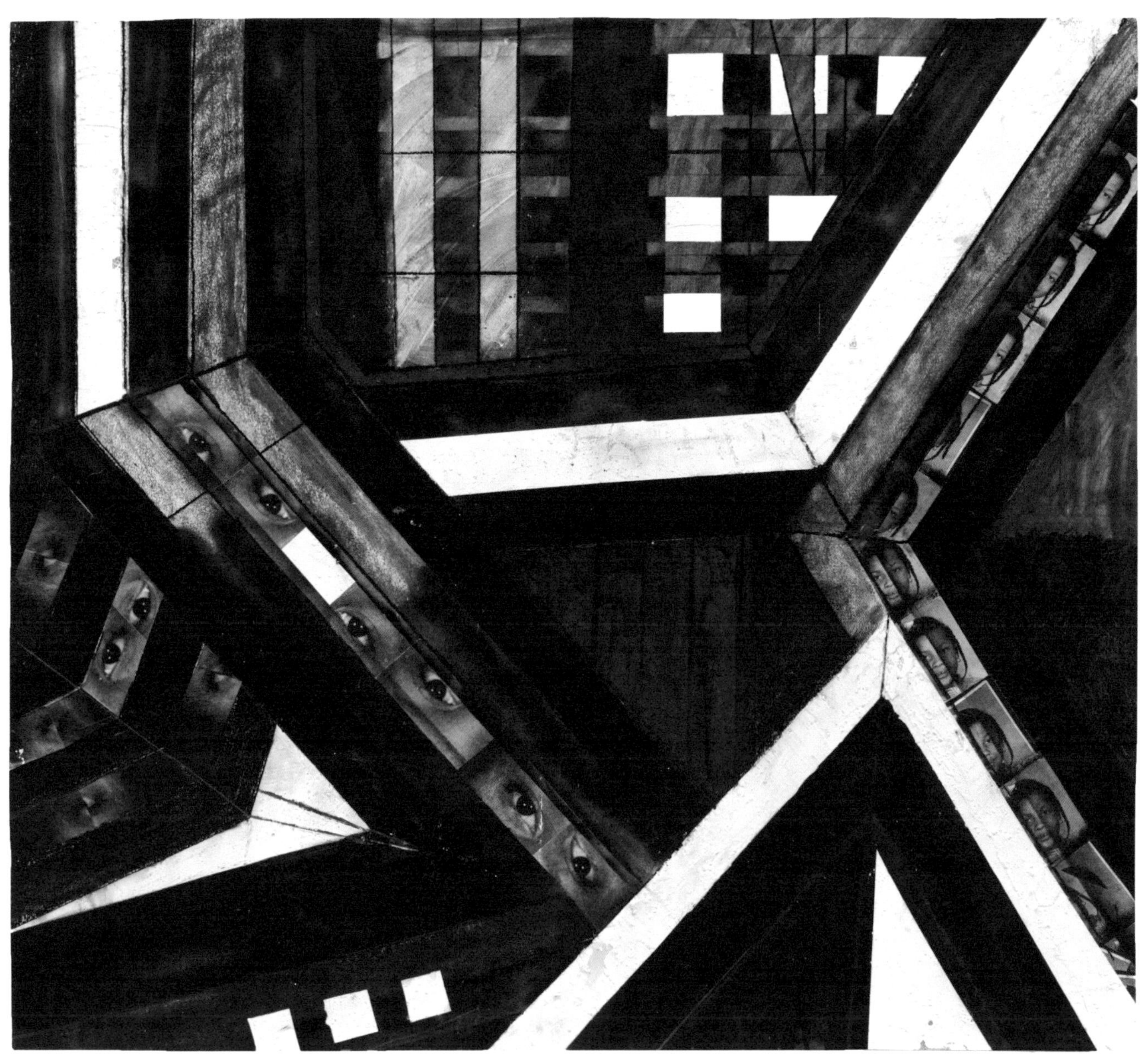

Demeter Persephone Downtown LA, 2014, mixed media on paper

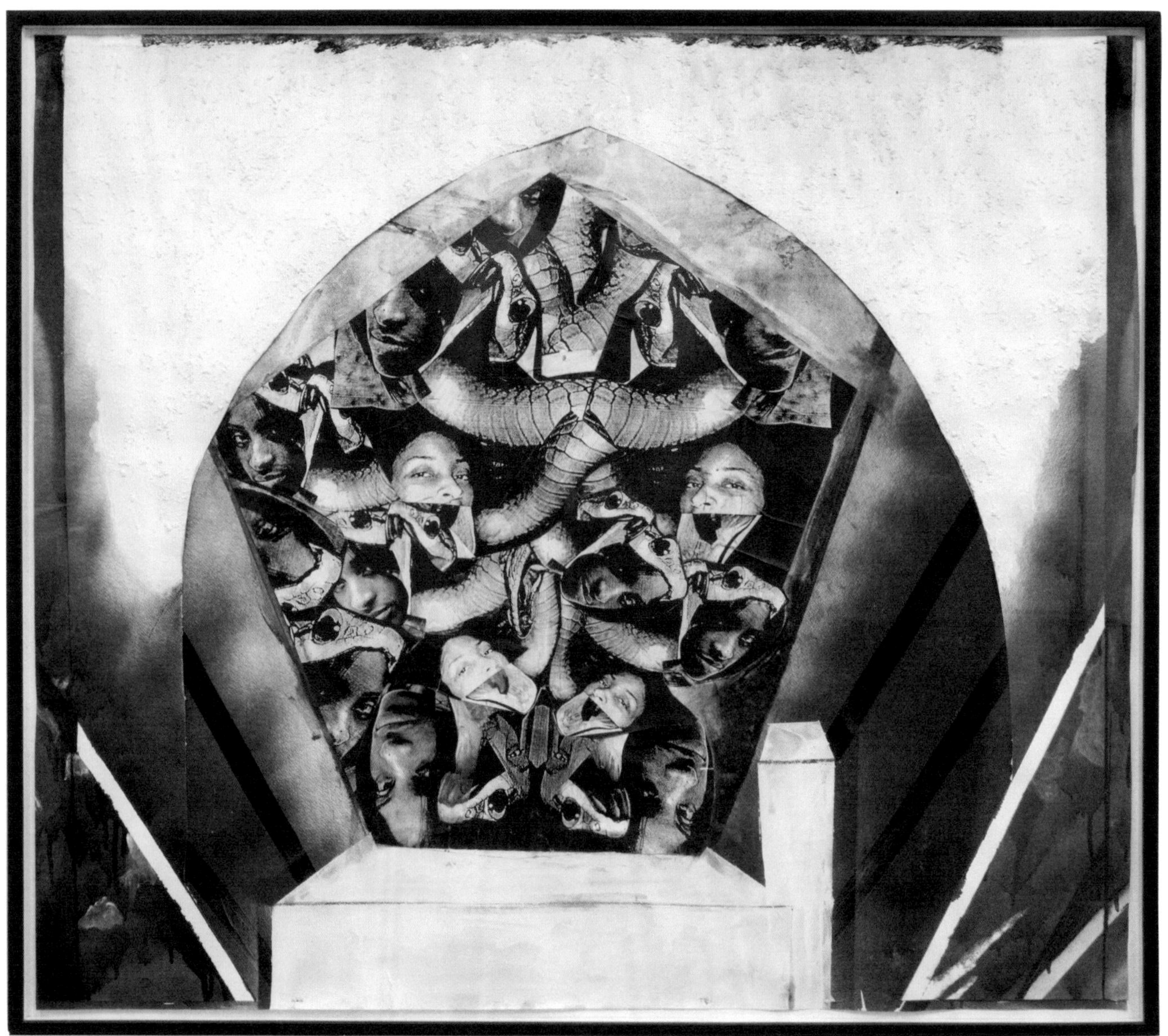

kid sister, 2014, mixed media on paper

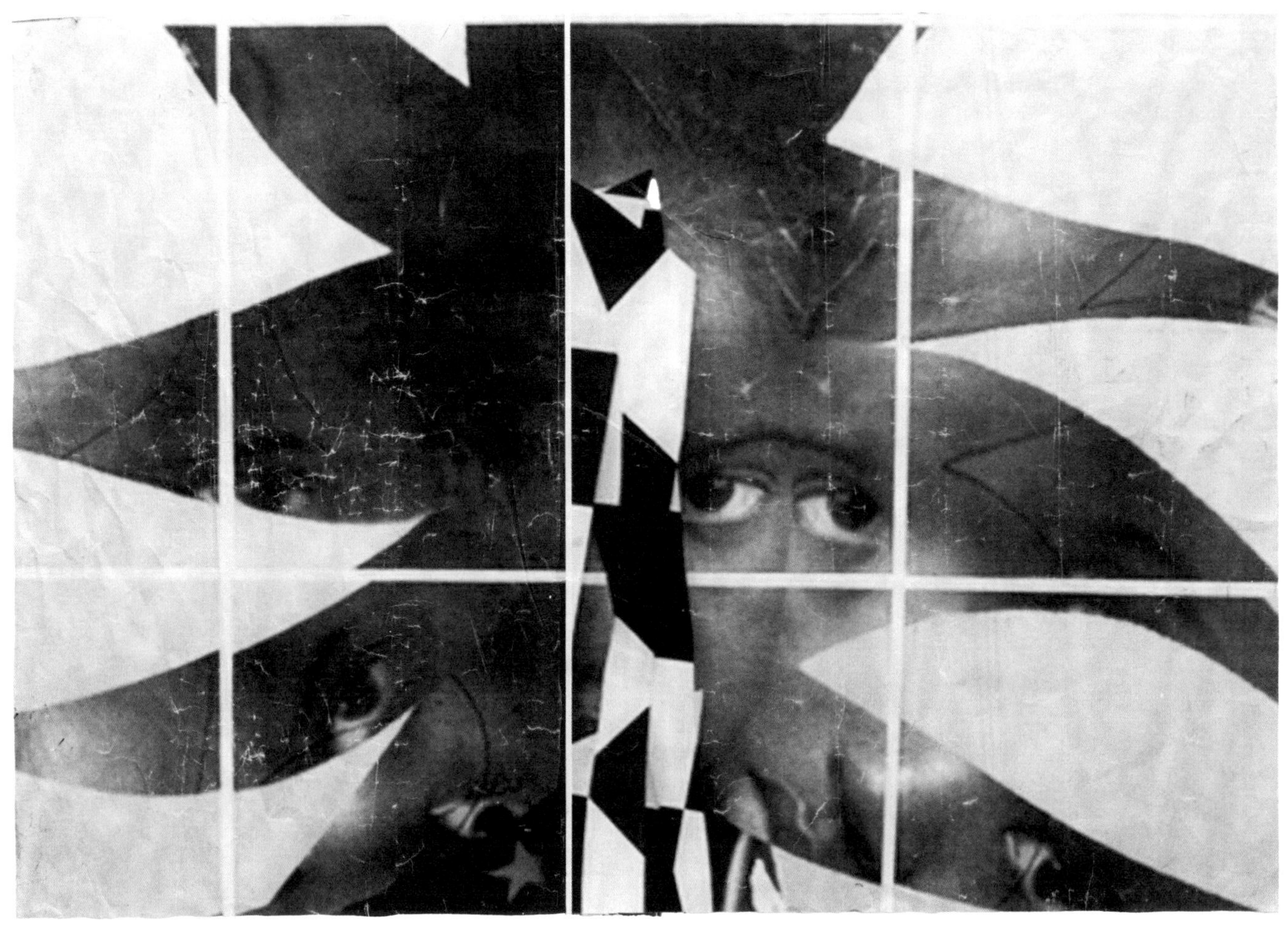

Study for Liza Jane (Unborn Daughter), 2015, collage on paper

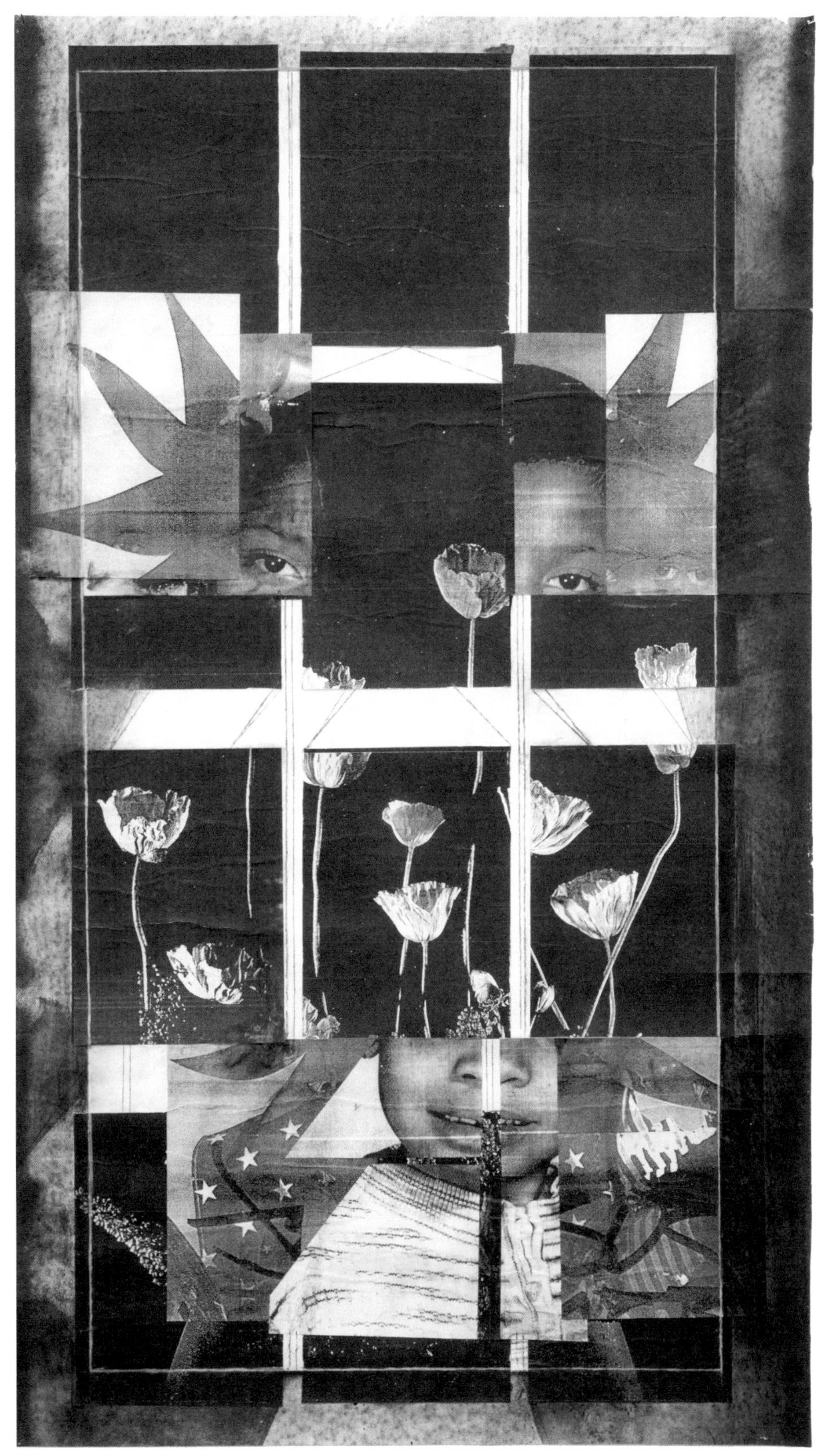

Mother sister sister anchor arrangement, 2013, xerox, charcoal, and acrylic on paper

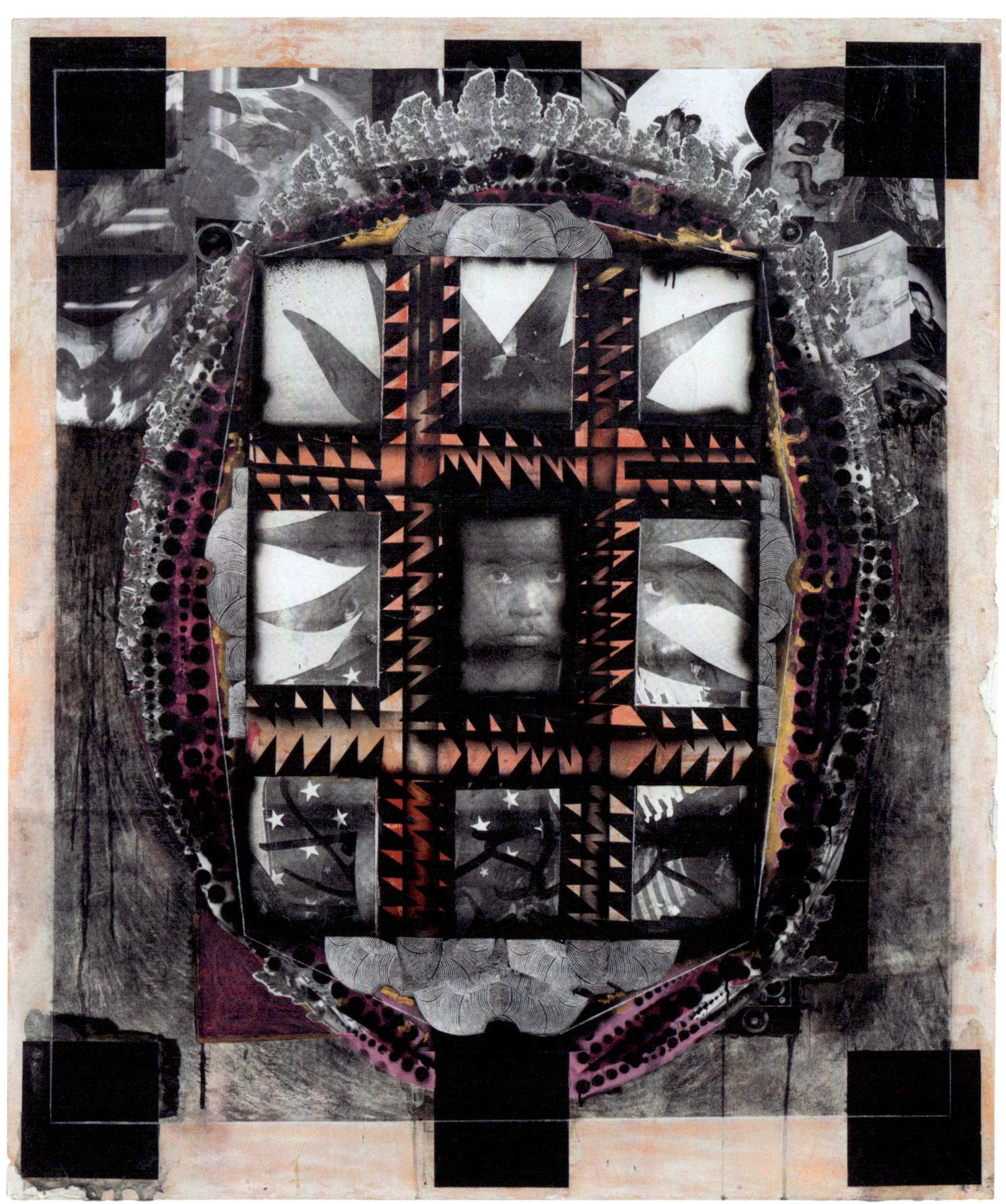

Study for Liza Jane (Unborn Daughter), 2015, mixed media on board

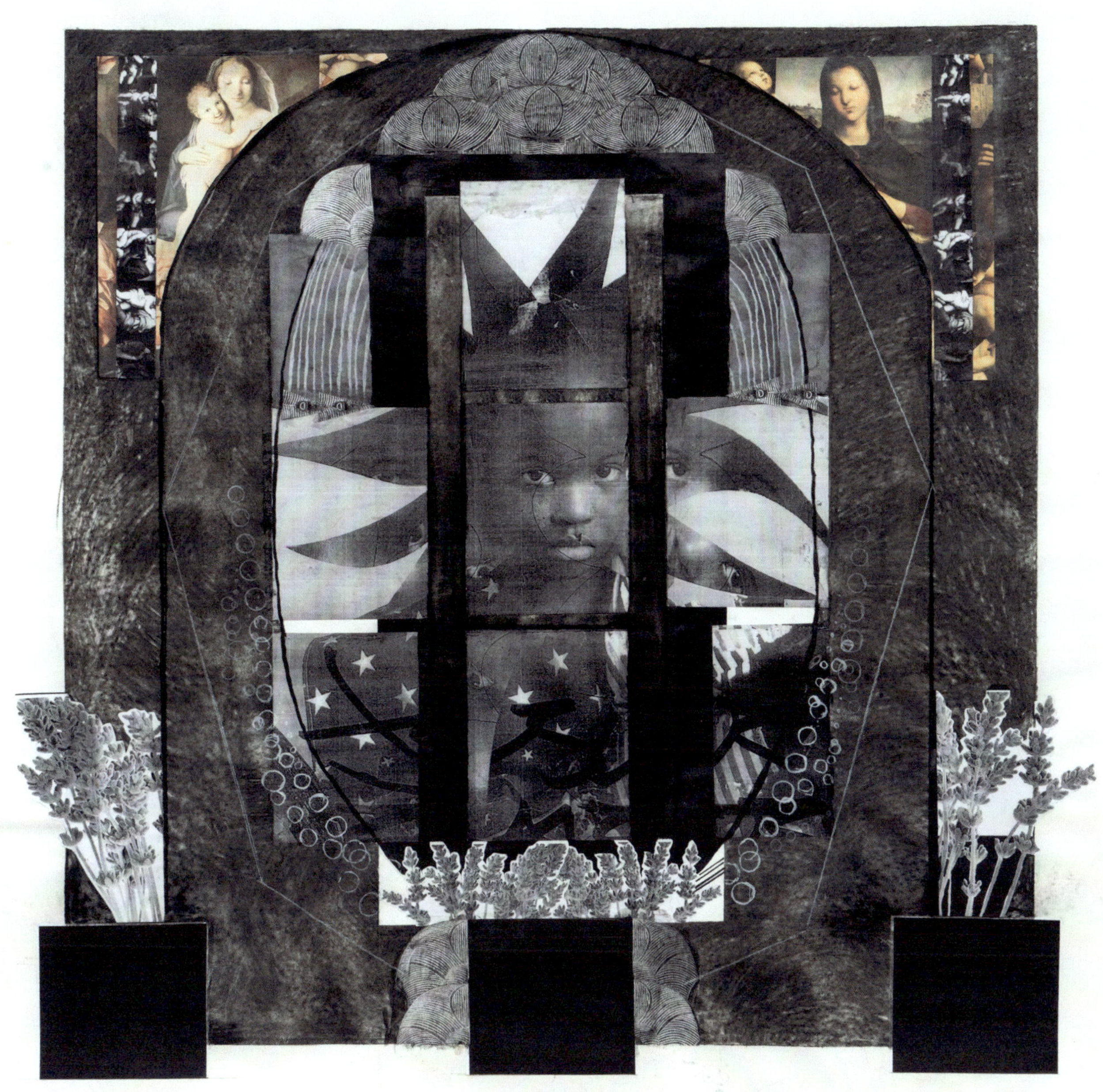

Study for Liza Jane (Unborn Daughter), 2015, acrylic paint, ink, and collage on paper

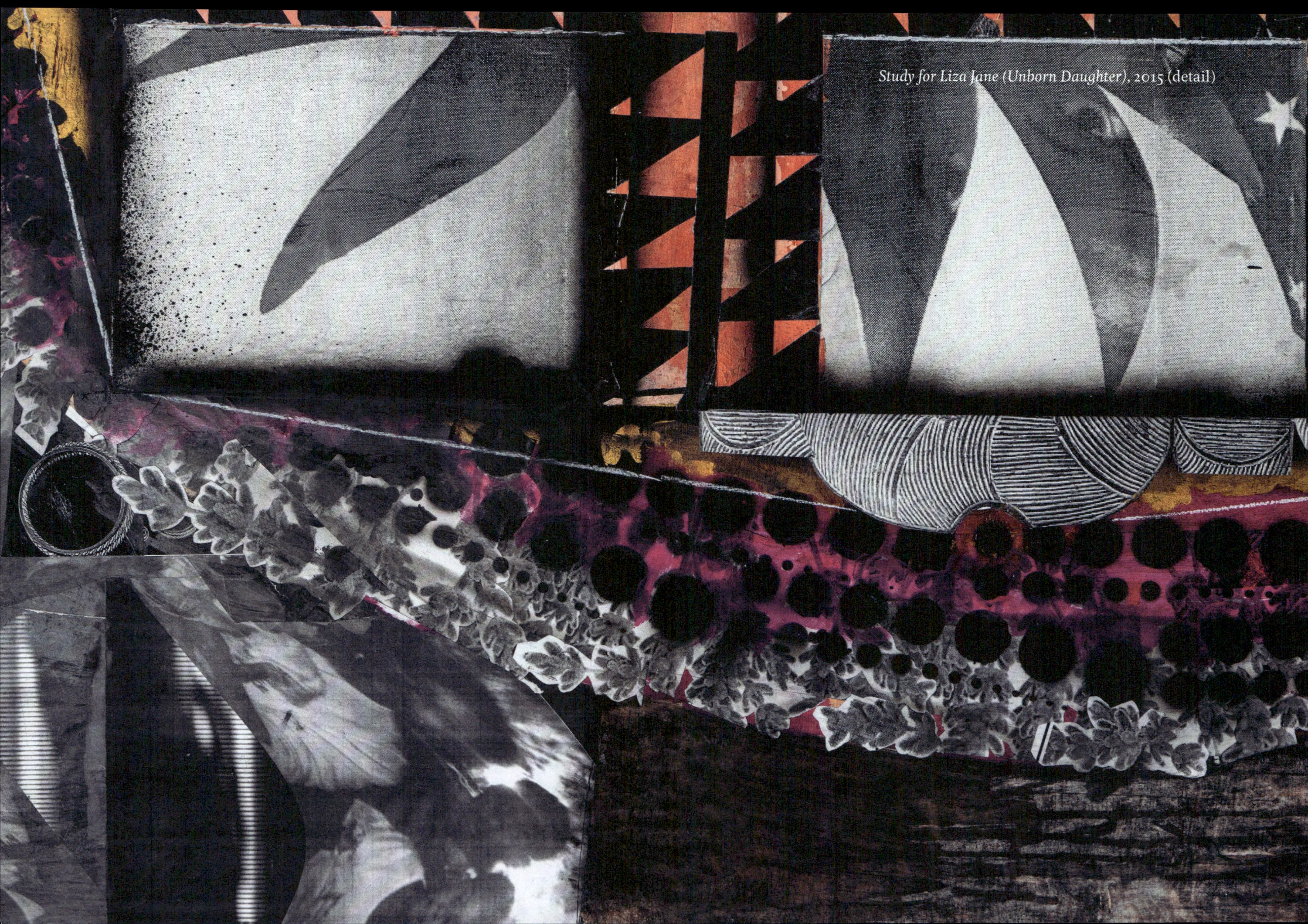

Study for Liza Jane (Unborn Daughter), 2015 (detail)

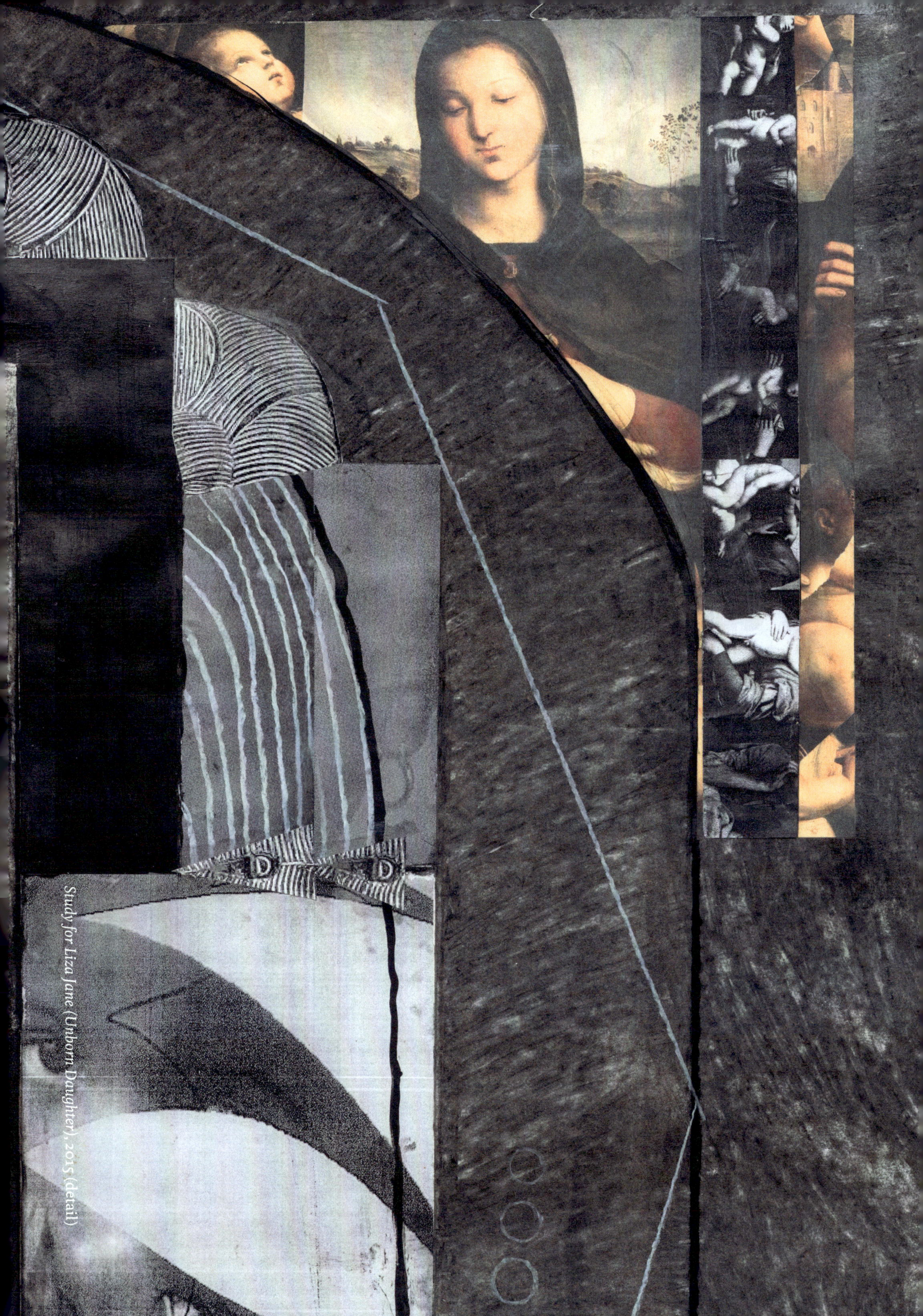

Study for Liza Jane (Unborn Daughter), 2015 (detail)

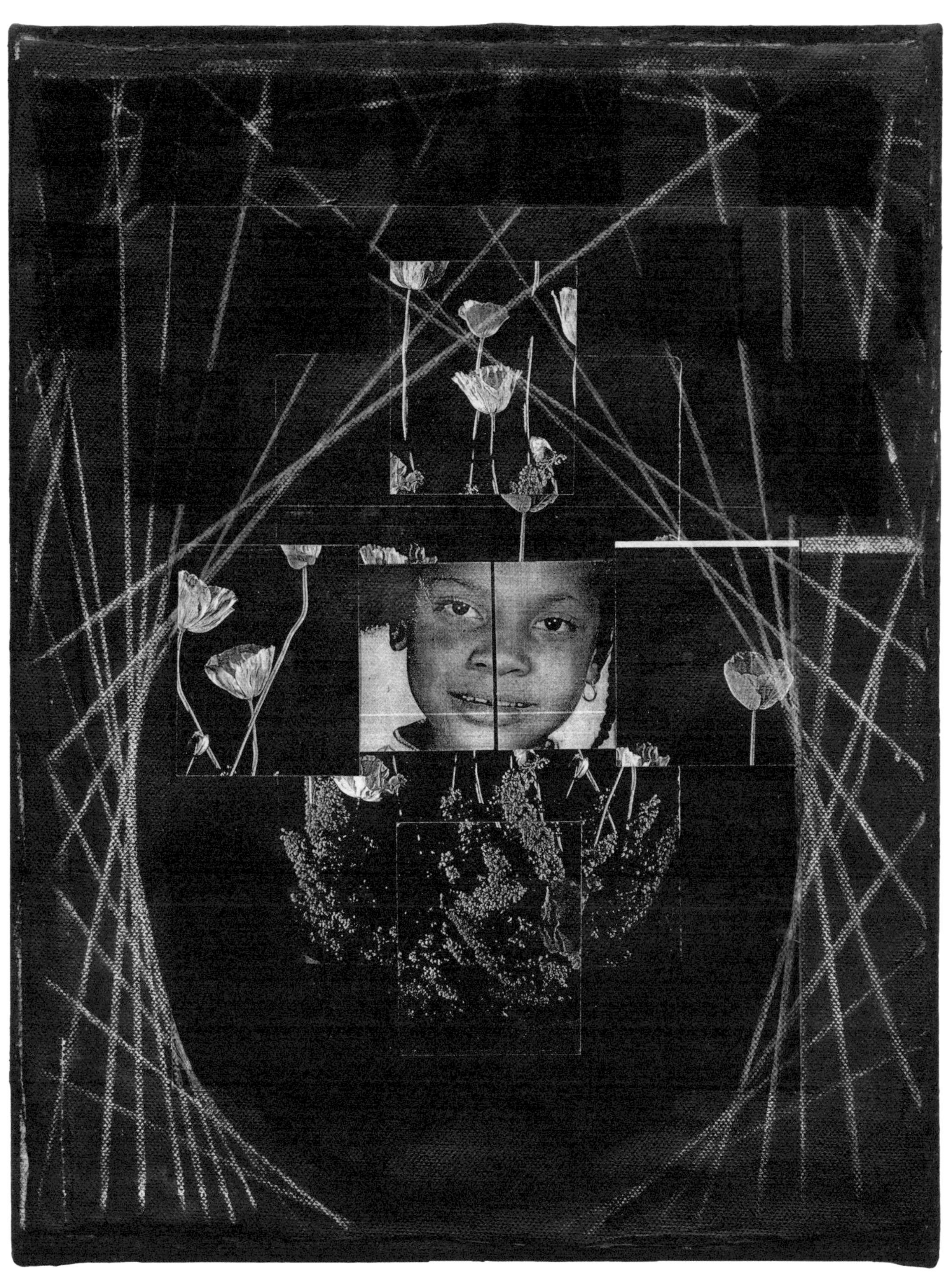

M/other 4, 2015, acrylic paint and collage on canvas

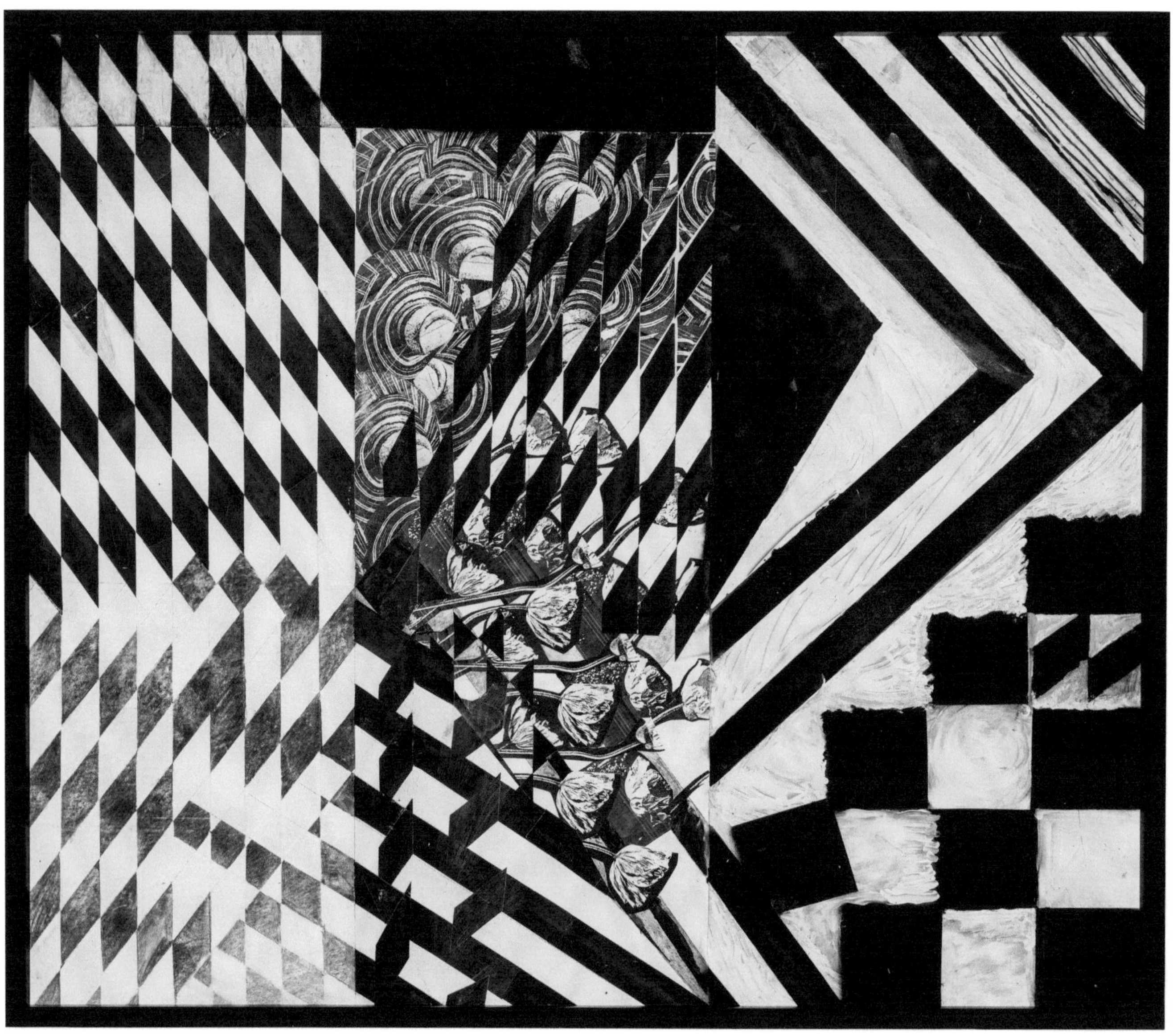

Songye Shield, 2015, acrylic paint, ink, and collage on panel

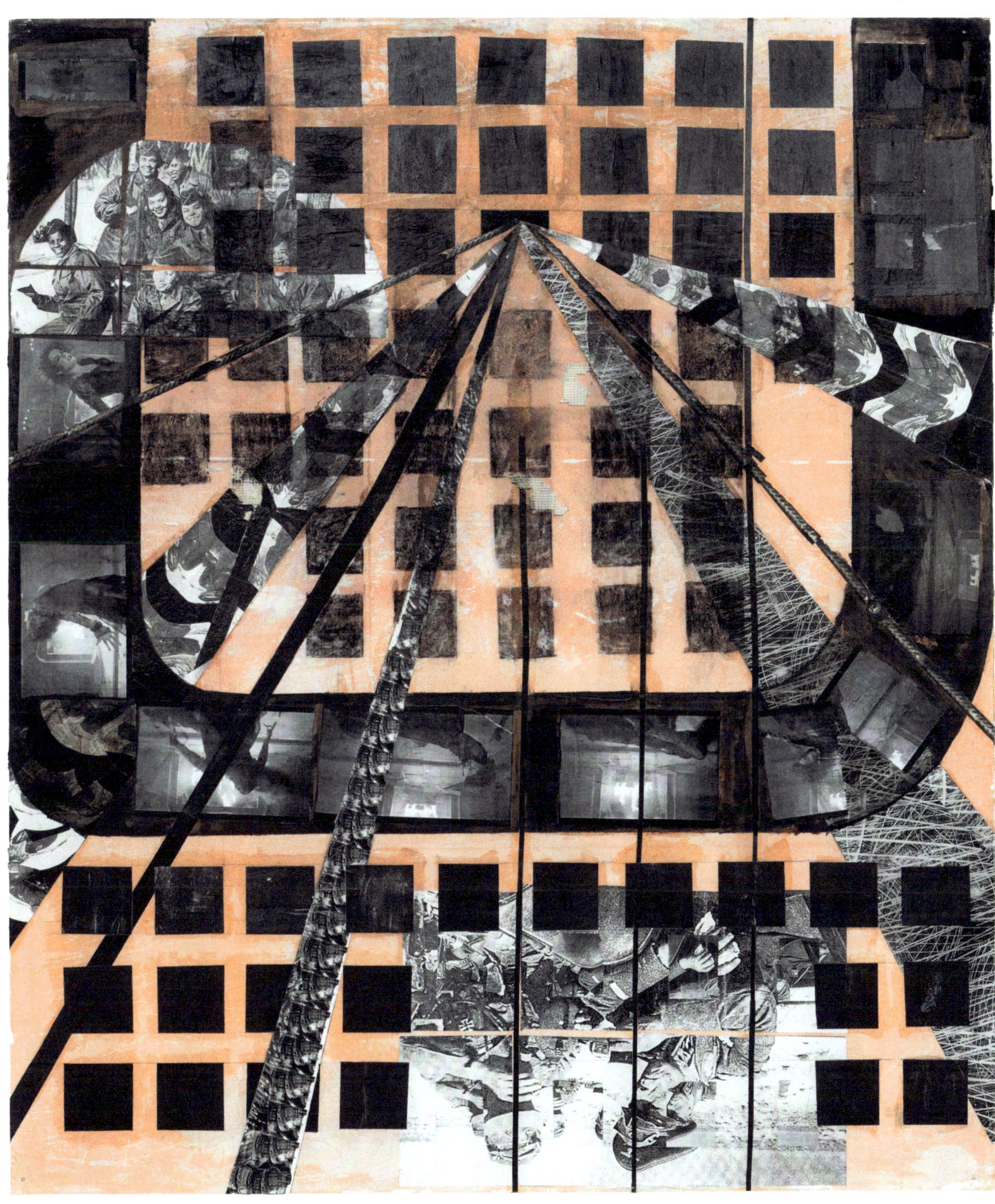

Study, 2015, mixed media on board

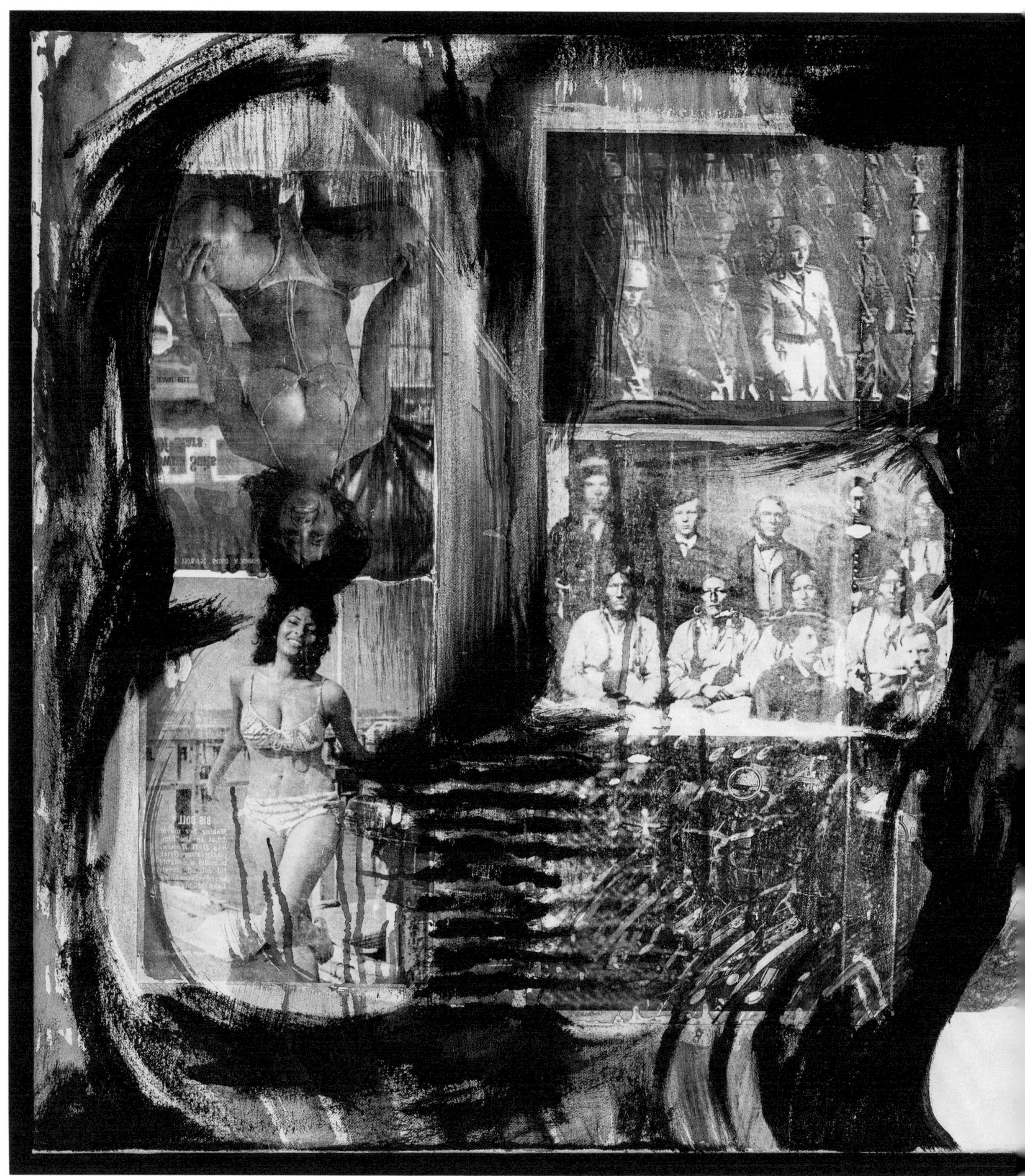

Study, 2015, acrylic paint, ink, and collage on canvas

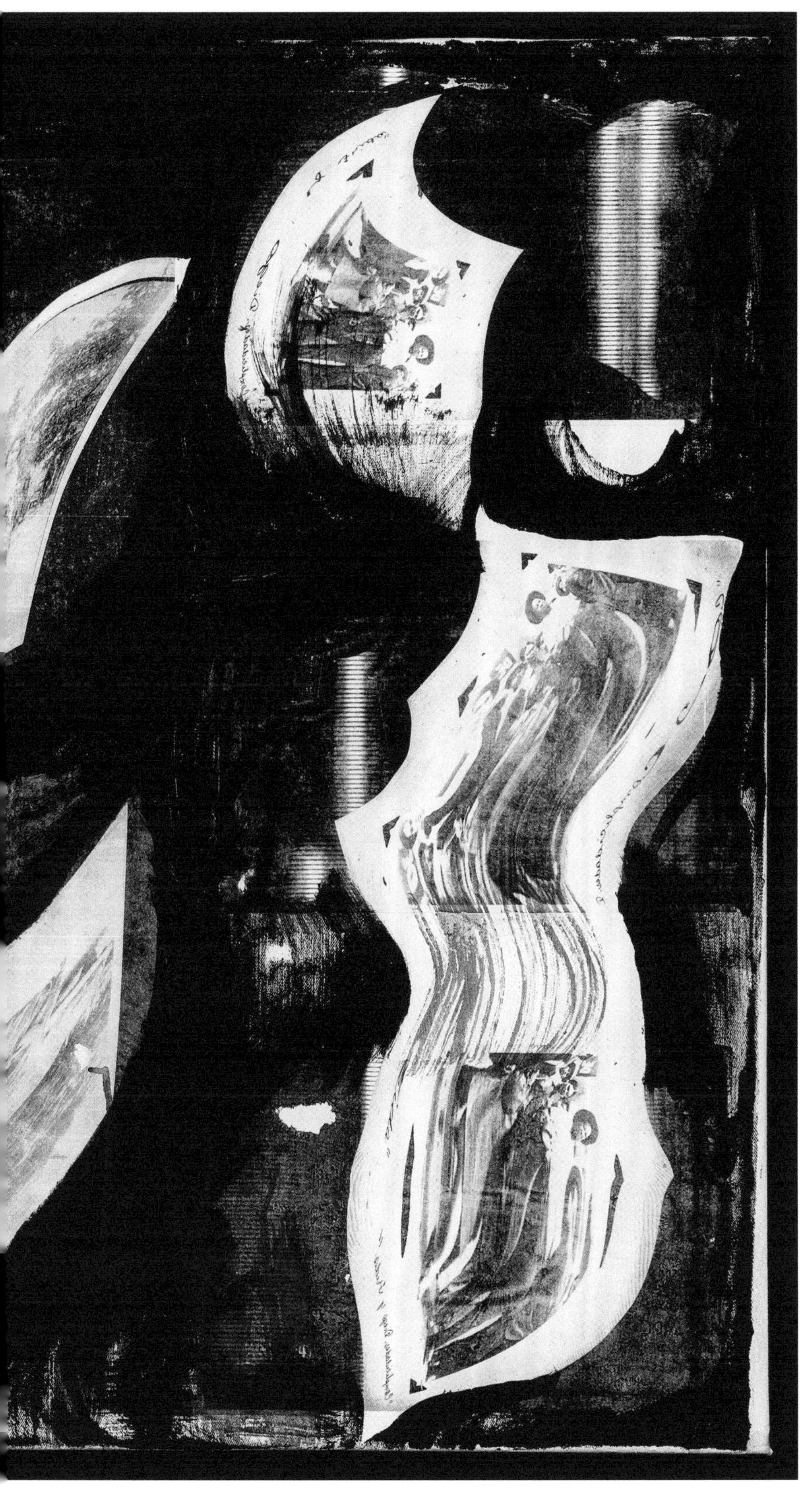

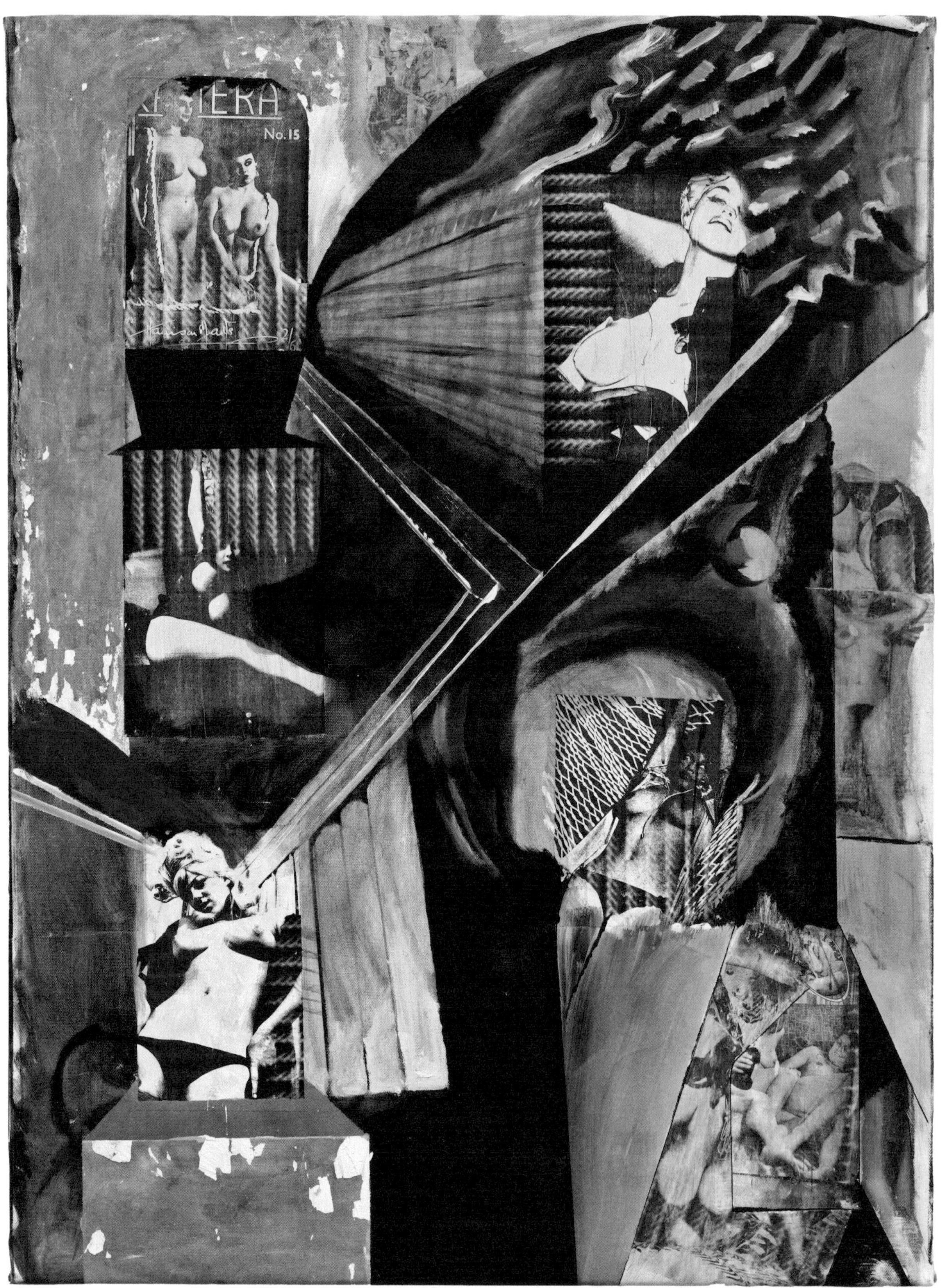

Study, 2015, acrylic paint, ink, and collage on canvas

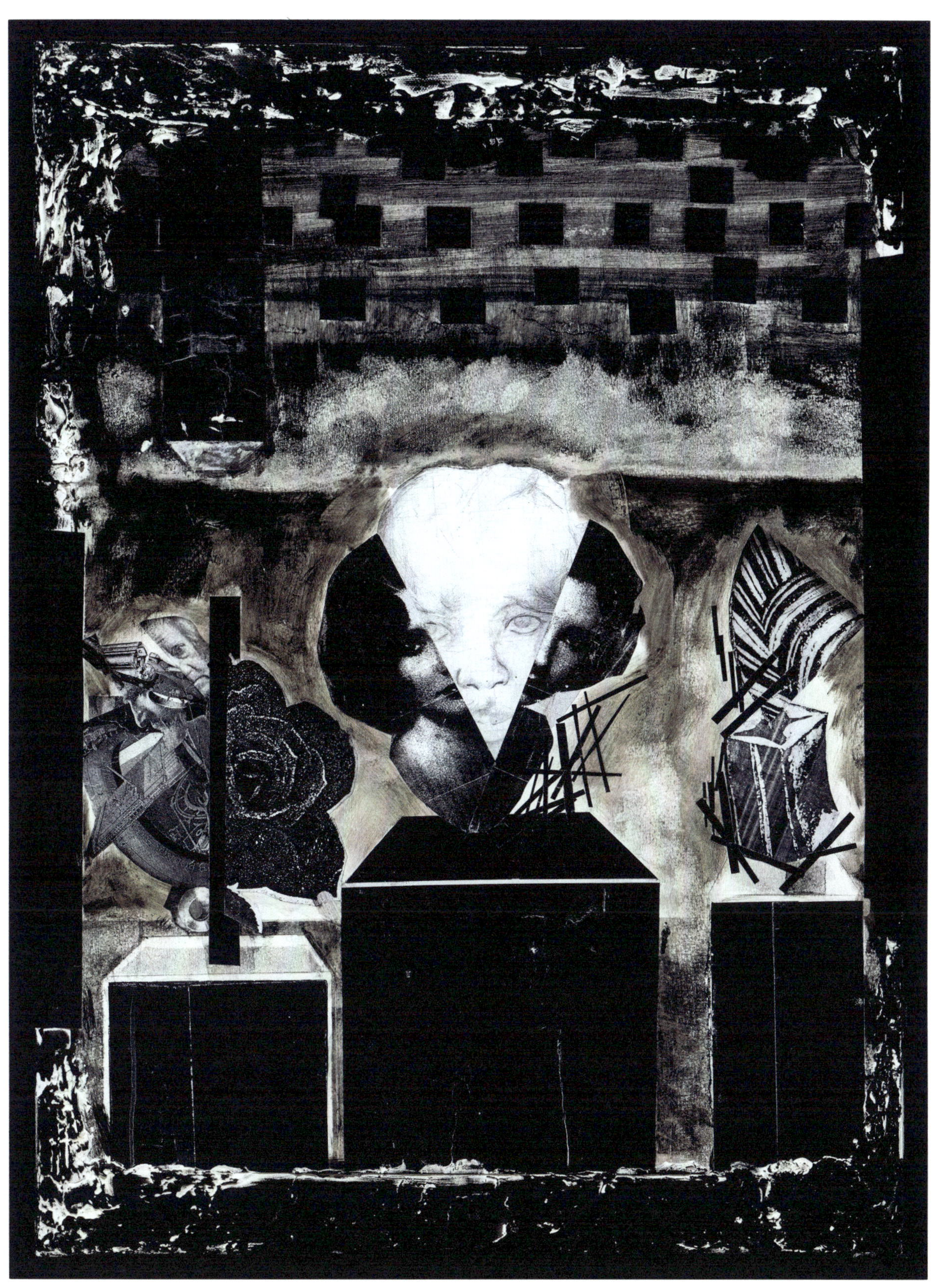

Study, 2015, acrylic paint, ink, and collage on canvas

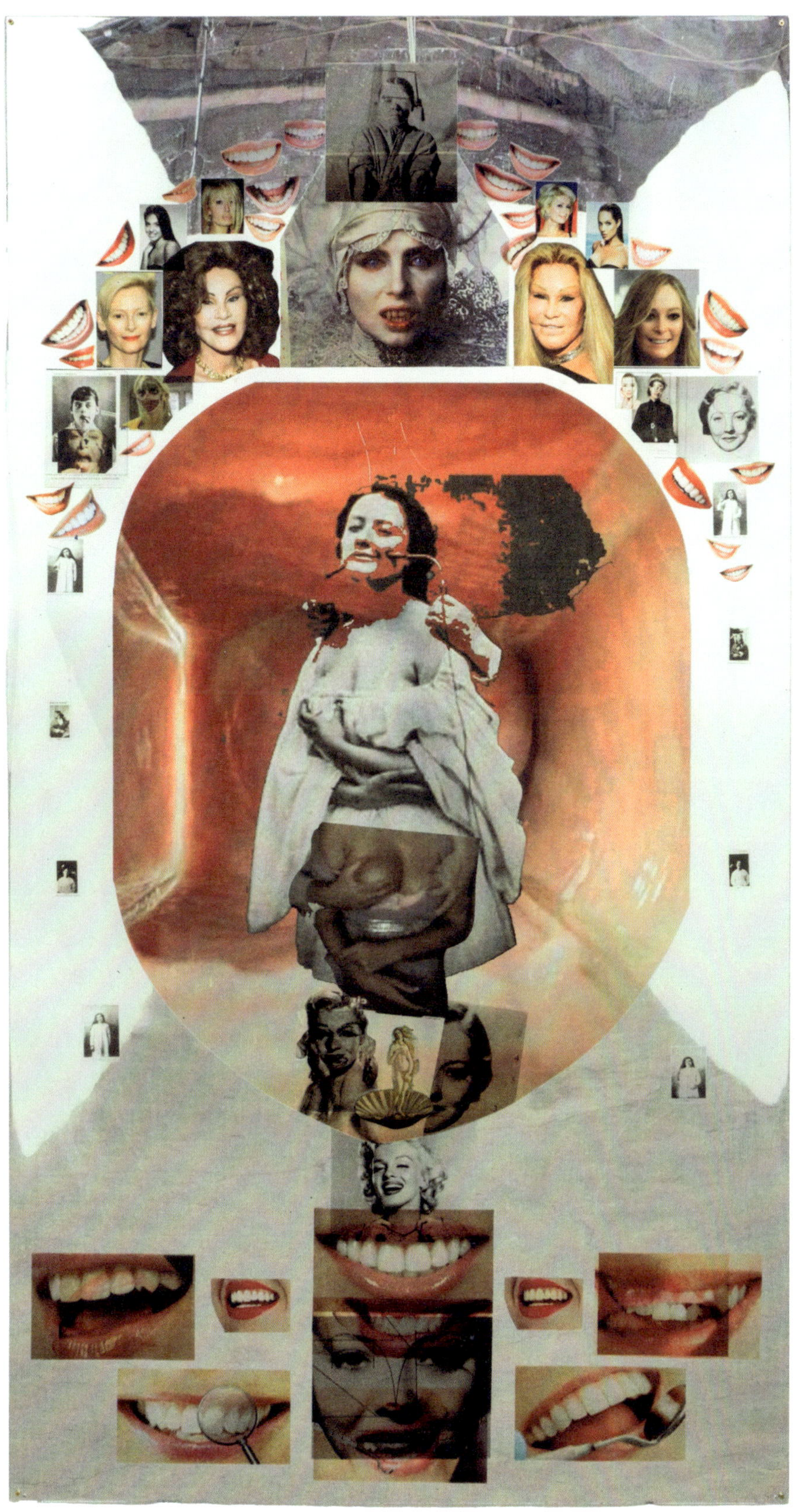

Cervical Smile, 2016, vinyl adhesive on plexiglass

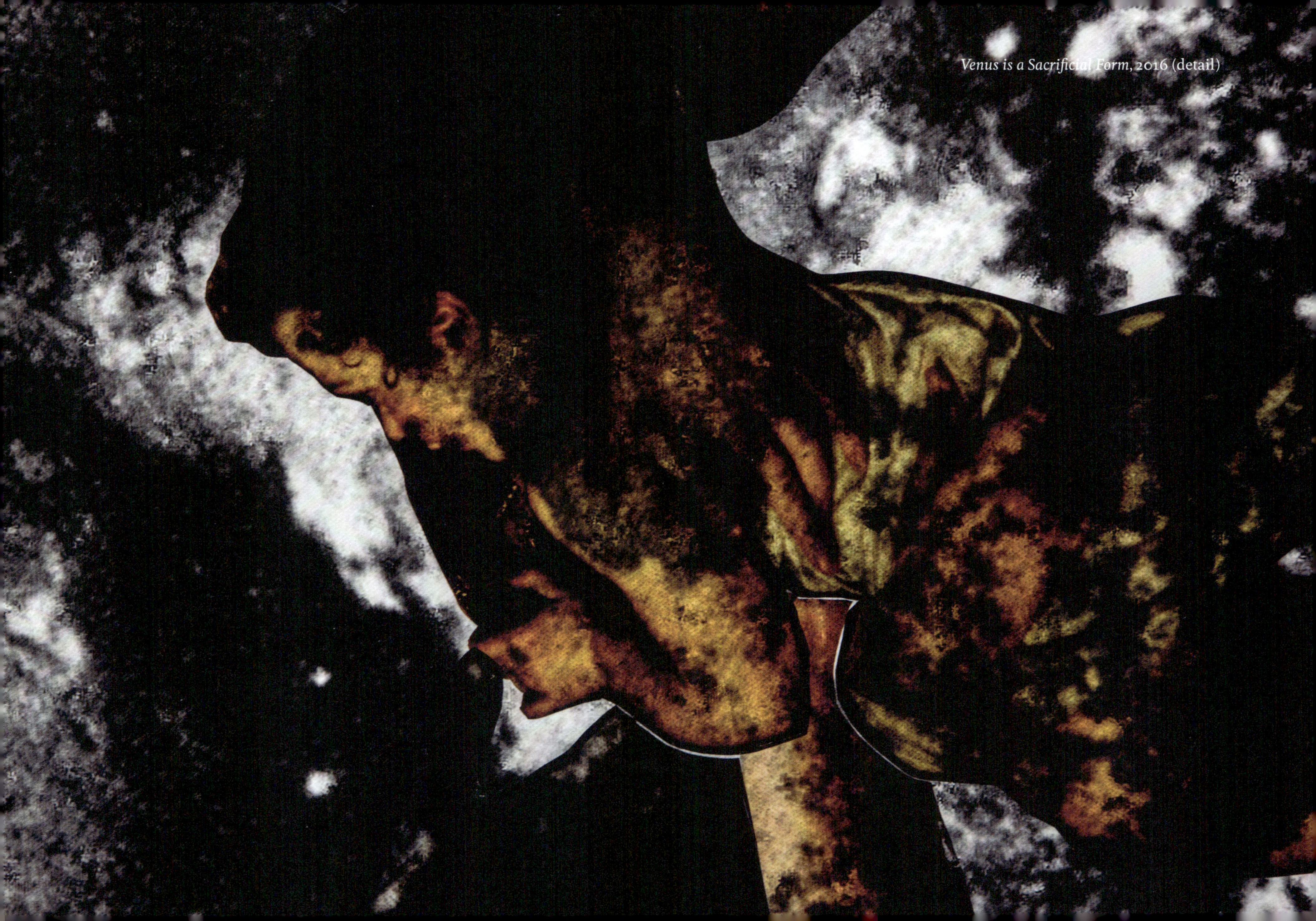

Venus is a Sacrificial Form, 2016 (detail)

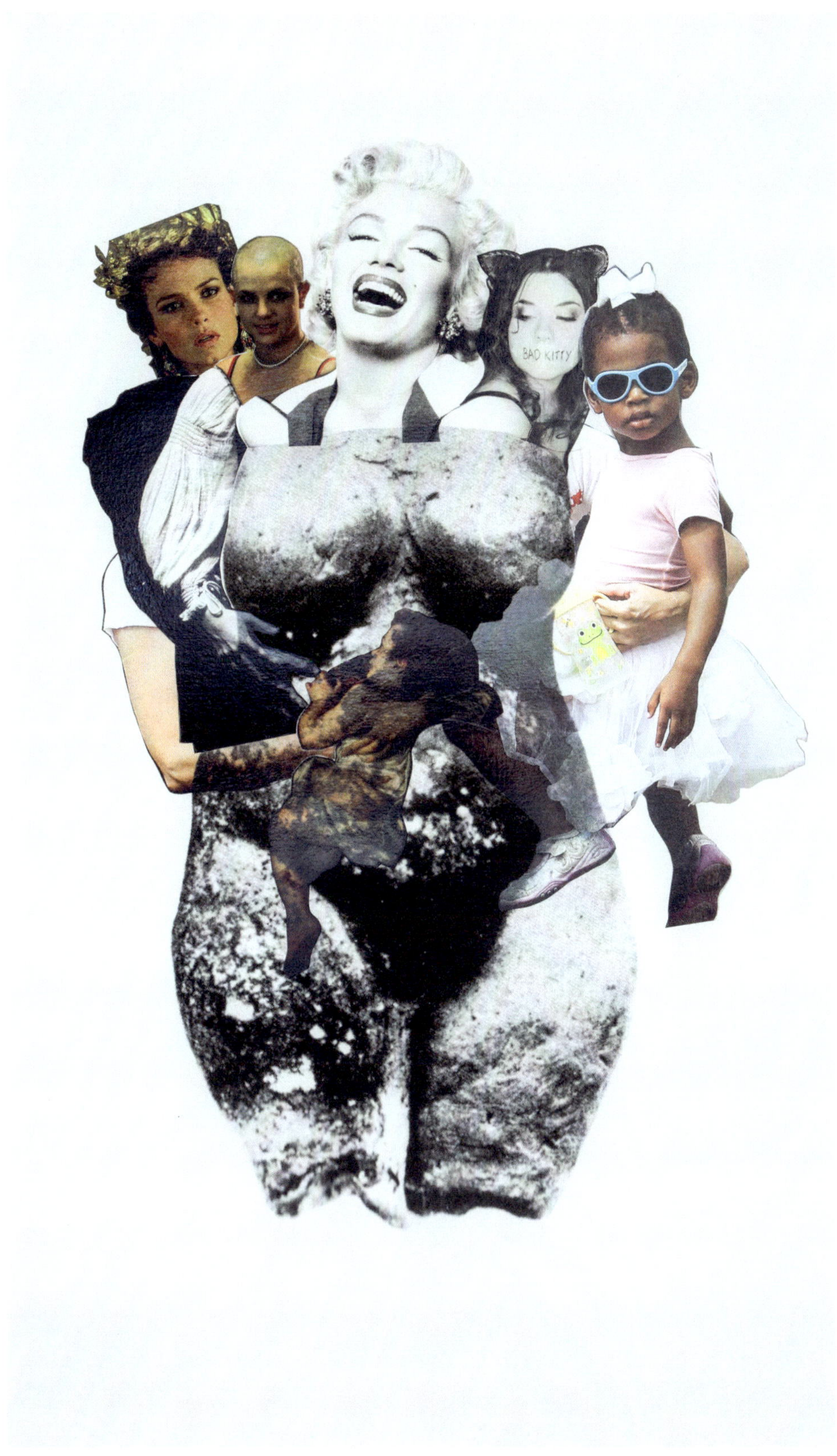

Venus is a Sacrificial Form, 2016, vinyl, phototransfer, and acrylic paint on canvas

Mothers and sisters seem here to have been revealed as the true love objects of these men. The words of the incest taboo have written "the water is wide, and they cannot get across." We now also have a way of understanding why "good" women have to be husband-less, why they have to be pale as death. It is their very suffering, their attitude of sacrifice, the traces of self denial on their faces, that give them their deathlike beauty. Why? Because the sons/brothers want it that way. They may produce one Red outrage after another as pretexts, but it's clear enough that they are the ones who want to see the "mask" on these women. The mothers/sisters are called upon to demonstrate that they, too, are consumed by suffering because they are unable to fall into the tender embrace of the sons/brothers. This is the only embrace that the sons/brothers believe the women really want. In short, it is the sons' merciless jealousy that has the husbands killed off (by the "Reds") and makes martyred angels of the mothers and sisters, 2017, vinyl adhesive on plexiglass

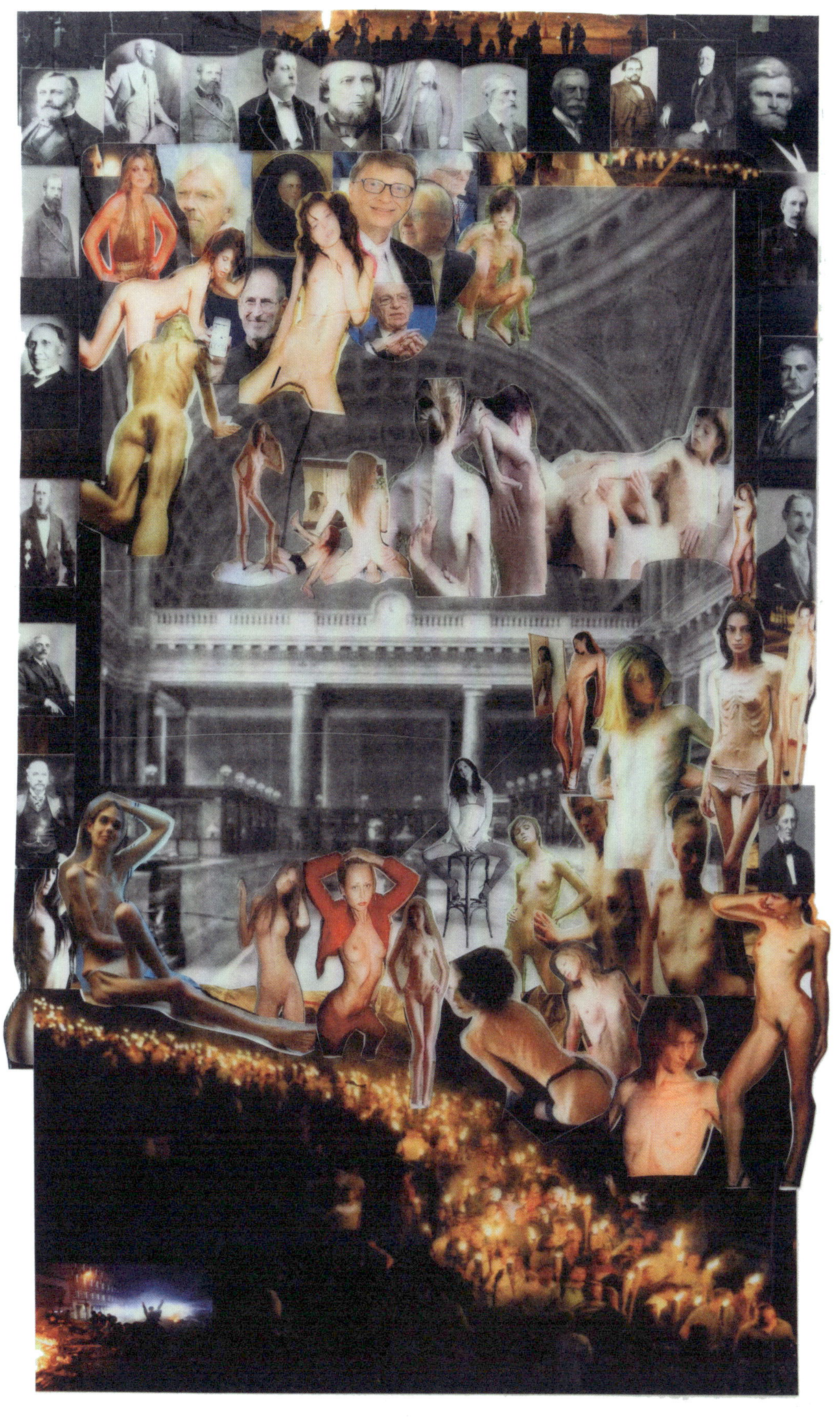

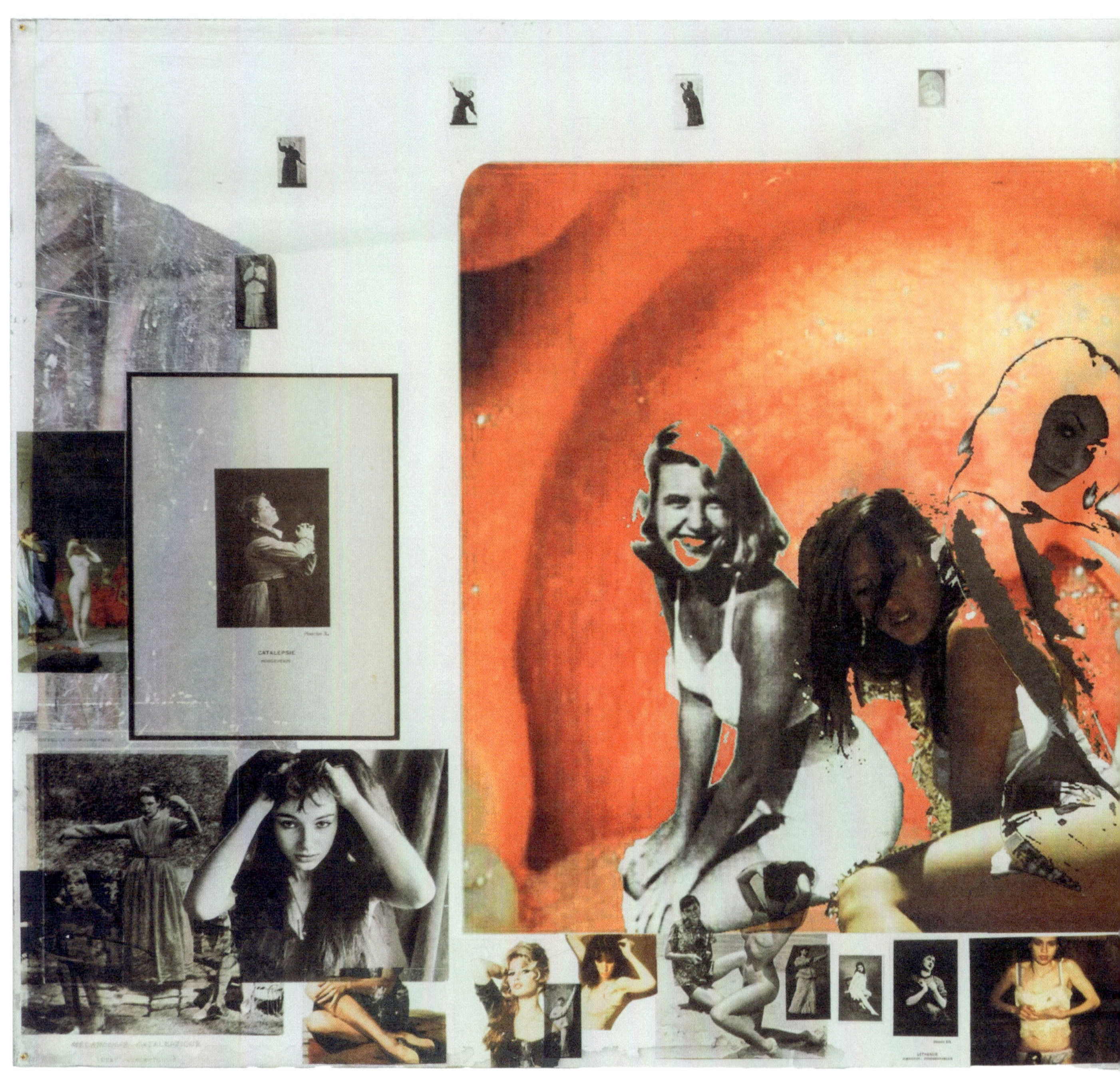

Esophagus Pin-Up, 2016, vinyl adhesive on plexiglass

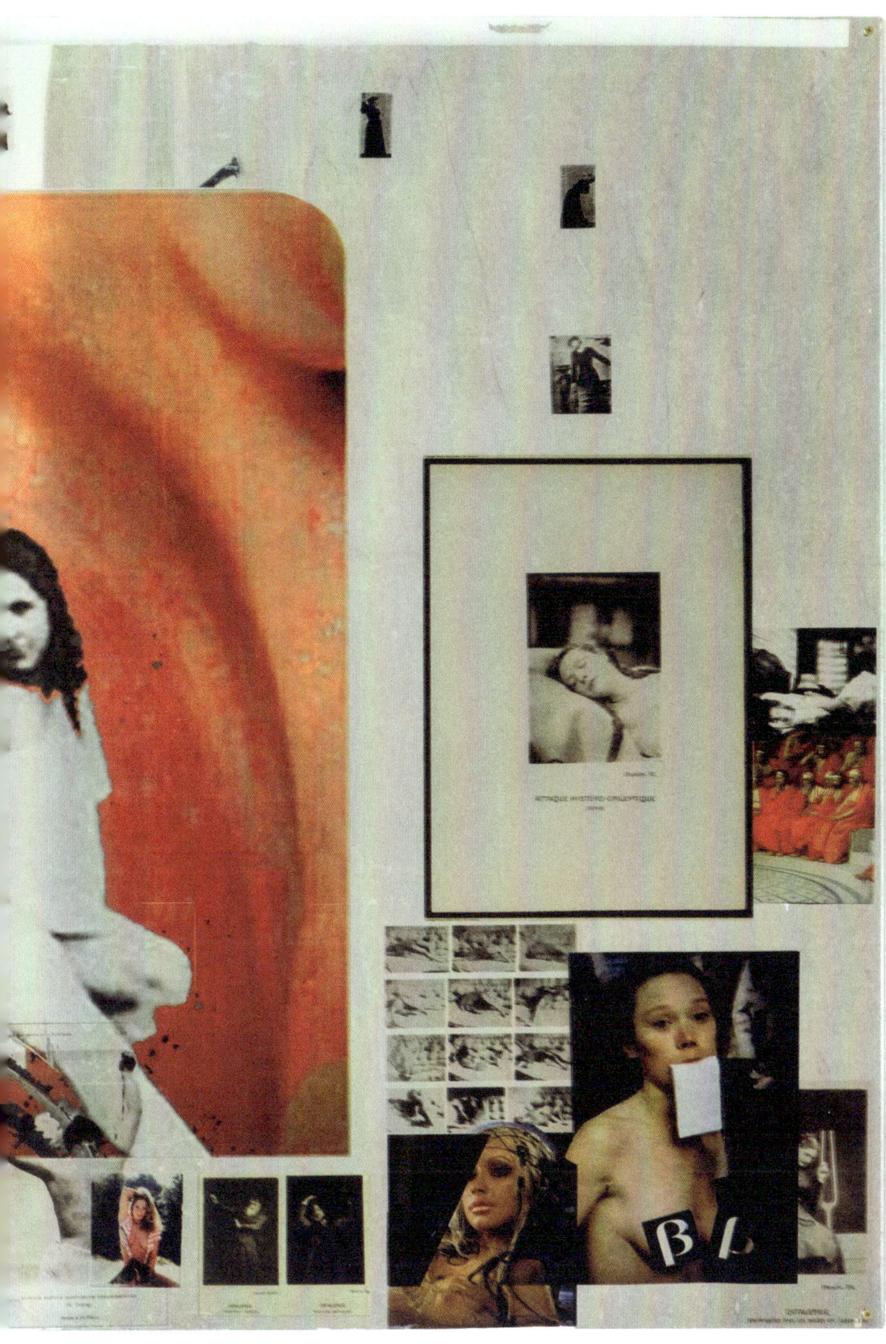

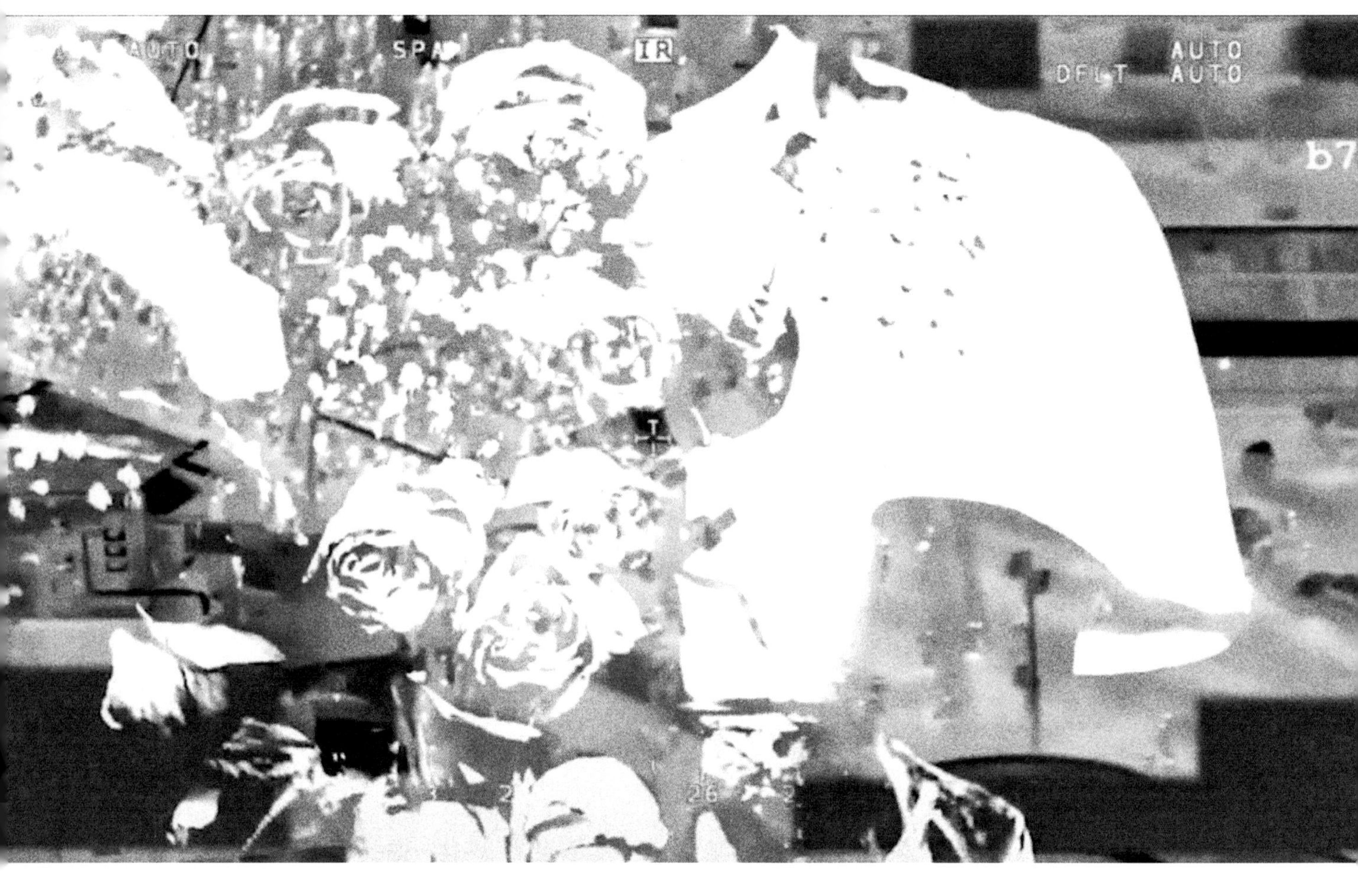

Eurydice, 2017–2021, two-channel HD video installation (color, sound) (video stills)

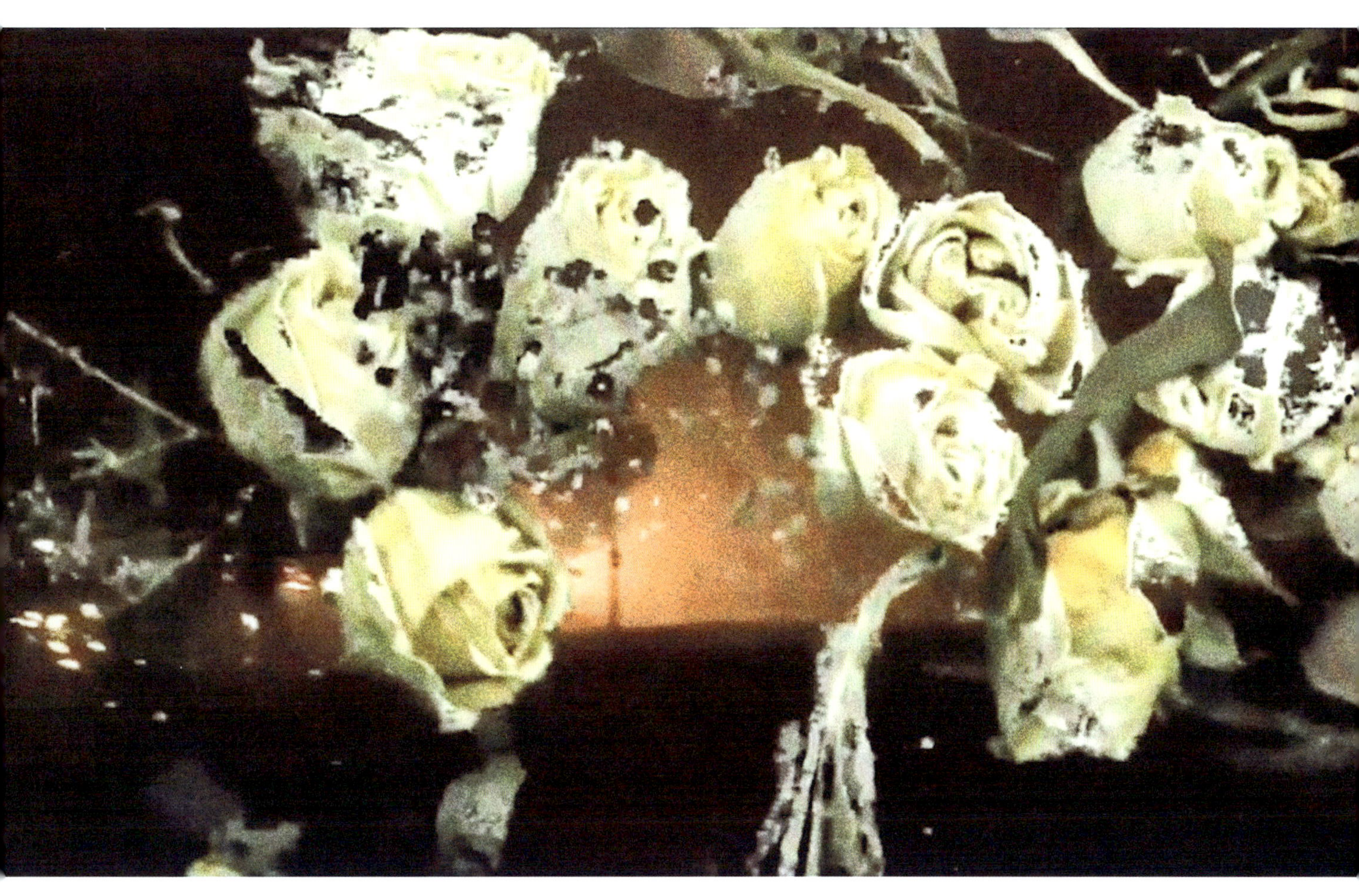

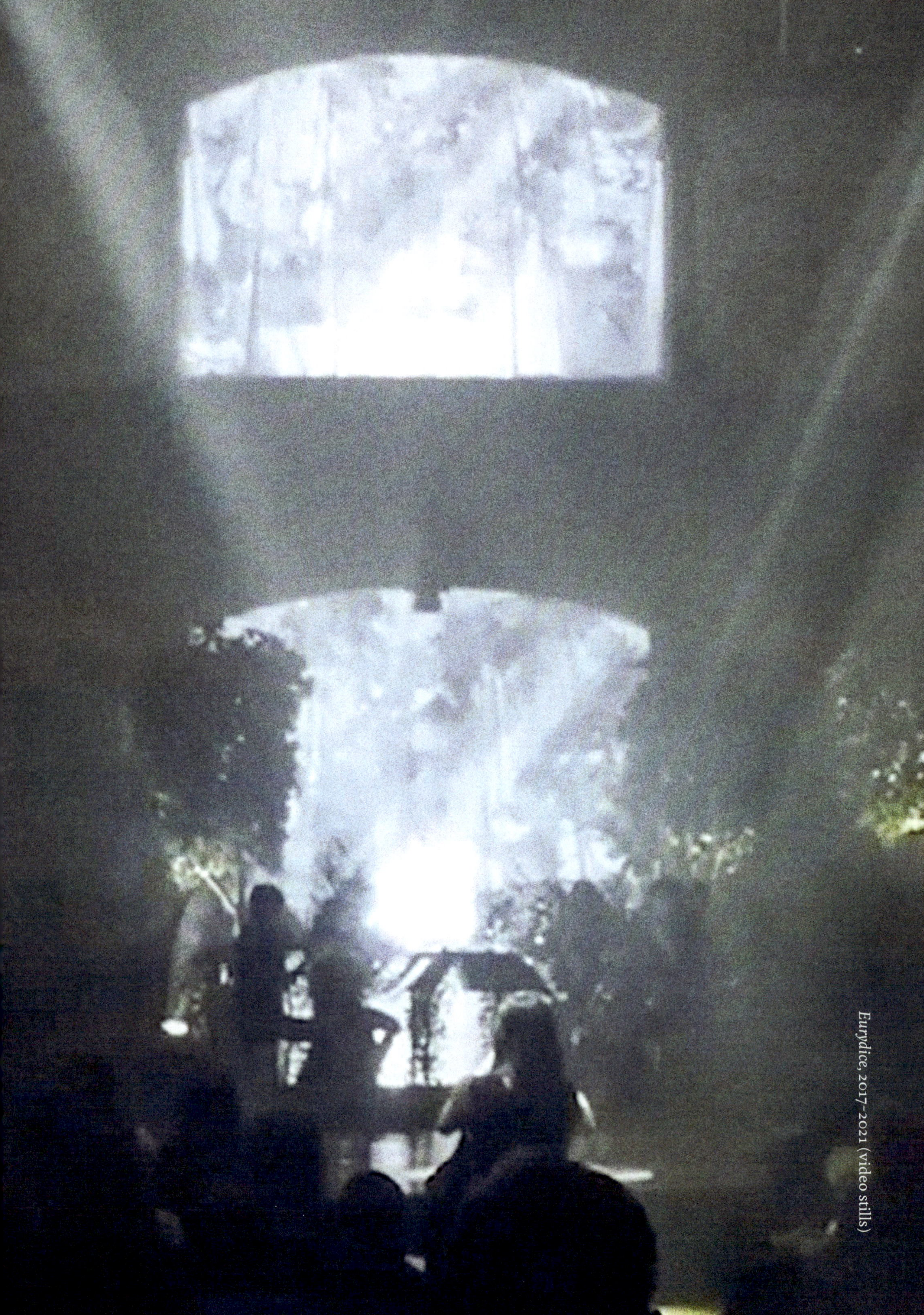

Eurydice, 2017–2021 (video stills)

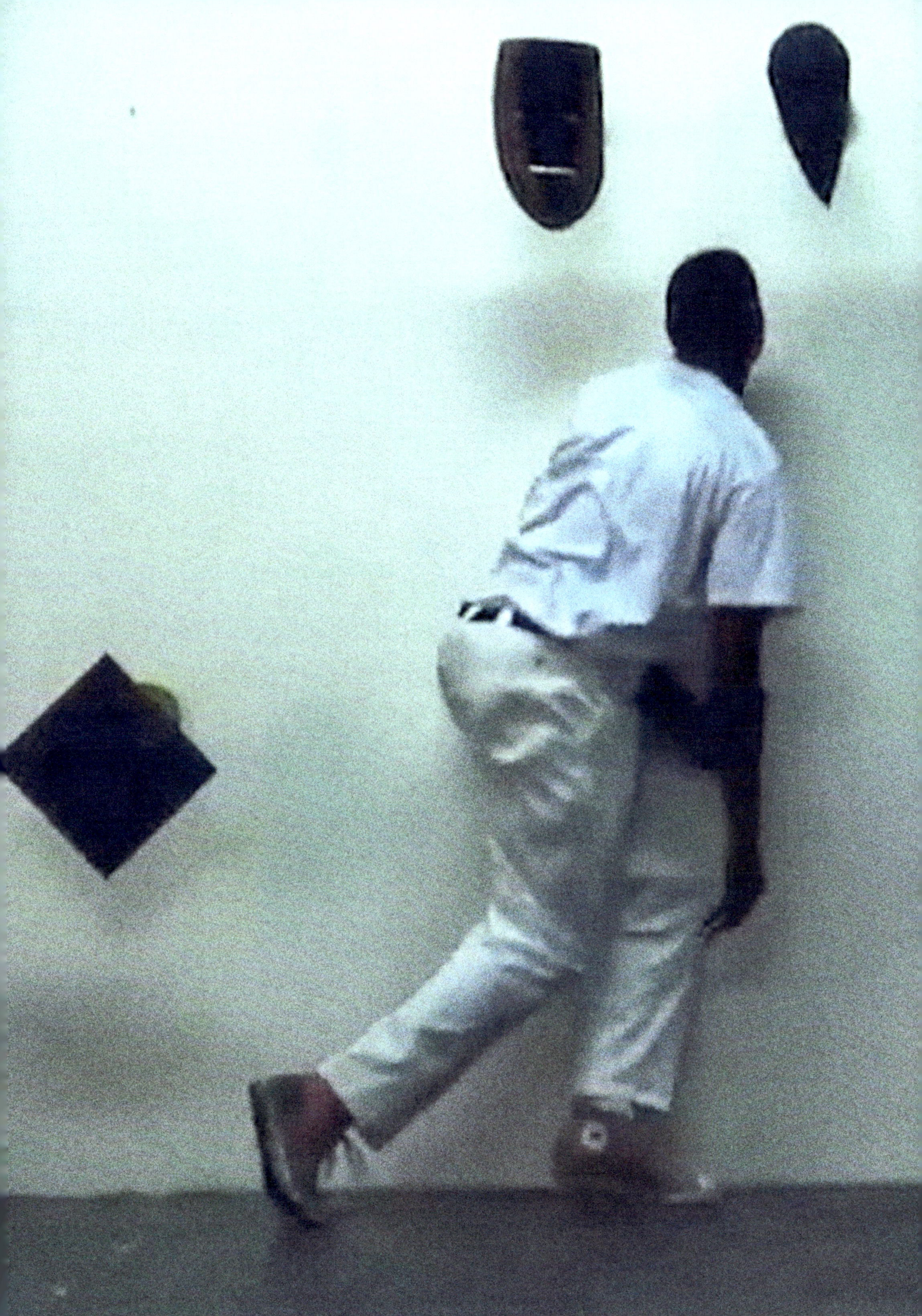

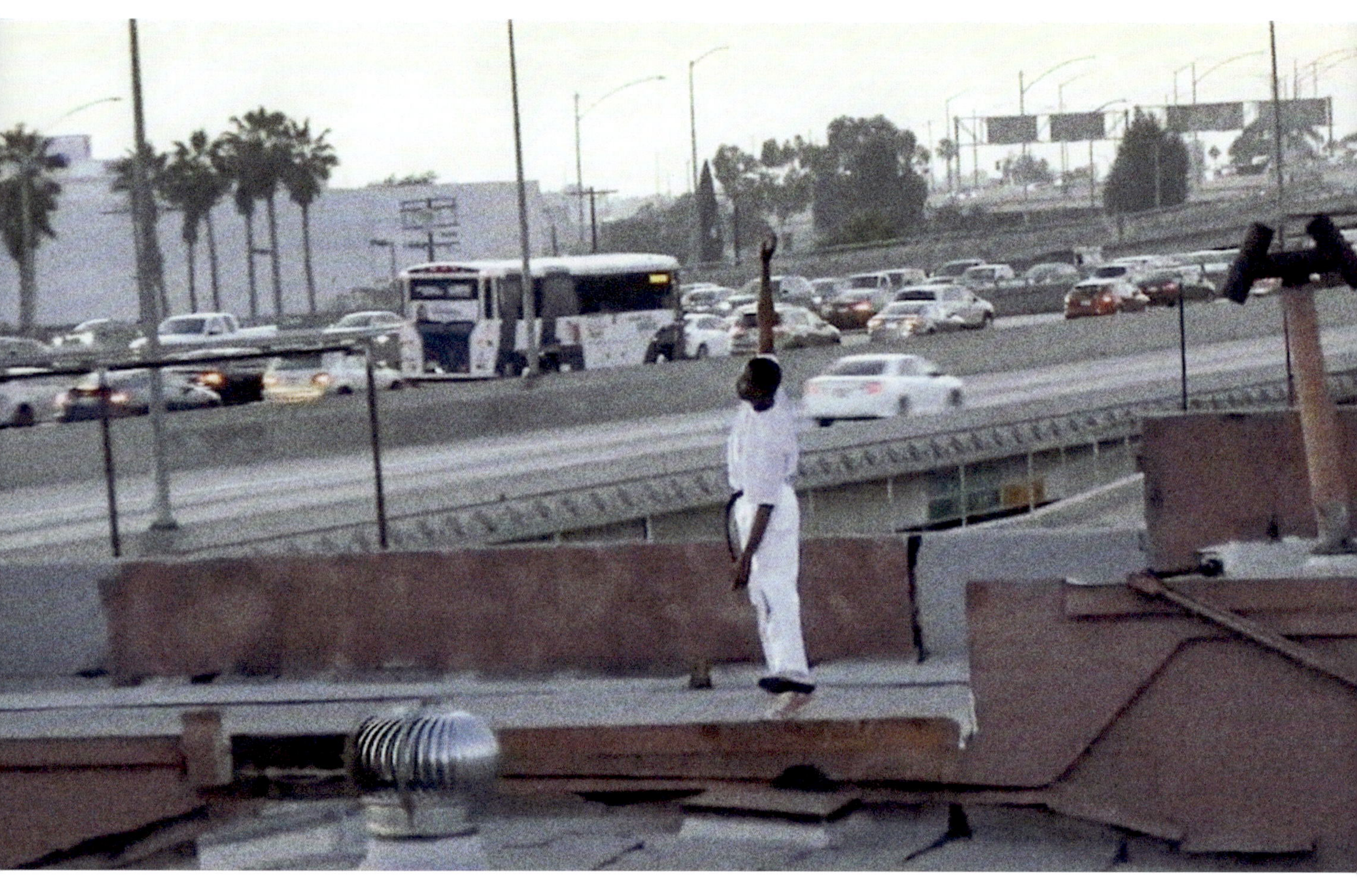

Eurydice, 2017–2021, two-channel HD video installation (color, sound) (video stills)

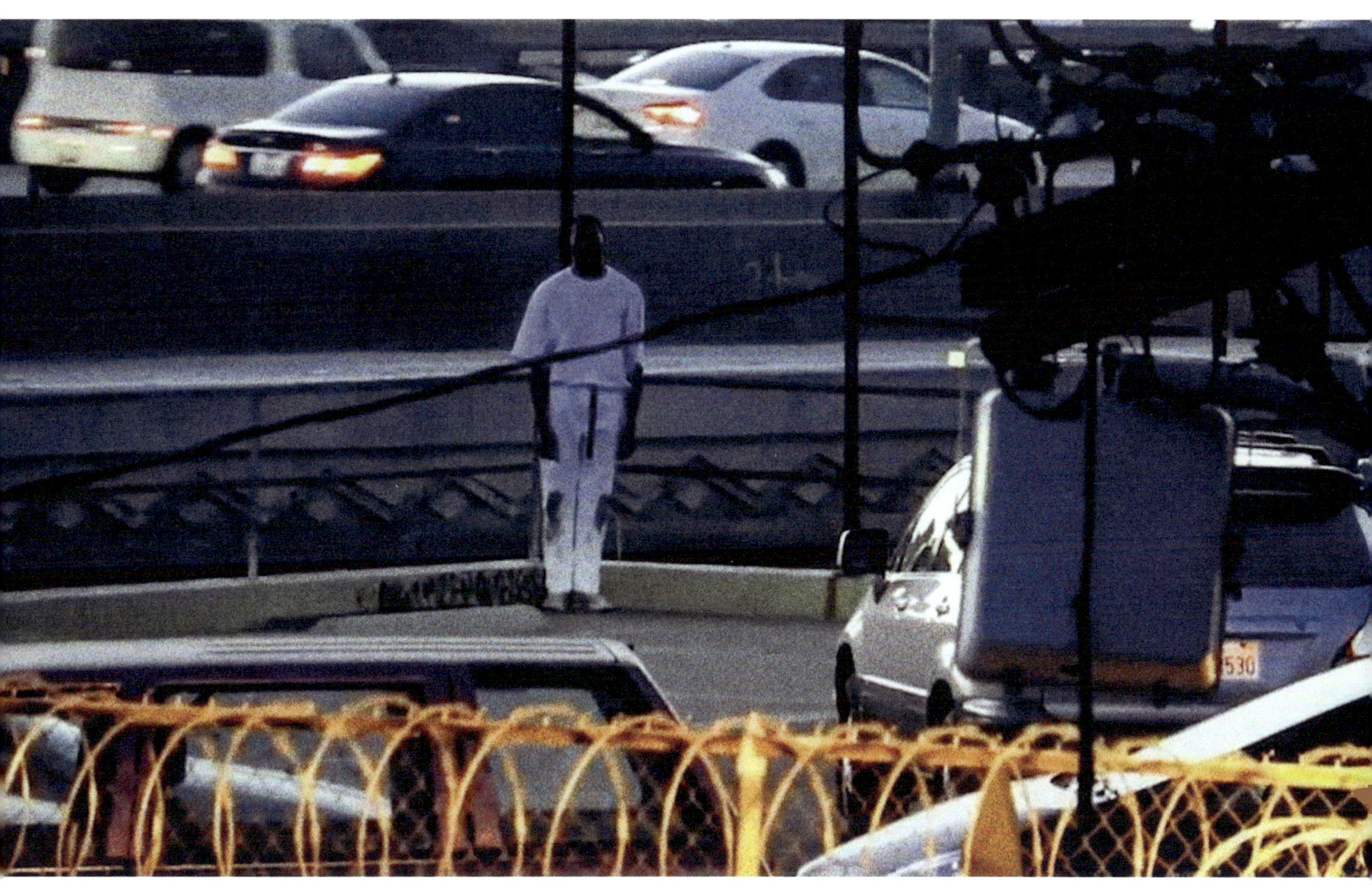

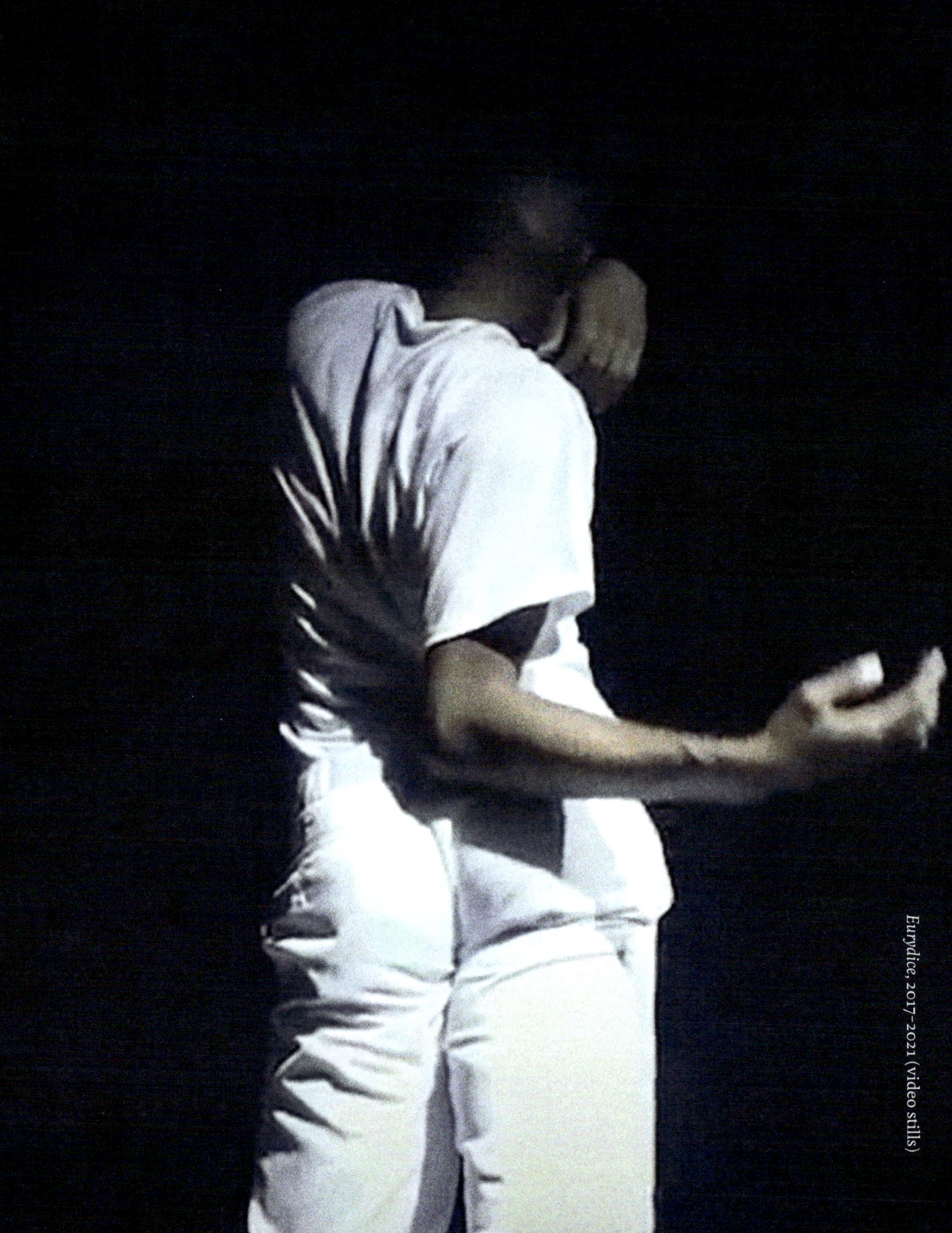

Eurydice, 2017–2021 (video stills)

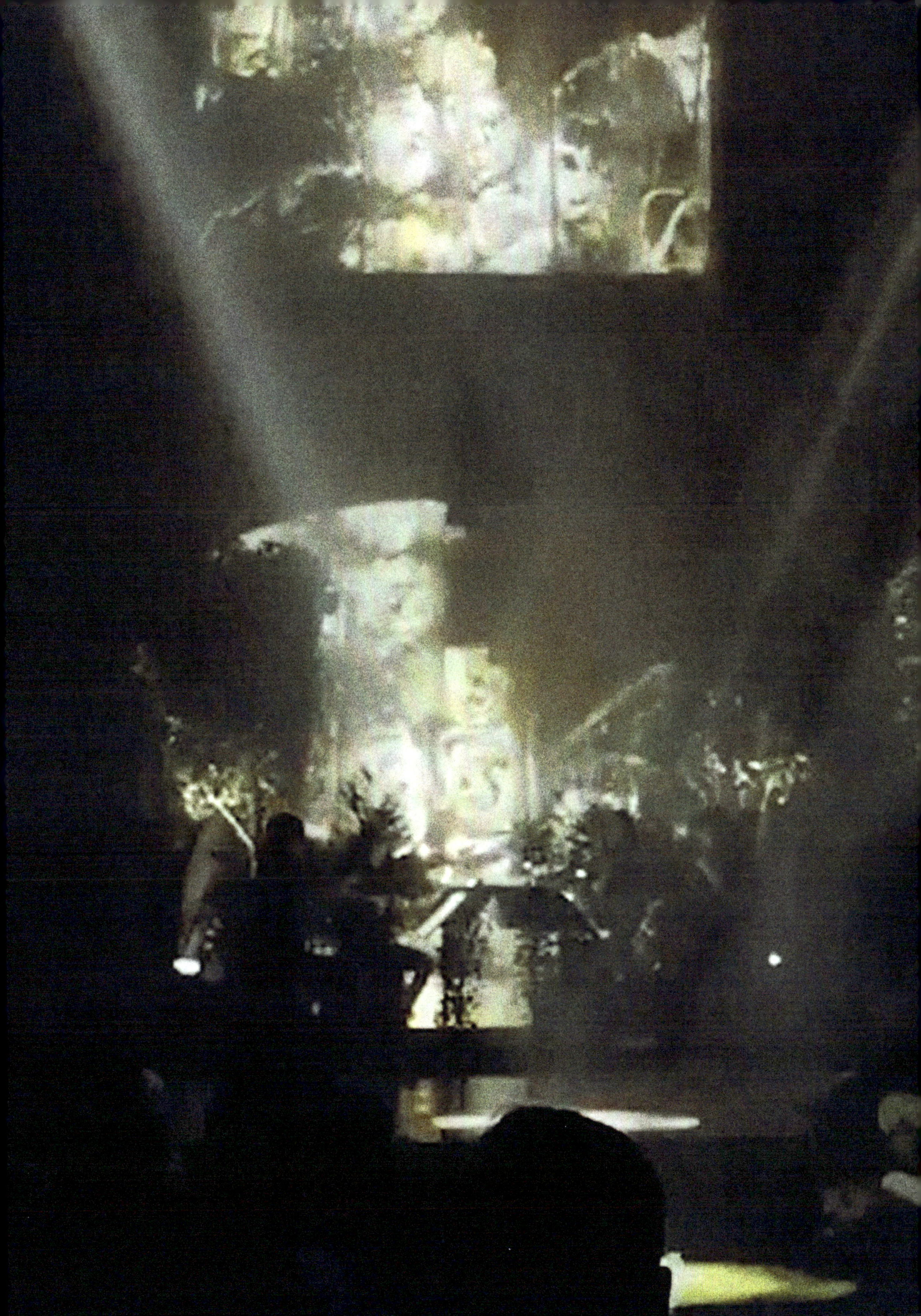

the set-up Out of the blackest part of my soul, across the zebra striping of my mind, surges this desire to be suddenly white. I wish to be acknowledged not as black but as white. Now—and this is a form of recognition that Hegel had not envisaged—who but a white woman can do this for me? By loving me she proves that I am worthy of white love. I am loved like a white man. I am a white man. Her love takes me onto the noble road that leads to total realization. . . . I marry white culture, white beauty, white whiteness. When my restless hands caress those white breasts, they grasp white civilization and dignity and make them mine., 2017, vinyl adhesive on mirror

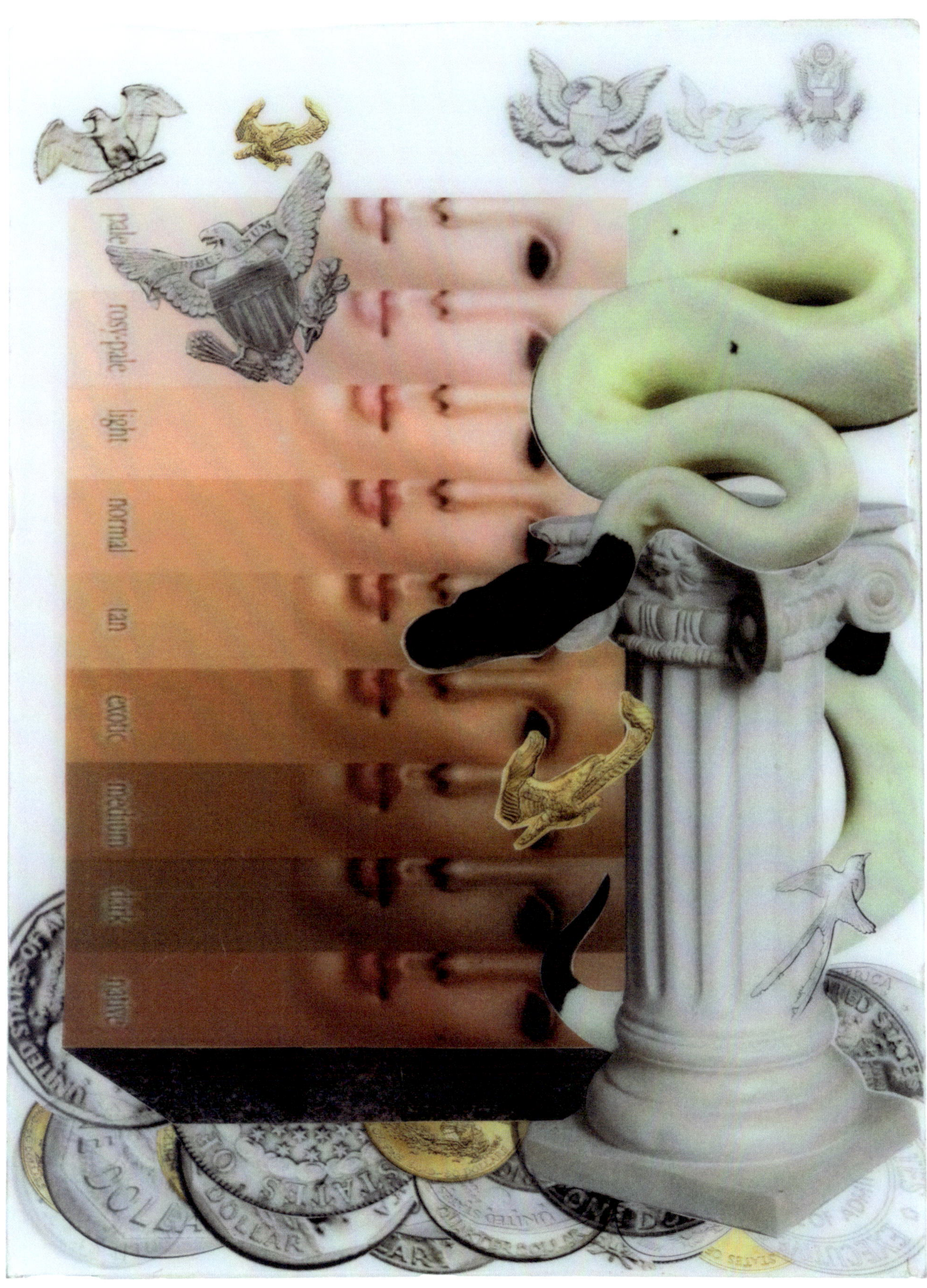
pale
rosy-pale
light
normal
tan
exotic
medium
dark
native

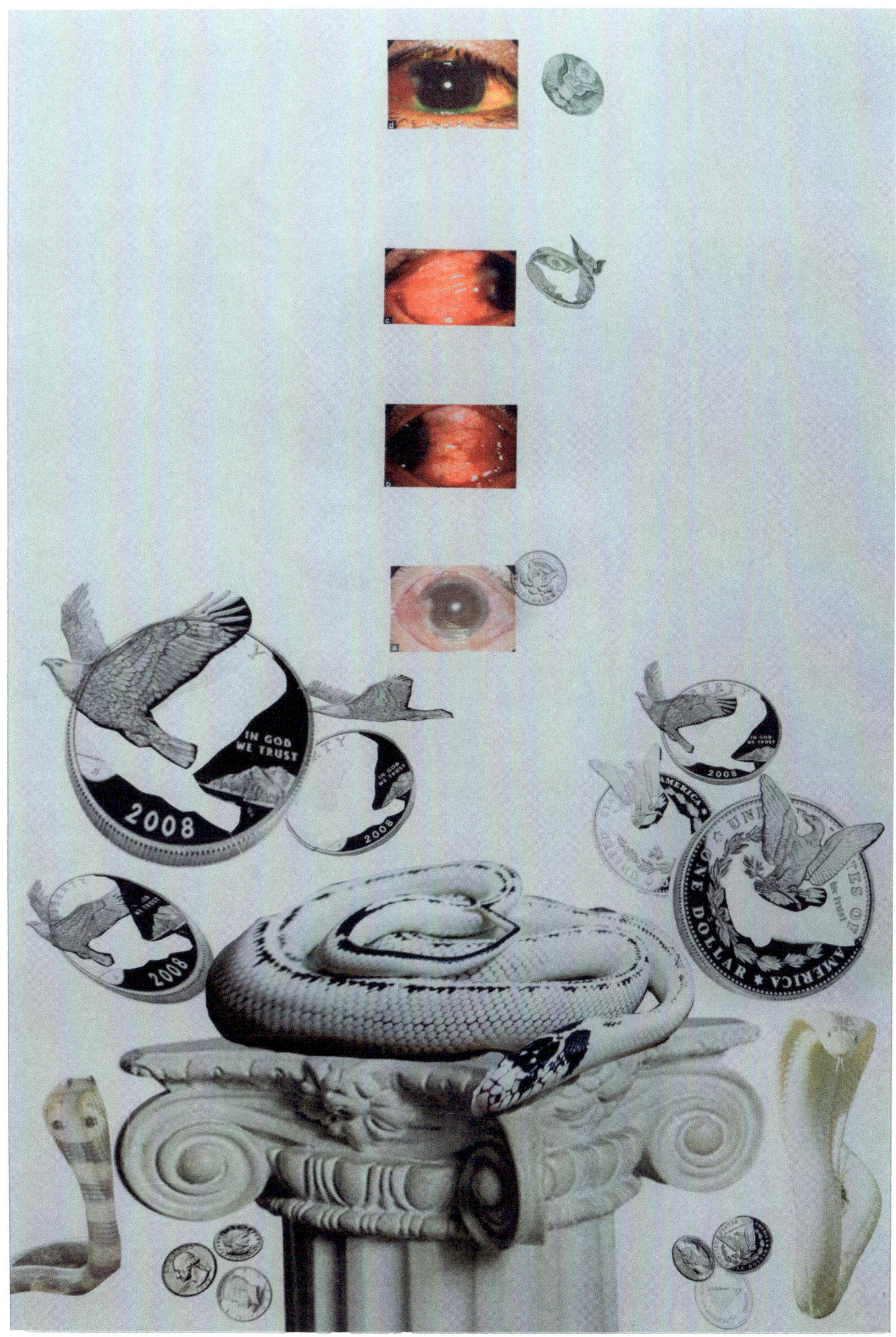

Snow, if sign value and exchange value (sign form and commodity form) really are implicated, by reason of their logical form, in the framework of a general political economy, we can claim no affinity of the same order linking symbolic exchange and use value; quite the contrary, because the former implies the transgression of the latter, the latter the reduction of the former, 2017, vinyl adhesive on mirror

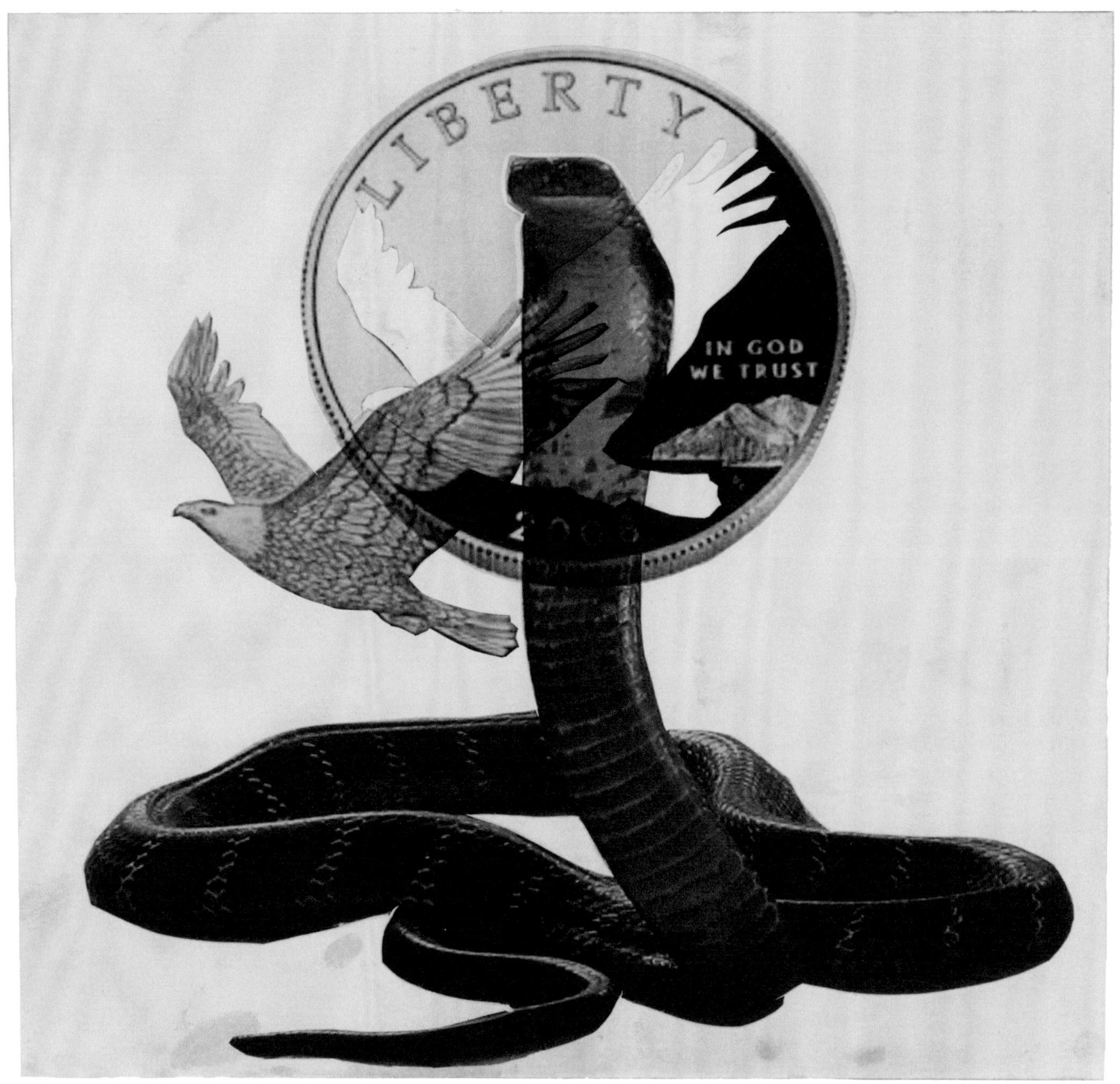

The Midnight Snack, Well-a, whosonever told it, that he told a- He told a dirty lie, babe. Well-a, whosonever told it, that he told a- He told a dirty lie, well-a. Well-a, whosonever told it, that he told a- He told a dirty lie, babe. Well the eagle on the dollar-quarter, He gonna rise and fly, well-a. He gonna rise and fly, sugar. He gonna rise and fly, well-a. Well the eagle on the dollar-quarter, He gonna rise and fly, well-a (Chorus) Sung by "22", Little Red, Tangle Eye, and Hard Hair, accompanied by double cutting axes, 2017, vinyl adhesive on mirror

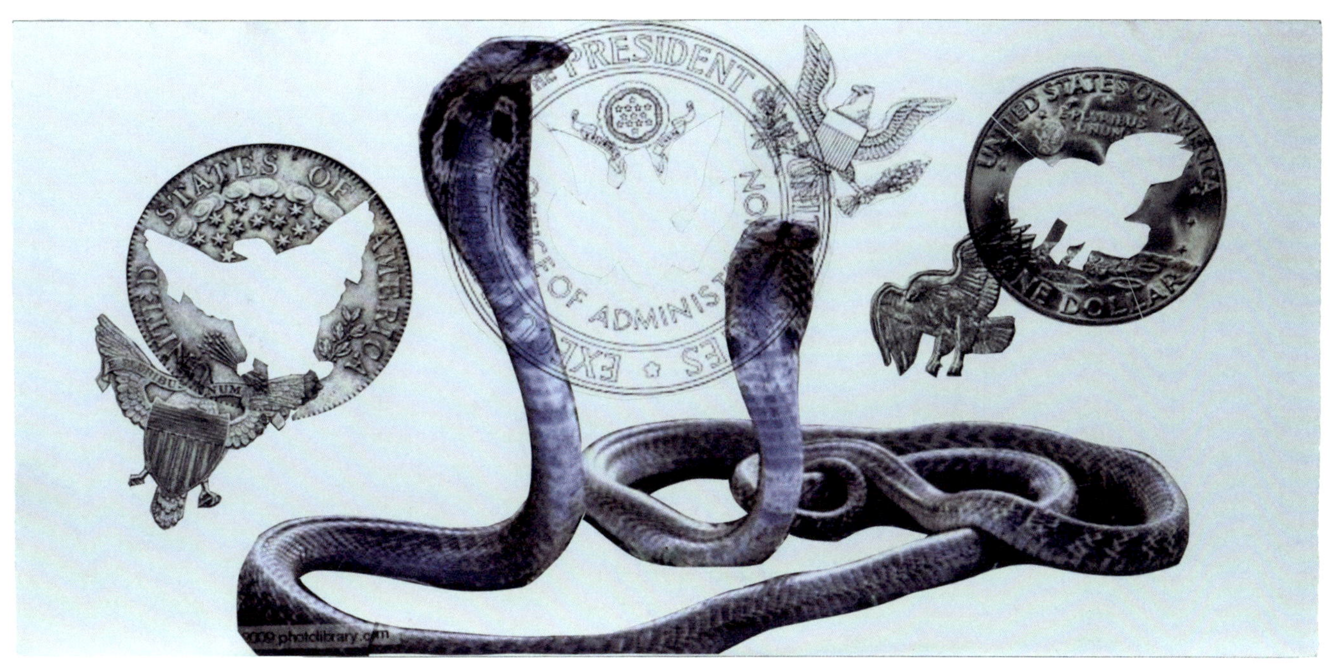

'We are too much in the habit of looking at falsehood in its darkest associations... That indignation which we profess to feel at deceit absolute, is indeed only at deceit malicious. We resent calumny, hypocrisy, and treachery because they harm us, not because they are untrue.' ruskin, 2017, vinyl adhesive on mirror

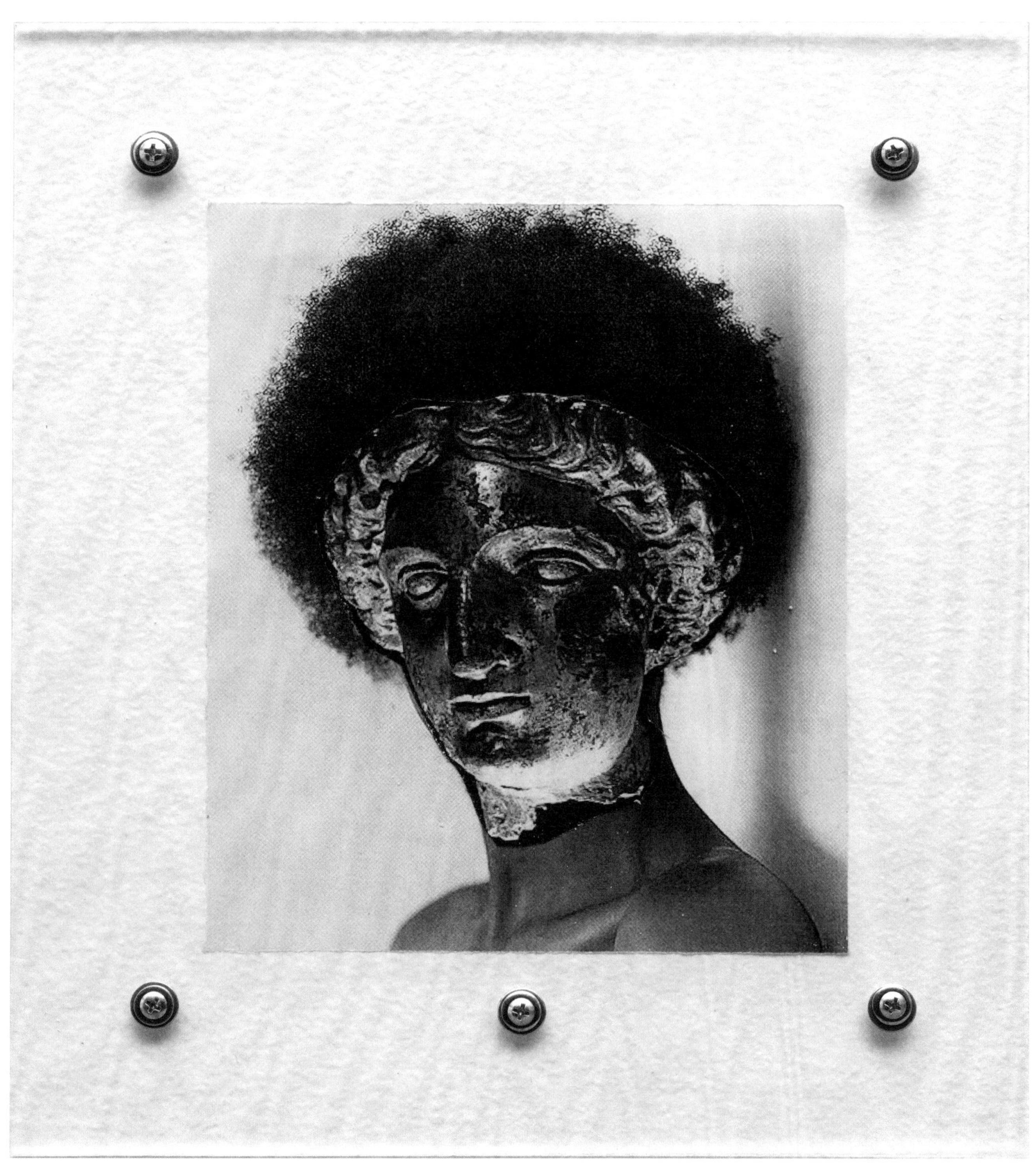

Styxx, 2018, paper, collage, and plexiglass

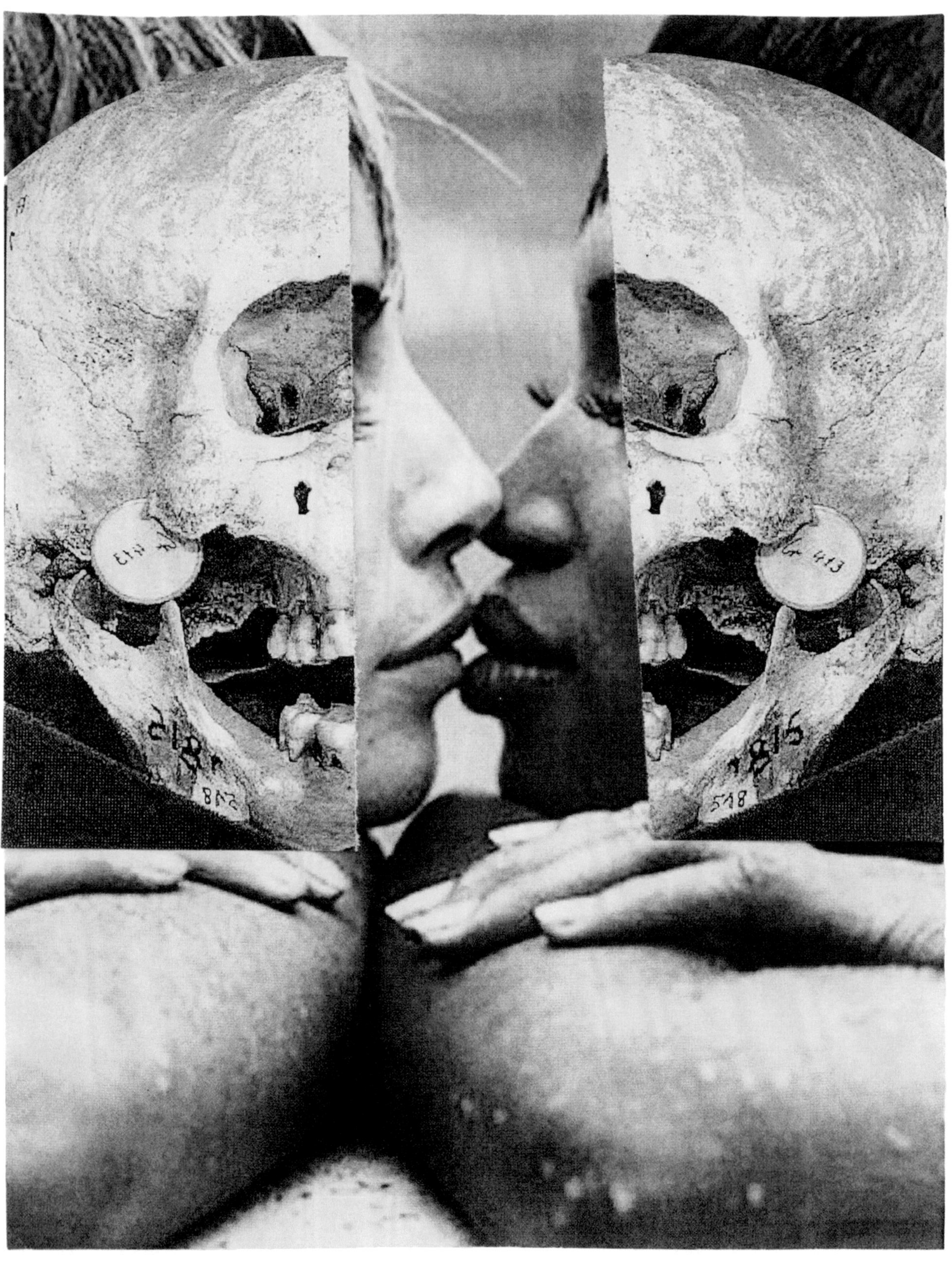

The Bathers of Acheron, 2018, paper, collage, and plexiglass

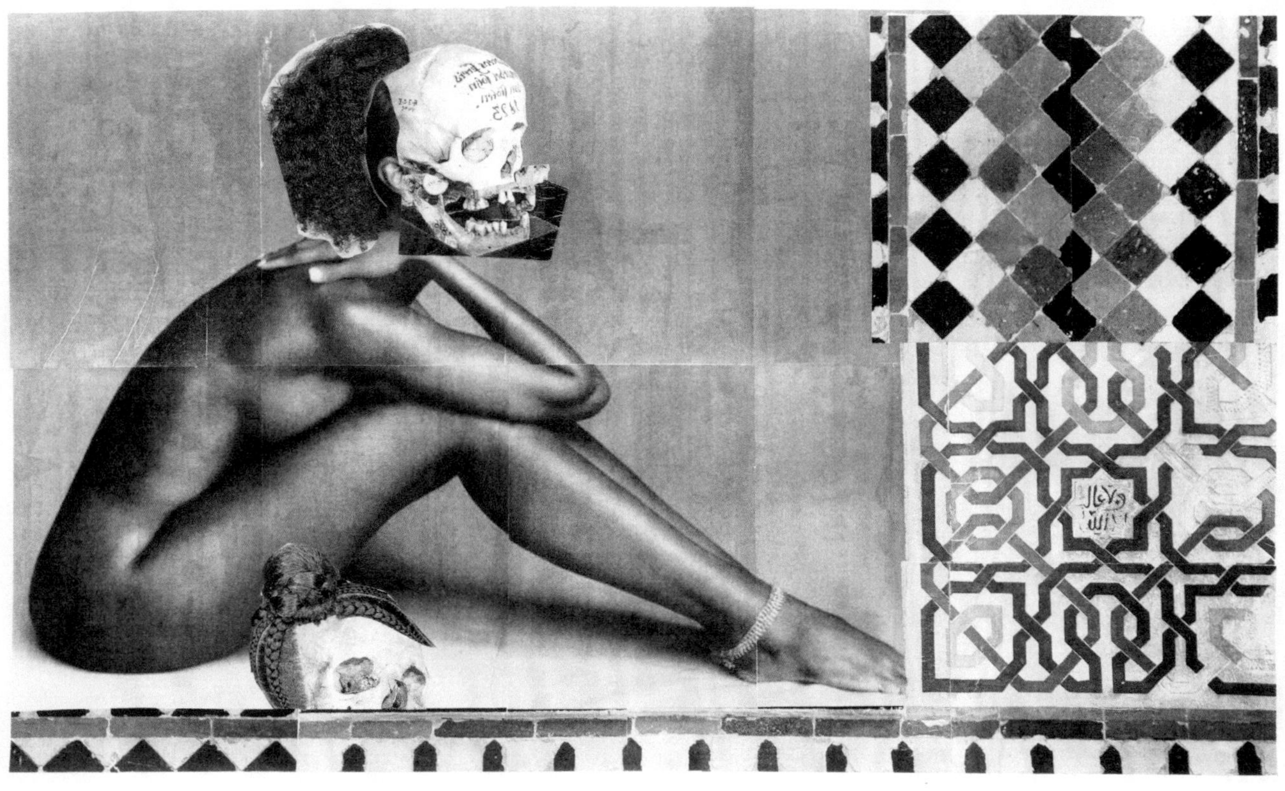

Iconic, the Face of, Death Mask I, 2018, paper, collage, and plexiglass

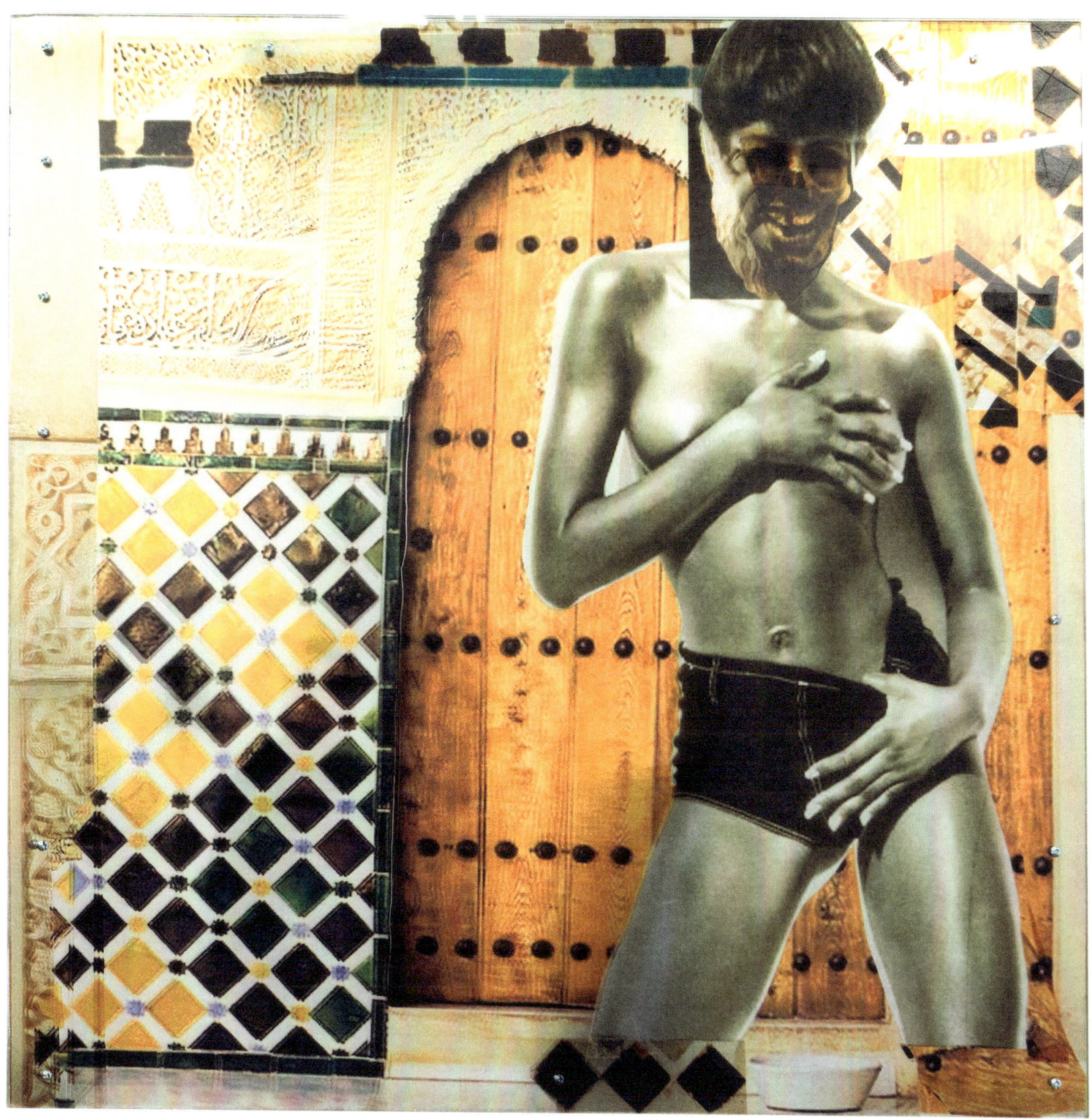

Acheron Death Mask II, 2018, sticker on mirror glass

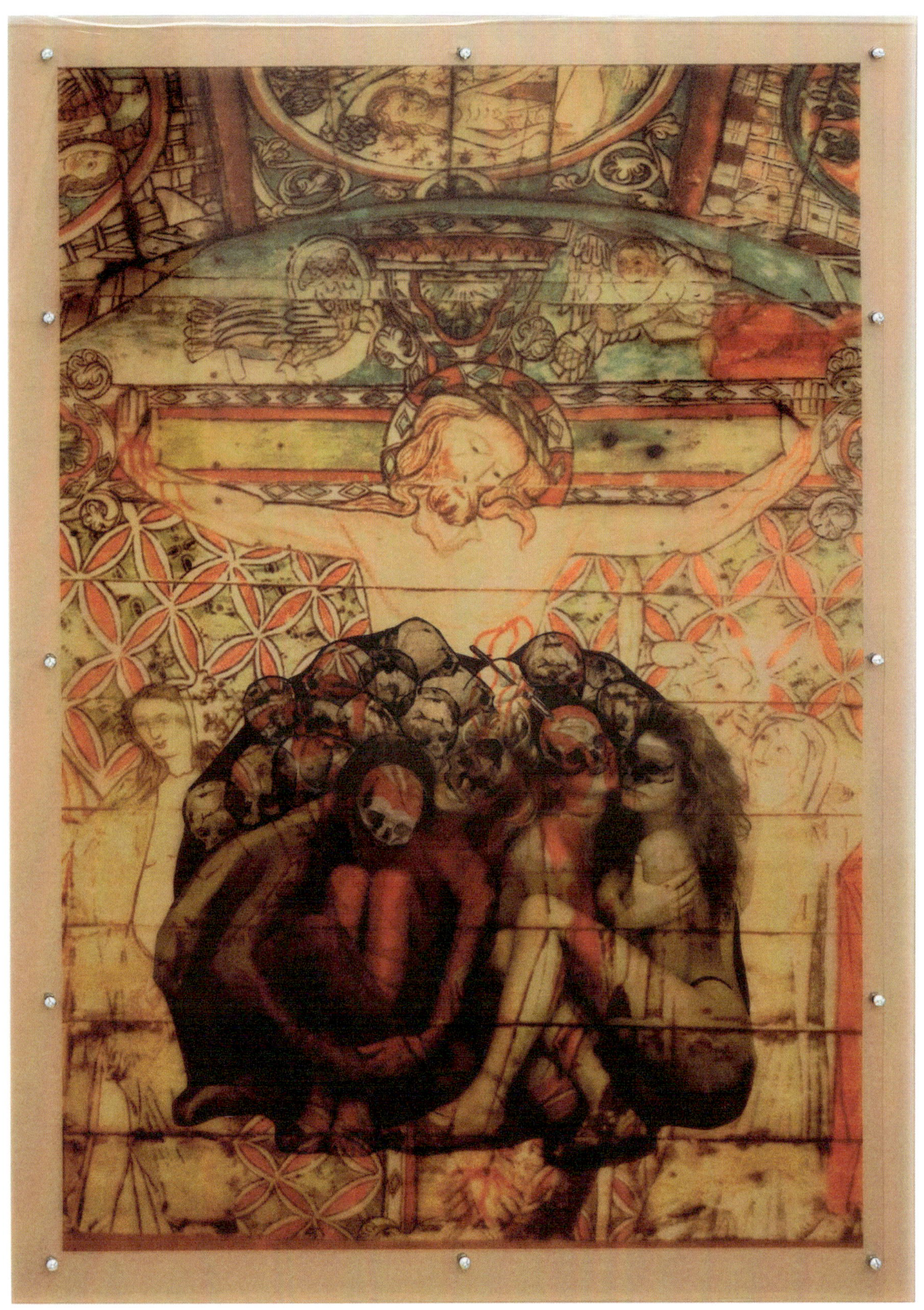

The Mother the Son and the Holy Spirit, 2018, printed plastic and plexiglass

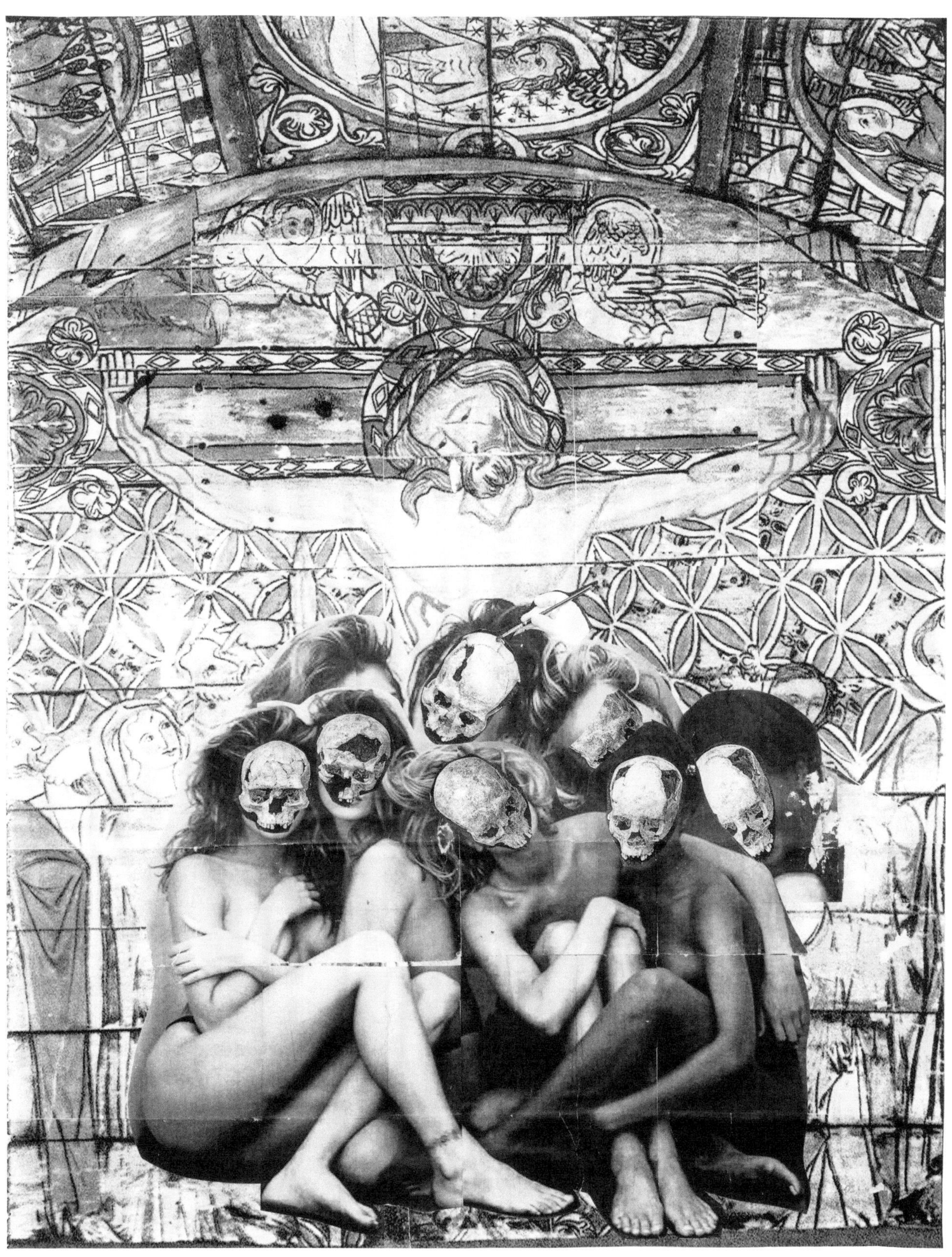

Her and love are the same, 2018, paper, collage, and plexiglass

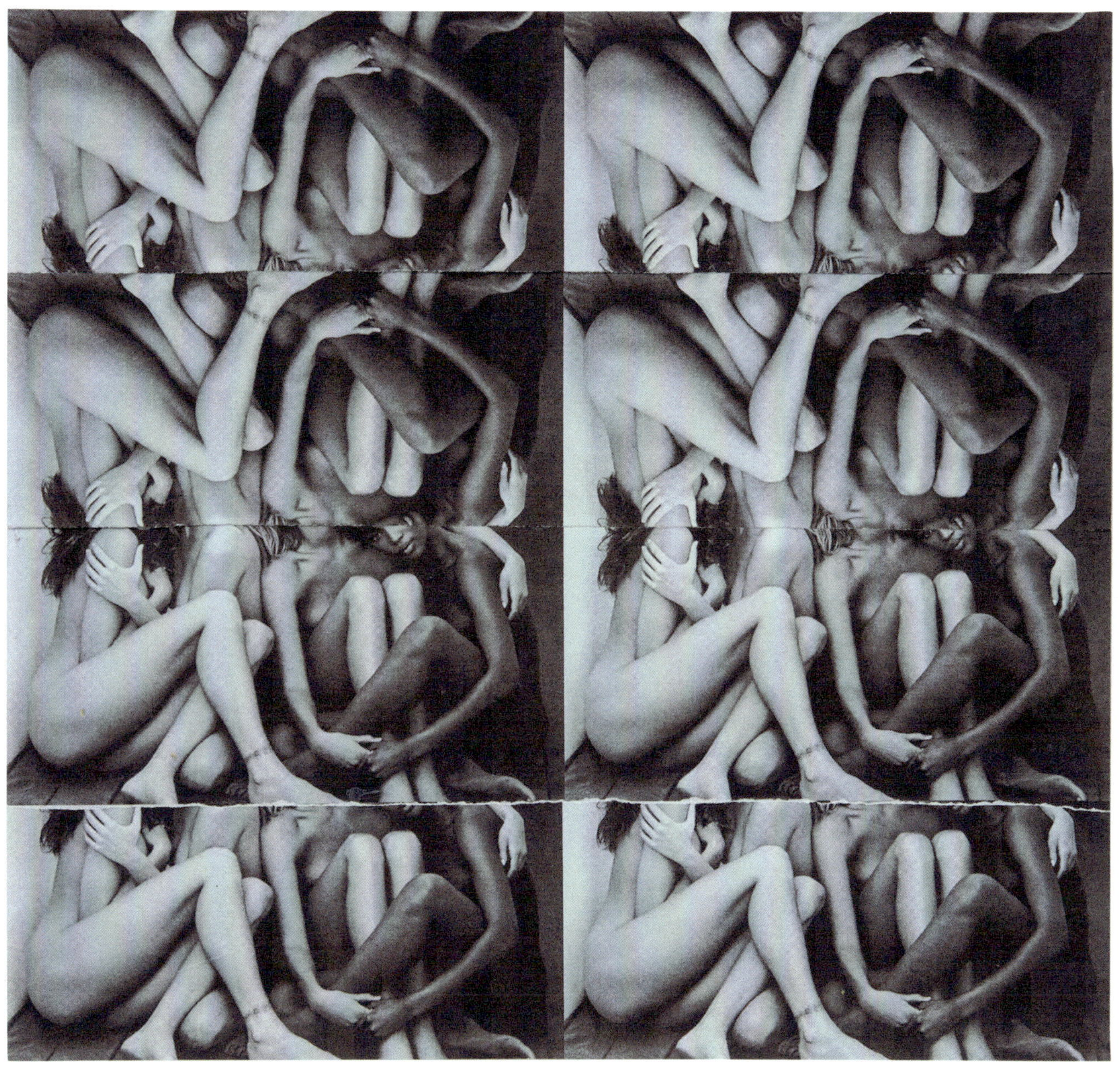

Collapse, Turn 'Round, 2018, paper and collage

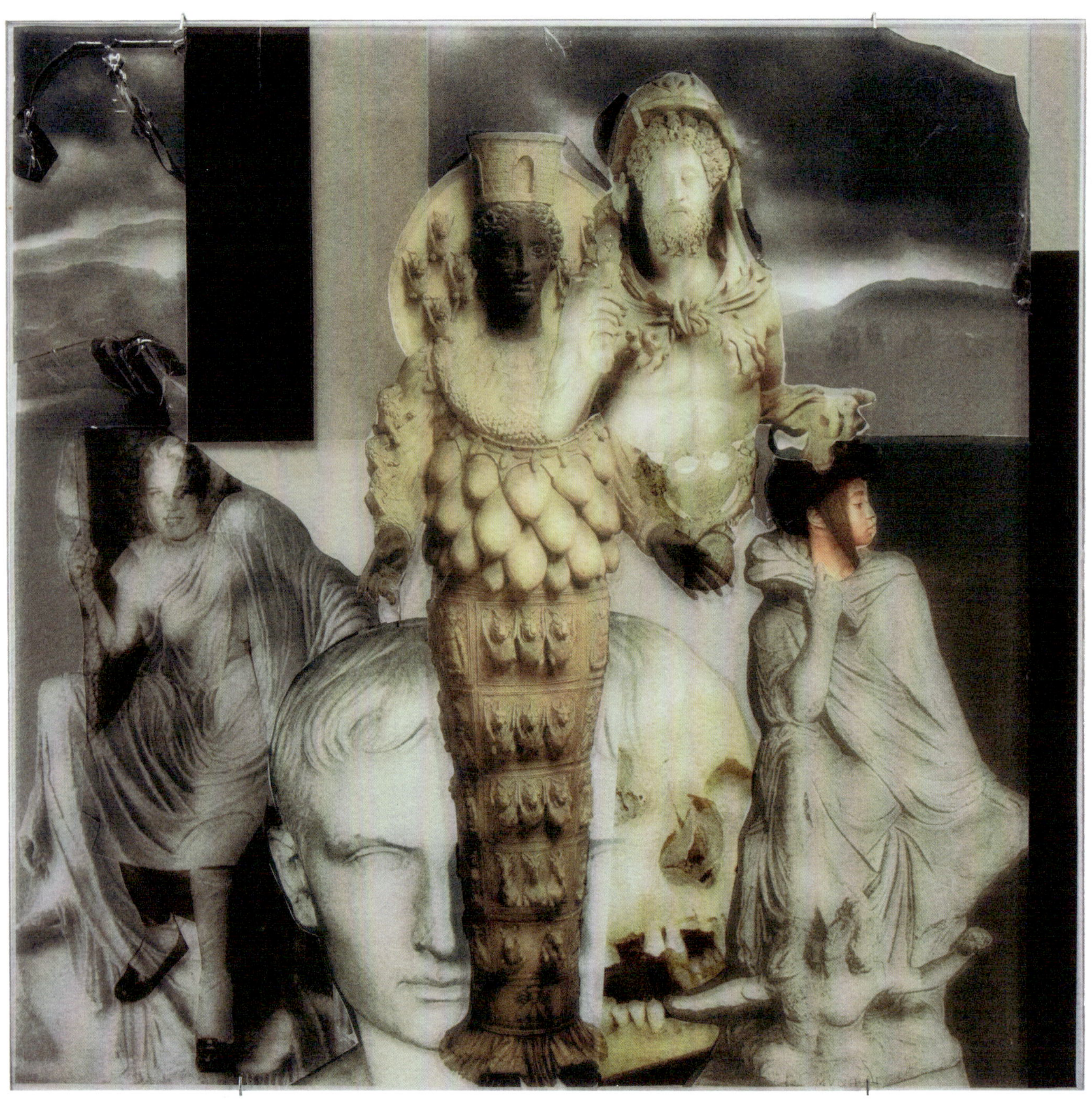

Landscape and RFD, 2018, sticker, collage, and plexiglass

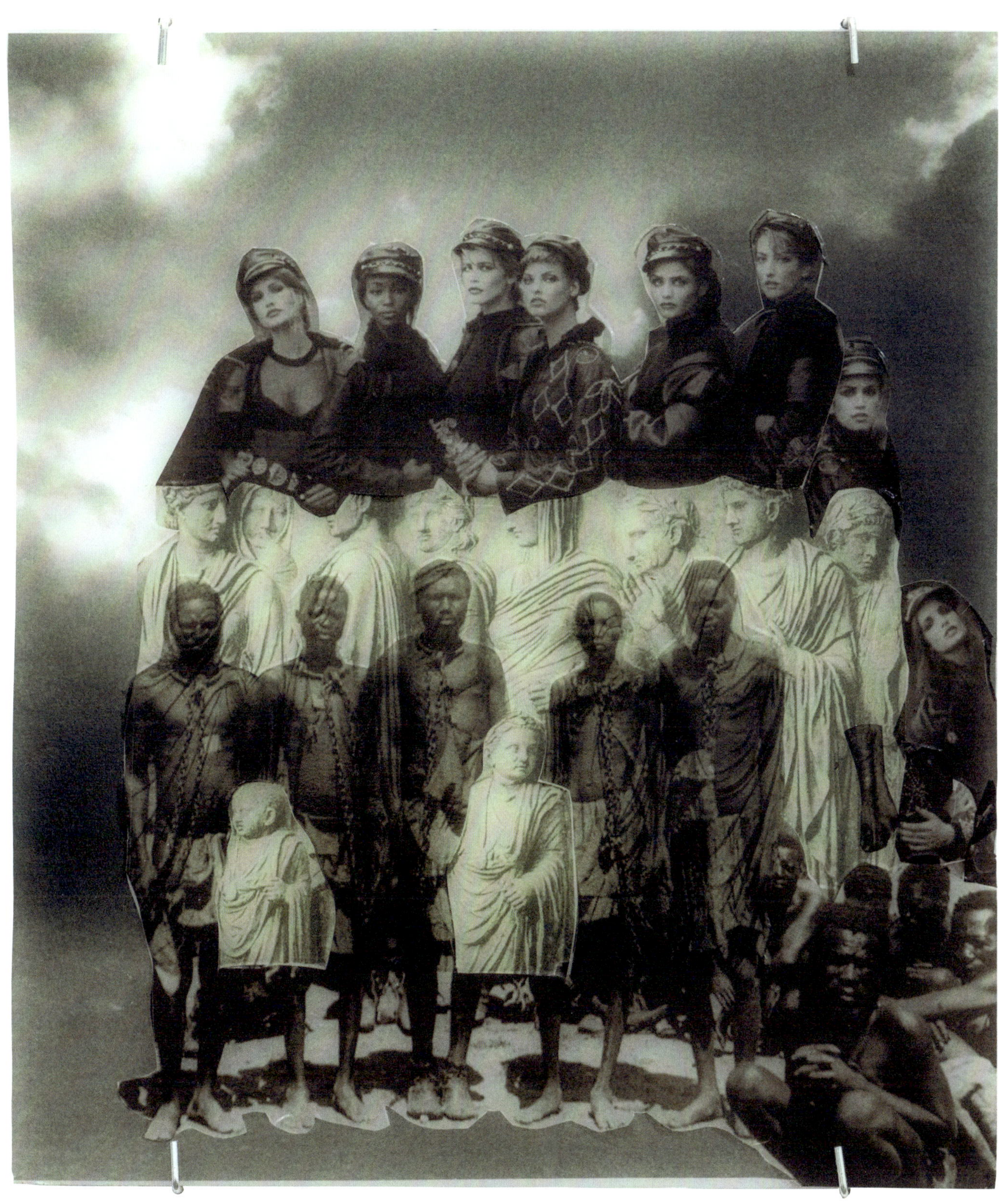

Crowd on the marshes of Lethe, 2018, sticker and plastic

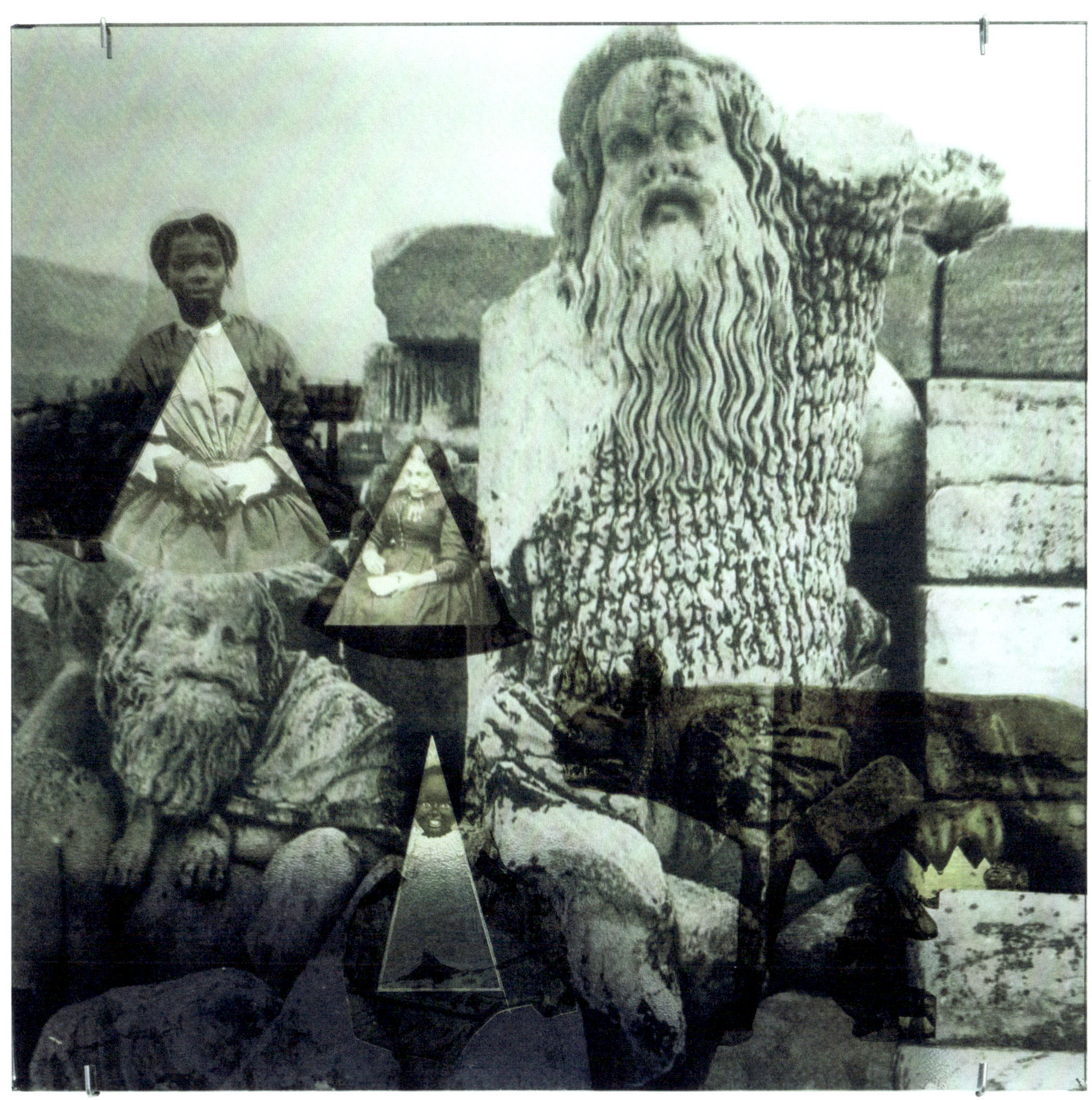

Cave before Cocytus, 2018, sticker on mirror glass

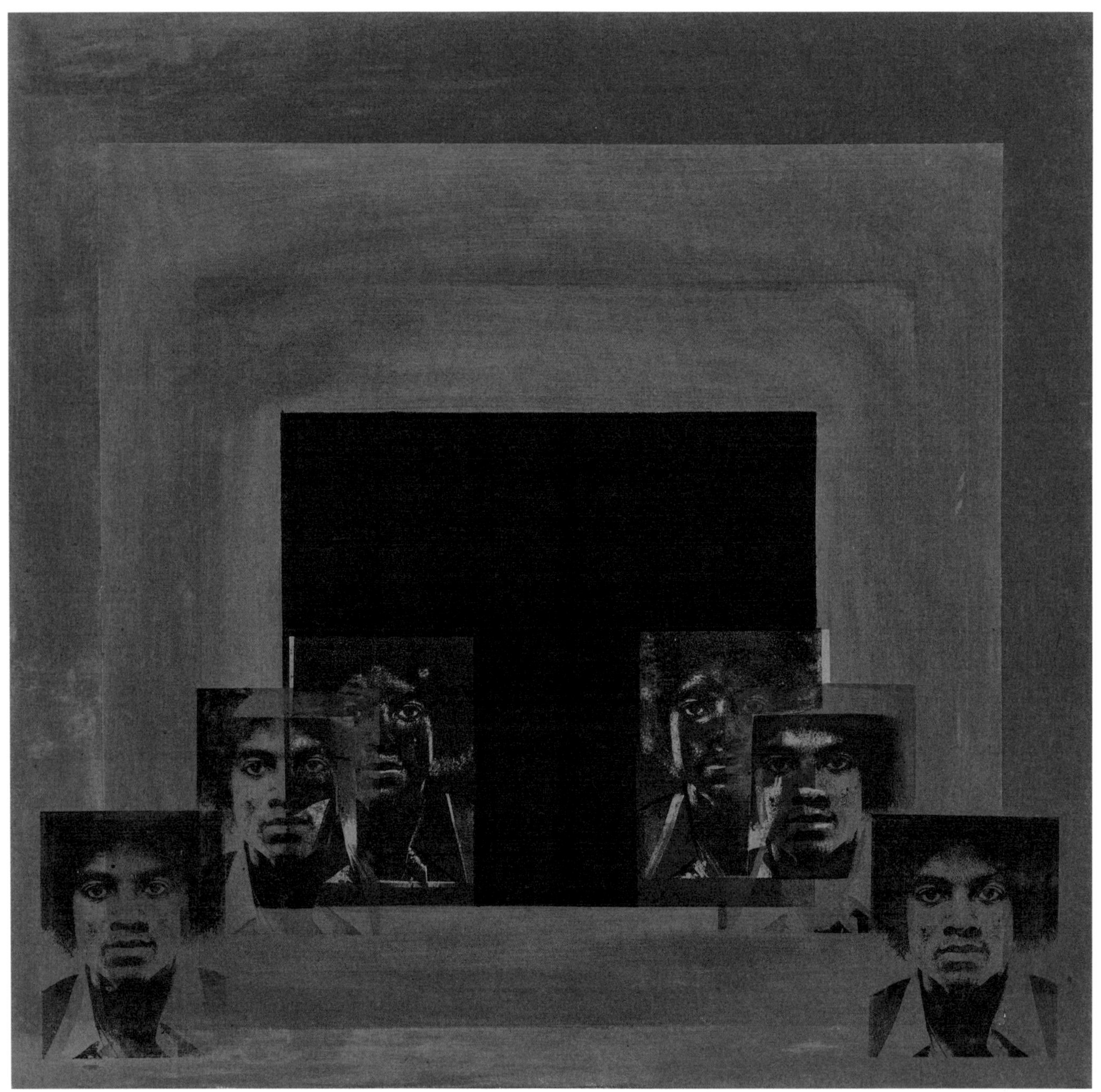

Modernity is not merely a compromise between novel forms of commercially driven social organization and this archaic cultural pattern of patrilineal exogamy, but more fundamentally, a deepening of the compromise already integral to any exogamy that is able to remain patrilineal, 2019, acrylic and dye on canvas and board

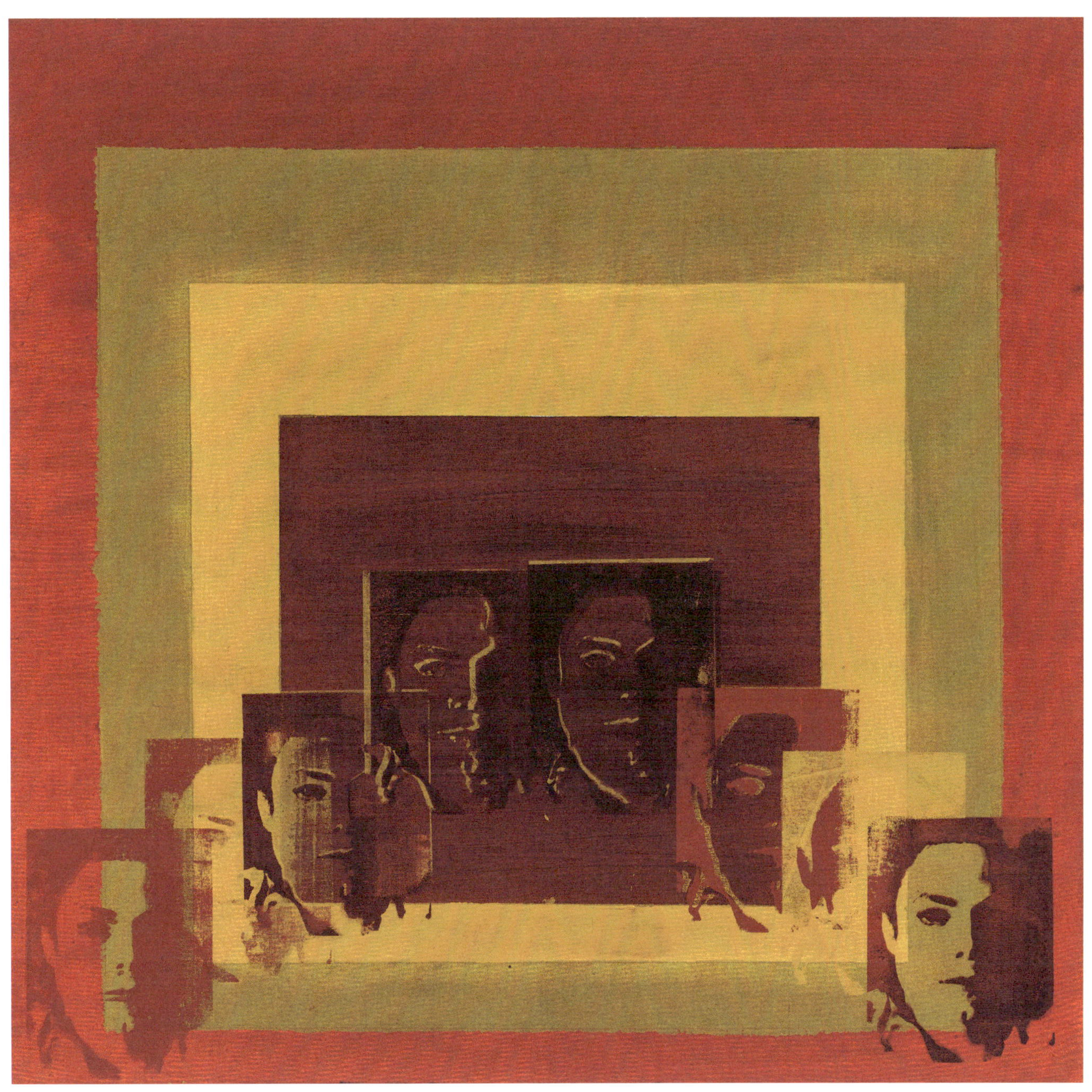

Primitive accumulation: Kant, Marx, Albers, Jackson, 2019, acrylic and dye on canvas and board

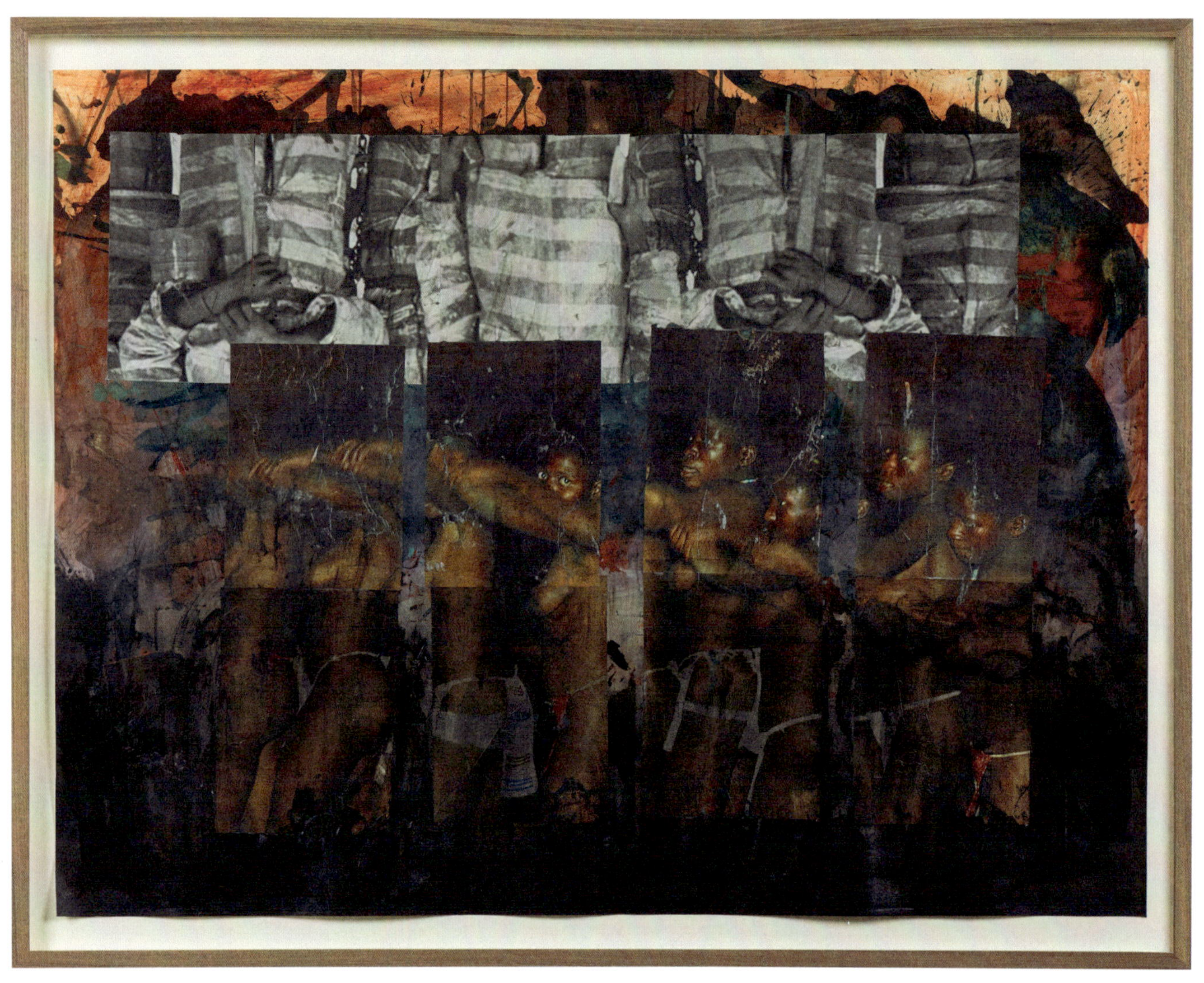

In an events-without-witness era, 2019, xerox collage and ink on paper, framed

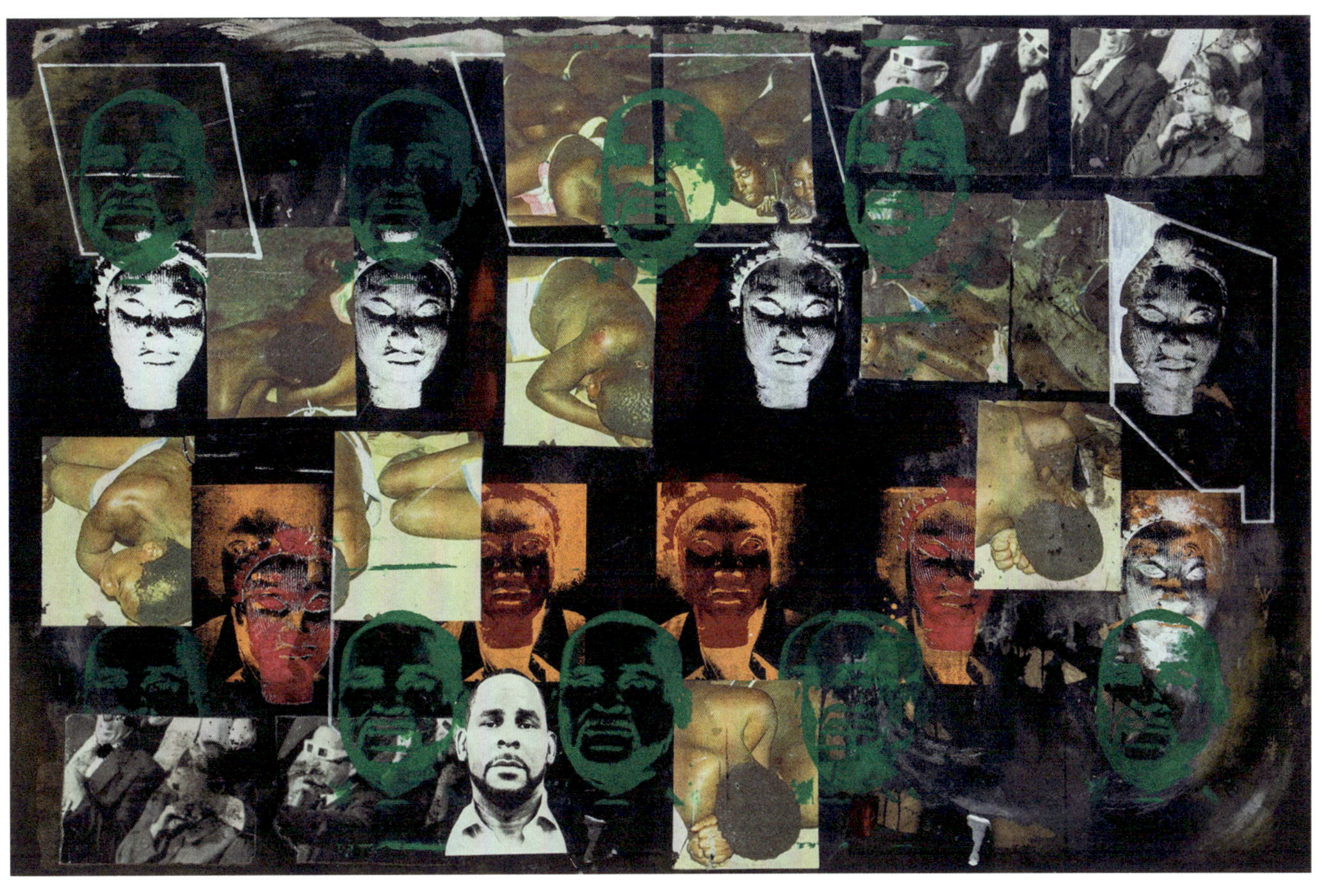

When the chief passes by, the dancers have 'to die': they throw themselves down, hiding their faces with their hands. Crafted during the Johnson, Nixon and Reagan administrations, the current federal "starve the beast" movement is designed to reestablish numerous forms of domination by comprehensively transforming key institutions within the national and international political economy, that is, 'deevolution' at home and 'neoliberalism' abroad, 2019, ink, dye, and collage on canvas

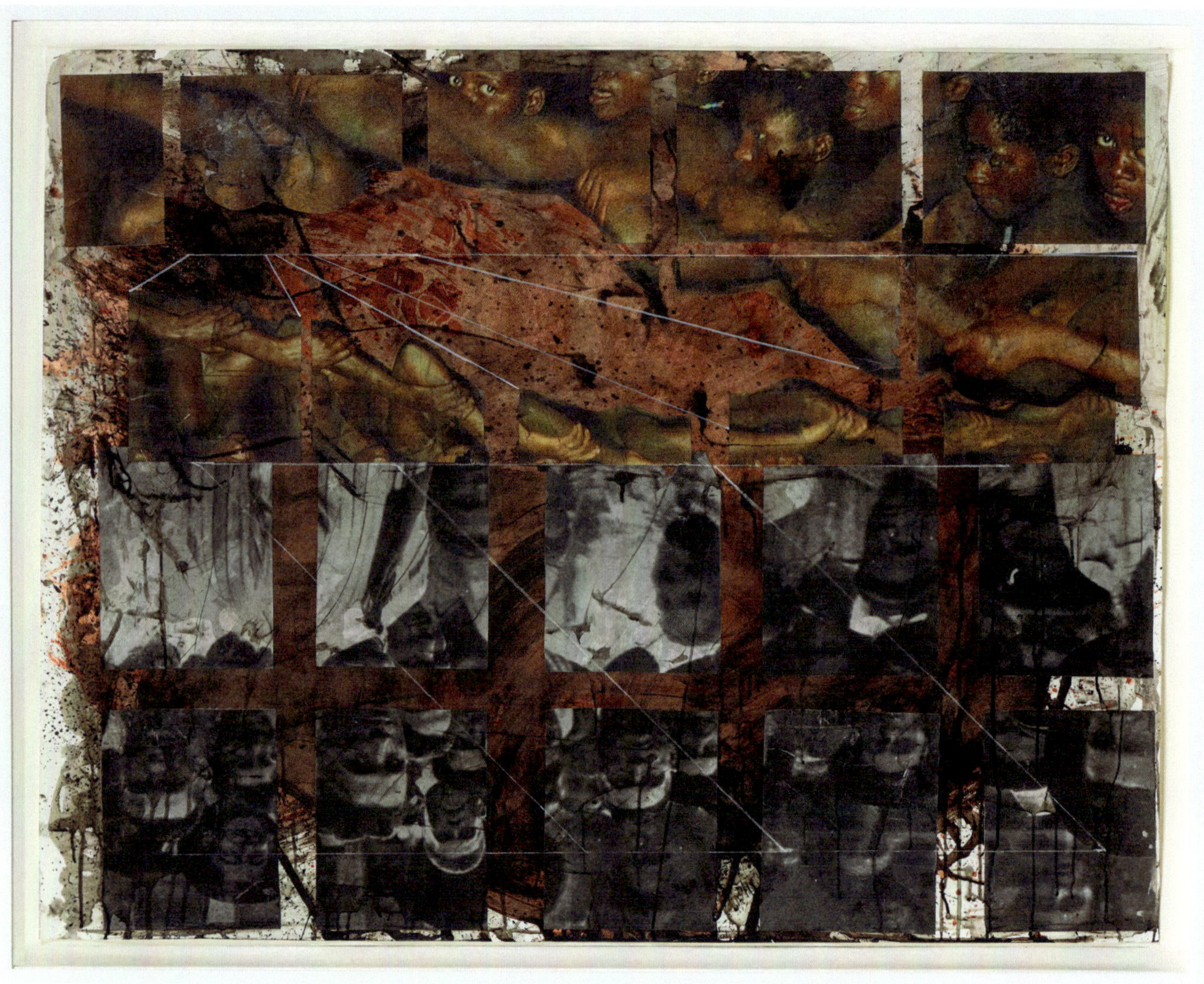

co-response-ability with/for the unknown Other, 2019, xerox collage and ink on paper, framed

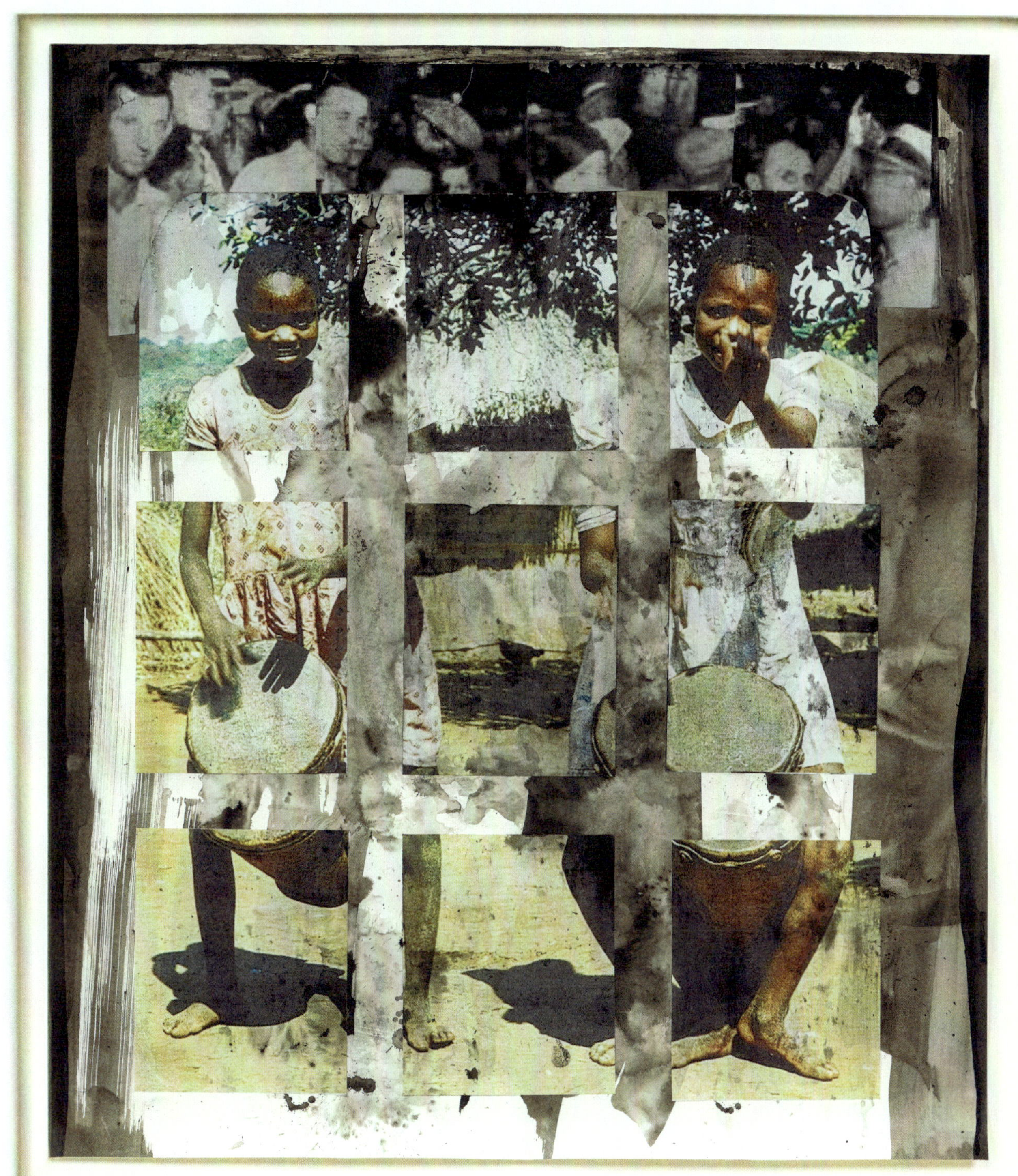

transformed relations-without-relating, 2019, xerox collage and ink on paper

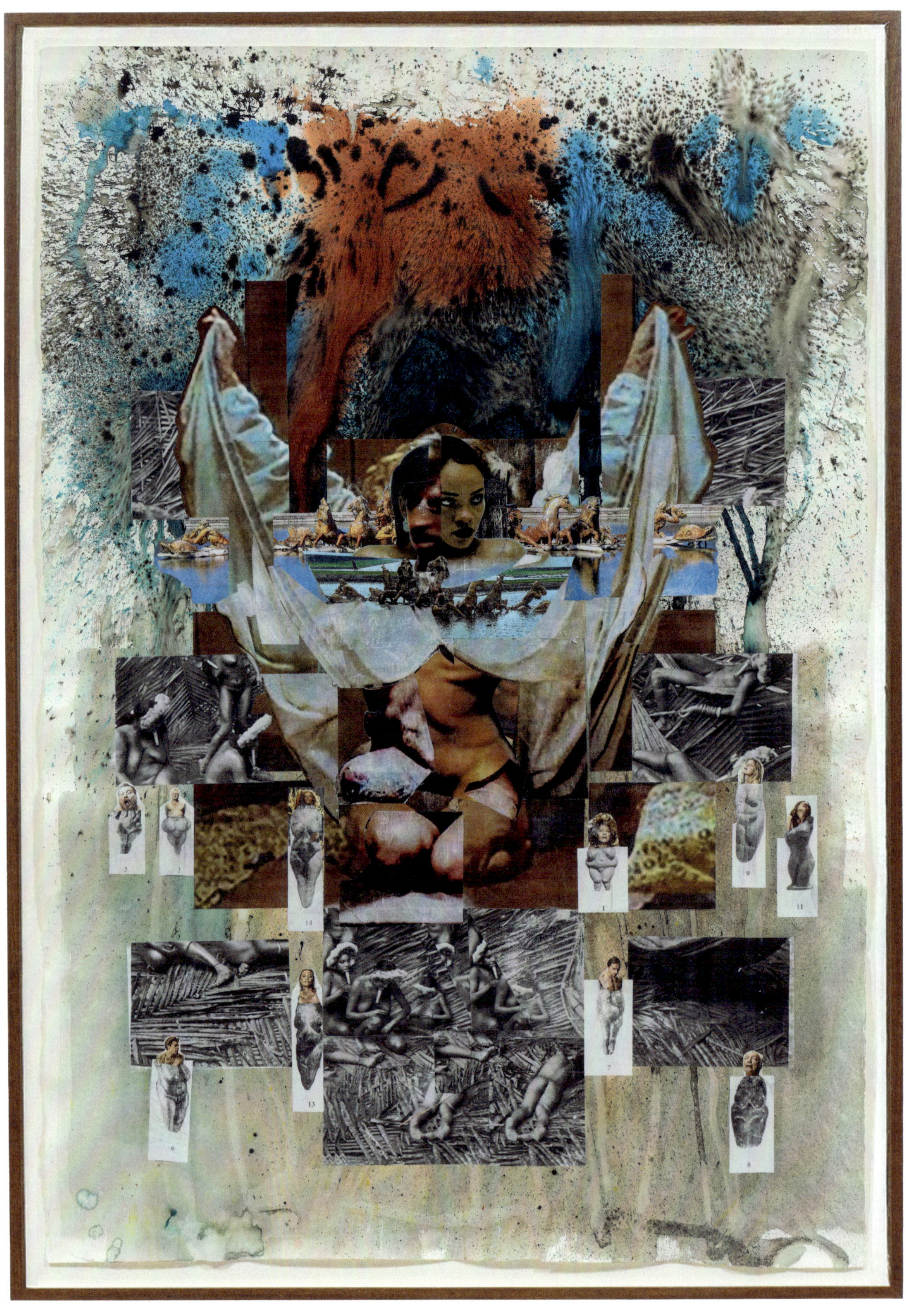

Belladonna Atropos. On the one hand, the plant appears to withdraw from a human economy of desire and hovers at the limits of our affective identification. But it also produces profound effects on us, including setting in motion our imagination. This oscillation is not only a defining characteristic of vegetality but functions as a key trait of speculative literature, giving this genre a power and agency that is inherently linked to the vibrancy of plant matter. can all the tight pussy gals step forward?, 2020, toner, ink, and acrylic medium on paper

We have spared no expense. scope, scalpel, axe, drill. The Sort of Thing You Should Not Admit: violent death, turns out to be puzzlingly complex and if you have a problem figuring out whether you're for me or, then you ain't black., 2020, ink and cut-and-pasted printed paper on paper

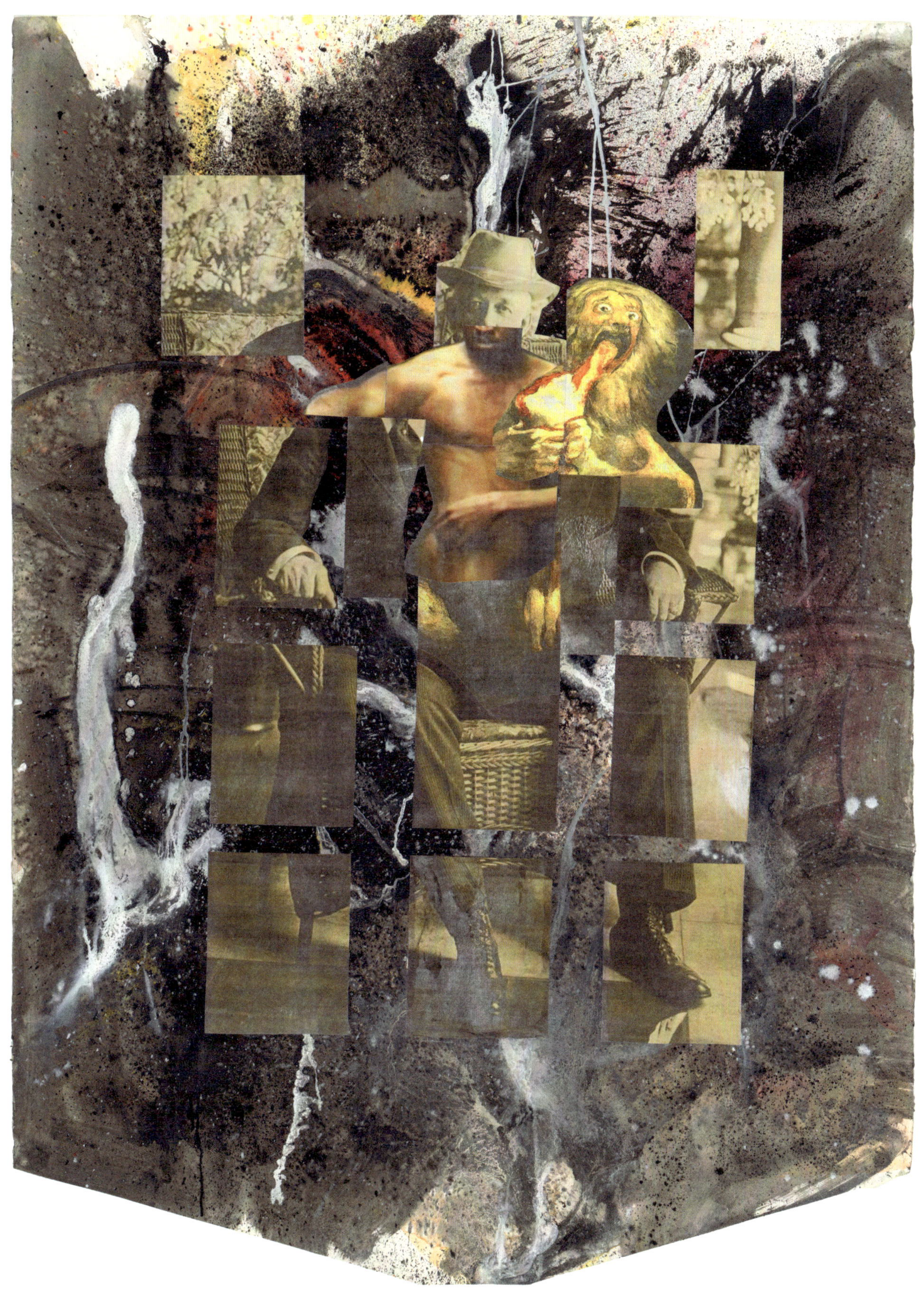

Nay, but tell me, am I not unlucky indeed, / To arise from the earth and be only a weed? / Ever since I came out of my dark little seed, / I have tried to live rightly, but still am a--weed! / To be torn by the roots and destroyed, this my meed, / And despised by the gardener, for being--a weed. / Ah! but why was I born, when man longs to be freed / Of a thing so obnoxious and bad as a--weed? / Now, the cause of myself and my brothers I plead, / Say, can any good come of my being a--weed? / Imagine smoking weed in the streets without cops harassin' / Imagine going to court with no trial / Lifestyle cruising blue behind my waters / No welfare supporters, more conscious of the way we raise our daughters / Days are shorter, nights are colder / Feeling like life is over, these snakes strike like a cobra / The world's hot my son got not / Evidently, it's elementary, they want us all gone eventually / Troopin' out of state for a plate, knowledge / If coke was cooked without the garbage we'd all have the top dollars / Imagine everybody flashin', fashion / Designer clothes, lacing your click up with diamond vogues / Your people holdin' dough, no parole / No rubbers, go in raw imagine, law with no undercovers / Just some thoughts. . ., 2020, xerox collage and ink on watercolor

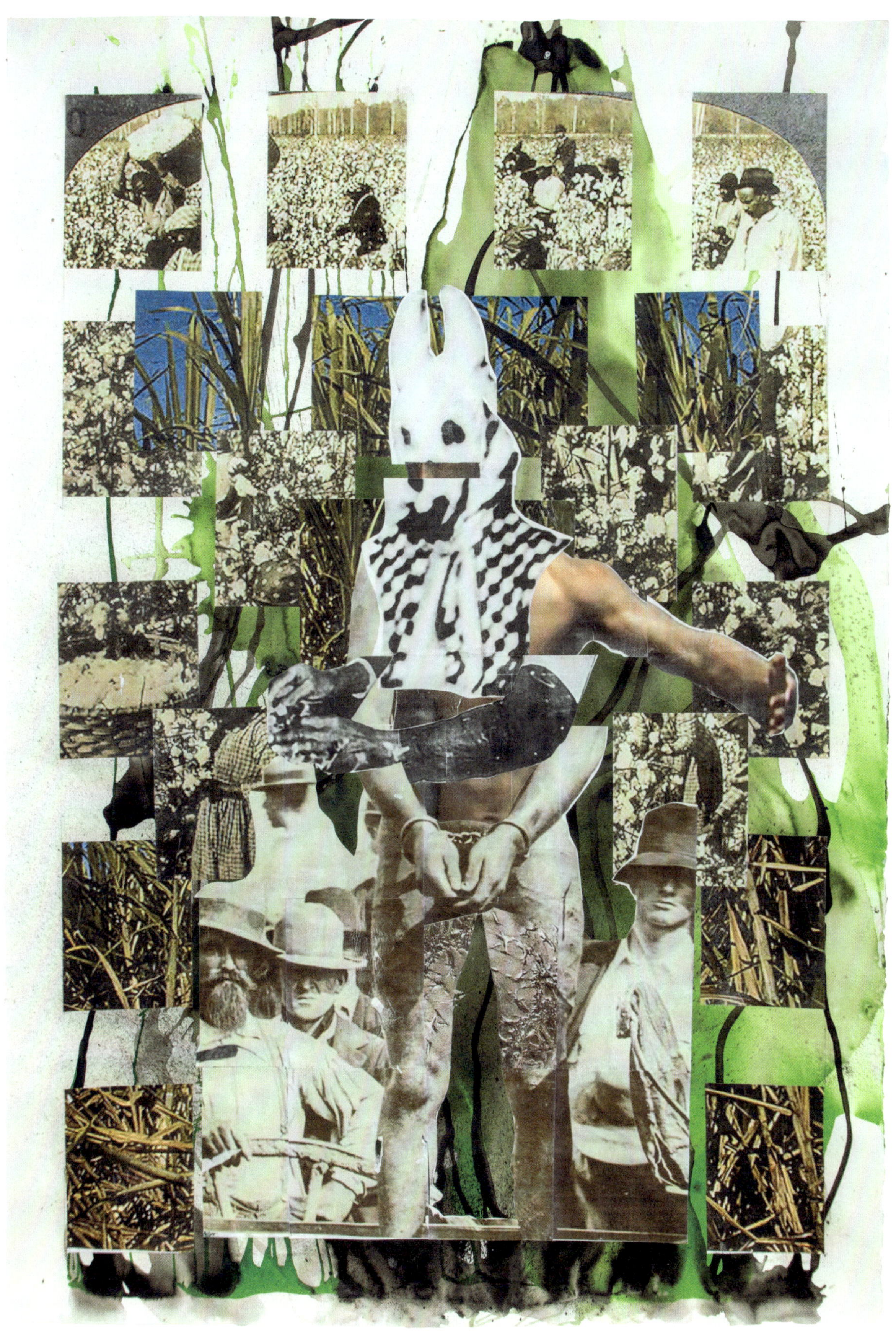

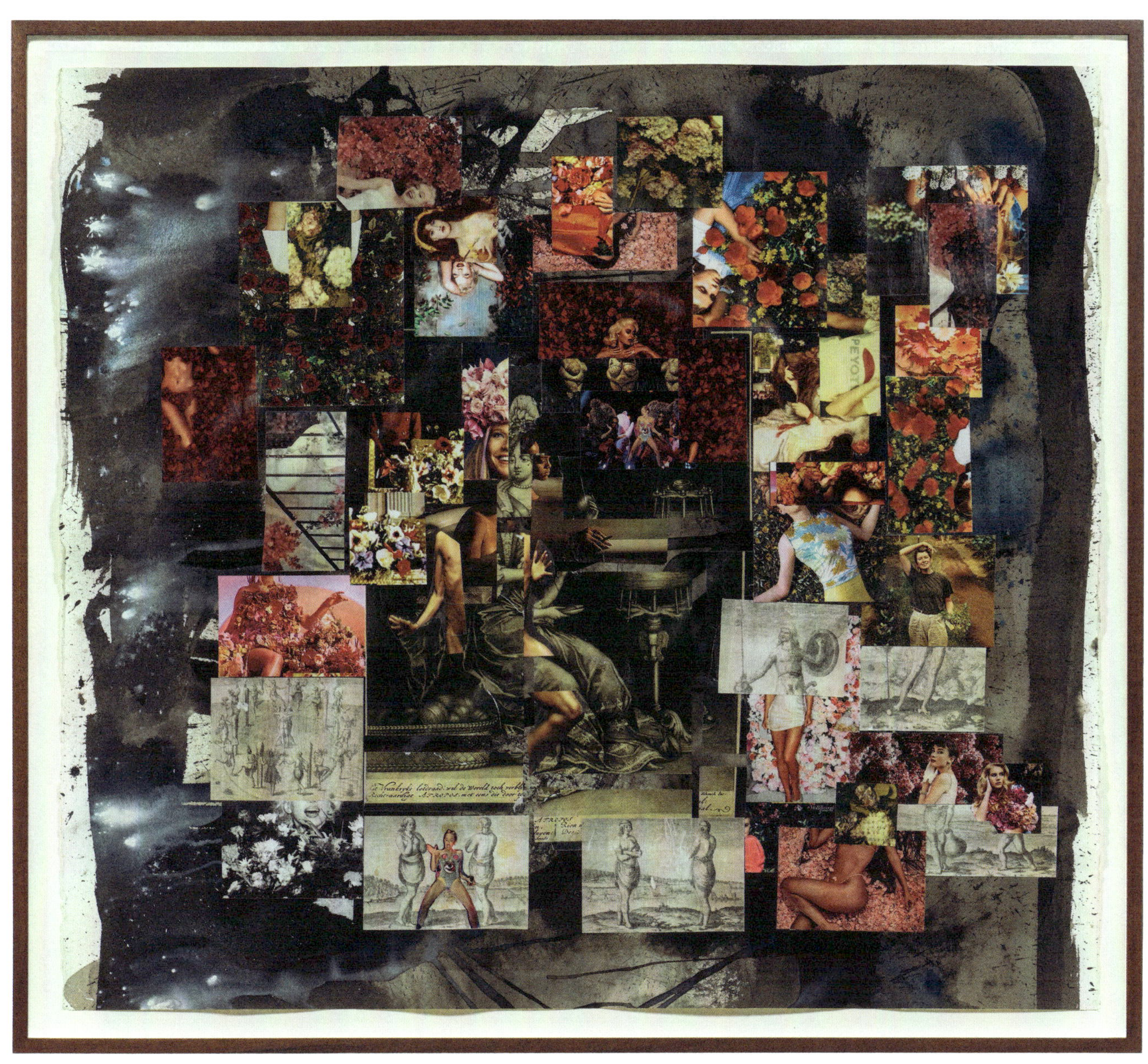

Because the forest is so densely grown with thistles and thorns, I had to send my slaves ahead of me with axes to hack out an opening for me to uncover specimens. Feet don't fail me now Take me to the finish line. Oh, my heart, it breaks every step that I take, But I'm hoping at the gates, they'll tell me athat you're mine., 2020, xerox collage and ink on watercolor paper

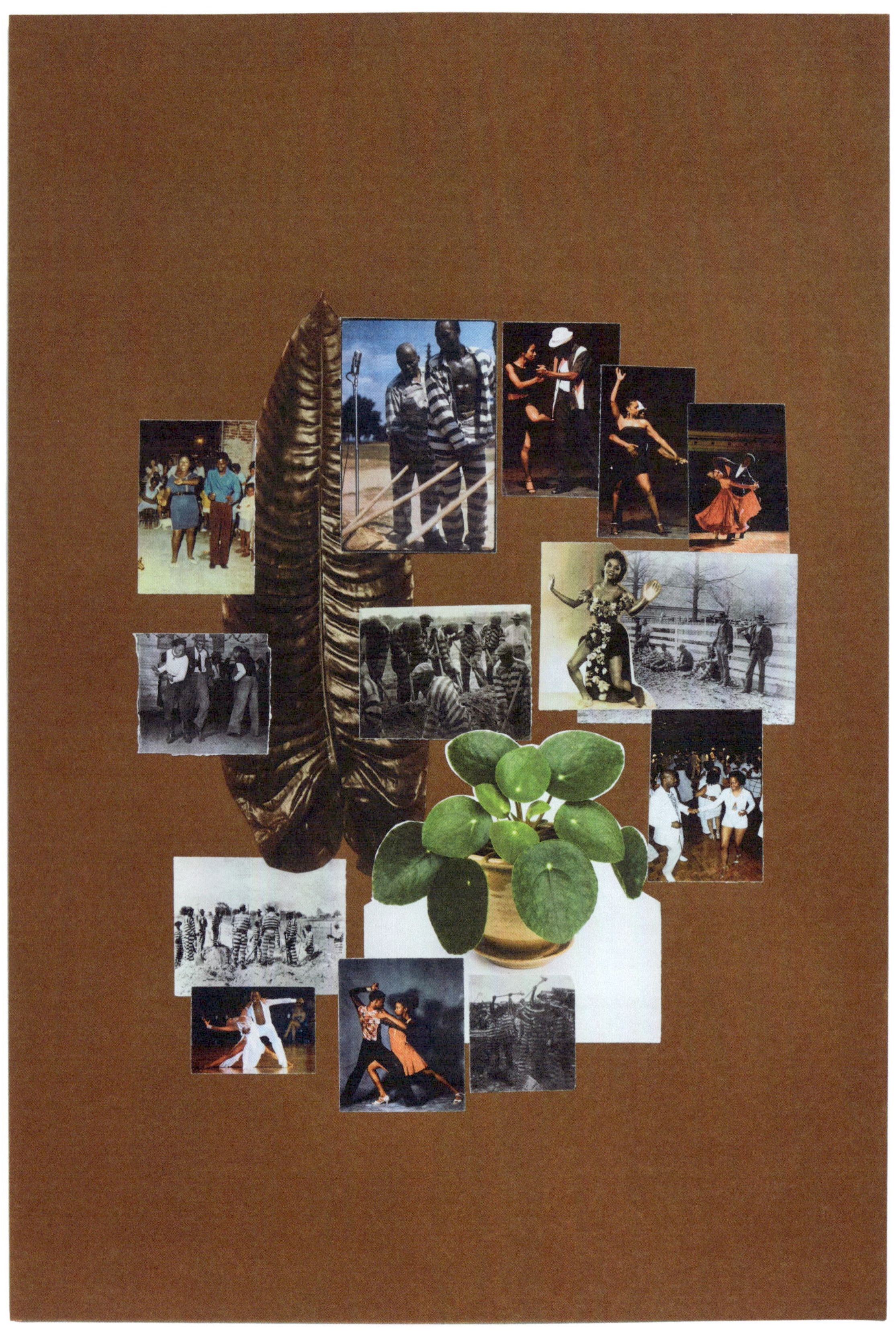

Transpositions, Sketch, Giant Tea Leaf and Money Plant, 2020, collage on paper

Transposition, Sketch, Monstera and Tumblr issued Tango, 2020, collage on paper

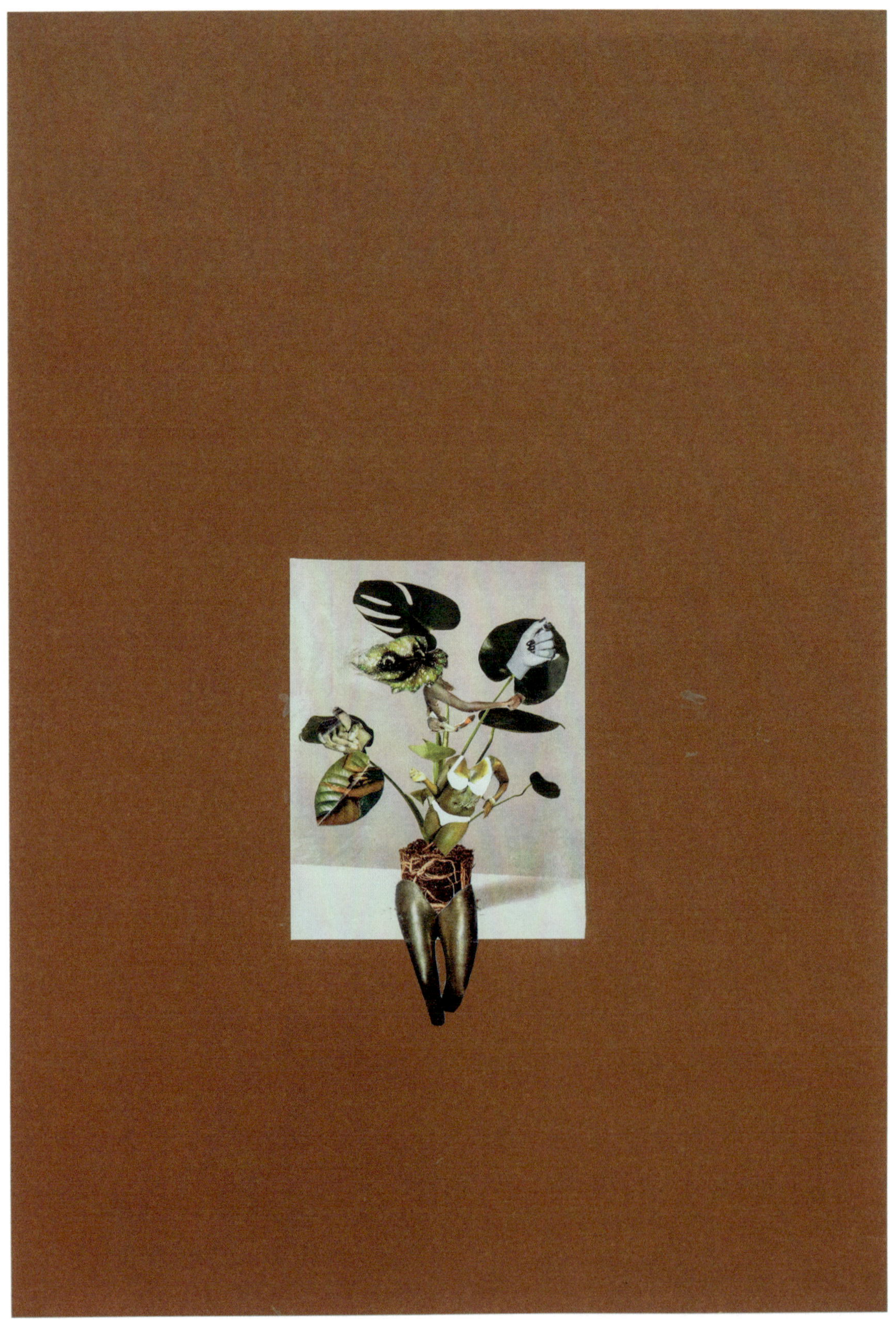

Transposition, Sketch, Swiss Monstera Candombe potted roots, 2020, collage on paper

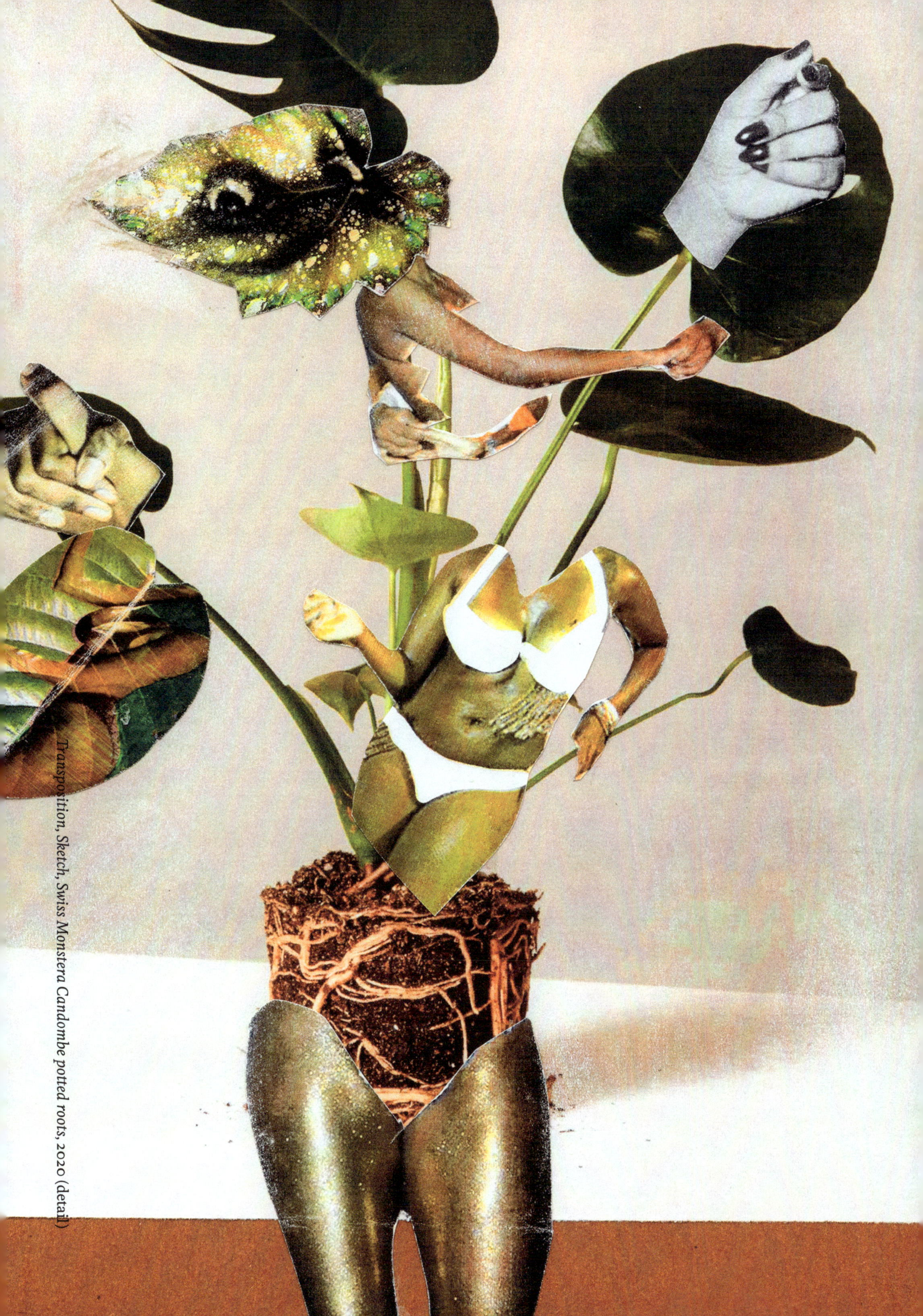

Transposition, Sketch, Swiss Monstera Candombe potted roots, 2020 (detail)

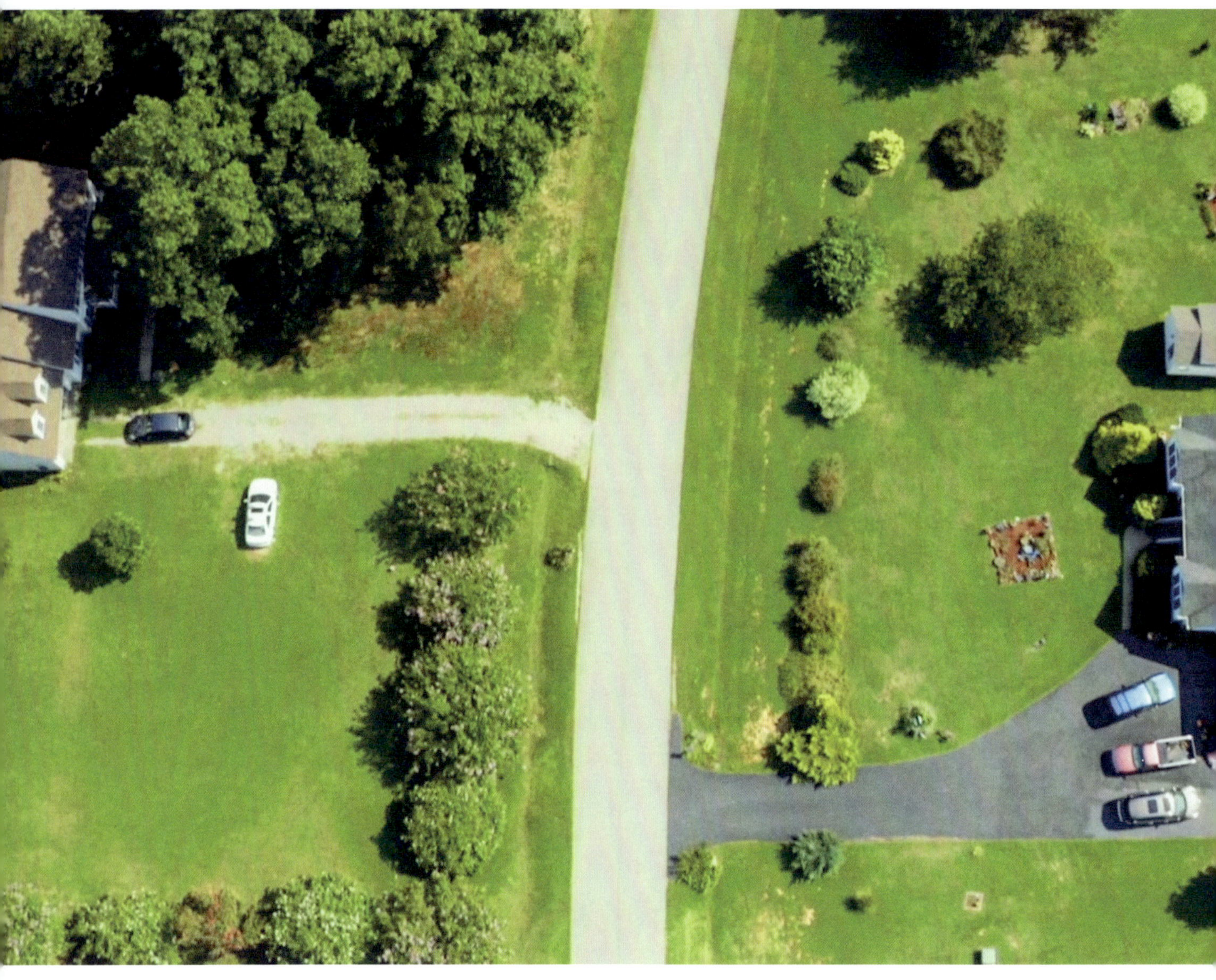

Annexation Tango, 2020, single-channel video (color, sound) (video still)

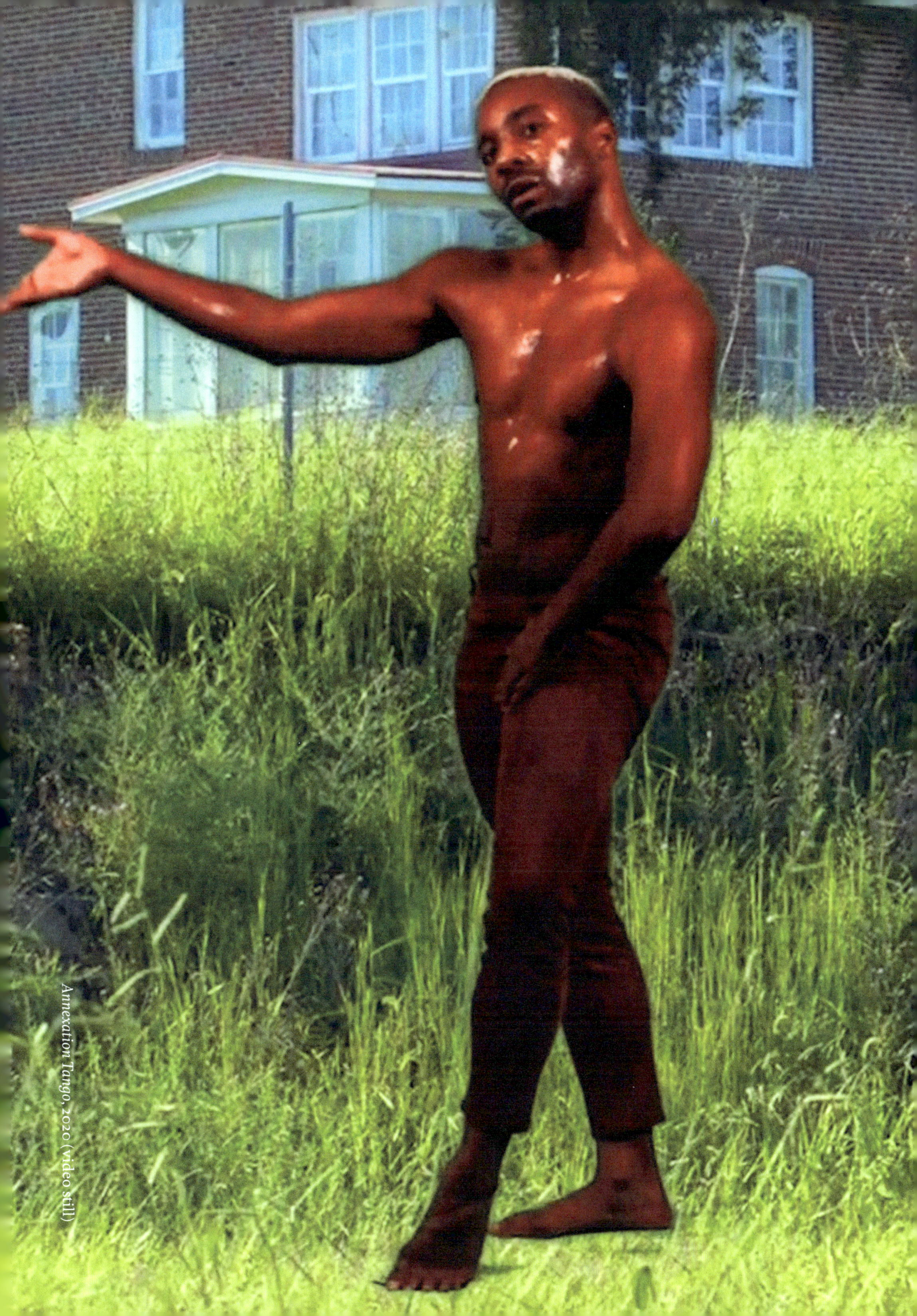

Annexation Tango, 2020 (video still)

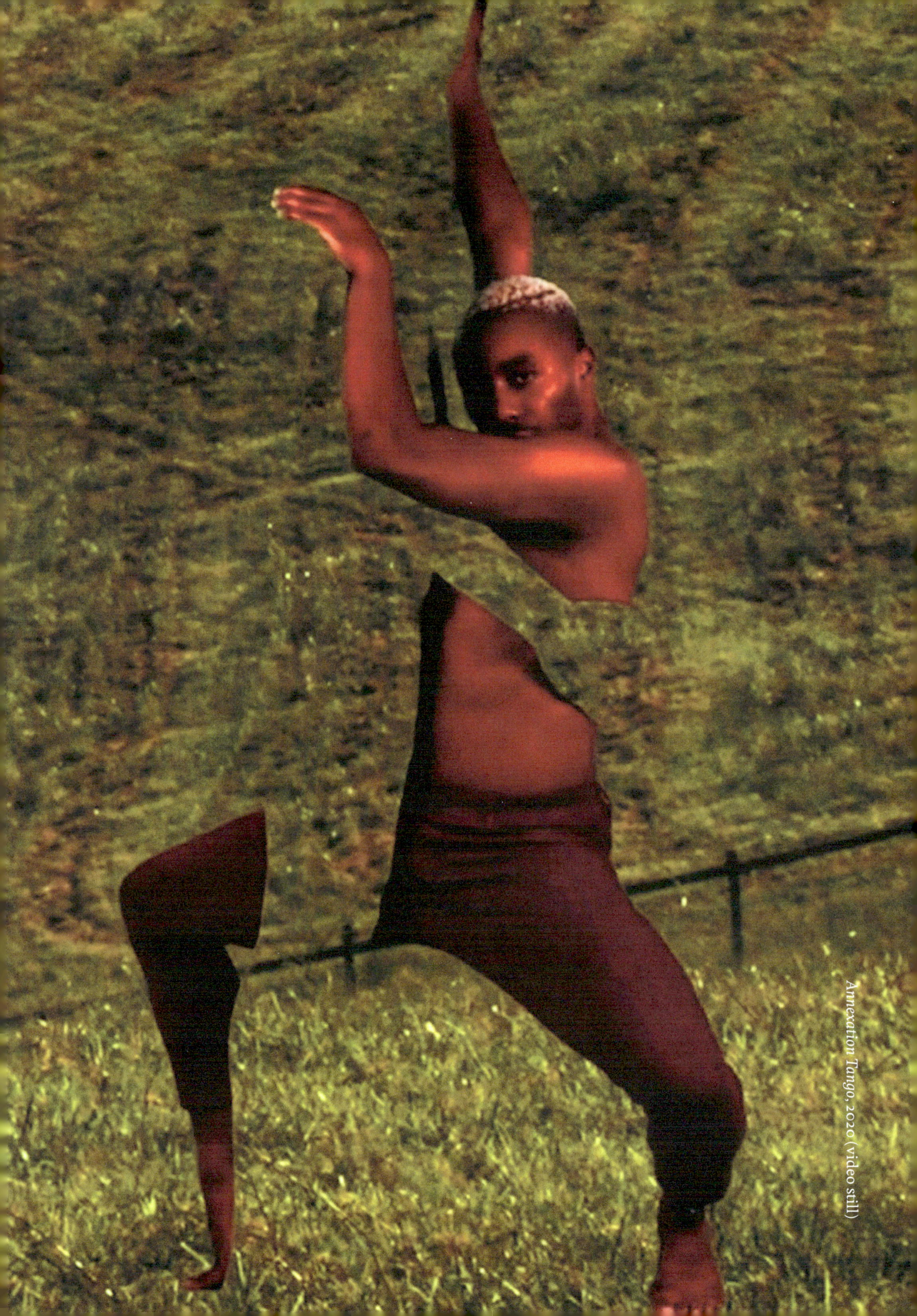

Annexation Tango, 2020 (video still)

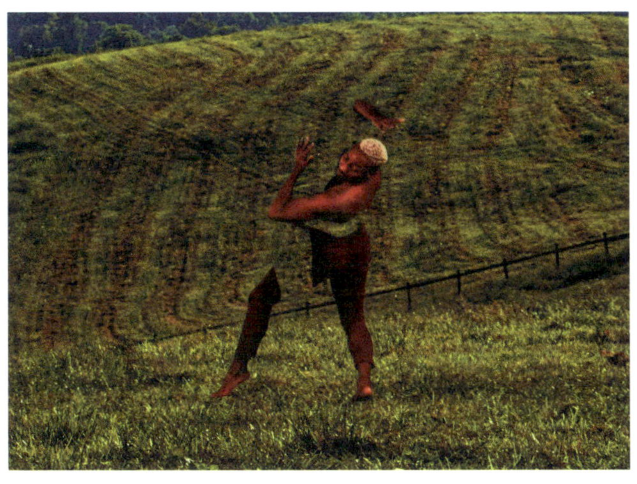

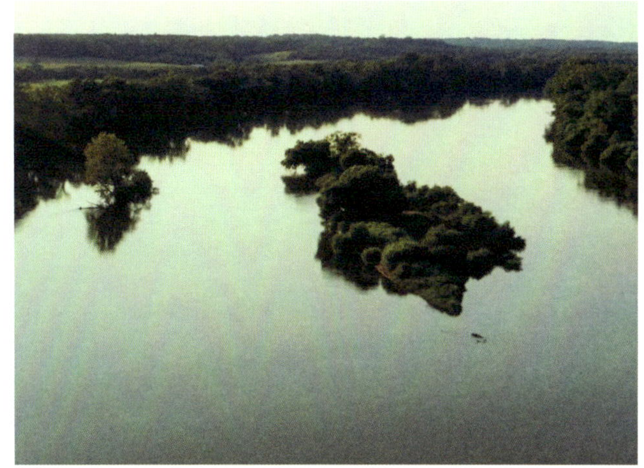

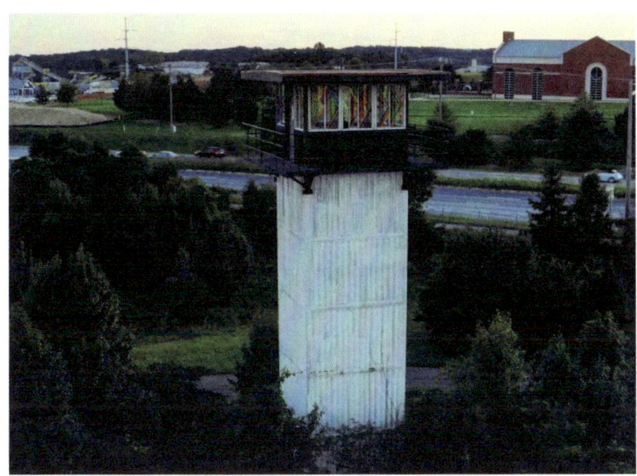

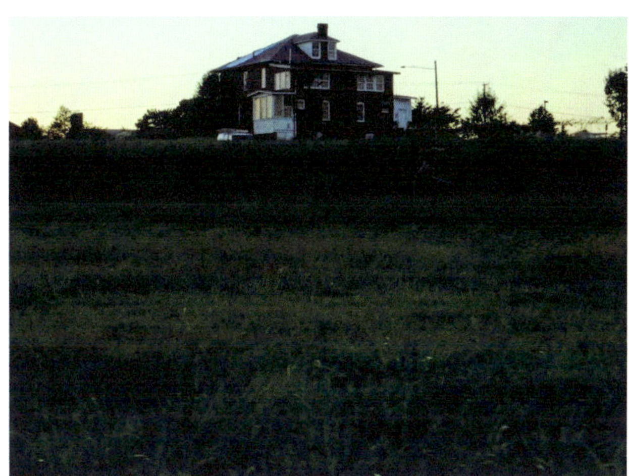

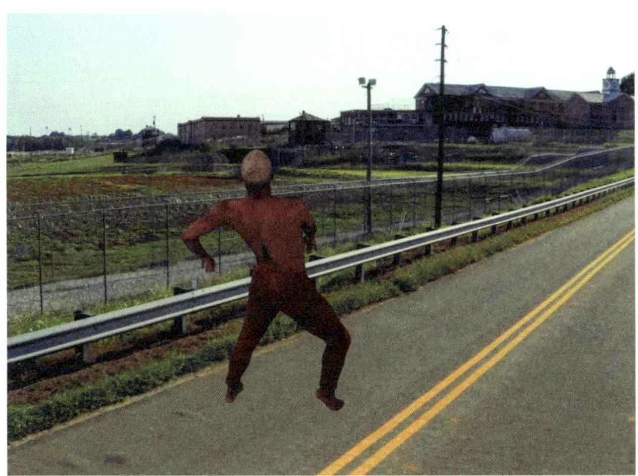

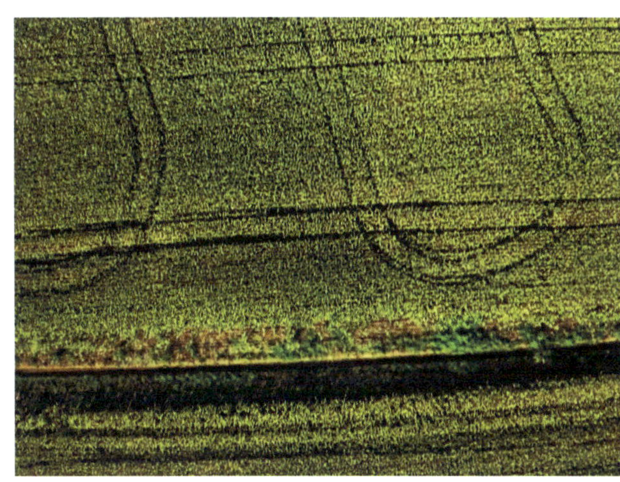

Annexation Tango, 2020, single-channel video (color, sound) (video stills)

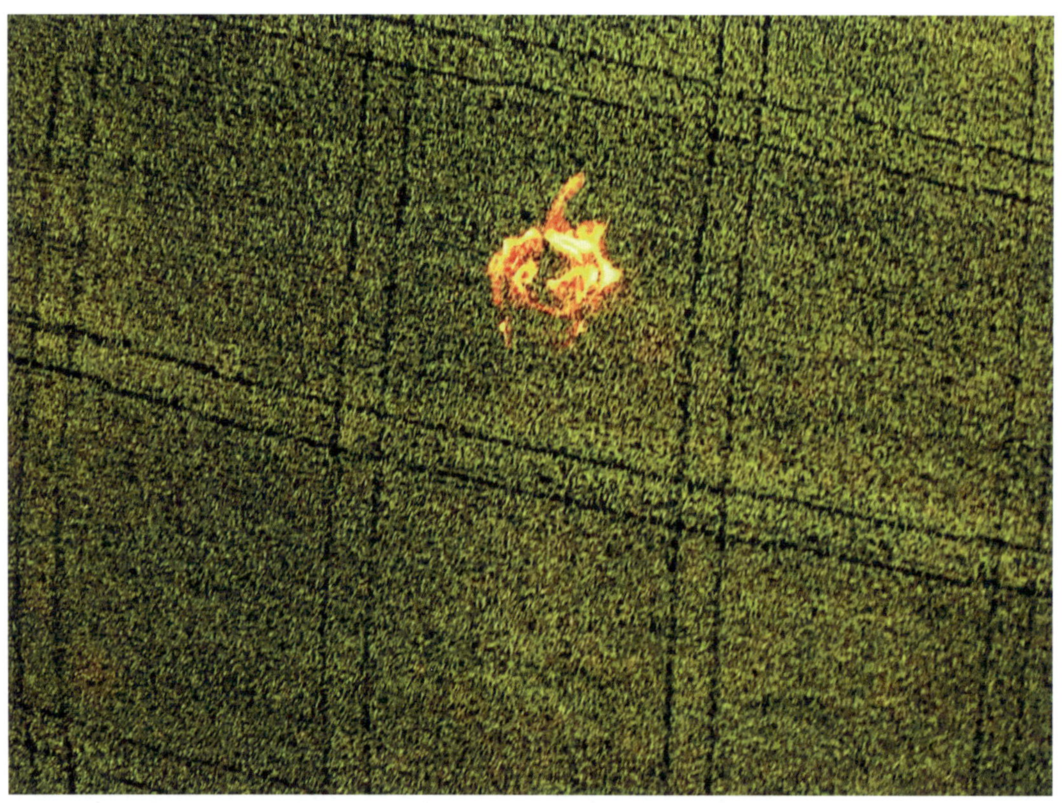

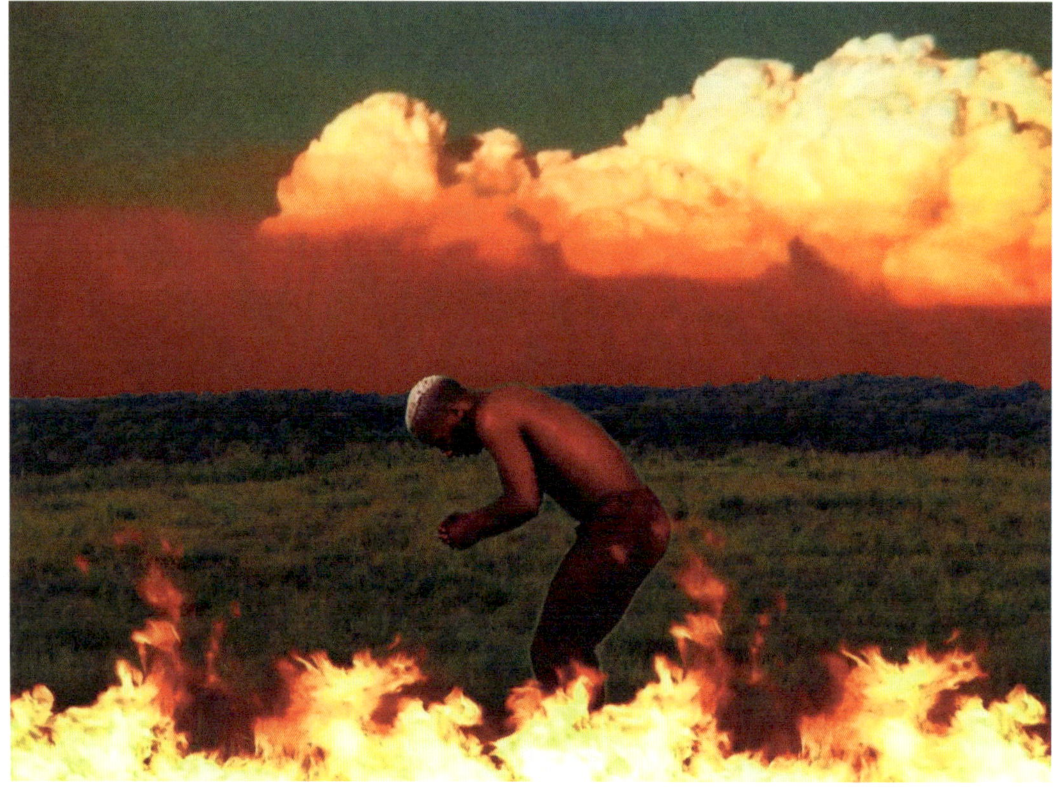

Annexation Tango, 2020, single-channel video (color, sound) (video stills)

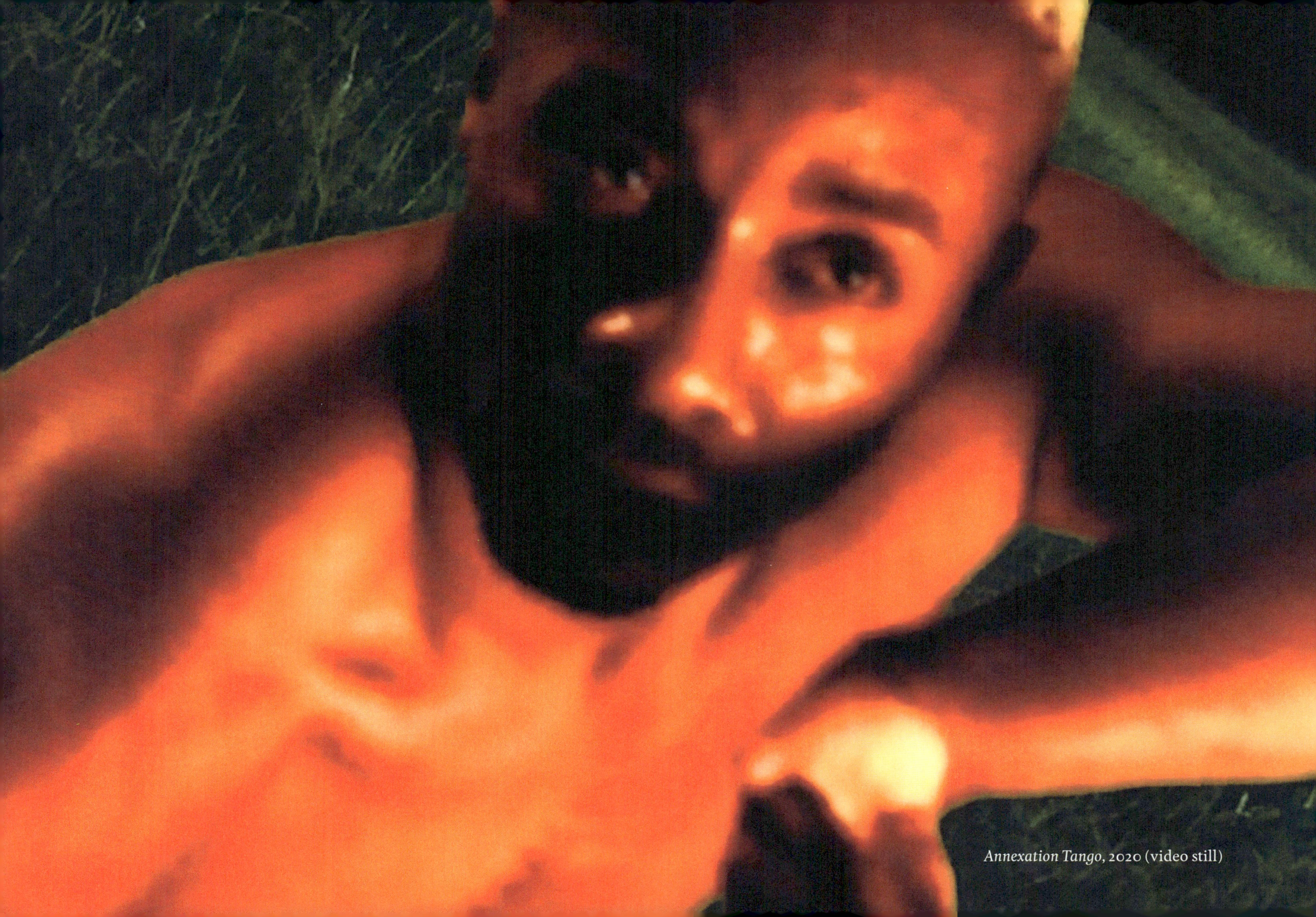

Annexation Tango, 2020 (video still)

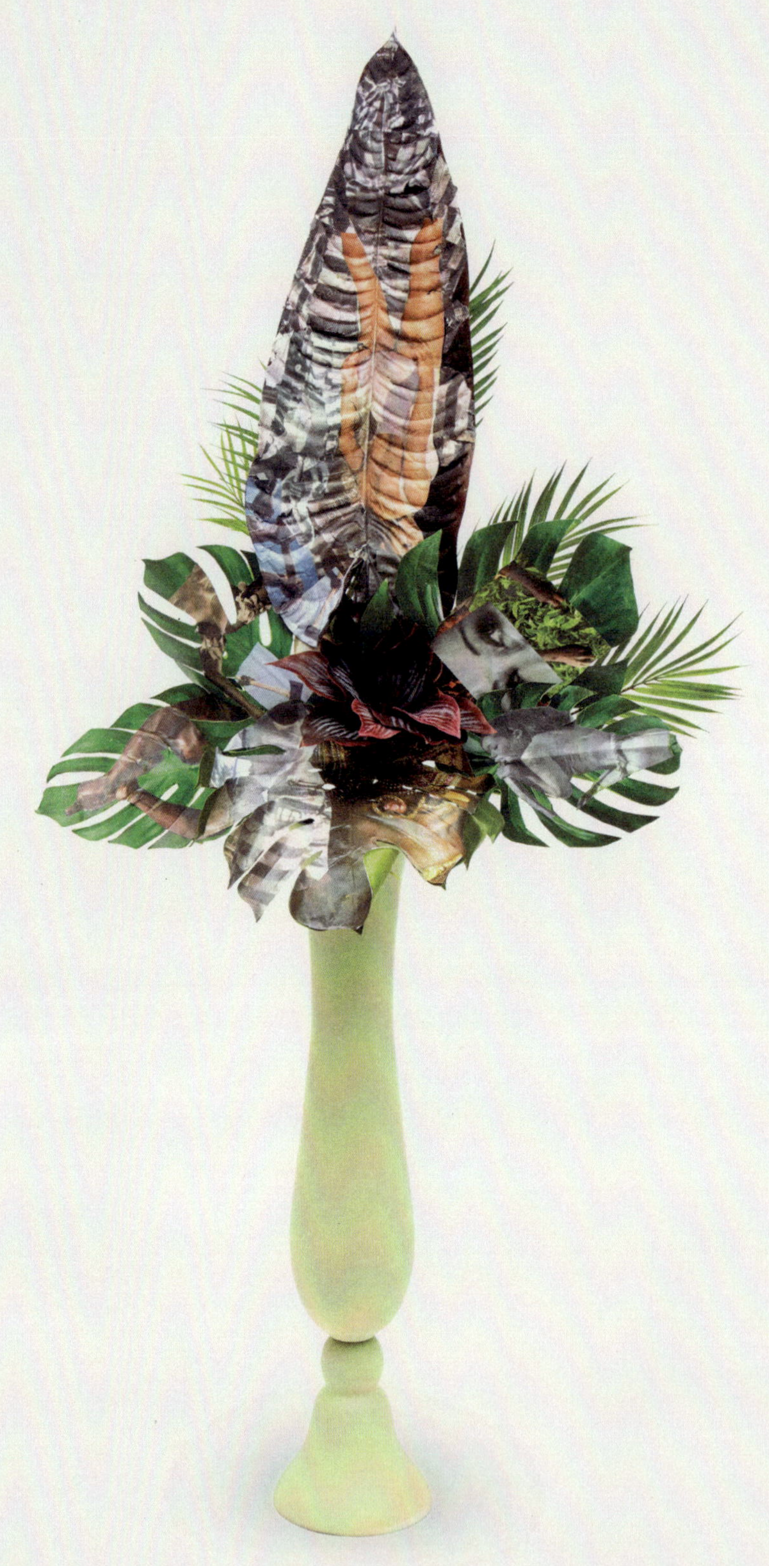

After birth all diligence is transferred to the calves; then the farmers brand them with their mark and the name of their breed And set aside those to rear to perpetuate their kind, to keep as sacred for the altar, or to cultivate earth and turn over the uneven field breaking its clods. the rest of the cattle pasture on green grasses, but train those that you'll prepare for work and service on the farm when they are still calves and set them on the path to dociling while their youthful spirits are willing, while their lives are tractable. some few women are born free, and some amid insult and scarlet letter achieve freedom [sic] with that freedom they are buying an untrammeled independence and dear as is the price they pay for it, it will in the end be worth every taunt and groan., 2020, sublimation prints on cotton paper, copper wire, plastic, and vase

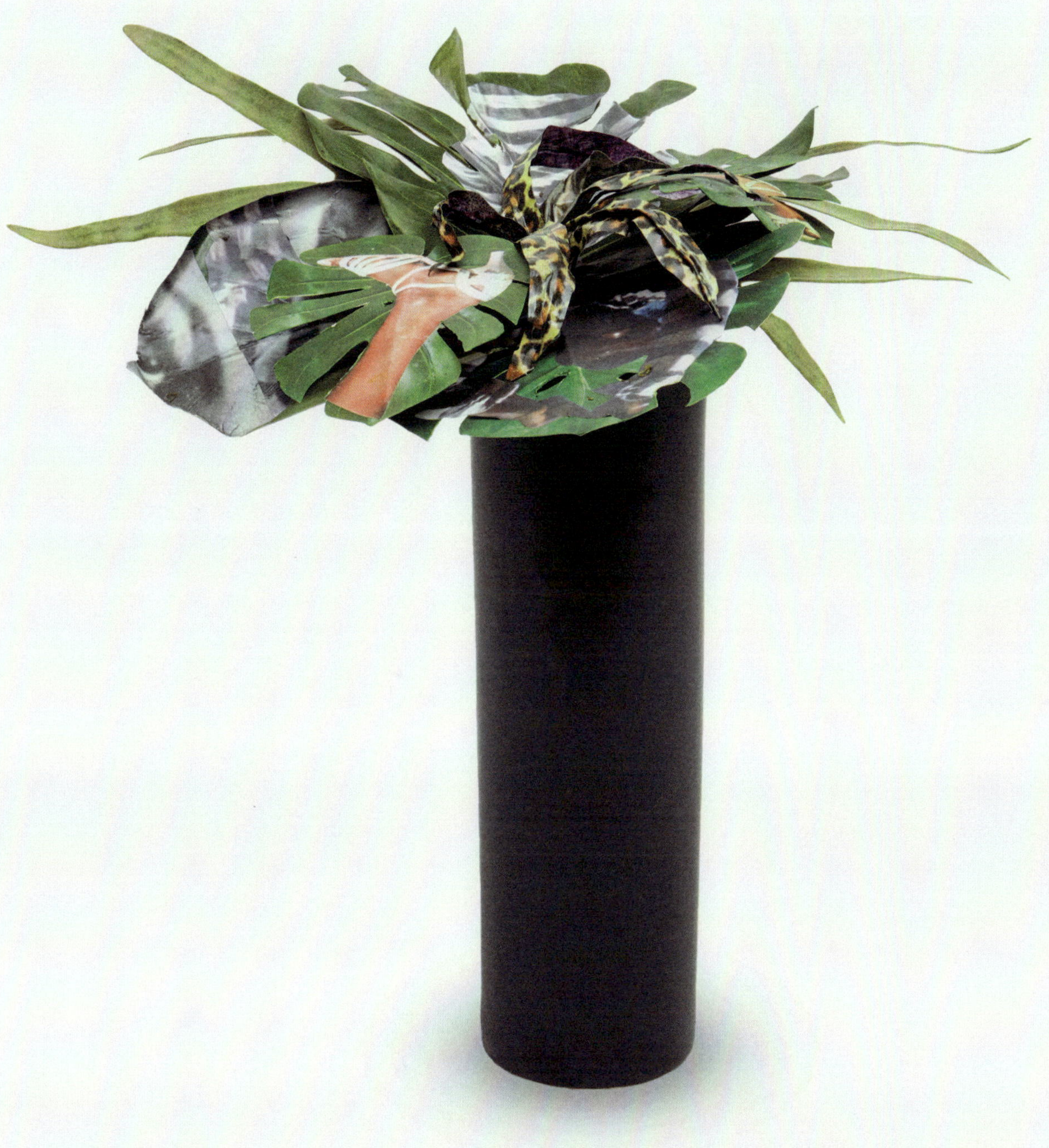

Exotica, 2020, sublimation prints on cotton paper, copper wire, plastic, sumi ink, and vase

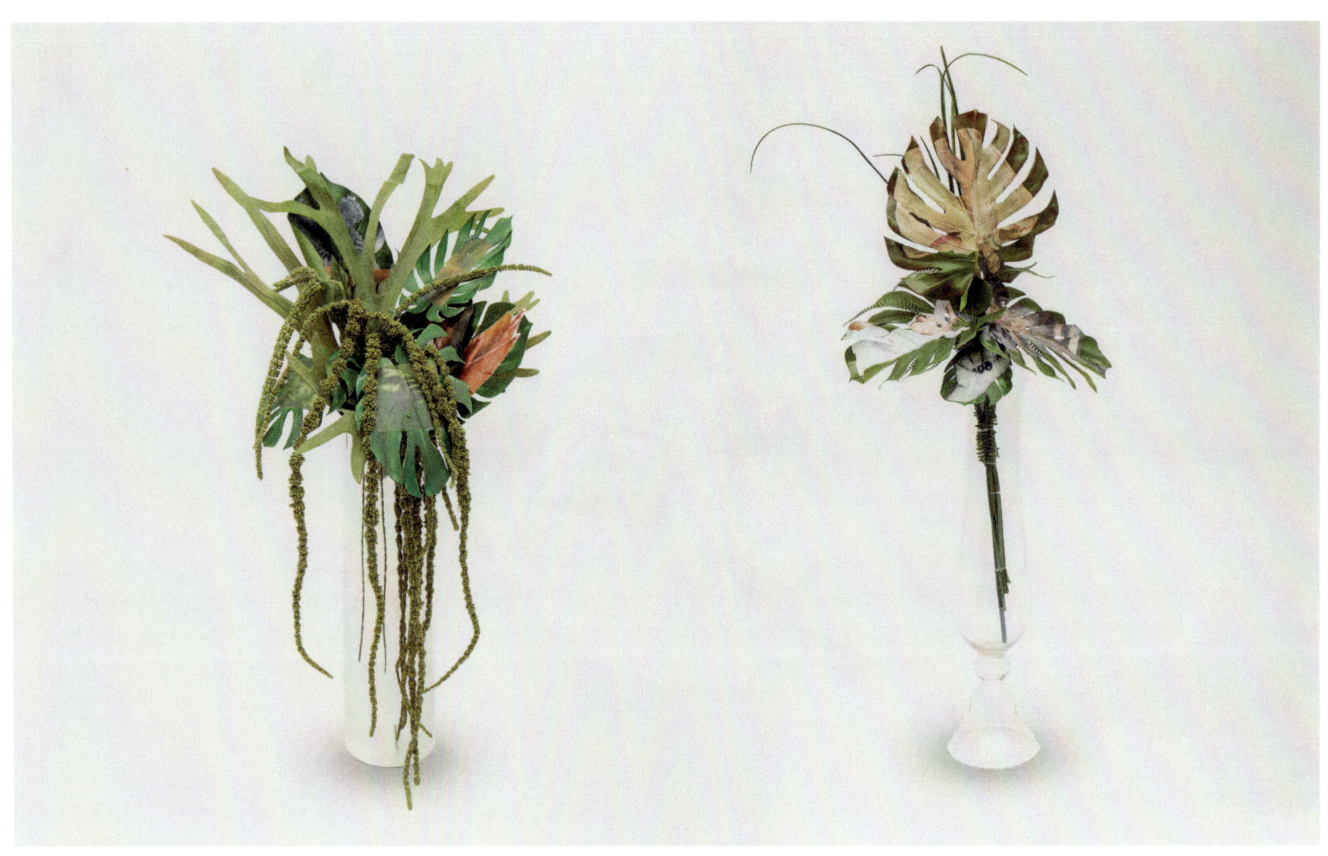

Left: *They go from a fence, or a closed place for slaves, to a dancing gathering of Africans in Latin America; from the beating of drums to the place where they danced to the sound of drums, even to the Hispanic-Arab-African dance they call tango andaluz. Kizomba, Semba, Sea Kelp and Hanging Amaranthus arrangement*, 2020, sublimation prints on cotton paper, copper wire, plastic, and vase

Right: *Exotica*, 2020, sublimation prints on cotton paper, copper wire, plastic, and vase

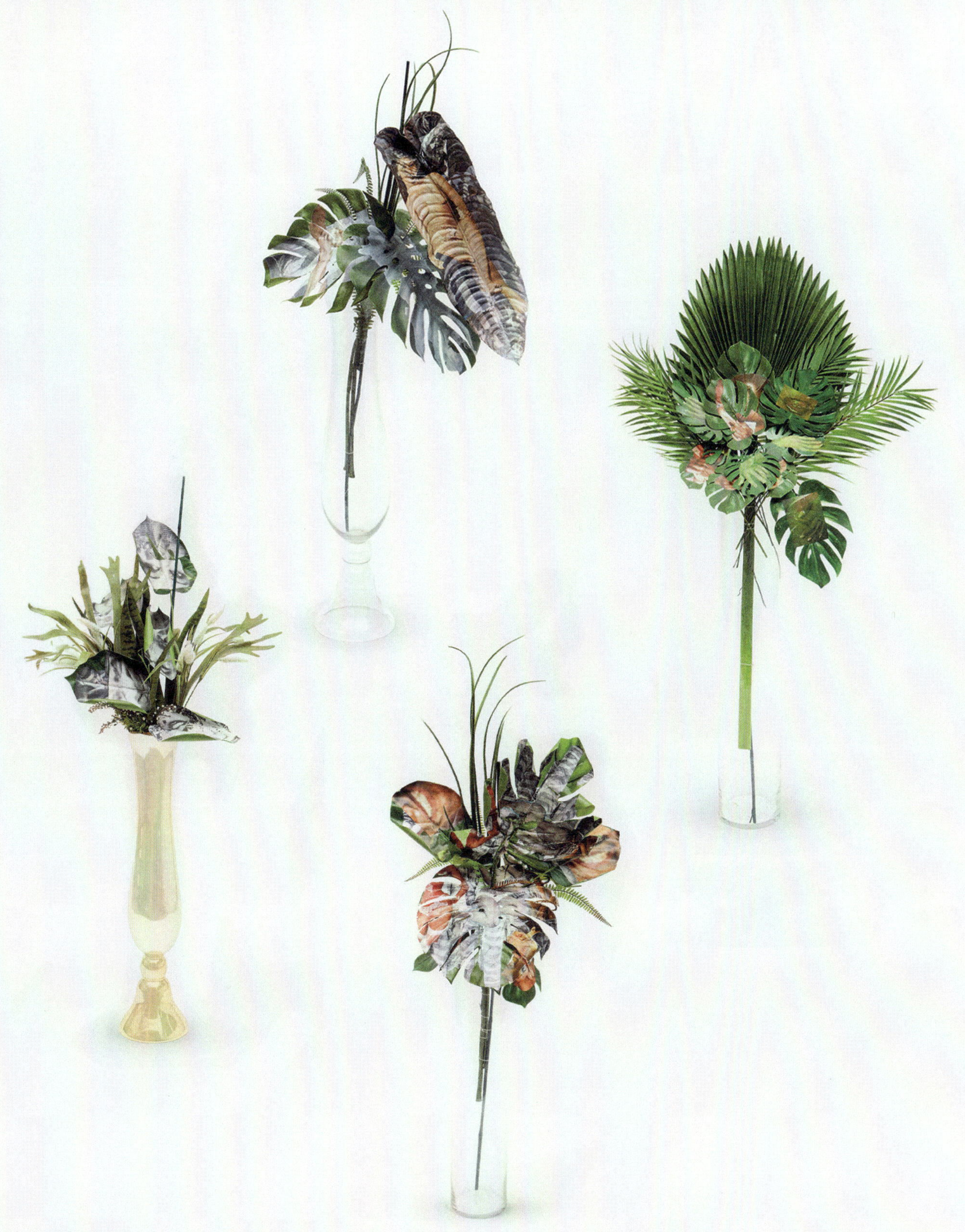

Clockwise from top:

Candombe Africano via Jitterbug to Virginia Georgia Mississippi, 2020, sublimation prints on cotton paper, copper wire, plastic, sumi ink, and vase

Calesita in monstera, fan palm, and fern arranged from Tango, Tarantella and Jitterbug, 2020, sublimation prints on cotton paper, copper wire, plastic, and vase

Exotica, 2020, sublimation prints on cotton paper, copper wire, plastic, and vase

Sea Kelp and Weeping Willow Bouquet, 2020, sublimation prints on cotton paper, copper wire, plastic, and vase

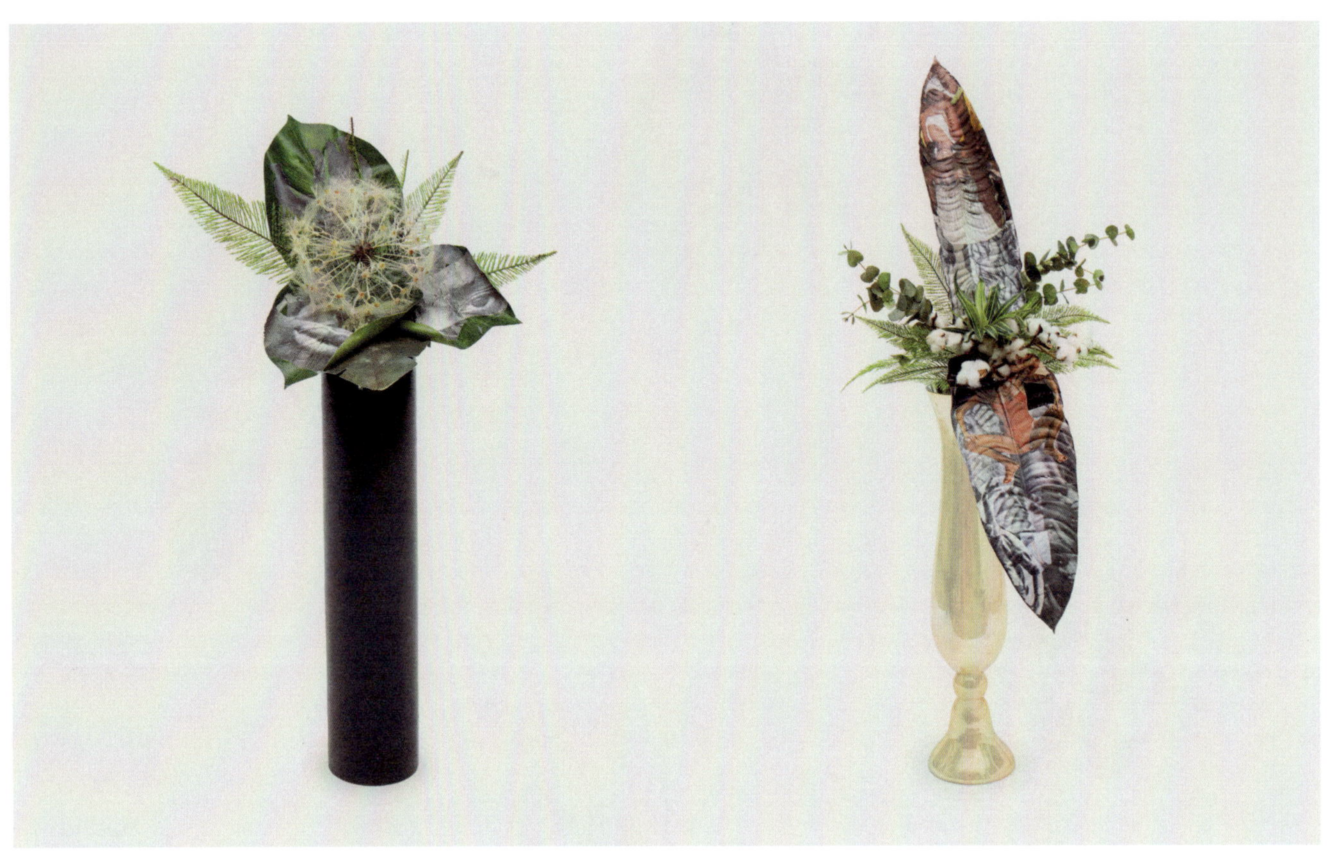

Left: *Convict leasing "depended upon the heritage of slavery and the allure of industrial capitalism," the combination of which produced a modern system in which capitalist development was forged through structures of antiblack racism and terror. Dandelion and Devil's Ivy arrangement- line, color, mass: death life and surveillance.*, 2020, sublimation prints on cotton paper, copper wire, plastic, sumi ink, and vase

Right: *Otto Preminger's Carmen Jones - October 28th 1954, Brown v. Board of Education-May 17th 1954*, 2020, sublimation prints on cotton paper, copper wire, plastic, and vase

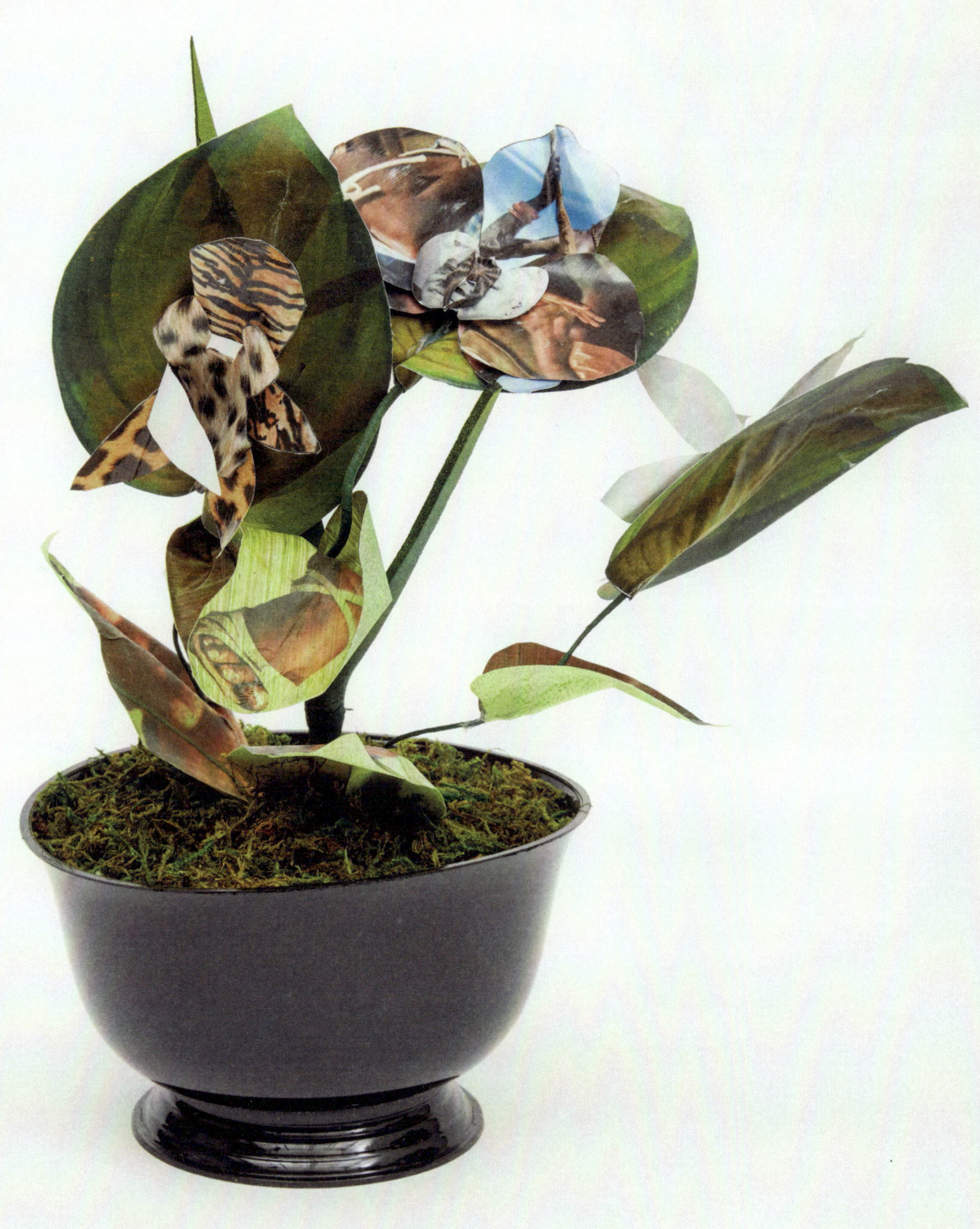

Exotica, 2020, collage on artificial plant, fabric grow bag with moss, and vase

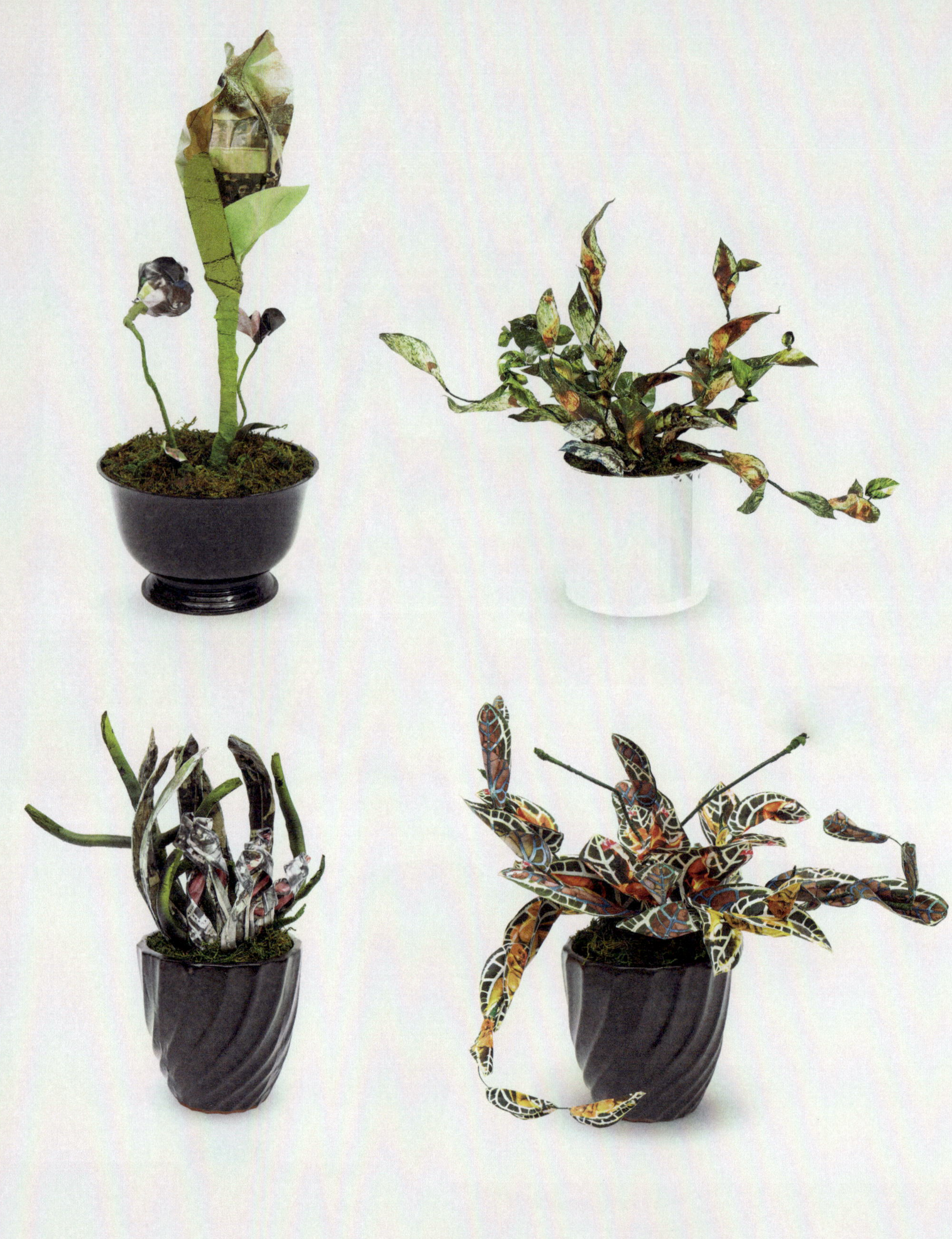

All: *Exotica*, 2020, collage on artificial plant, fabric grow bag with moss, and vase

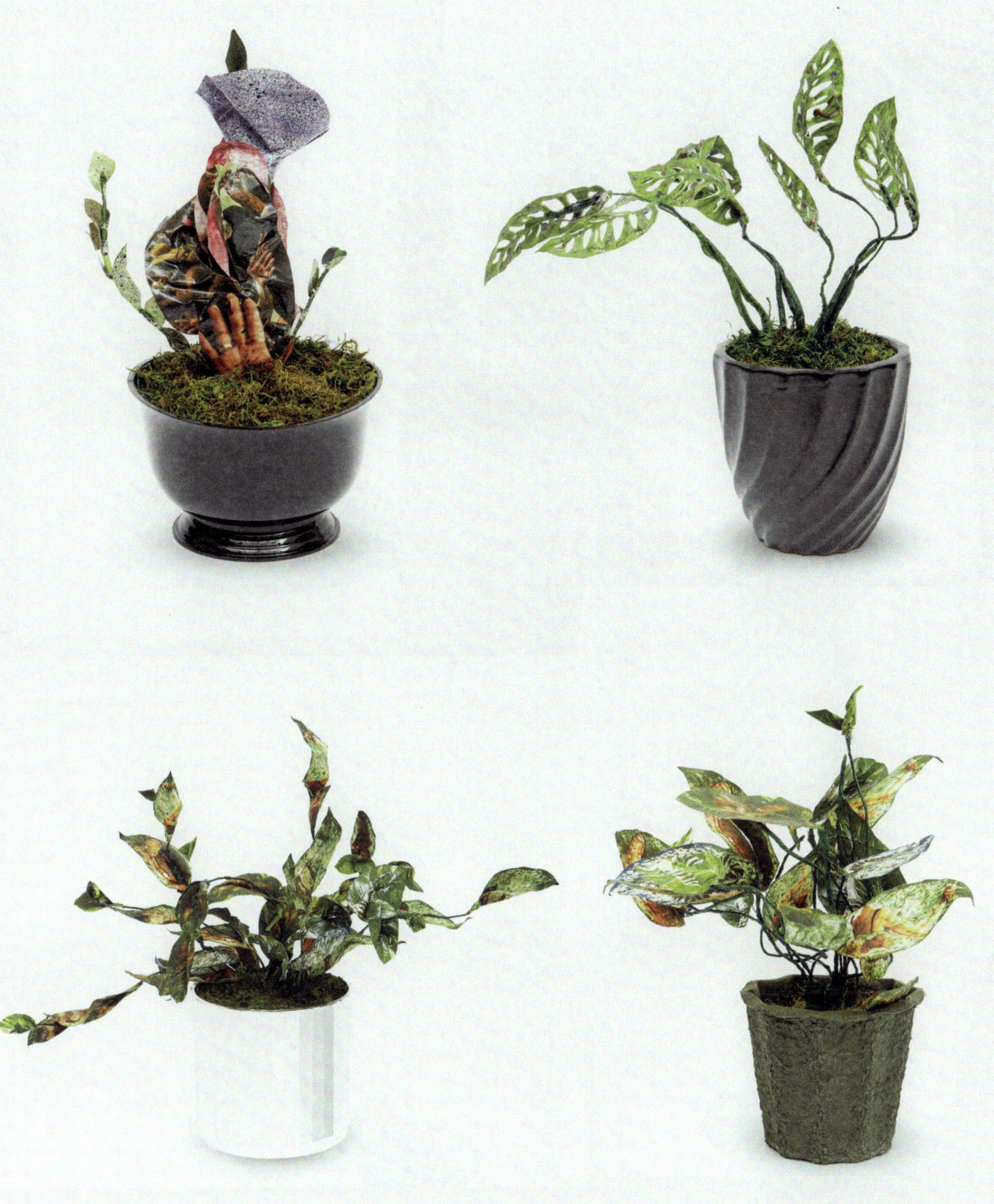

Top left: *Exotica*, 2020, collage on artificial plant, fabric grow bag with moss, and vase

Top right: *Malandro Mississippi CHAIN GANG Monstera adansonii*, 2020, sublimation prints on cotton paper, copper wire, plastic, moss, and vase

Bottom left and right: *Exotica*, 2020, collage on artificial plant, fabric grow bag with moss, and vase

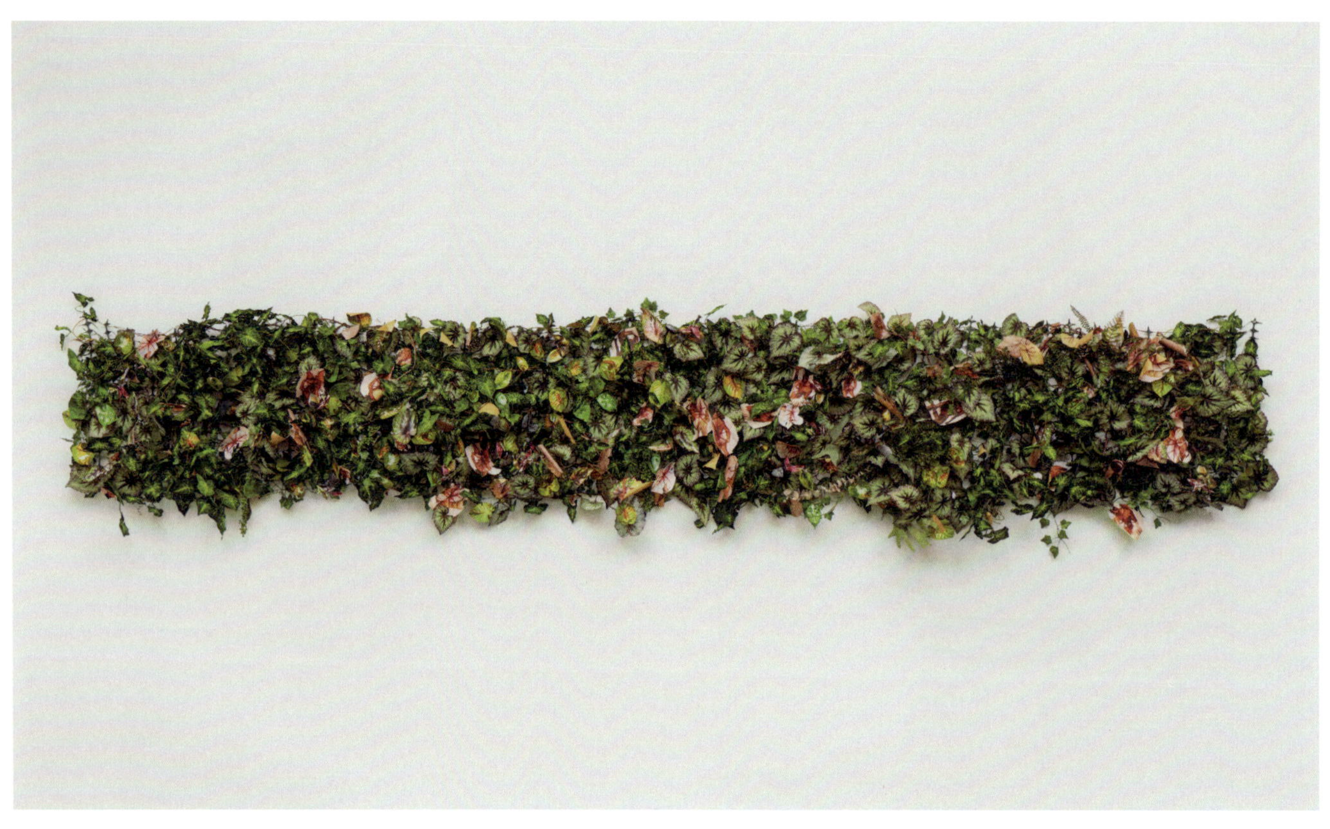

Toxic Exotica, 2020, sublimation prints on cotton paper, copper wire, and plastic

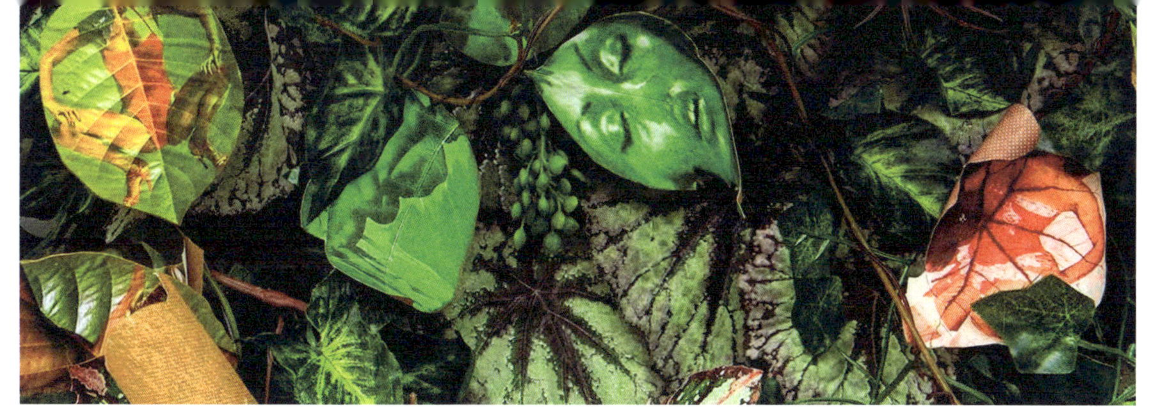

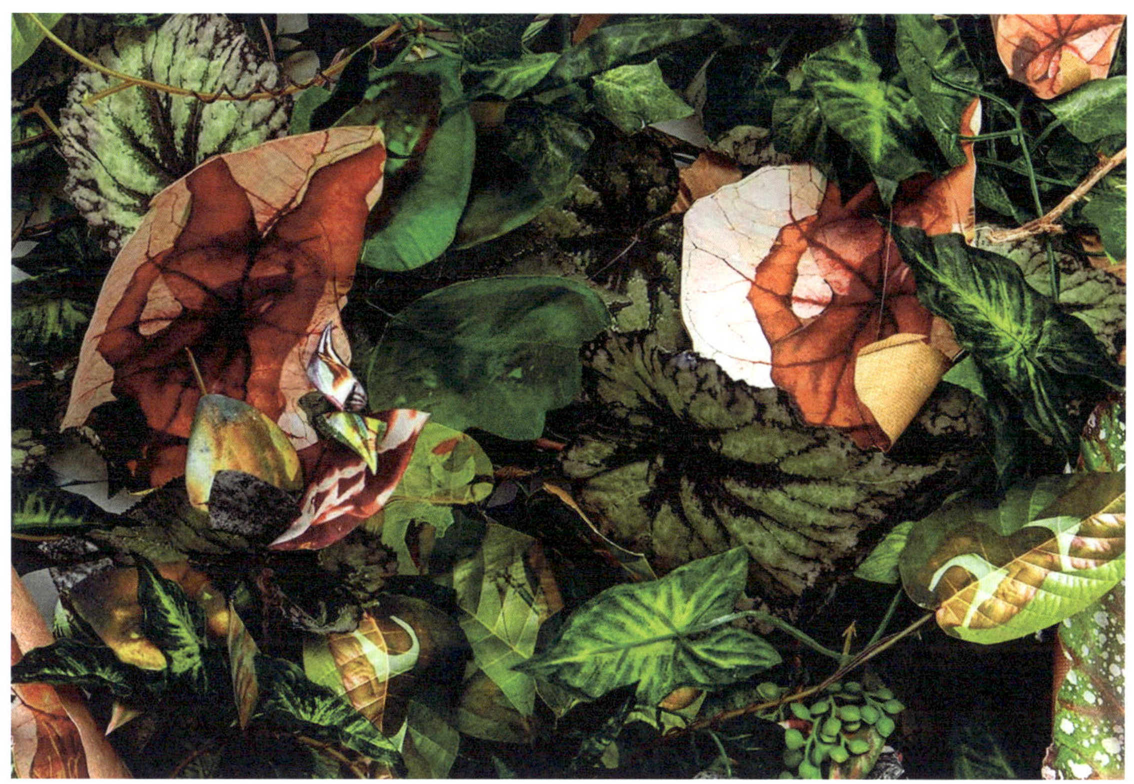

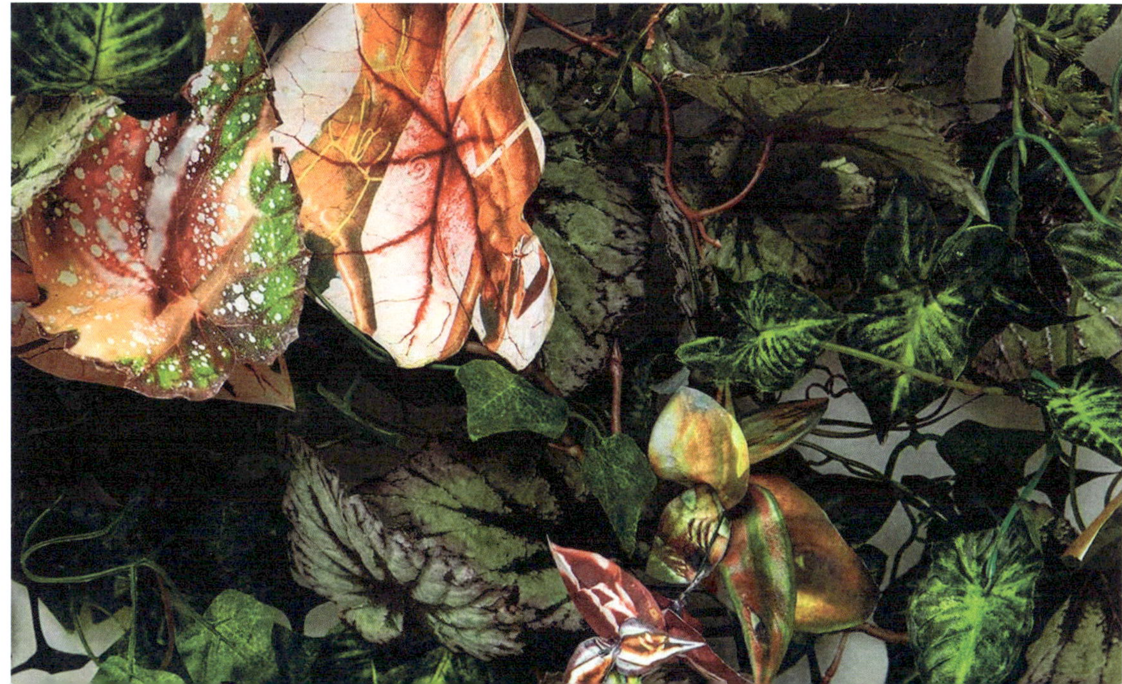

Toxic Exotica, 2020 (details)

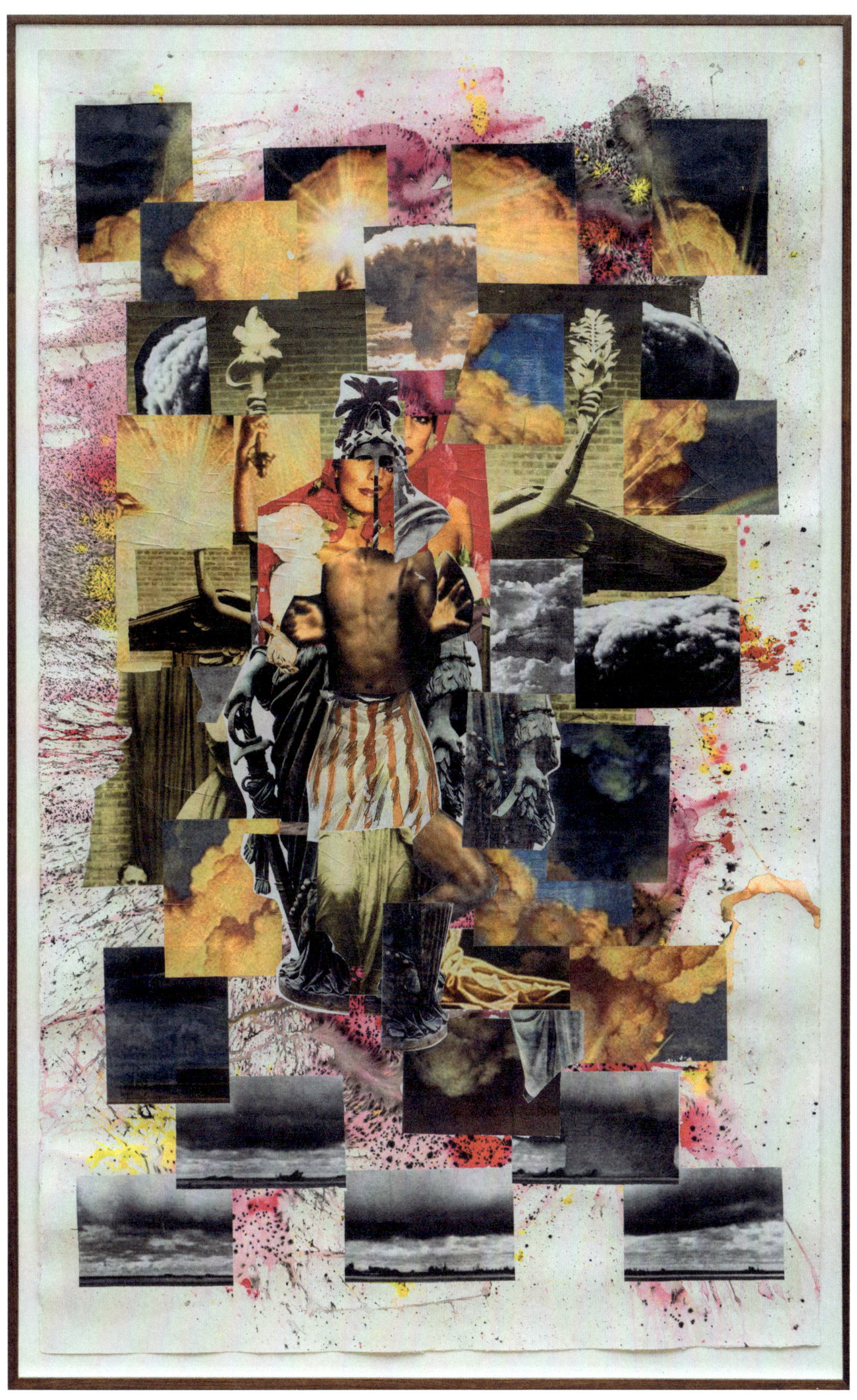

Atomic Karen, 2021, xerox collage and ink on watercolor paper

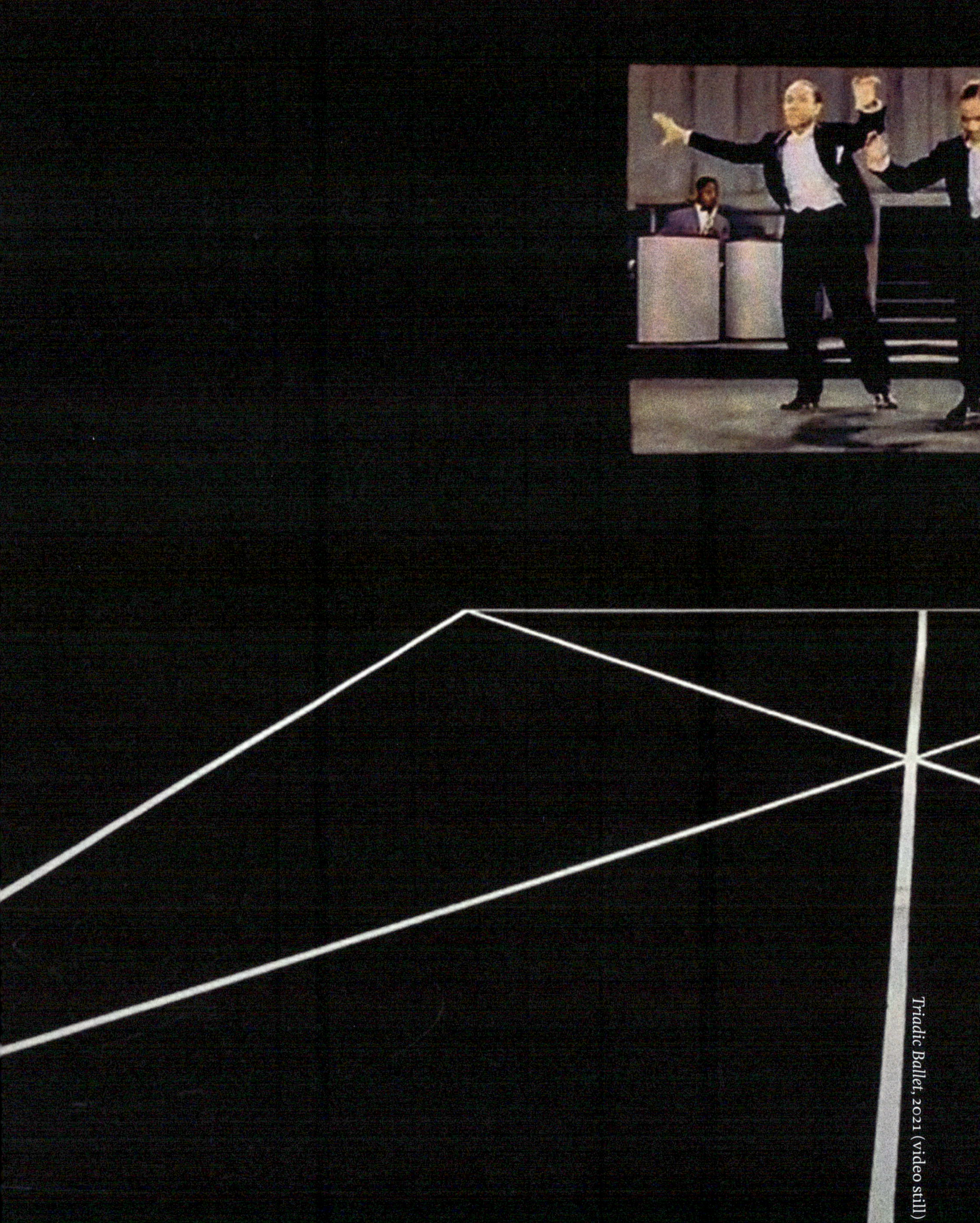

Triadic Ballet, 2021 (video still)

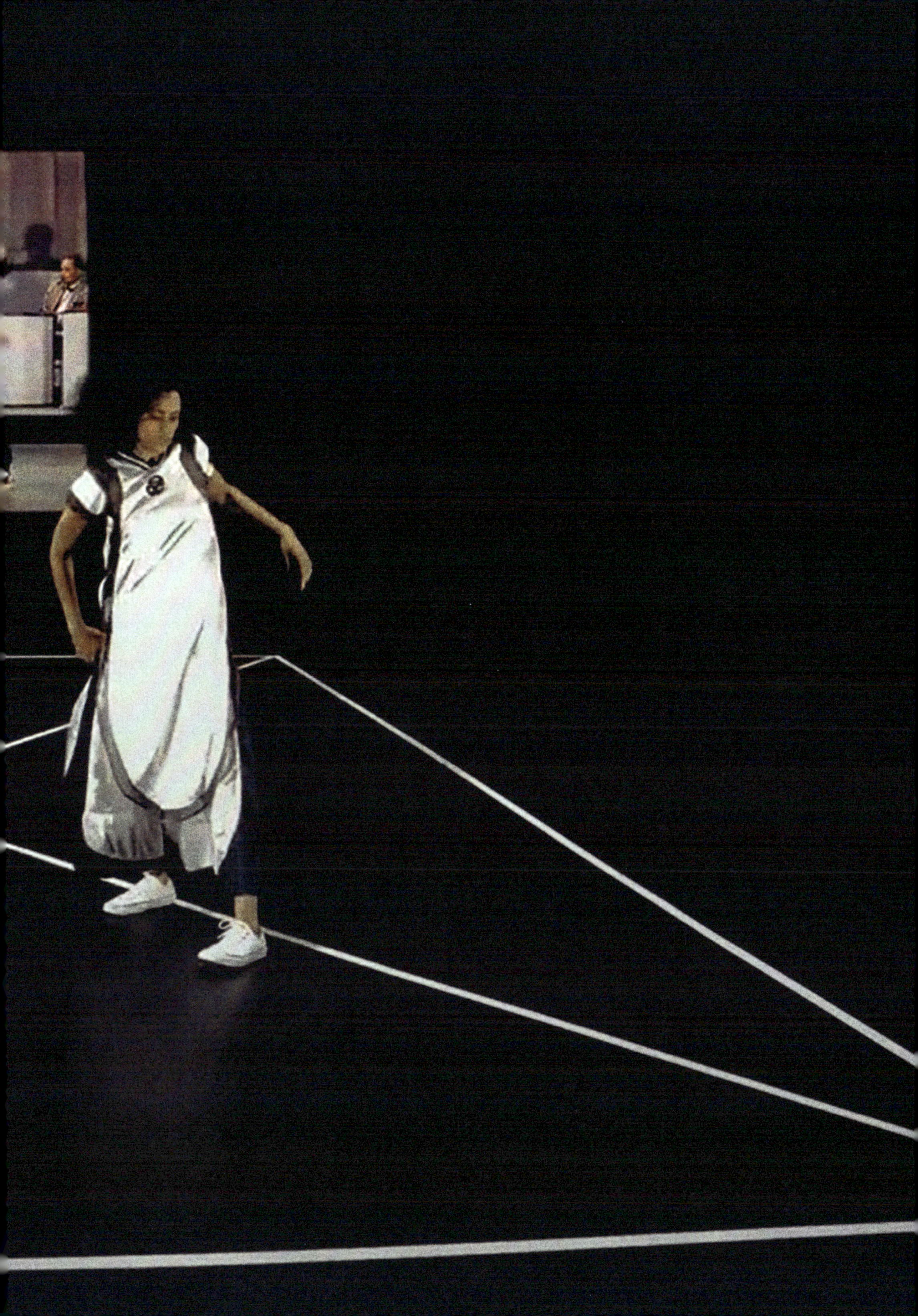

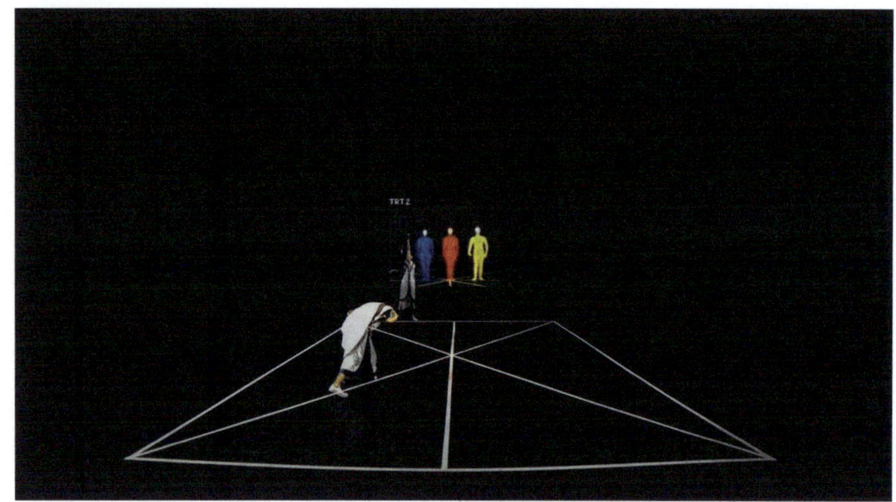

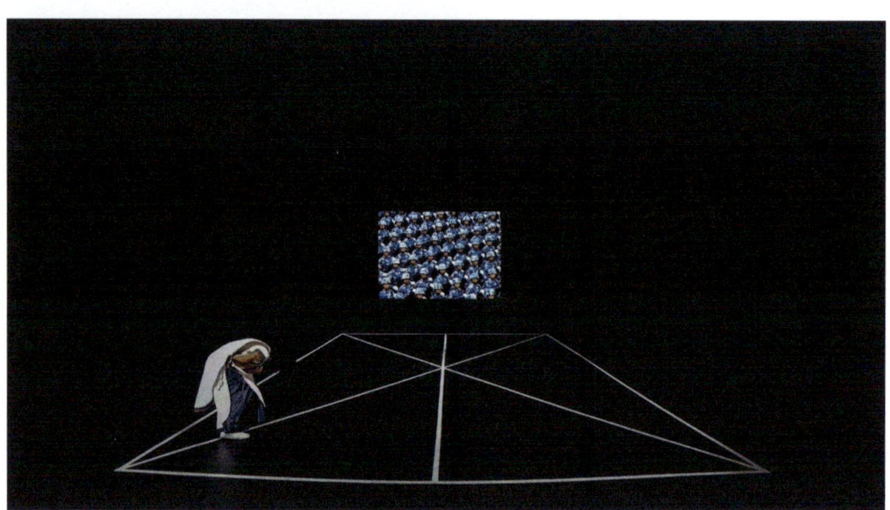

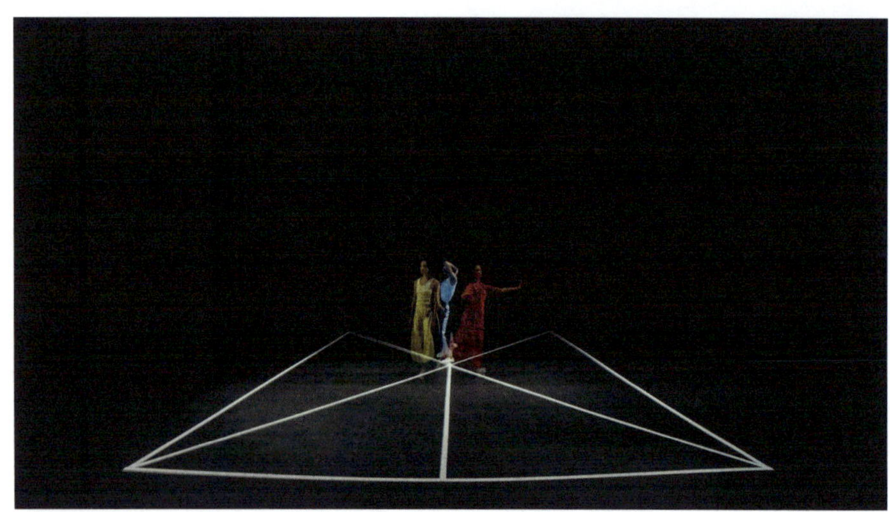

Triadic Ballet, 2021, variable-channel video (color, sound) (video stills)

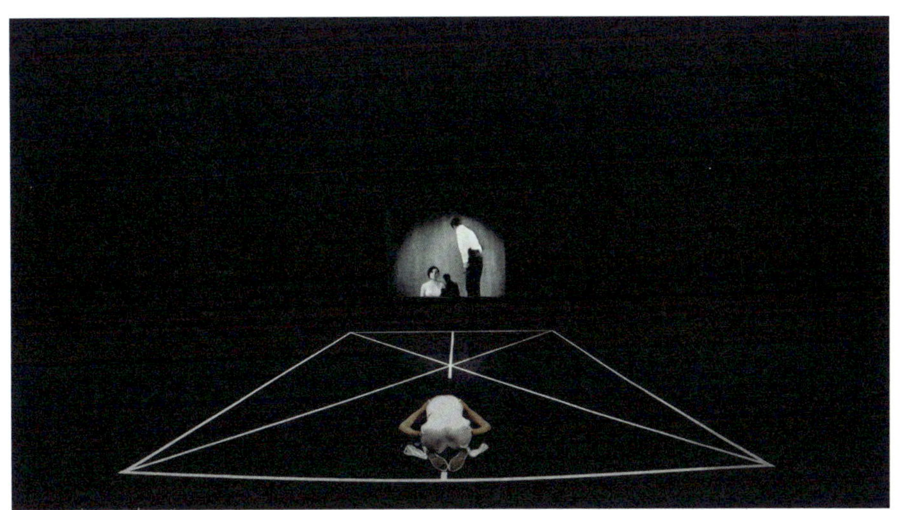

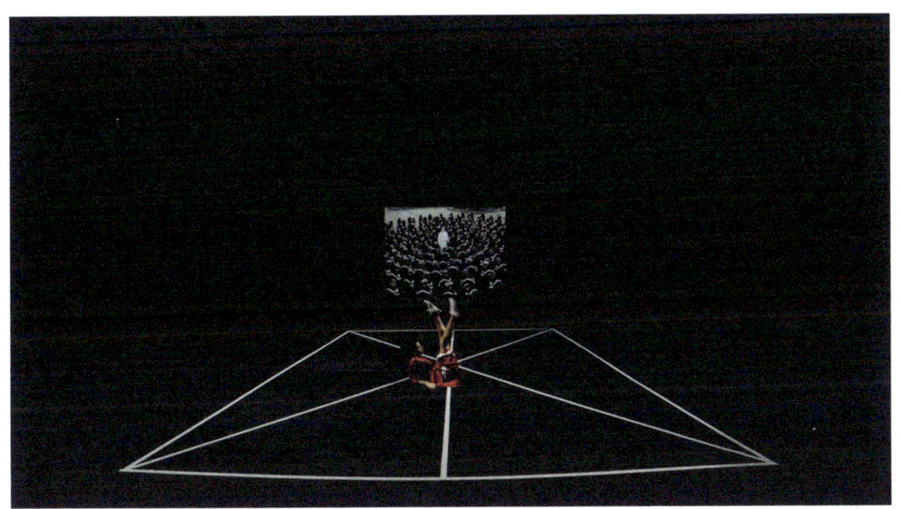

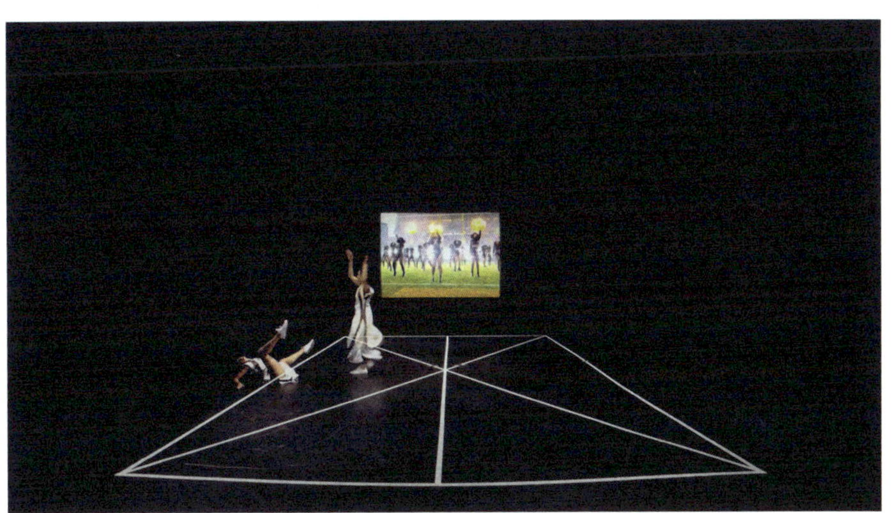

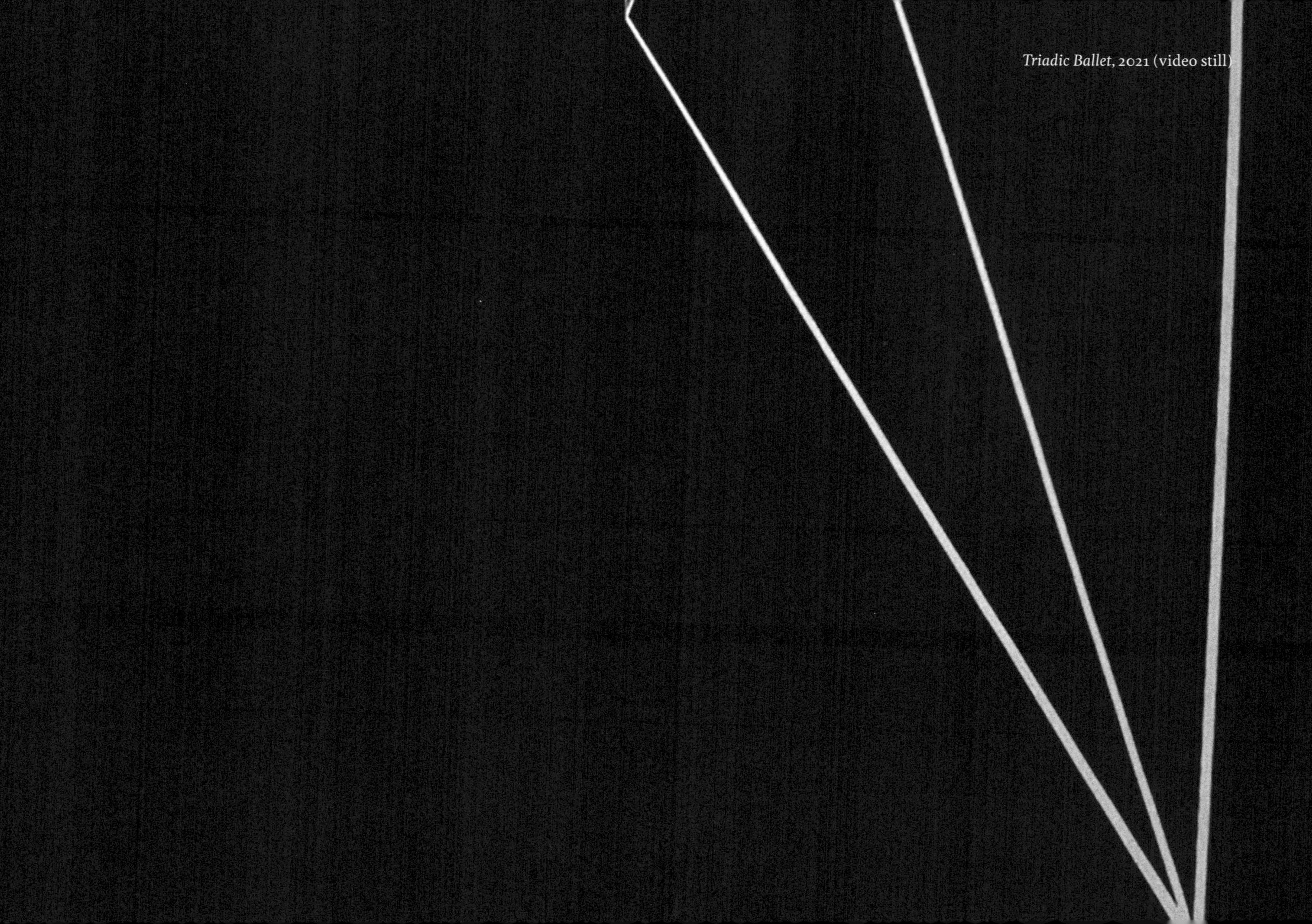

Triadic Ballet, 2021 (video still)

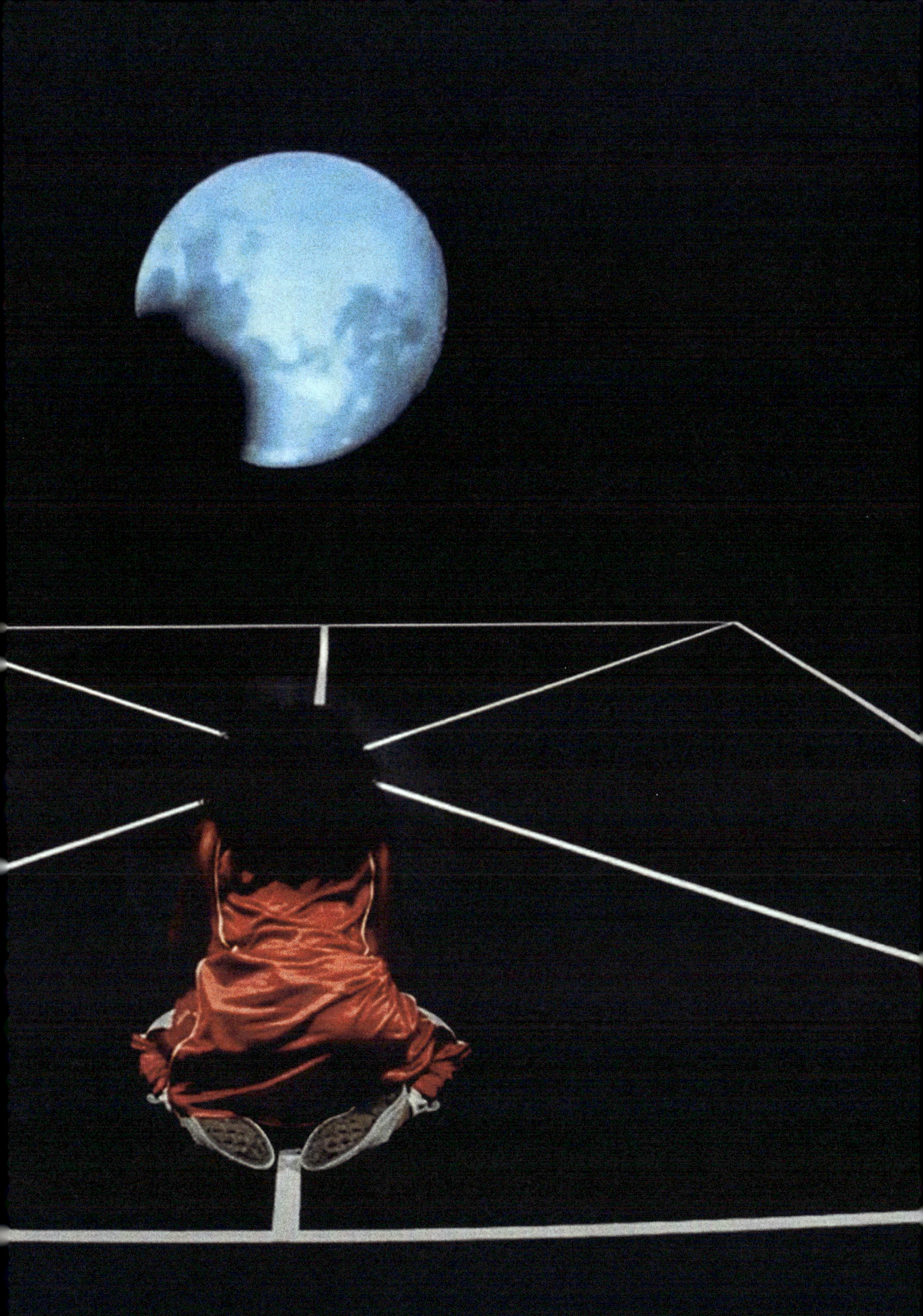

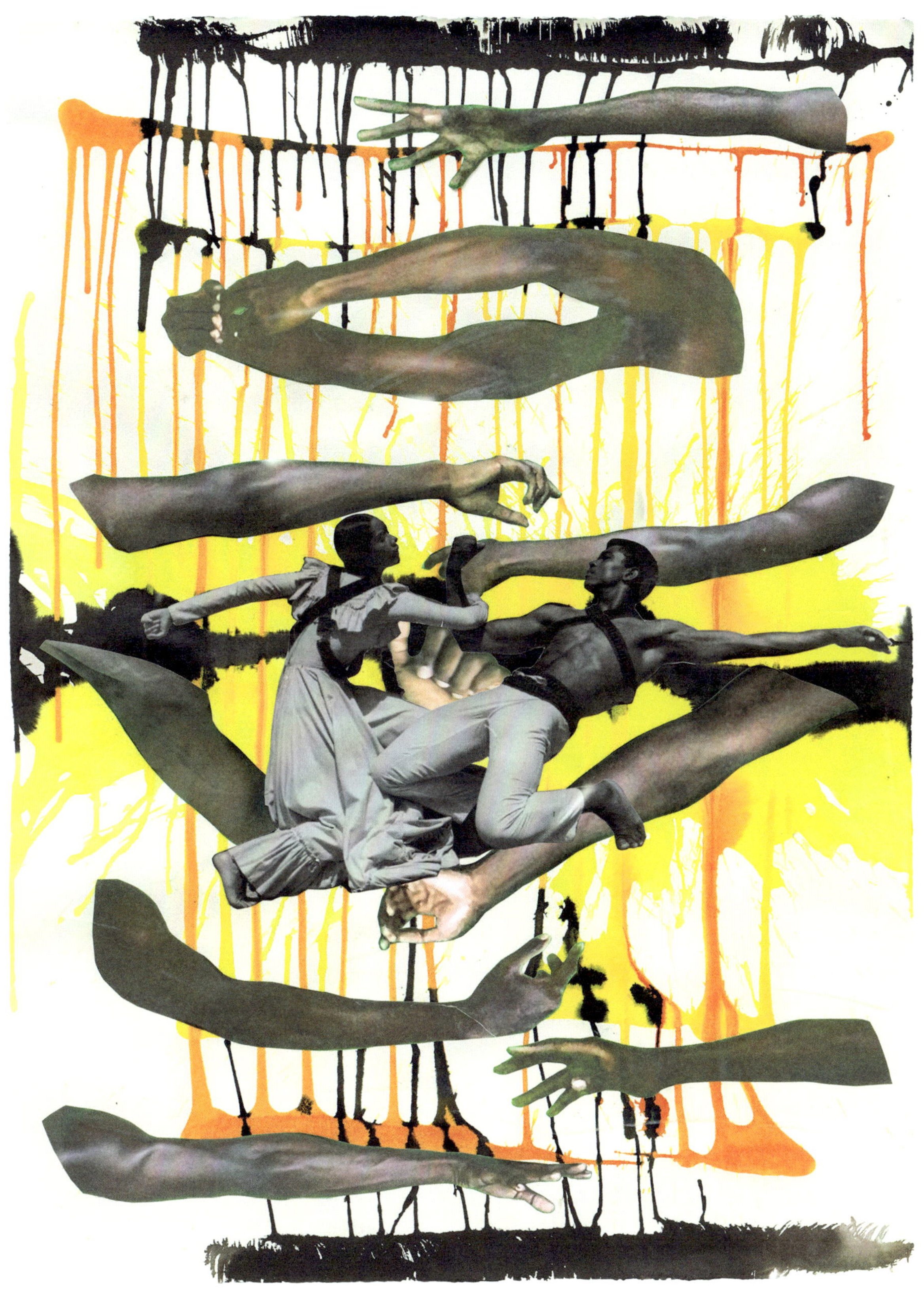

Black Box, 4 points: Horton, Ailey, McKayle contractions and expansions of drama from vernacular— arms outstretched and entangle, 2021, xerox collage and ink on paper

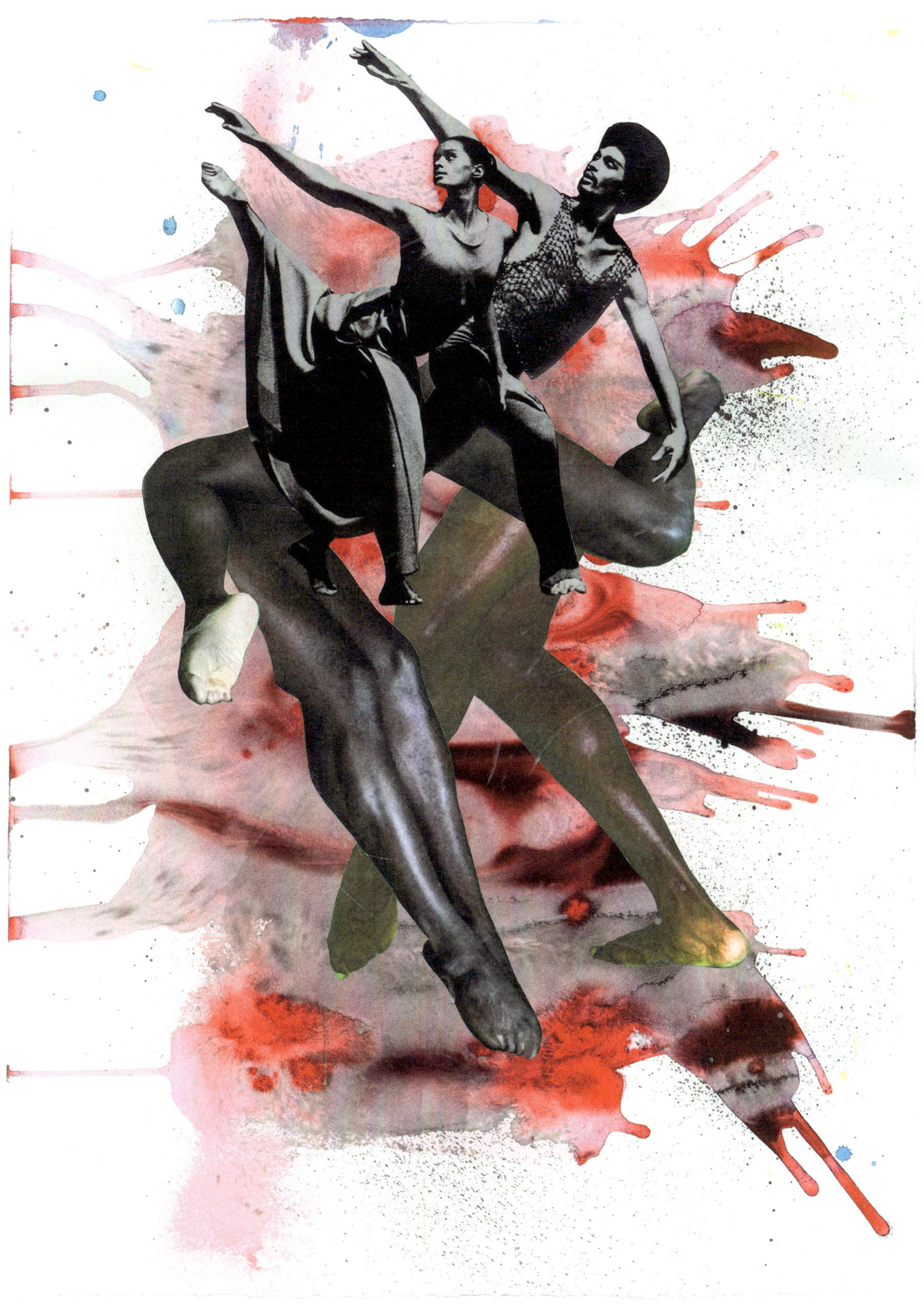

Black Box, 4 points: Wading in water, Archipelago, Myth, Revelations—B. Gottschild principle—muffled lines and ruptures—hyper-interpretation of Africanist presence(s), 2021, xerox collage and ink on paper

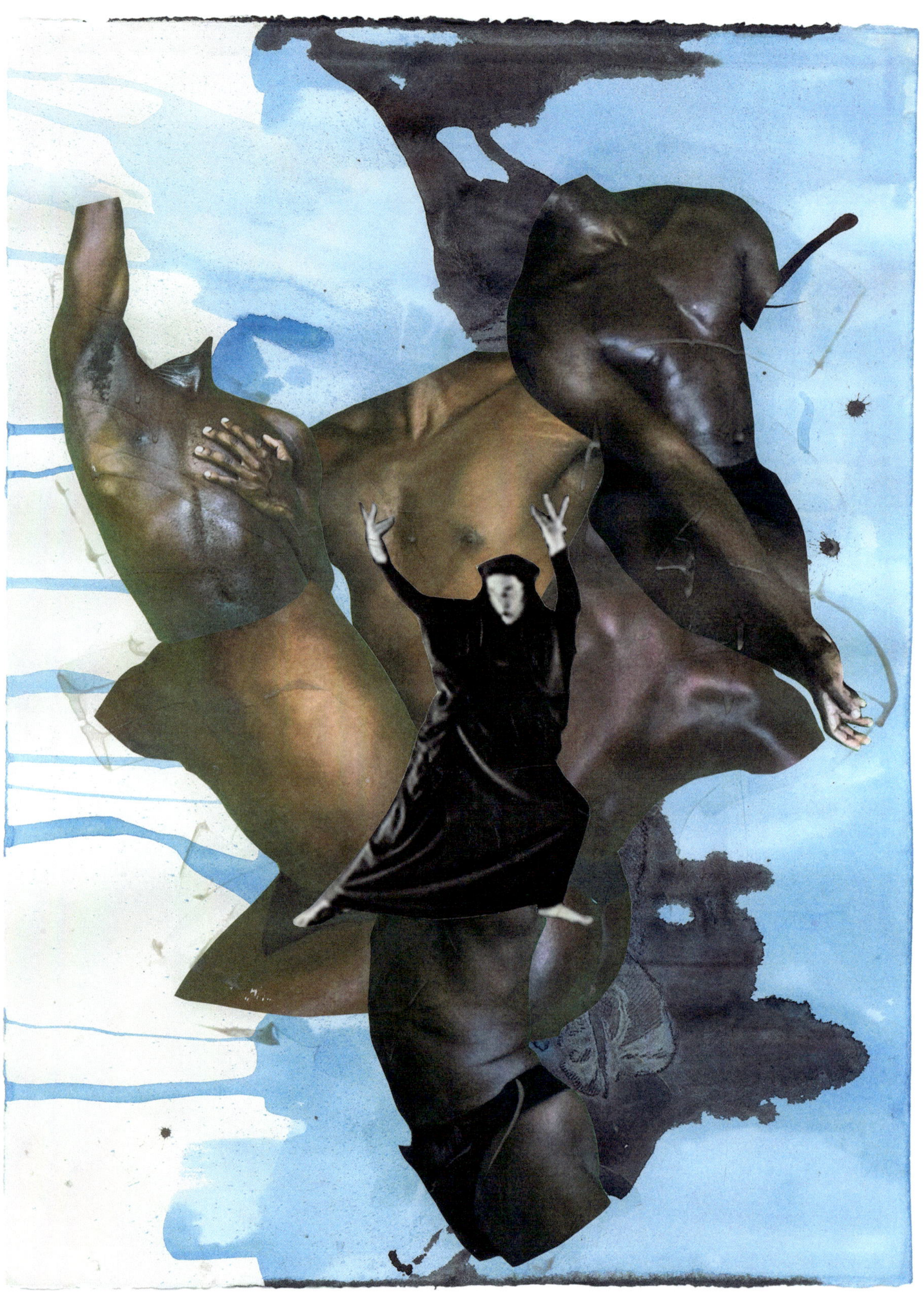

Black Box, 4 points: Ausdruckstanz and Körperkultur holds Orientalism, Primitivism, Islamophobia, and Anti-Indigenous Ideologies, 2021, xerox collage and ink on paper

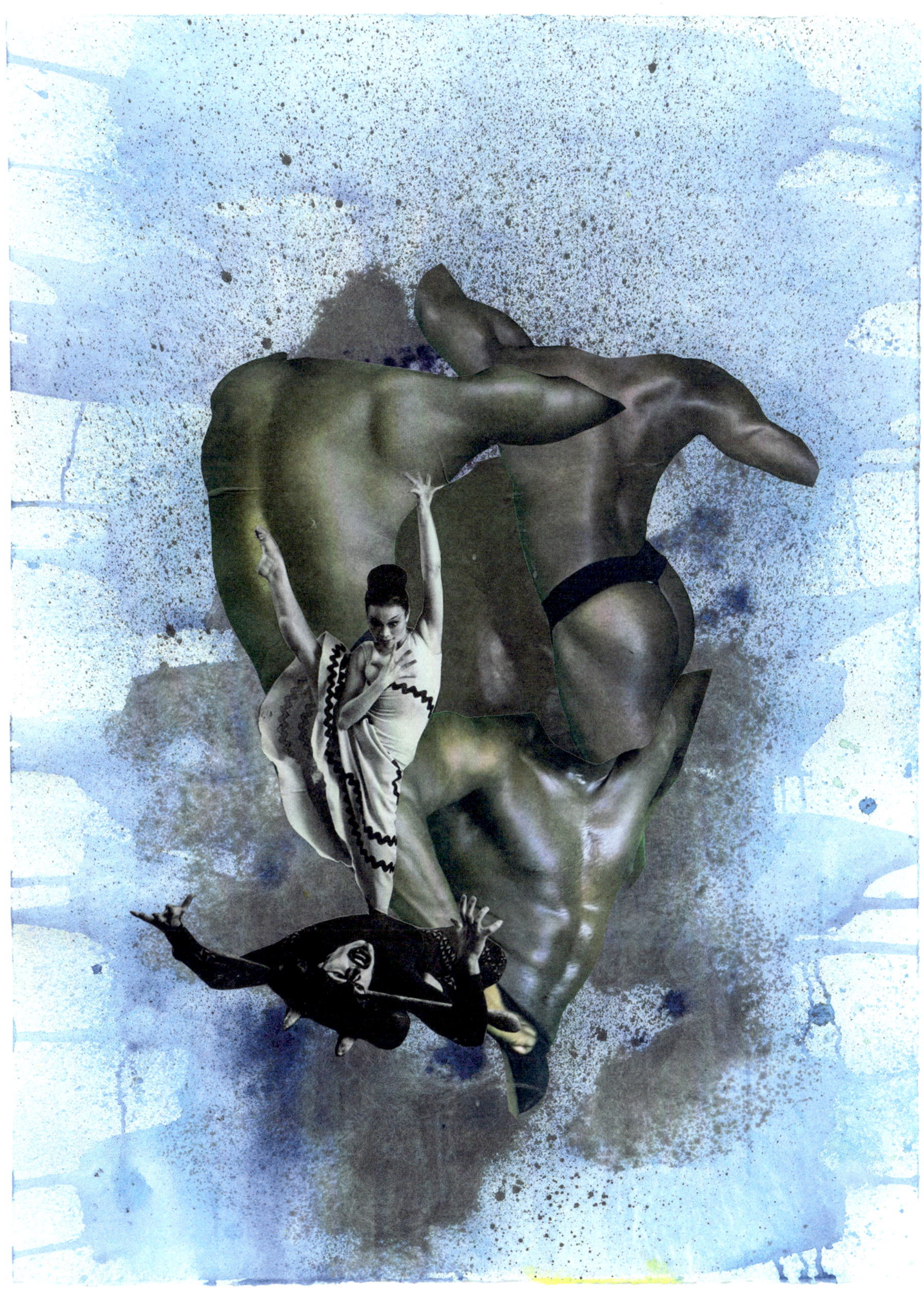

Black Box, 4 points: Greco Biblical Impulse—Clytemnestra, Eurydice, Princes, Queens, and Holofernes, 2021, xerox collage and ink on paper

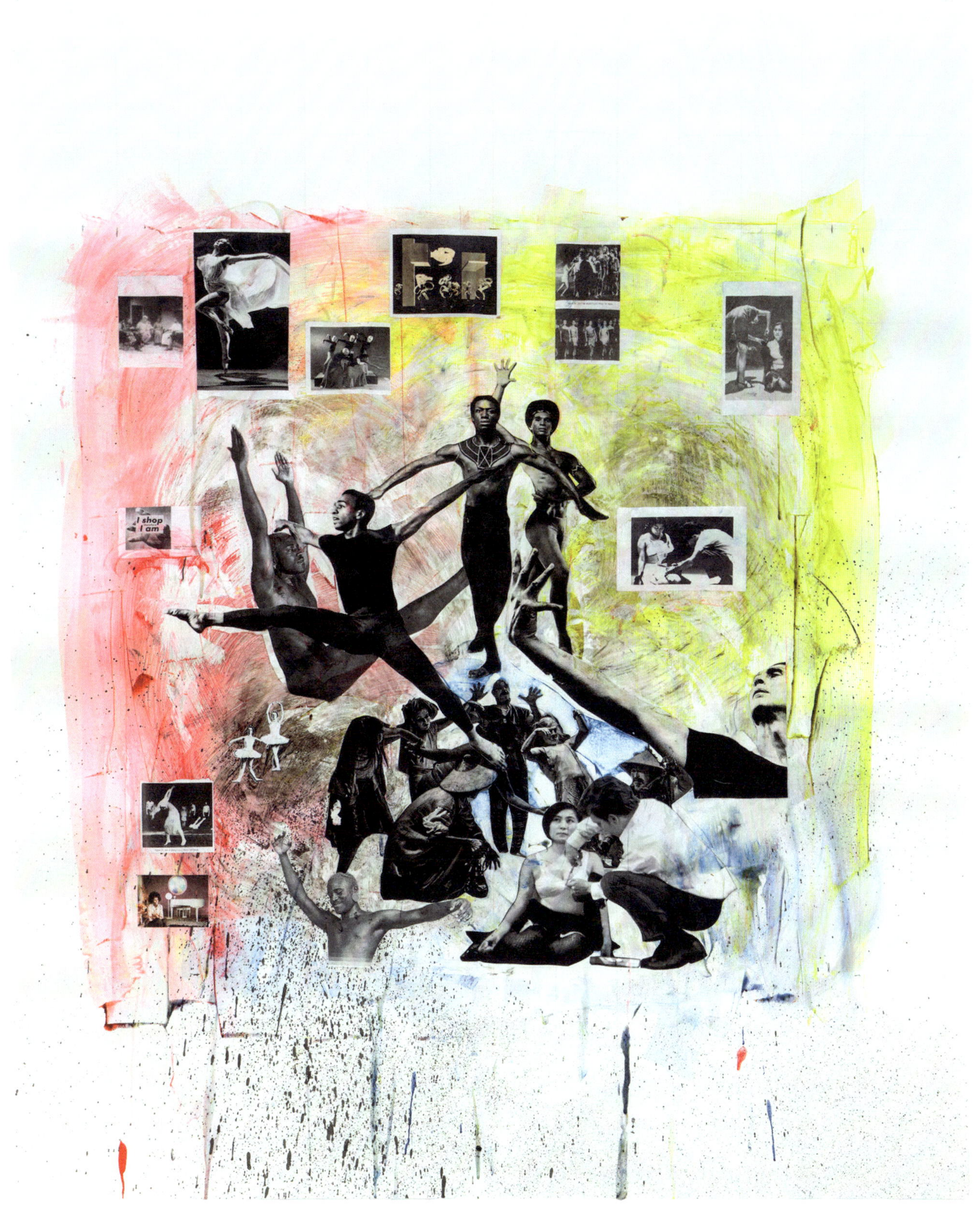

Notes for Stage, Cult, and Popular Entertainment according to place, person, genre, speech, music, and dance, 2021, xerox collage and ink on paper

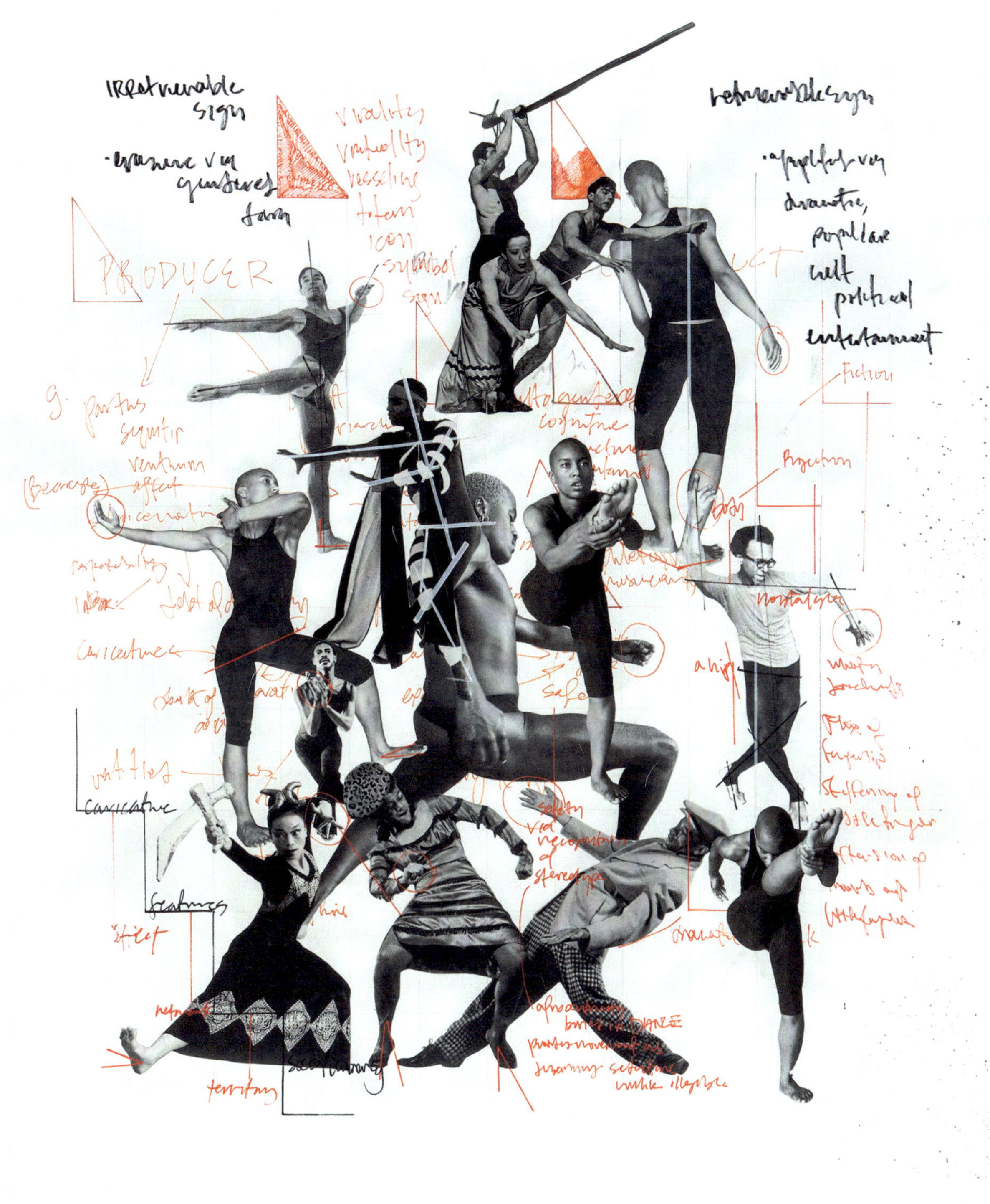

Bolshoi to Harlem: Diaghilev to Dunham, certainly fictions—caste, stereotype, gender, and race—are a primary means of production, 2021, xerox collage and ink on paper

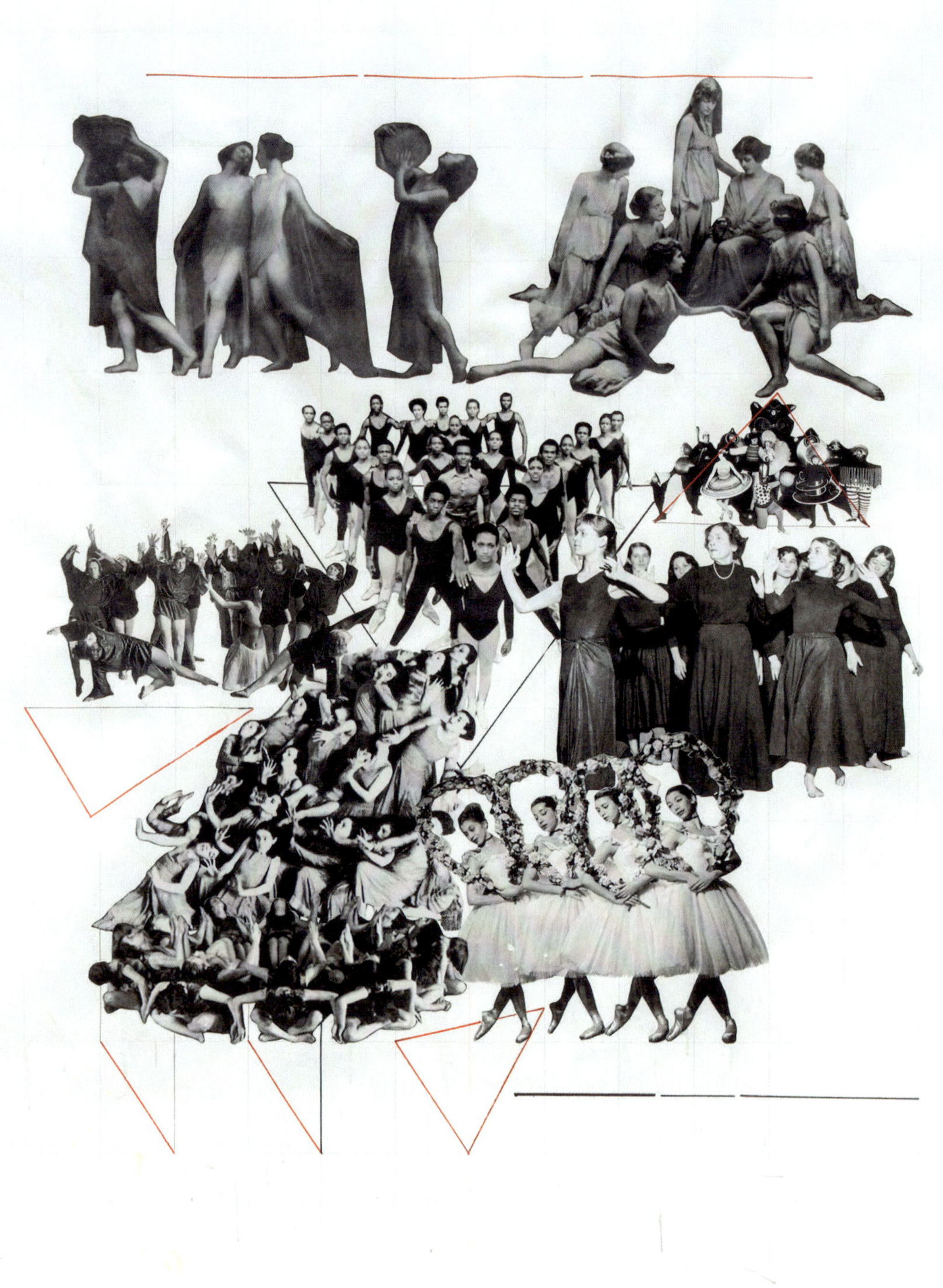

Triadic Ensemble: stacked erasures, Russes de Monte Carlo, Harlem Dance, Wigman and Duncan, 2021, xerox collage and ink on paper

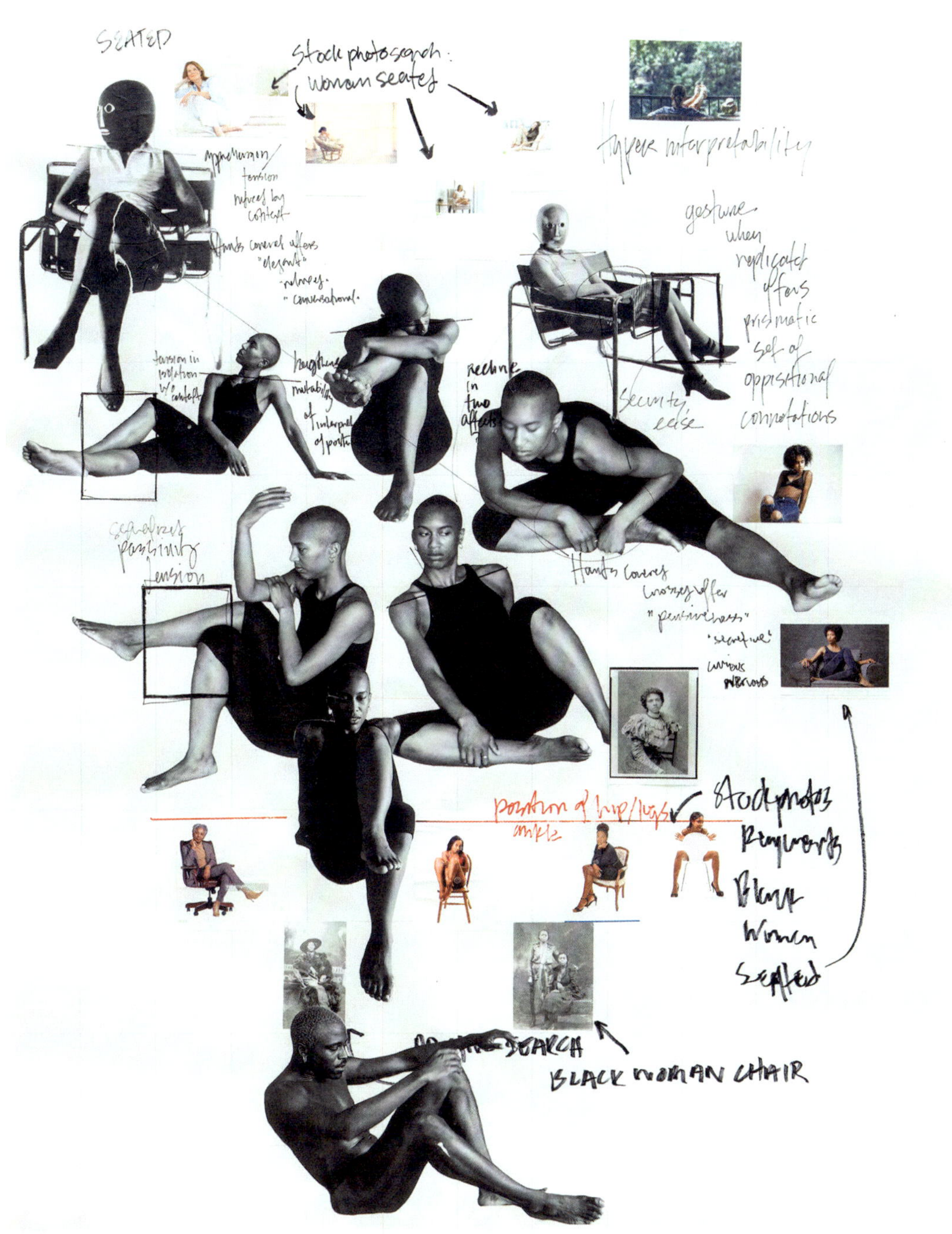

Hyper-interpretation—to be seated—figures sexualized and anonymized at rest, en largesse to stereotyping distribution, 2021, xerox collage and ink on paper

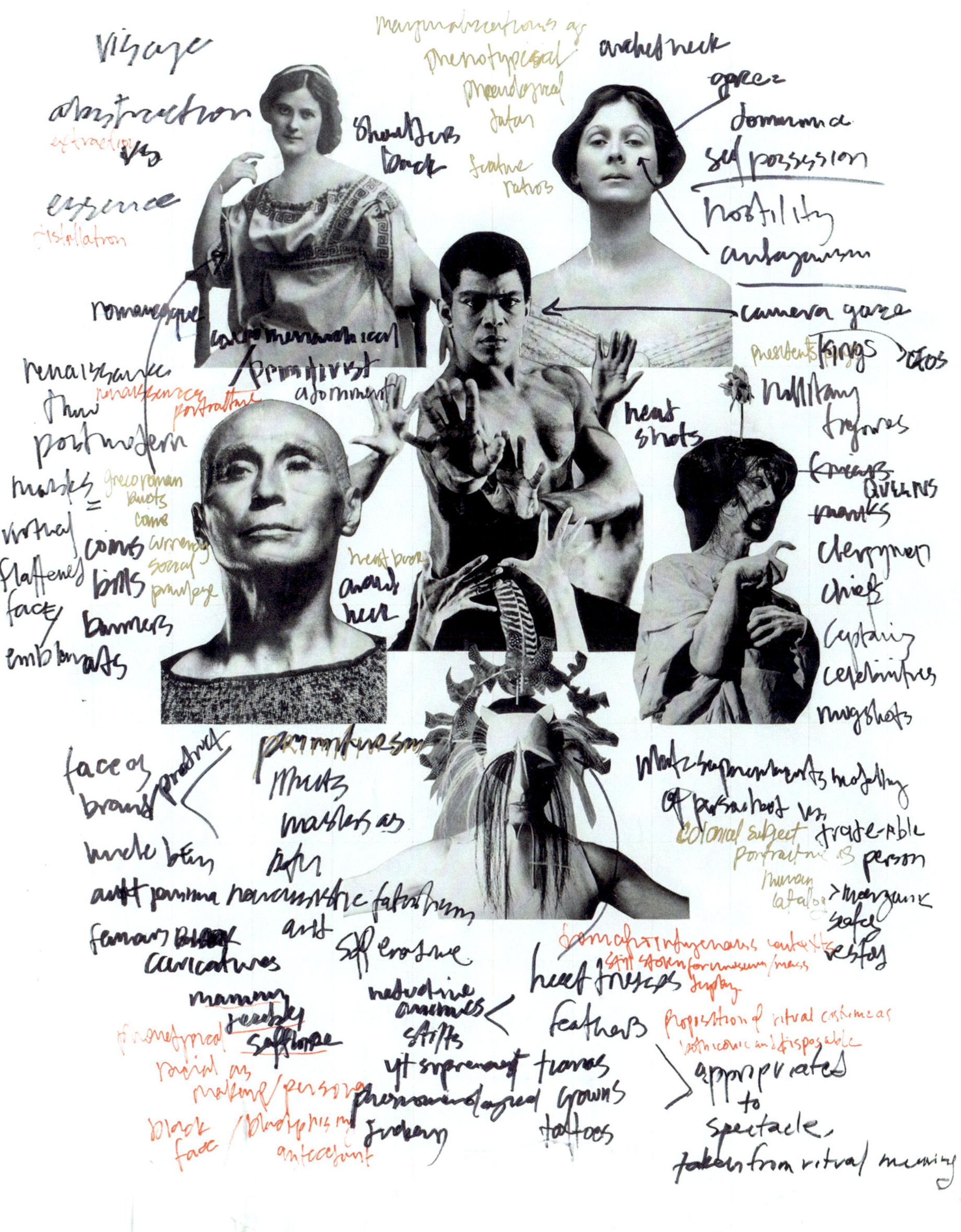

Visage, uses of portrait and mask from rulers to icons through Primitivism and phenotypical hierarchy, 2021, xerox collage and ink on paper

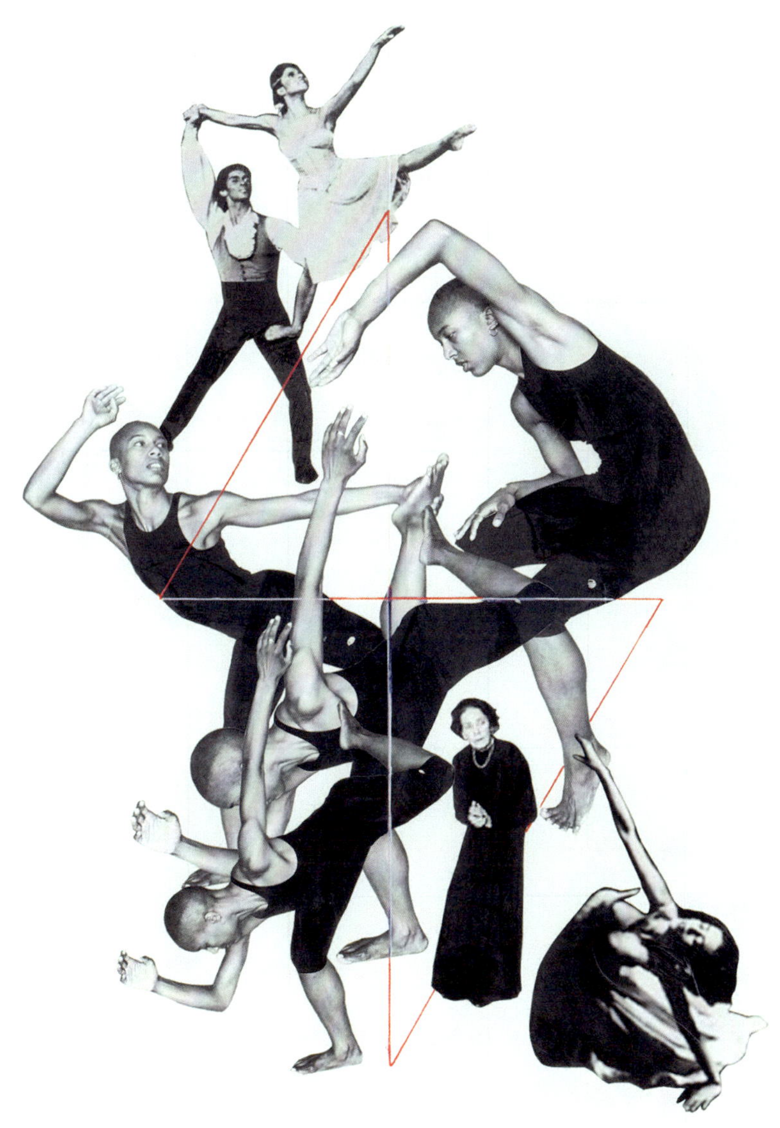

A Lift and a Kick conflated, 2021, xerox collage and ink on paper

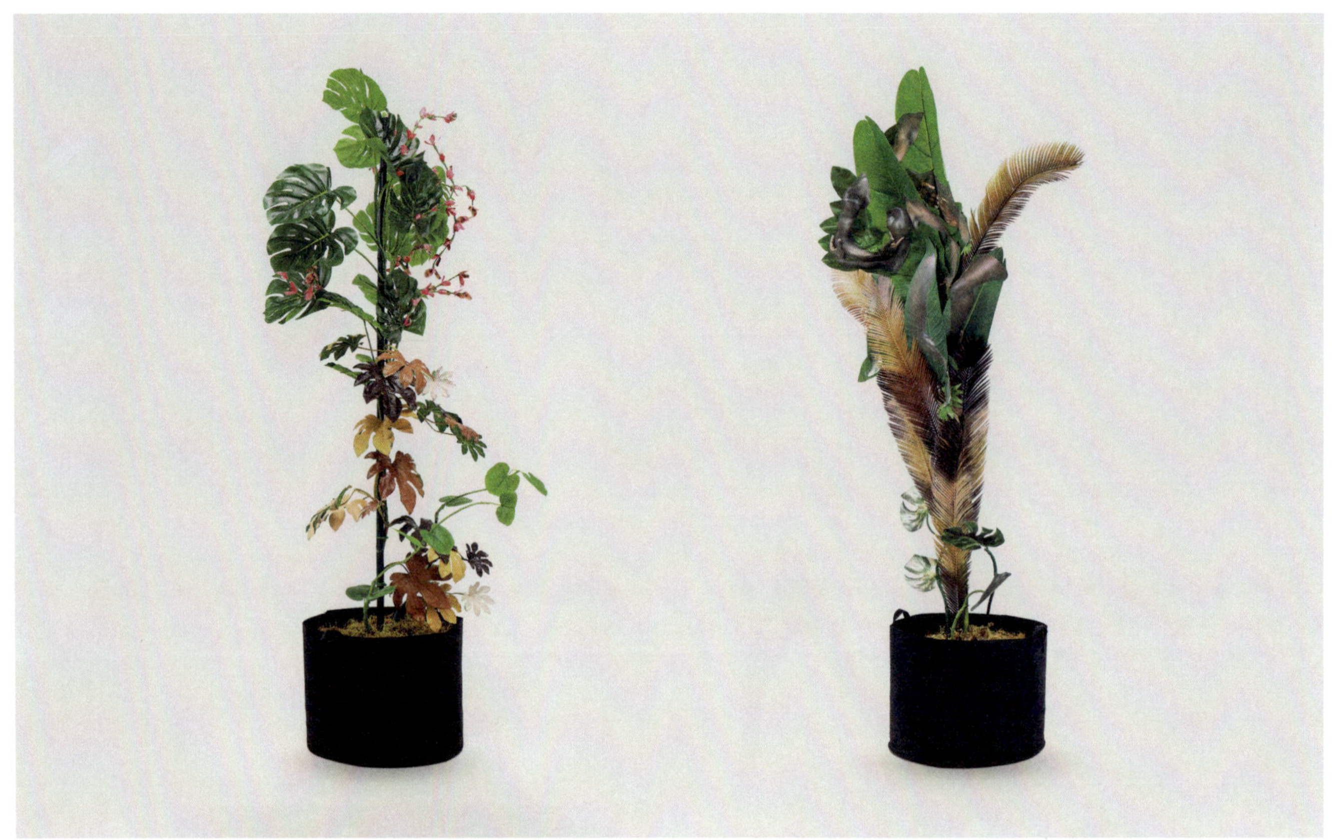

Left: *On the contrary, a legend gradually formed, which was neither investigated nor questioned. The legend covered the past with a blanket of oblivion: there had been no modern dance, it seems, under the Nazis, just a bit of ballet at the most. Modern German Dance, the so-called Ausdruckstanz, Expressive Dance, it was claimed, belonged to the great tradition of the artistic avantgarde in the early 20th century and hence was by definition progressive. Each instance of its performance according to how well it manifests the intention and the detail of the choreography, might then be thought to have a form outside of performance and that form pre-exists any written documents. Writing about and on behalf of black artists, Locke refused the responsibilities and limits of politics in artwork in favor of "expression." He argued that the purpose of black artwork was not to correct white supremacist misrepresentations of black life or history or to "demonstrate" that black people were, in fact, worthy of social and political inclusion. (That he took for granted, just as he should have.) Rather, Locke thought that (black) artwork should be "expressive of" "Negro life," in all its variety and vitality. Expressiveness was for Locke the mark of the most successful modern art*, 2021, collage on artificial plant, fabric grow bag with moss, acrylic paint, and plastic

Right: *Genes, Not Genius: Another aspect of the colonial educational and cultural patterns which needs investigation was expressed not only by hostility to African culture but by paternalism and by praise of negative and static social features. There were many colonialists who wished to preserve in perpetuity everything that was African, if it appeared quaint or intriguing to them*, 2021, collage on artificial plant, fabric grow bag with moss, acrylic paint, and plastic

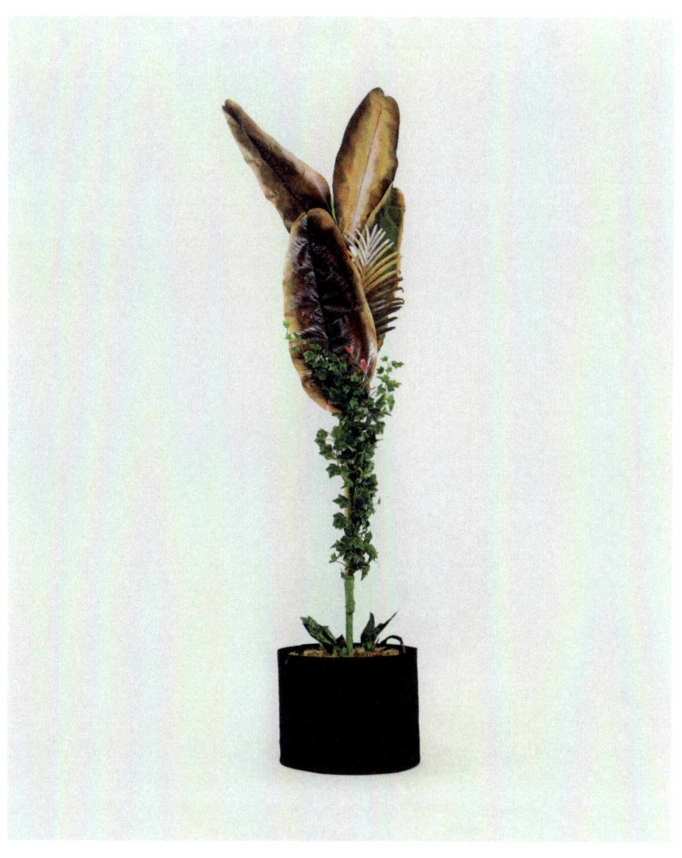

Where copyright law grants protection to "original works of authorship fixed in a tangible medium of expression," white mainstream culture has historically dismissed African American artistic forms like the blues and jazz as the product of "natural" expression rather than original authorship, that is, as "genes, not genius"—B. Gottschild / the term "vernacular" dancers to refer to those performers who appeared primarily in social clubs, nightclubs, and vaudeville stages, rather than on the high-art concert stage. That modern artists collaborated with Nazism reveals an important aspect of modernism, uncovers the bizarre bureaucracy which controlled culture, and tells the histories of great figures who became enthusiastic Nazis and lied about it later, 2021, collage on artificial plant, fabric grow bag with moss, acrylic paint, and plastic

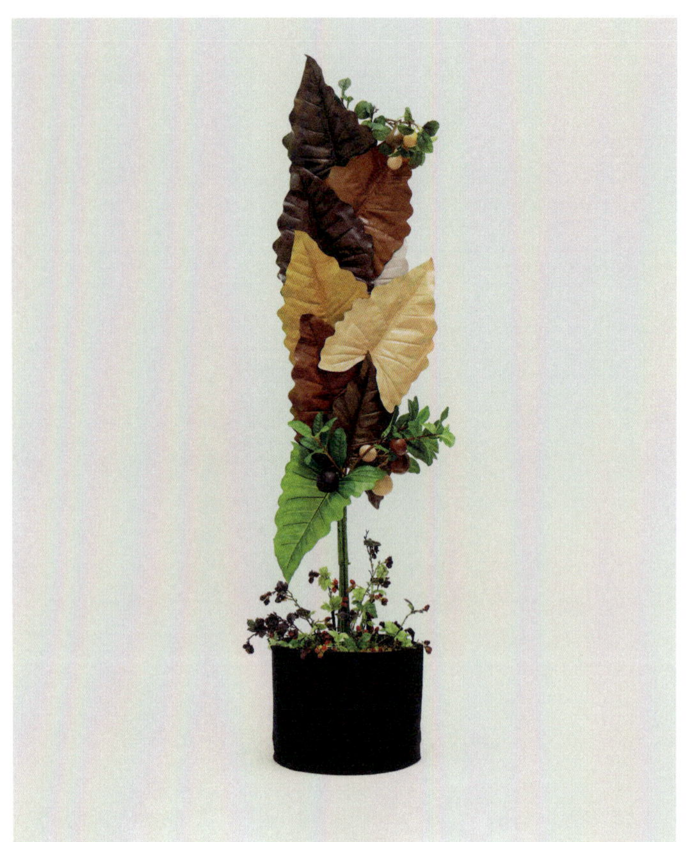

"Britannica" now: choreography, the art of creating and arranging dances. The word derives from the Greek for "dance" and for "write." In the 17th and 18th centuries, it did indeed mean the written record of dances. In the 19th and 20th centuries, however, the meaning shifted, inaccurately but universally, while the written record came to be known as dance notation. In biological taxonomy, race is an informal rank in the taxonomic hierarchy for which various definitions exist. Sometimes it is used to denote a level below that of subspecies, while at other times it is used as a synonym for subspecies. A race is a grouping of humans based on shared physical or social qualities into categories generally viewed as distinct by society.[1] The term was first used to refer to speakers of a common language and then to denote national affiliations. By the 17th century the term began to refer to physical (phenotypical) traits. Modern science regards race as a social construct, an identity which is assigned based on rules made by society. [2] While partially based on physical similarities within groups, race does not have an inherent physical or biological meaning. [1][3][4] Dance notation, the recording of dance movement through the use of written symbols. Dance notation is to dance what musical notation is to music and what the written word is to drama. In dance, notation is the translation of four-dimensional movement (time being the fourth dimension) into signs written on two-dimensional paper. A fifth "dimension"—dynamics, or the quality, texture, and phrasing of movement—should also be considered an integral part of notation, although in most systems it is not, 2021, artificial plant, fabric grow bag with moss, acrylic paint, and plastic

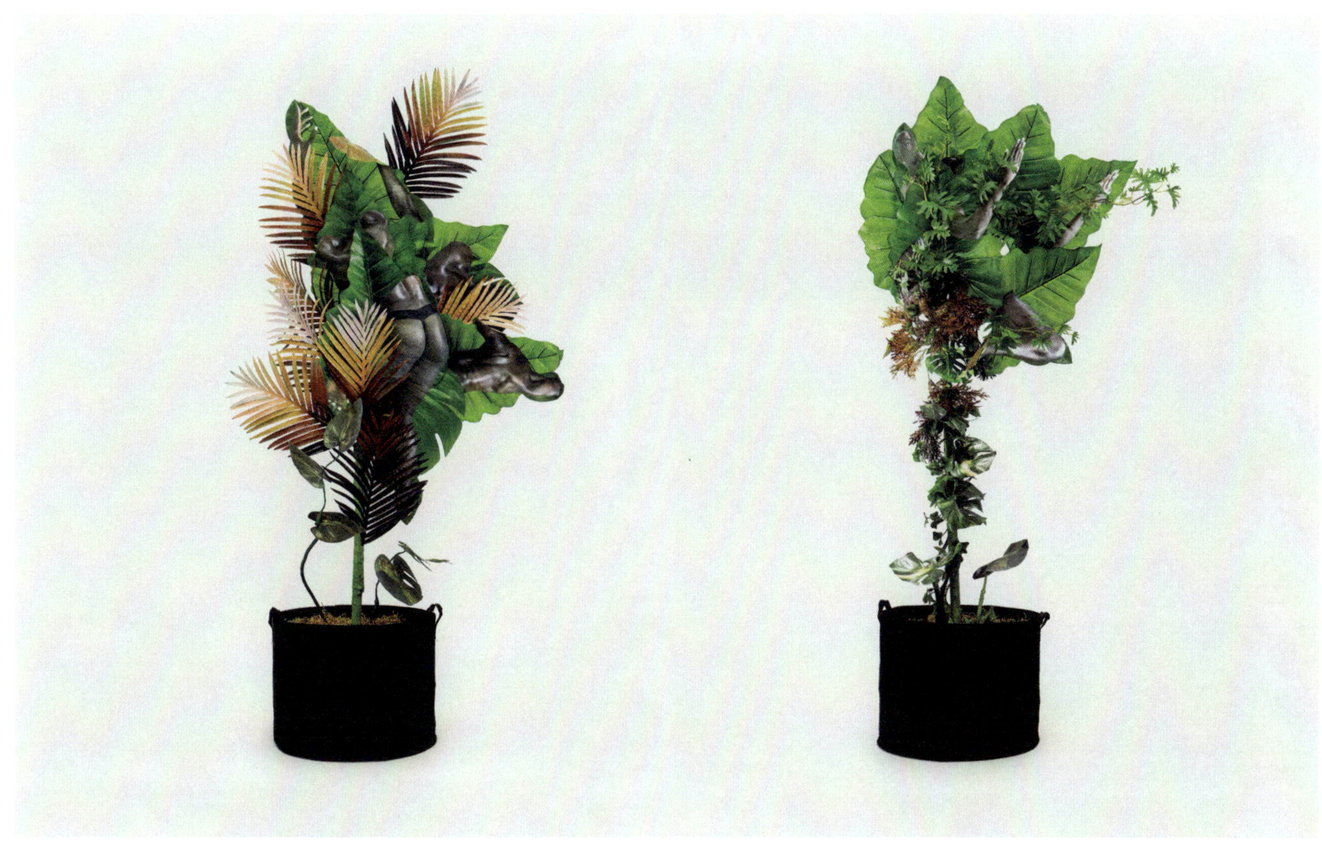

Left: *Genes, not Genius: For jazz is orgasm, it is the music of orgasm, good orgasm and bad, and so it spoke across a nation, it had the communication of art even where it was watered, perverted, corrupted, and almost killed, it spoke in no matter what laundered popular way of instantaneous existential states to which some whites could respond, it was indeed a communication by art because it said, "I feel this, and now you do too." Virtuosity is bound to colorism, tokenism, trophyism, and the ruptures of interraciality on legacies of rape and social distortion of dark skin, reverse colorism is not real. The importance of dance in courtship and social gatherings is probably older than its use as recreation and entertainment*, 2021, collage on artificial plant, fabric grow bag with moss, acrylic paint, and plastic

Right: *Genes, not Genius: The overlying purpose is to address how the social production of biologically determinist racial scripts—which extend from a biocentric conception of the human—can be dislodged by bringing studies of blackness in/and science into conversation with autopoiesis, black Atlantic livingness, weights and measures, and poetry. A biocentric conception of the human, it should be noted up front, refers to the law-like order of knowledge that posits a Darwinian narrative of the human—that we are purely biological and bioevolutionary beings—as universal; elegance is elimination*, 2021, collage on artificial plant, fabric grow bag with moss, acrylic paint, and plastic

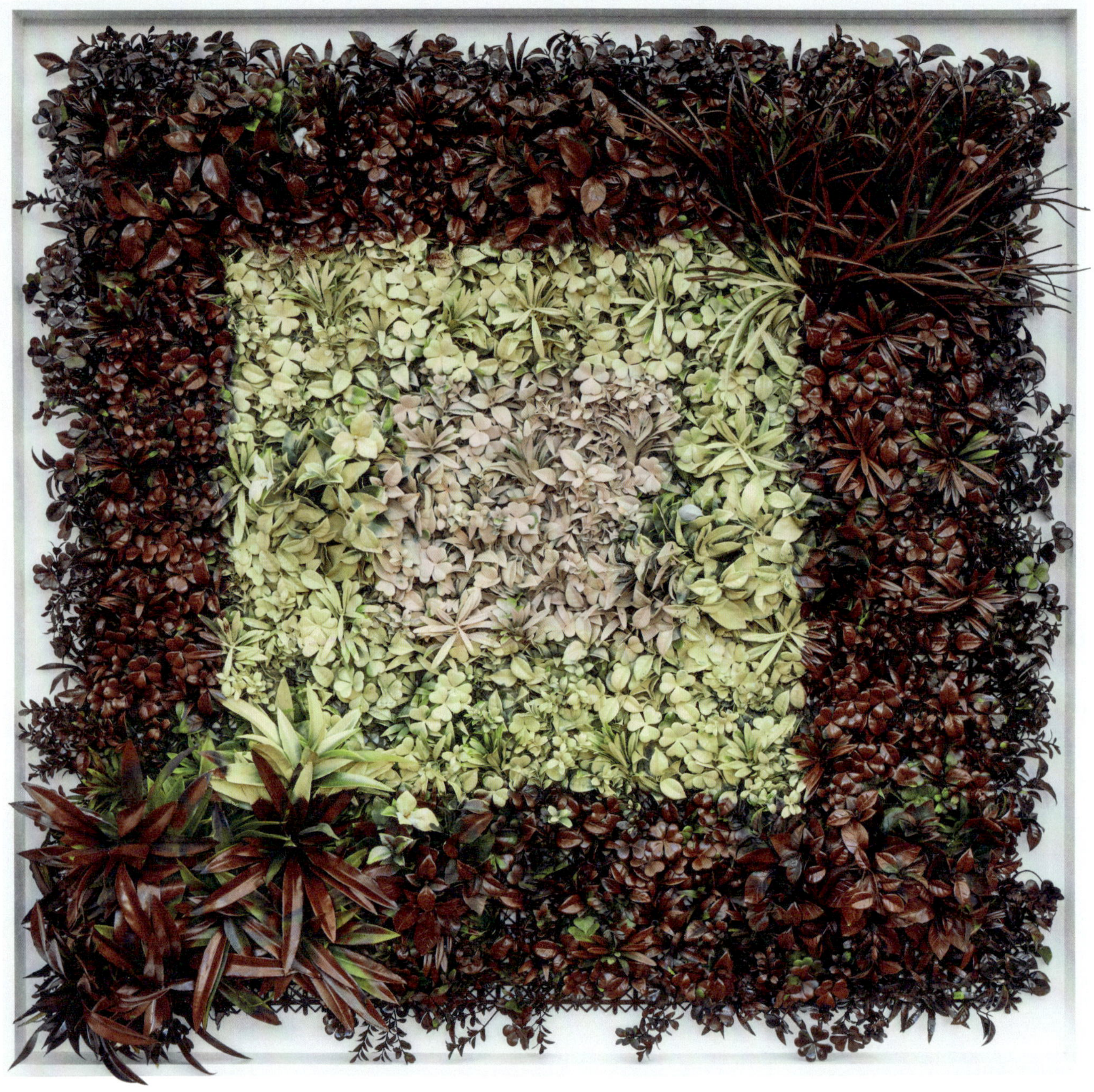

Bitter Arrangement IV: Overseers, Aerial, apprehension and authorization, 2021, aerosol spray and plastic

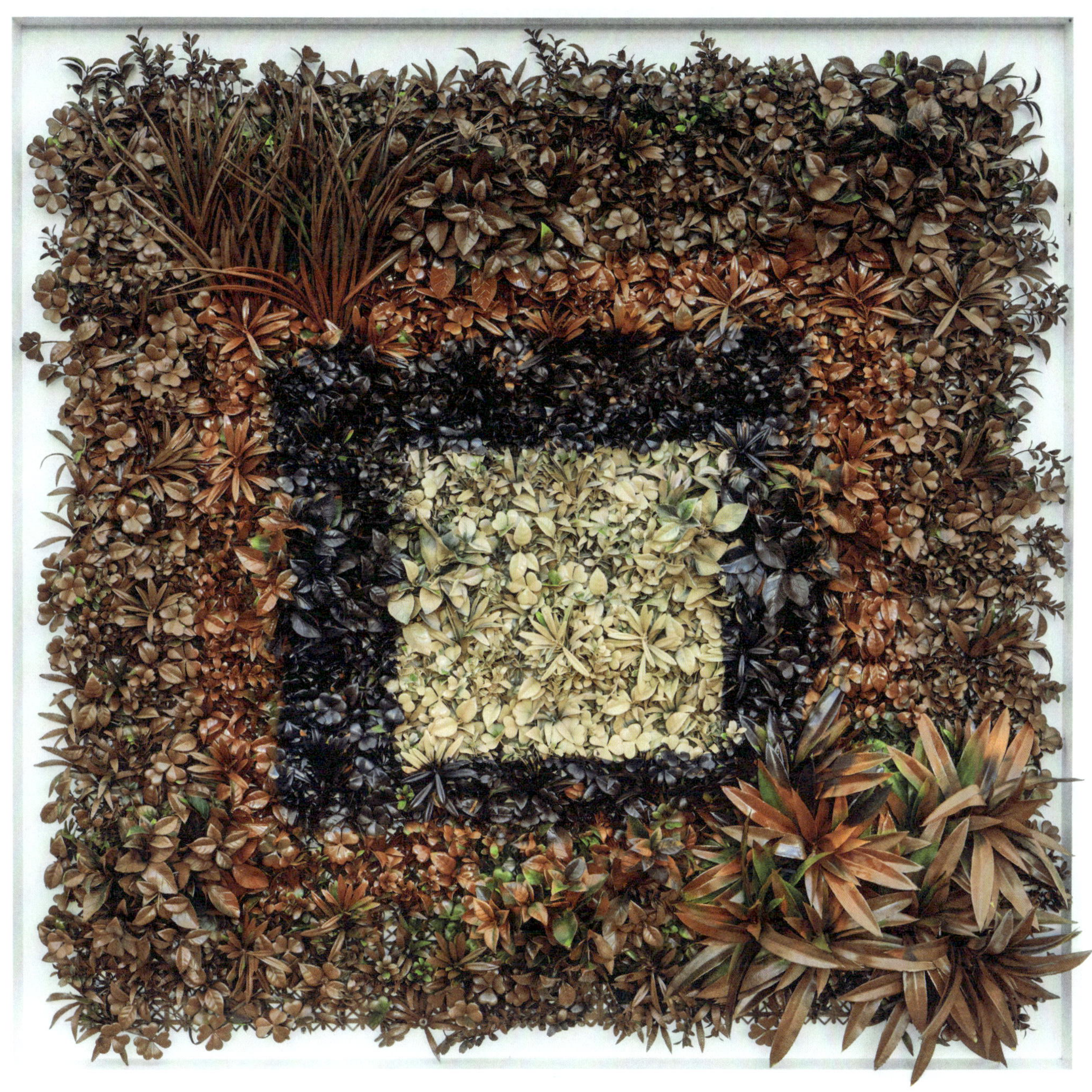

Bitter Arrangement V: Descending, subjectivization with/in/out compassion, 2021, aerosol spray and plastic

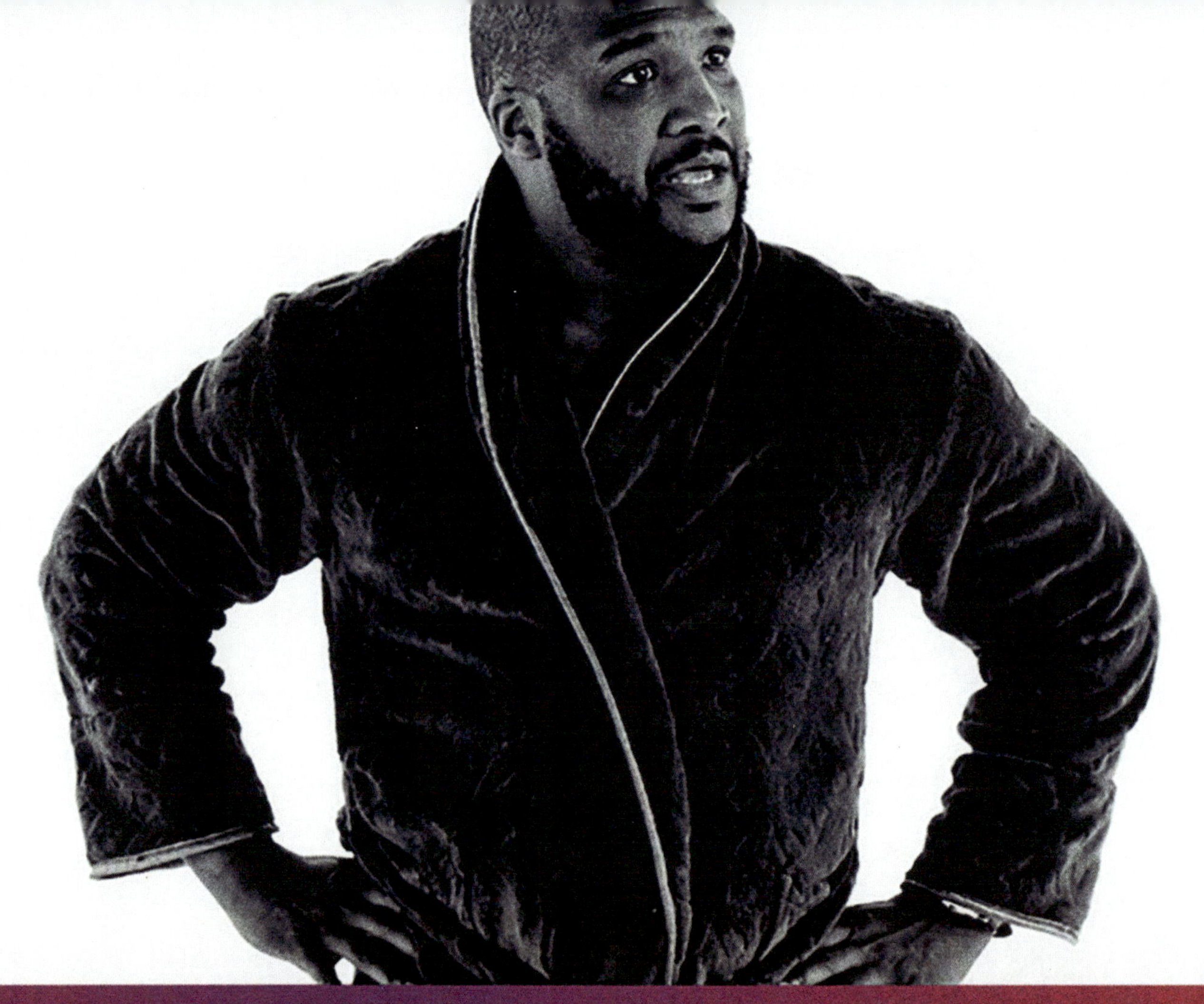

Death of A, 2022, four-channel HD video installation (color, sound) (video stills)

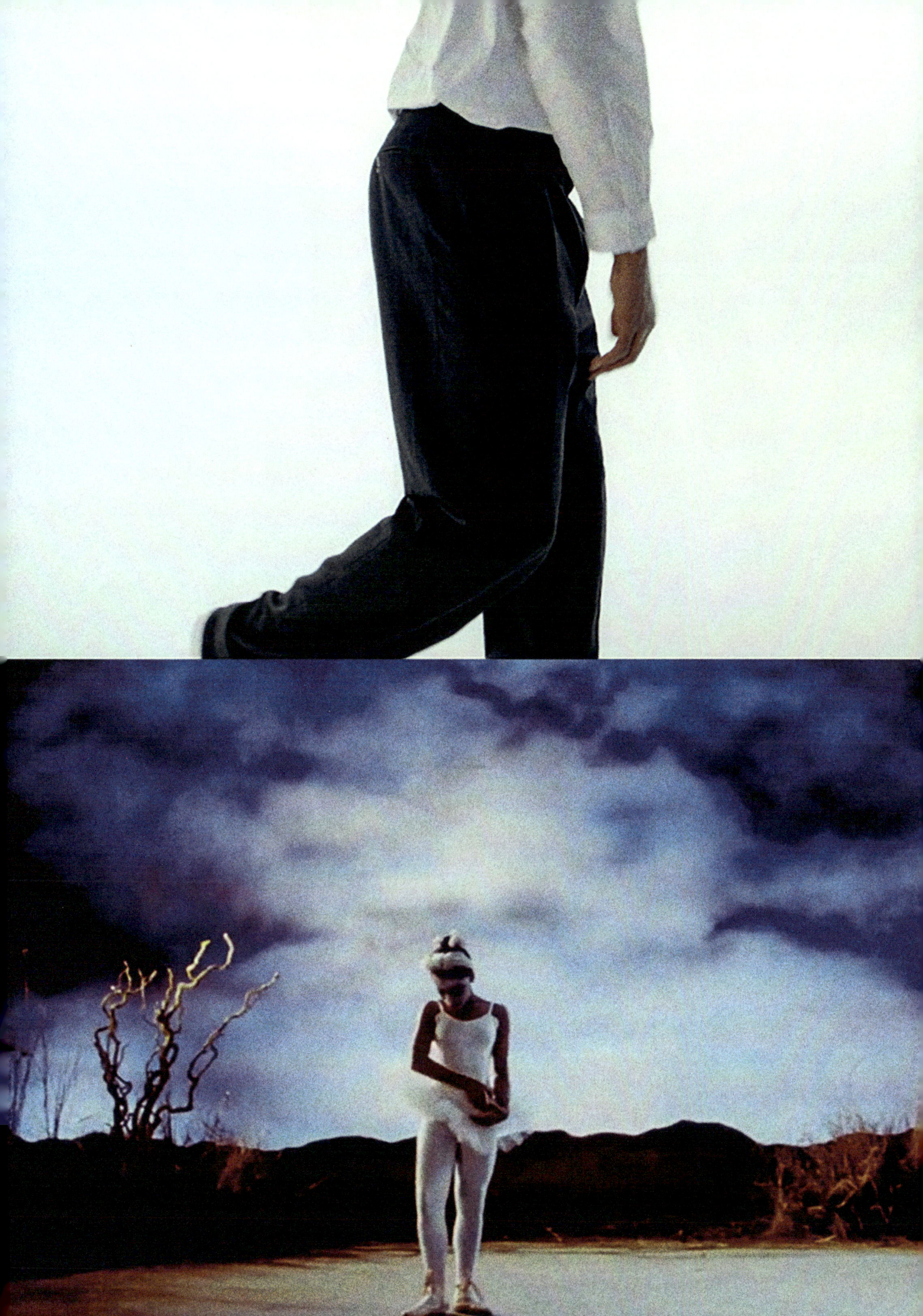

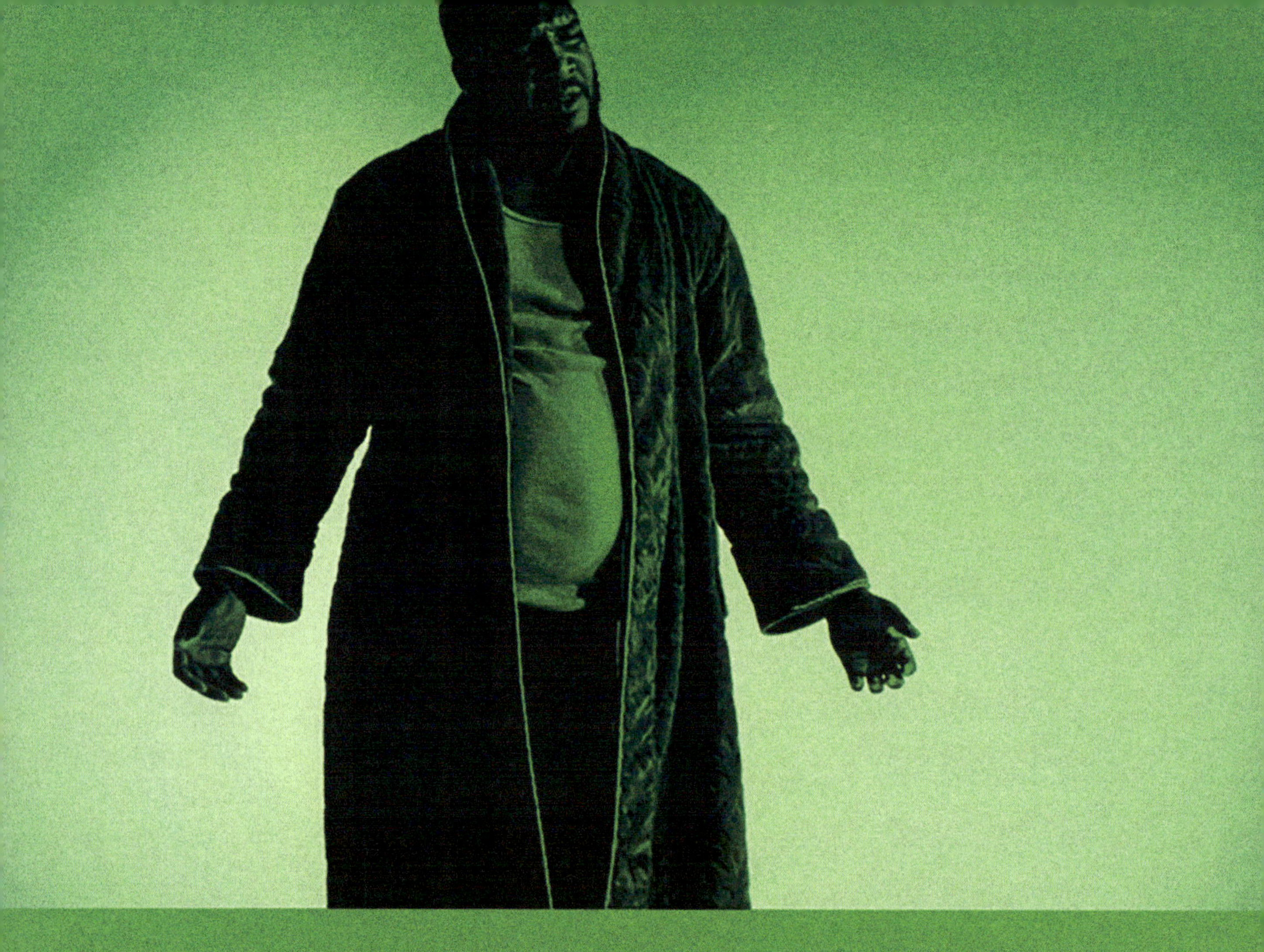

Death of A, 2022, four-channel HD video installation (color, sound) (video stills)

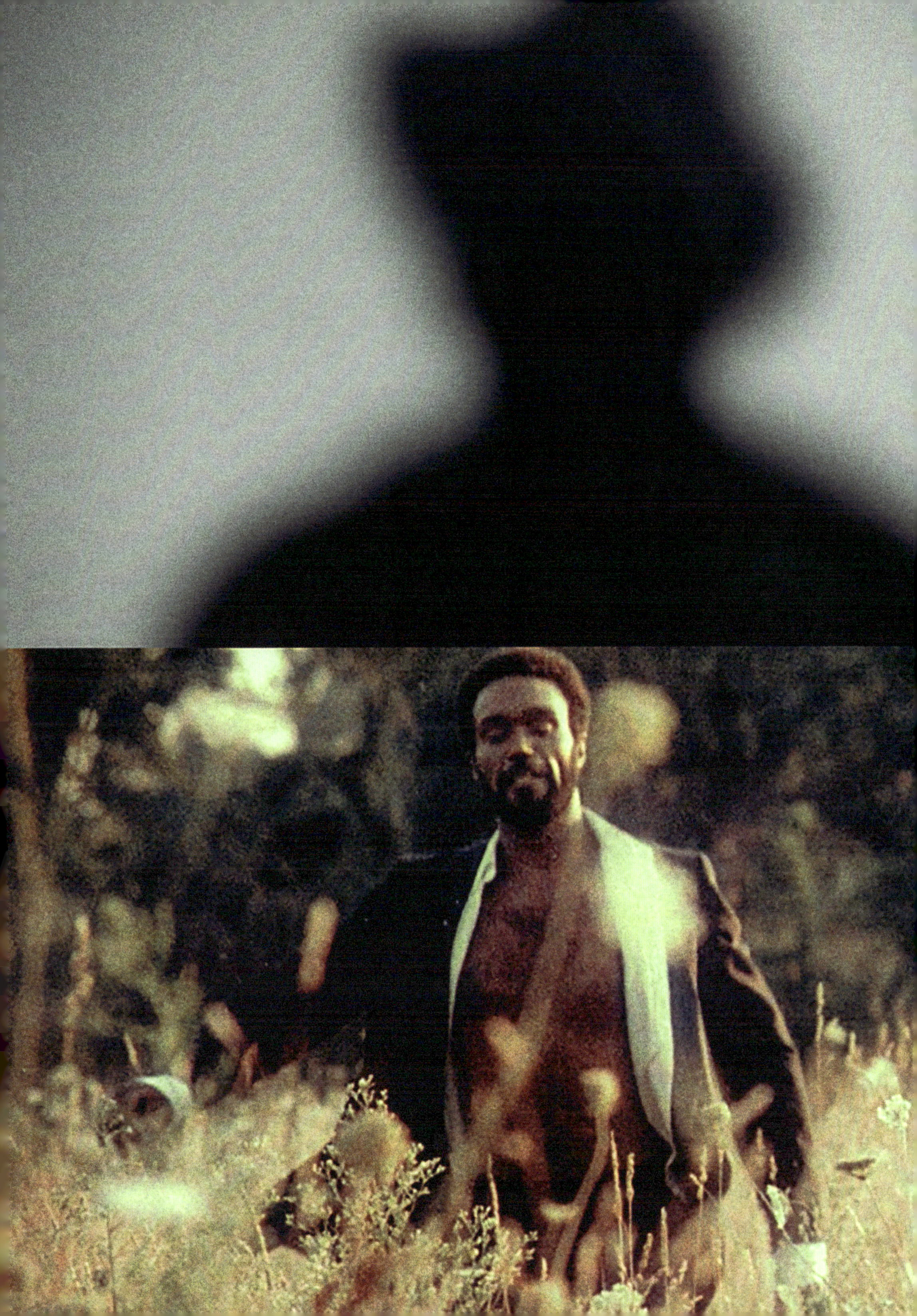

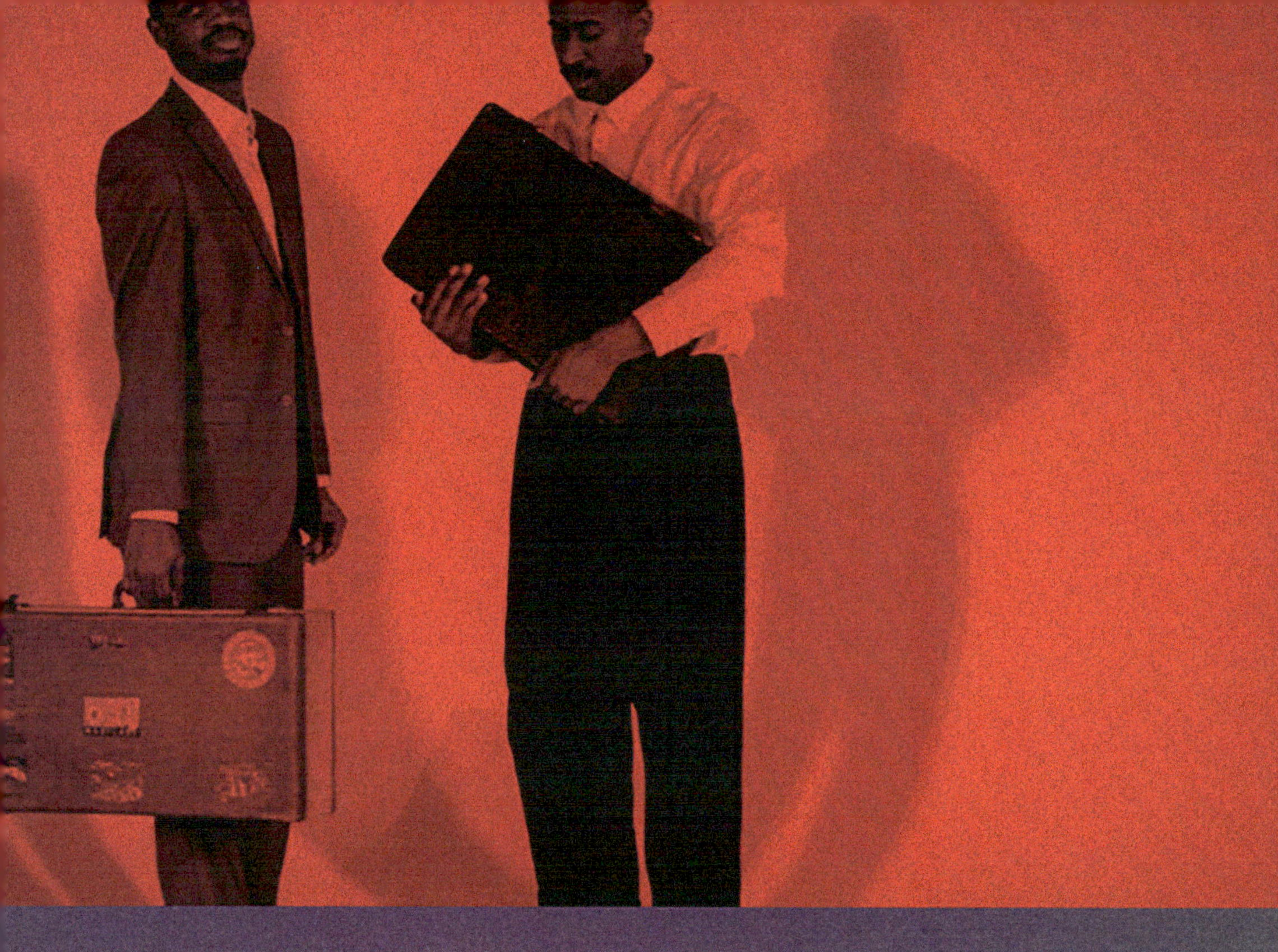

Death of A, 2022, four-channel HD video installation (color, sound) (video stills)

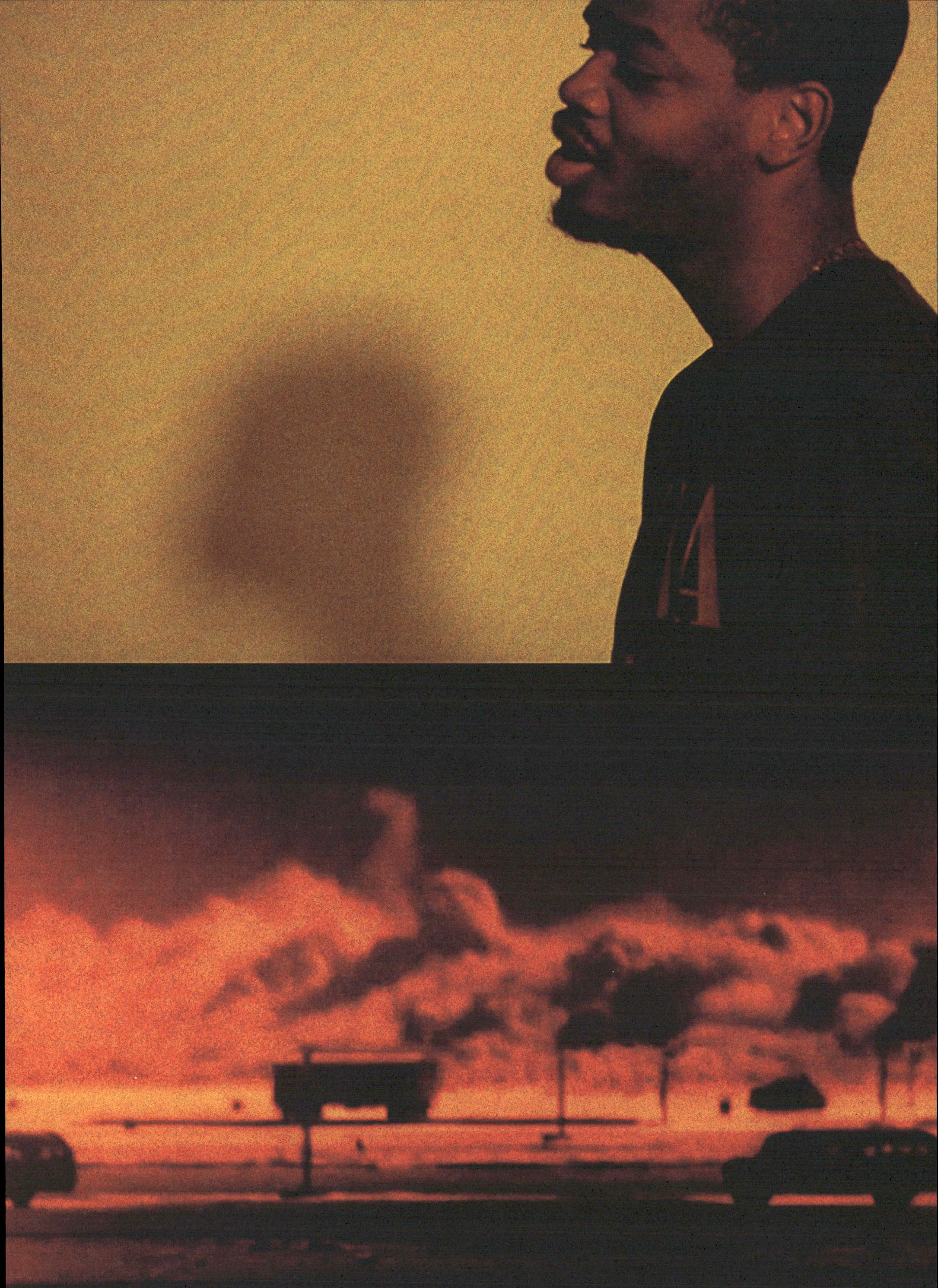

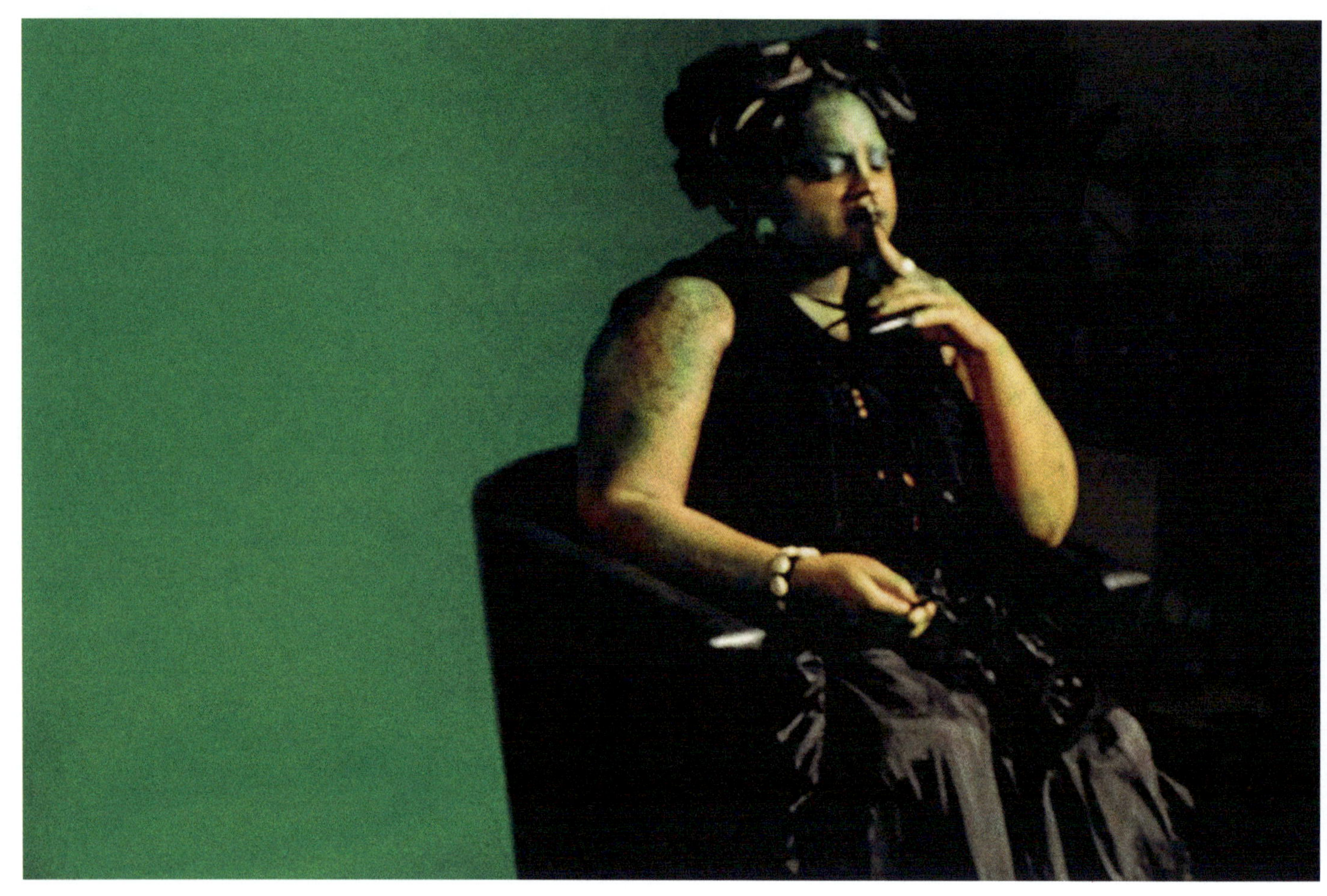

Medusa, 2023, single-channel video (color, sound) (video stills)

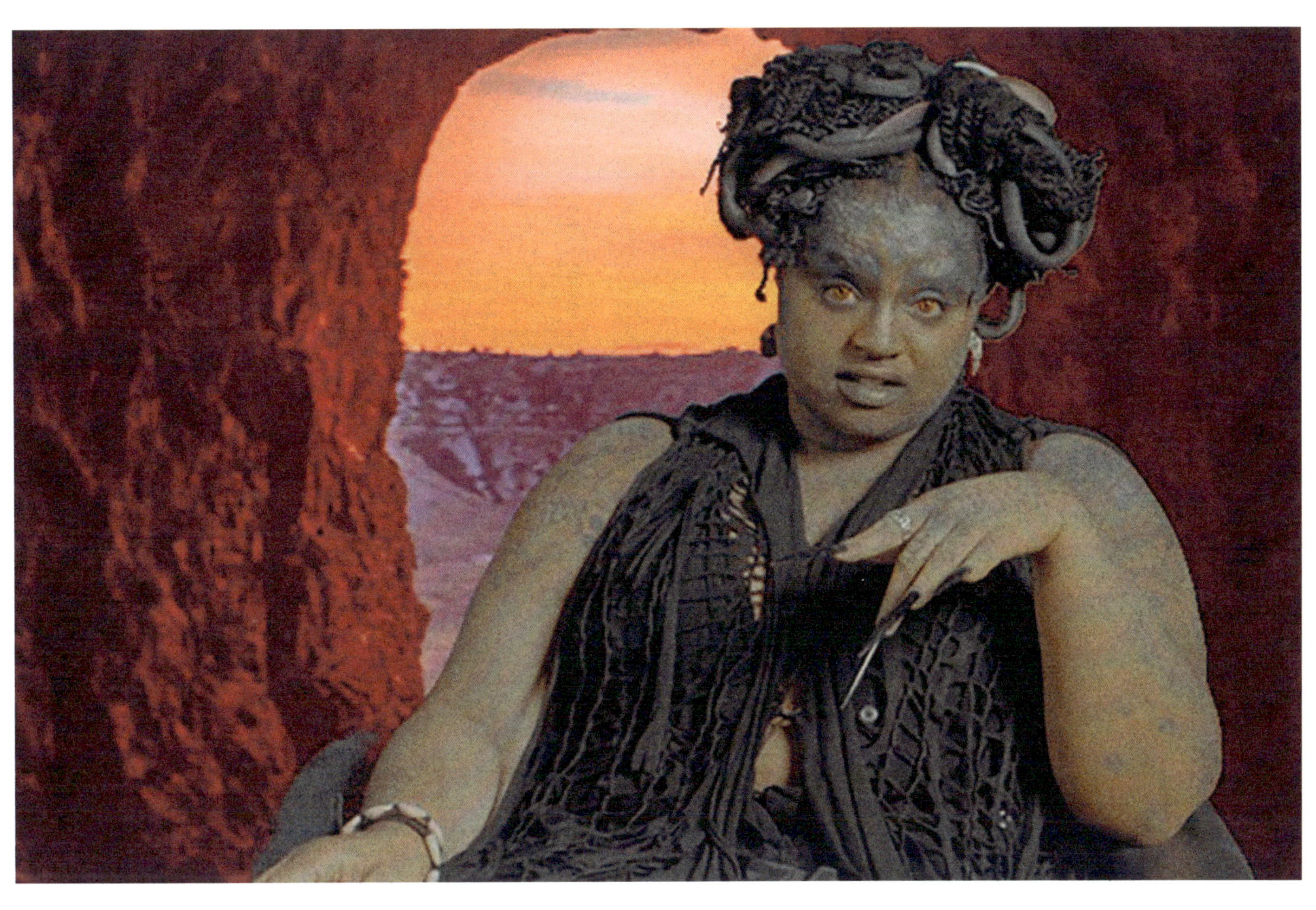

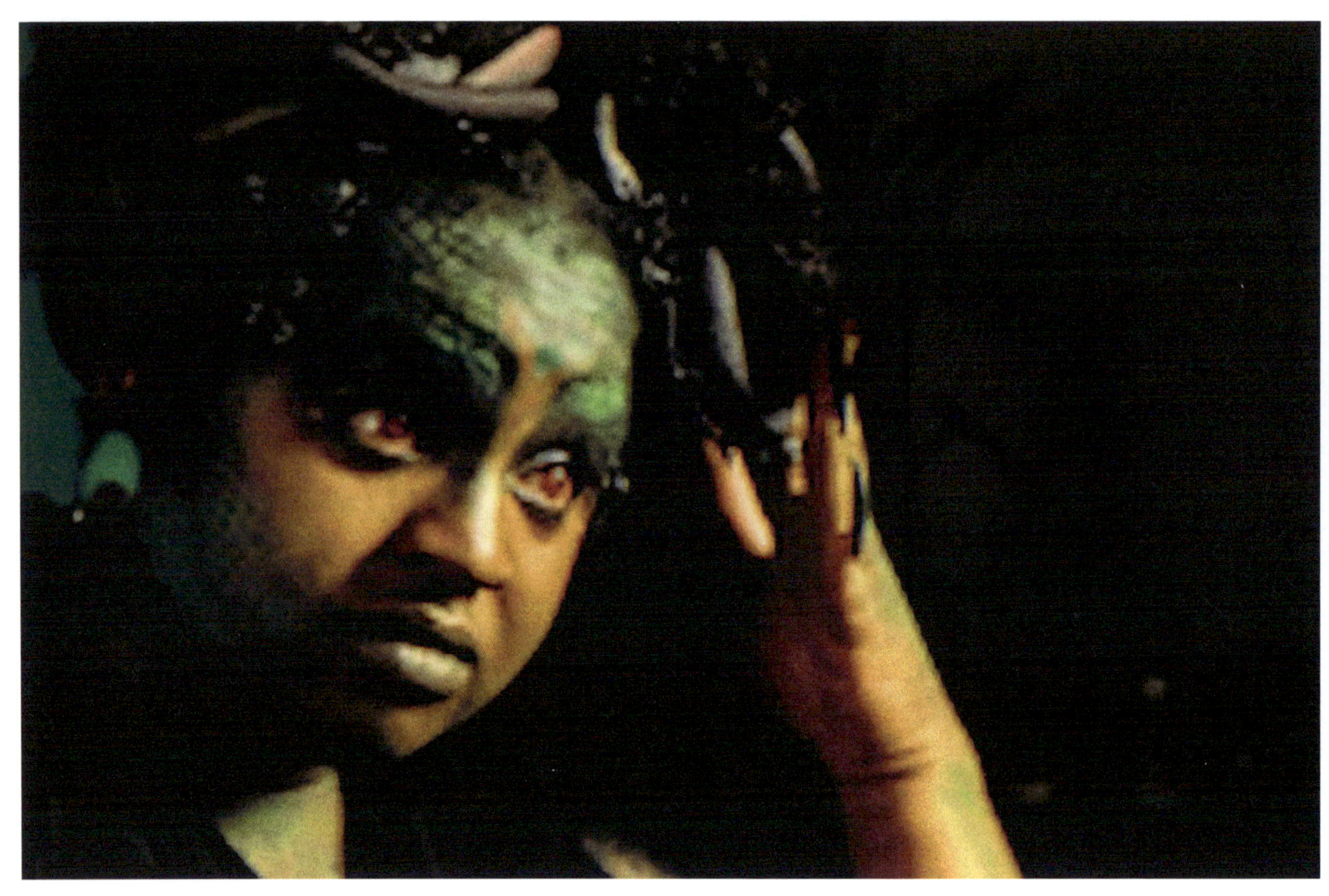

Medusa, 2023, single-channel video (color, sound) (video stills)

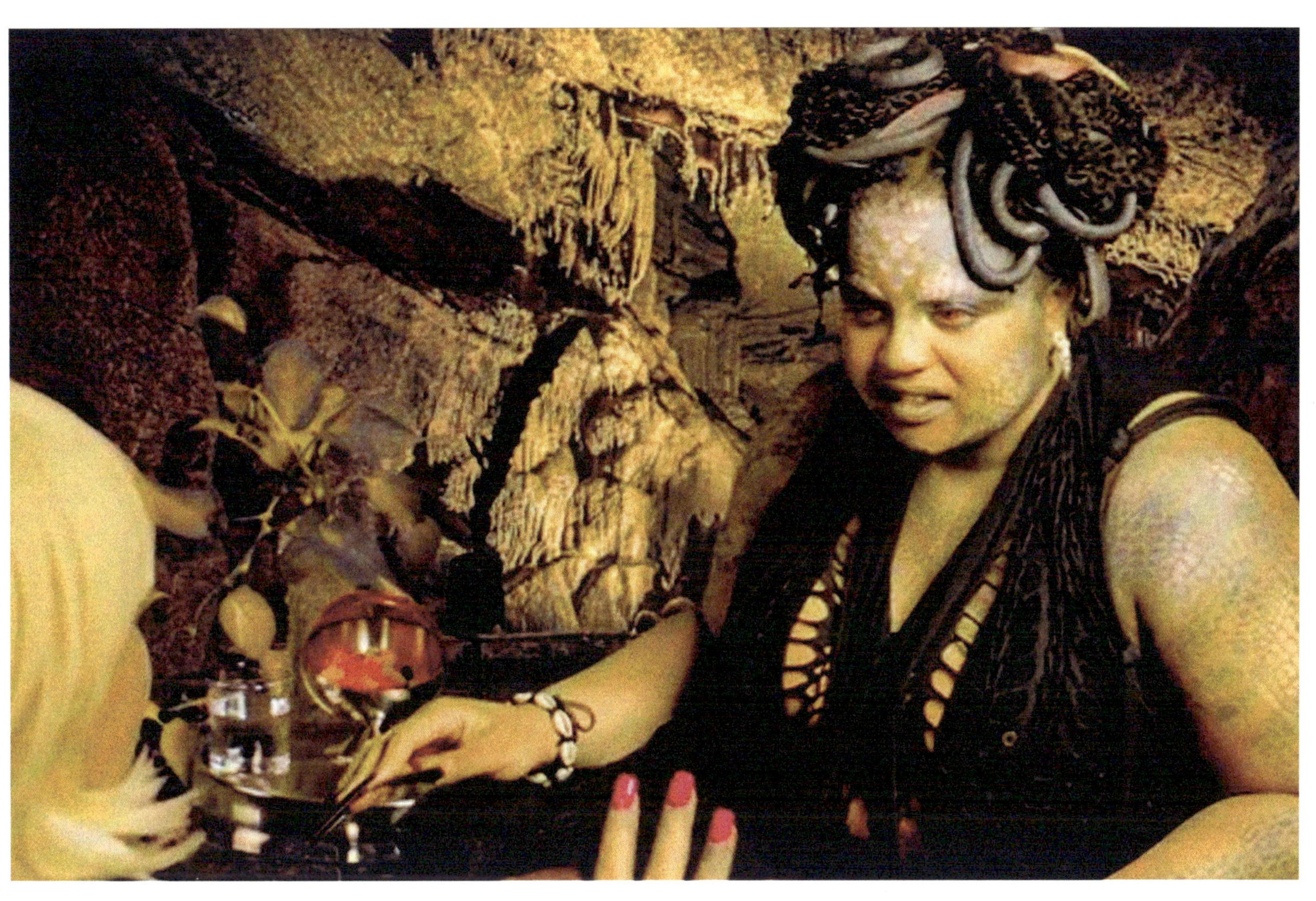

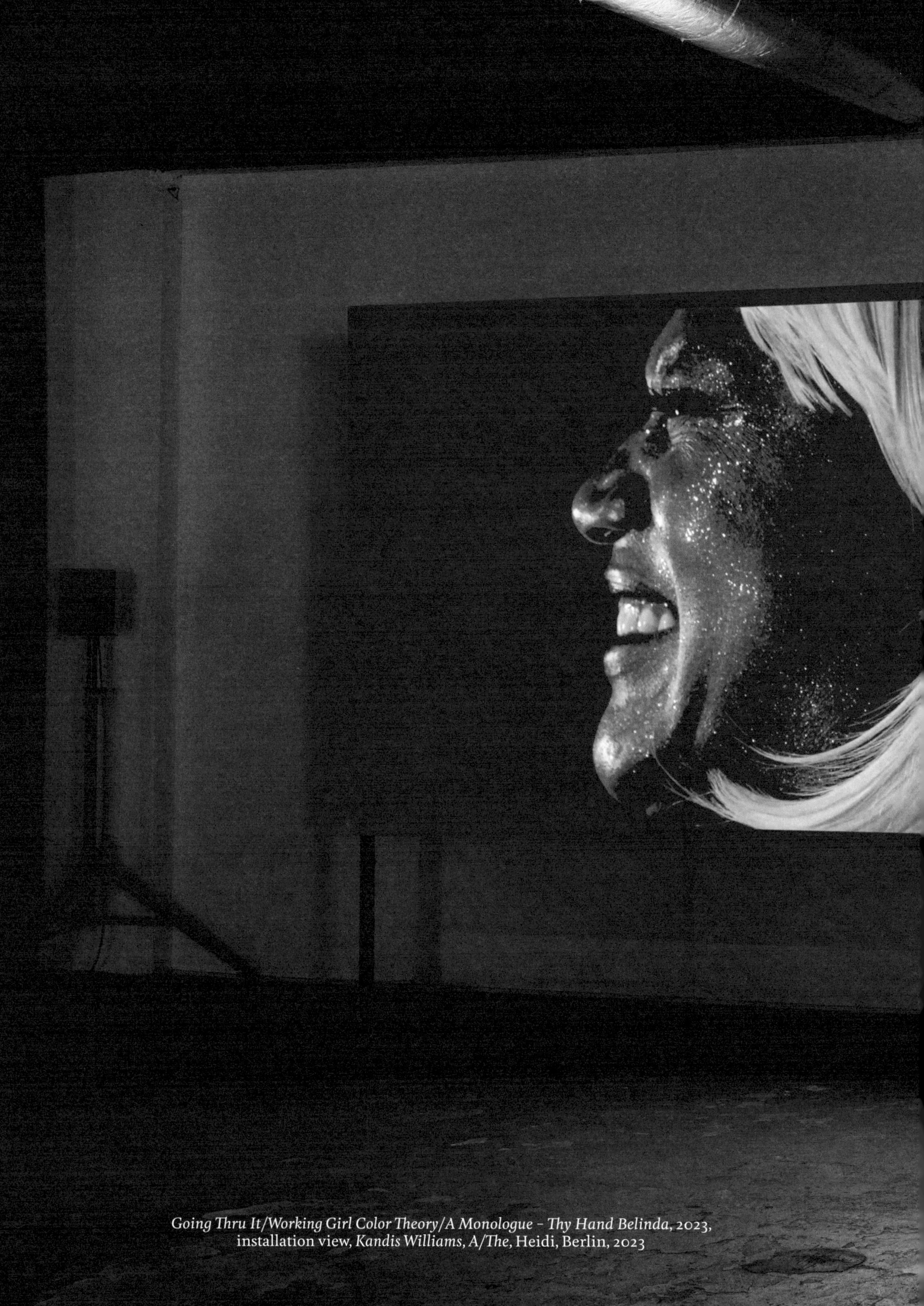

Going Thru It/Working Girl Color Theory/A Monologue – Thy Hand Belinda, 2023, installation view, *Kandis Williams, A/The*, Heidi, Berlin, 2023

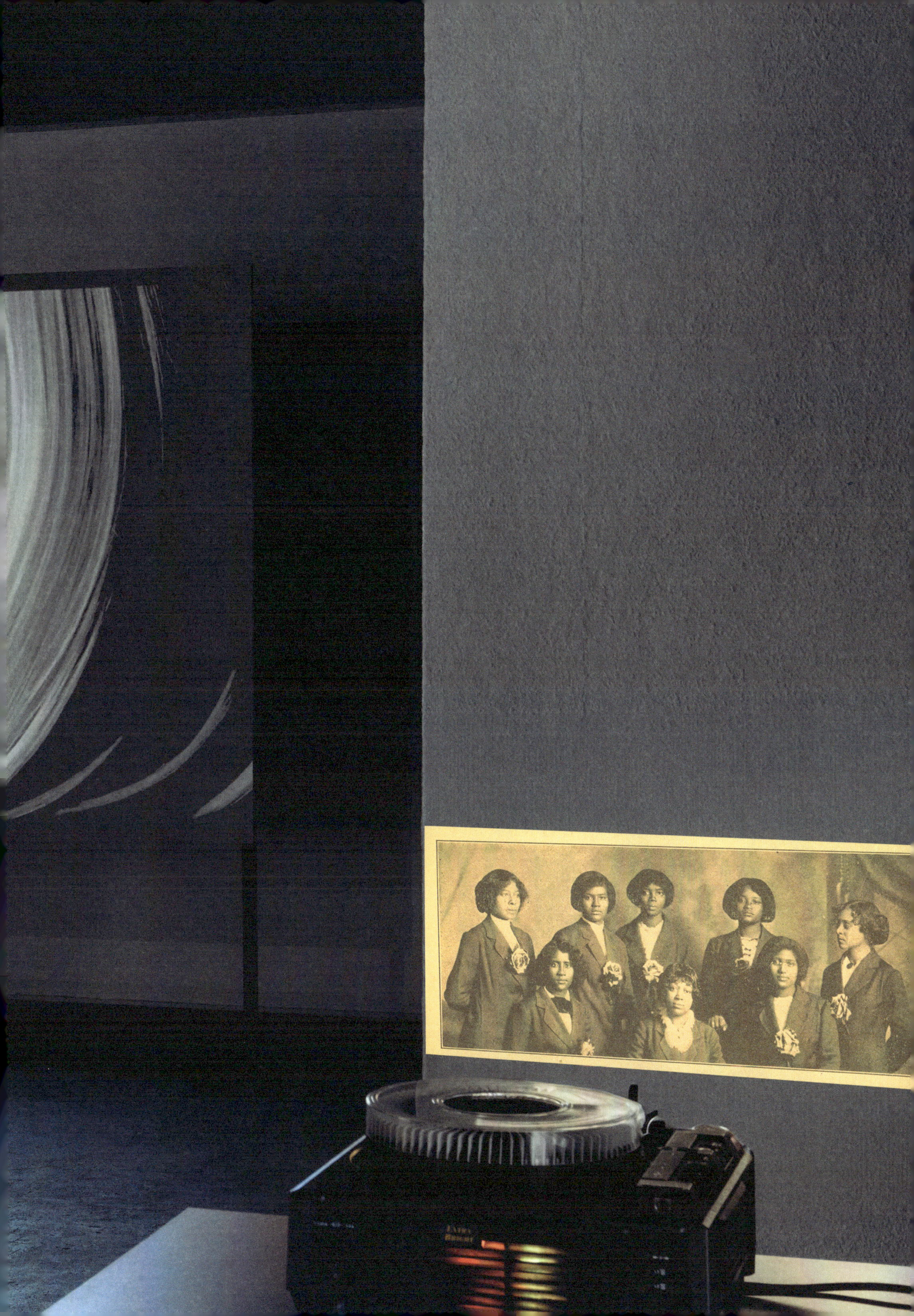

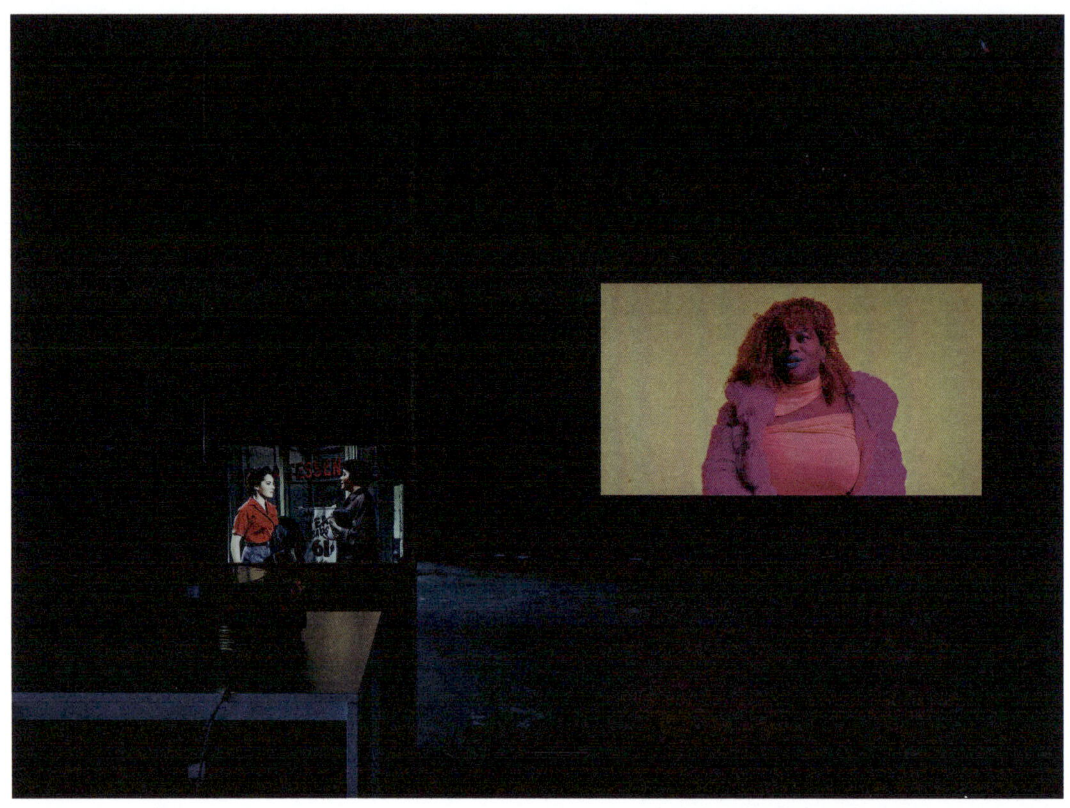

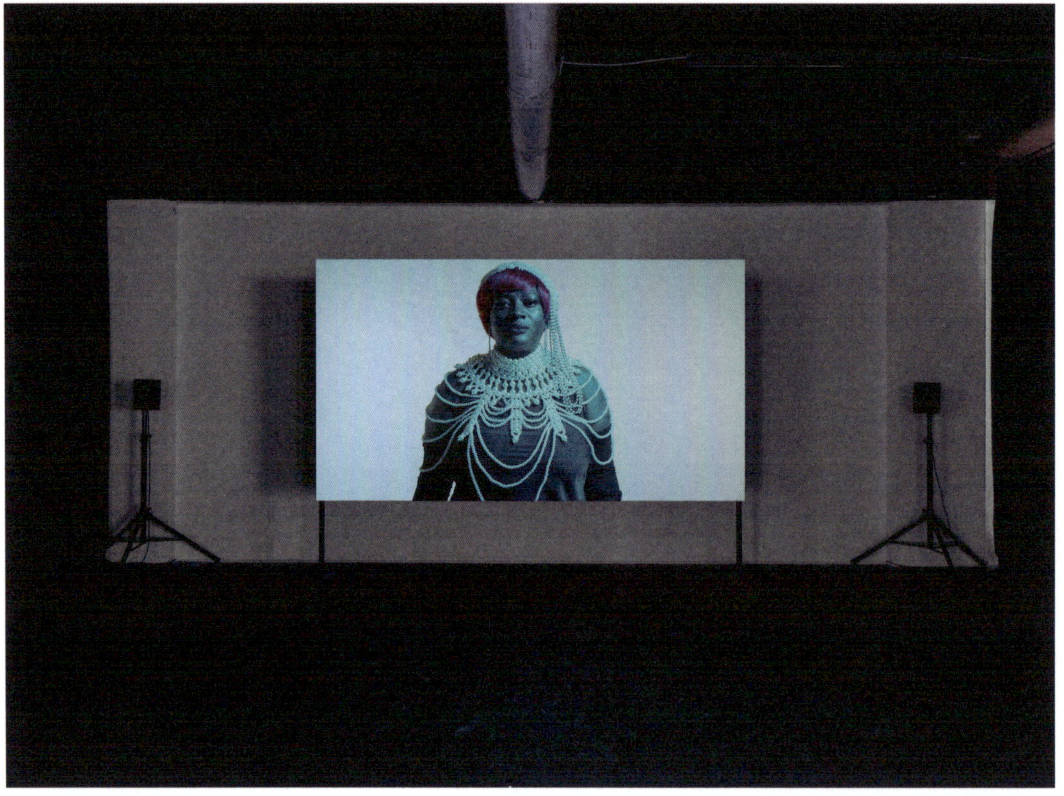

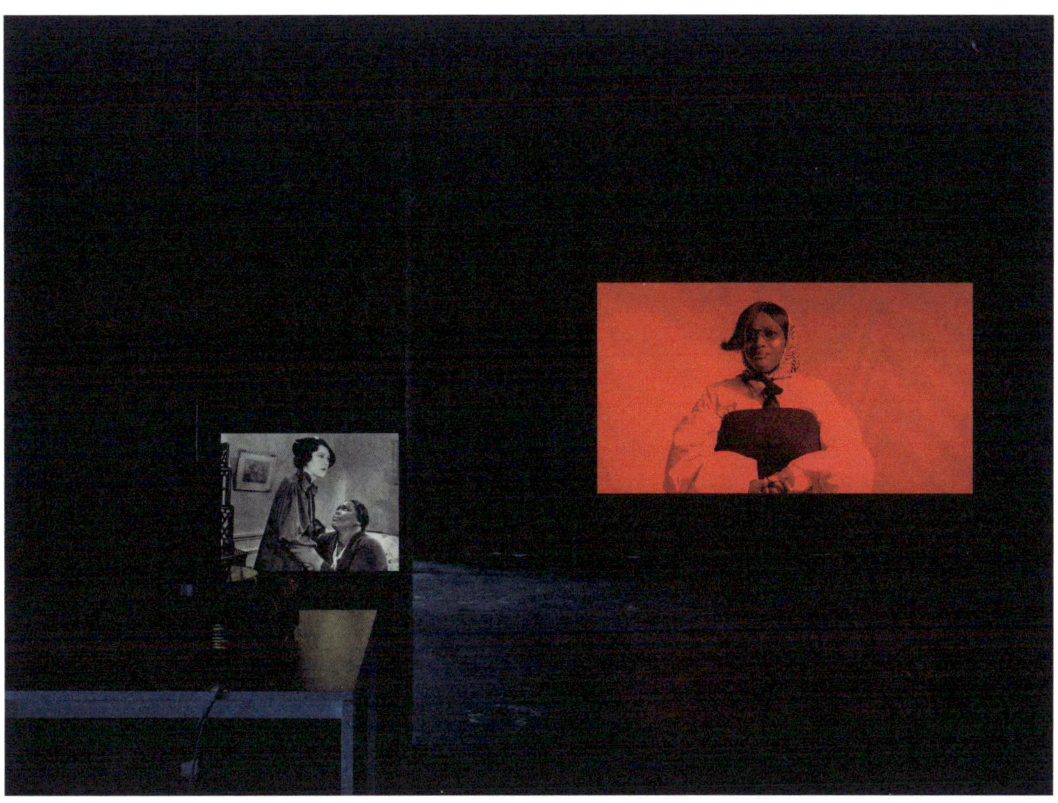

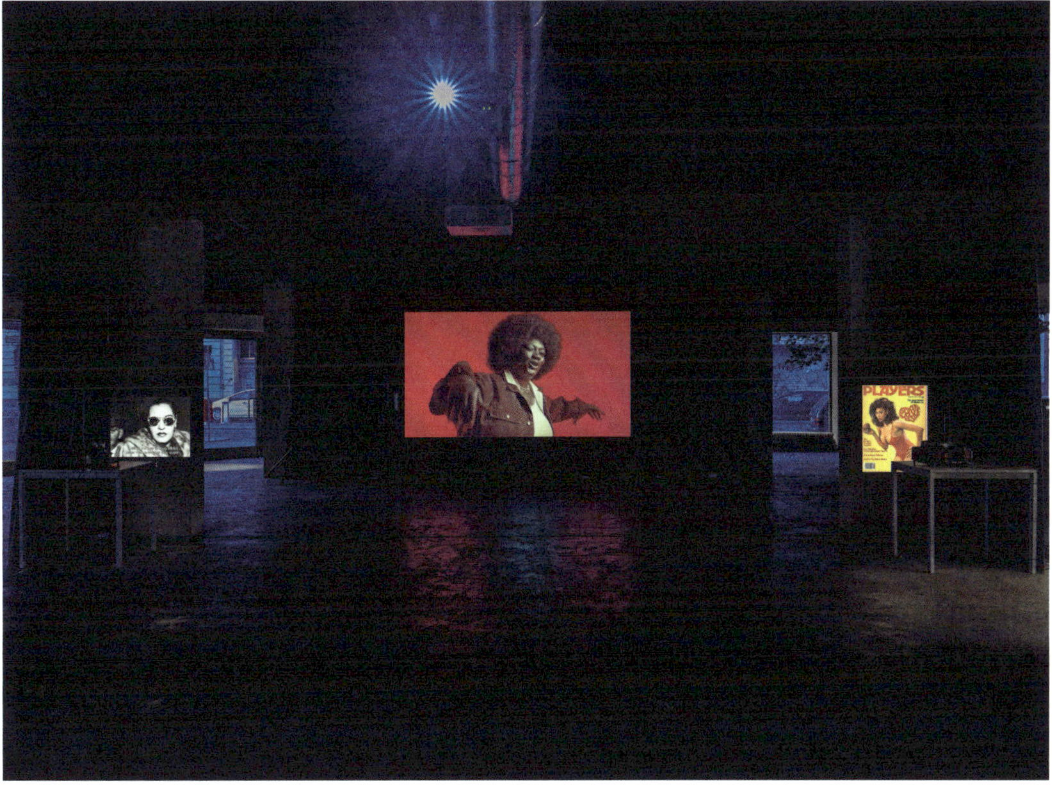

Going Thru It/Working Girl Color Theory/A Monologue – Thy Hand Belinda, 2023, installation views, *Kandis Williams, A/The*, Heidi, Berlin, 2023

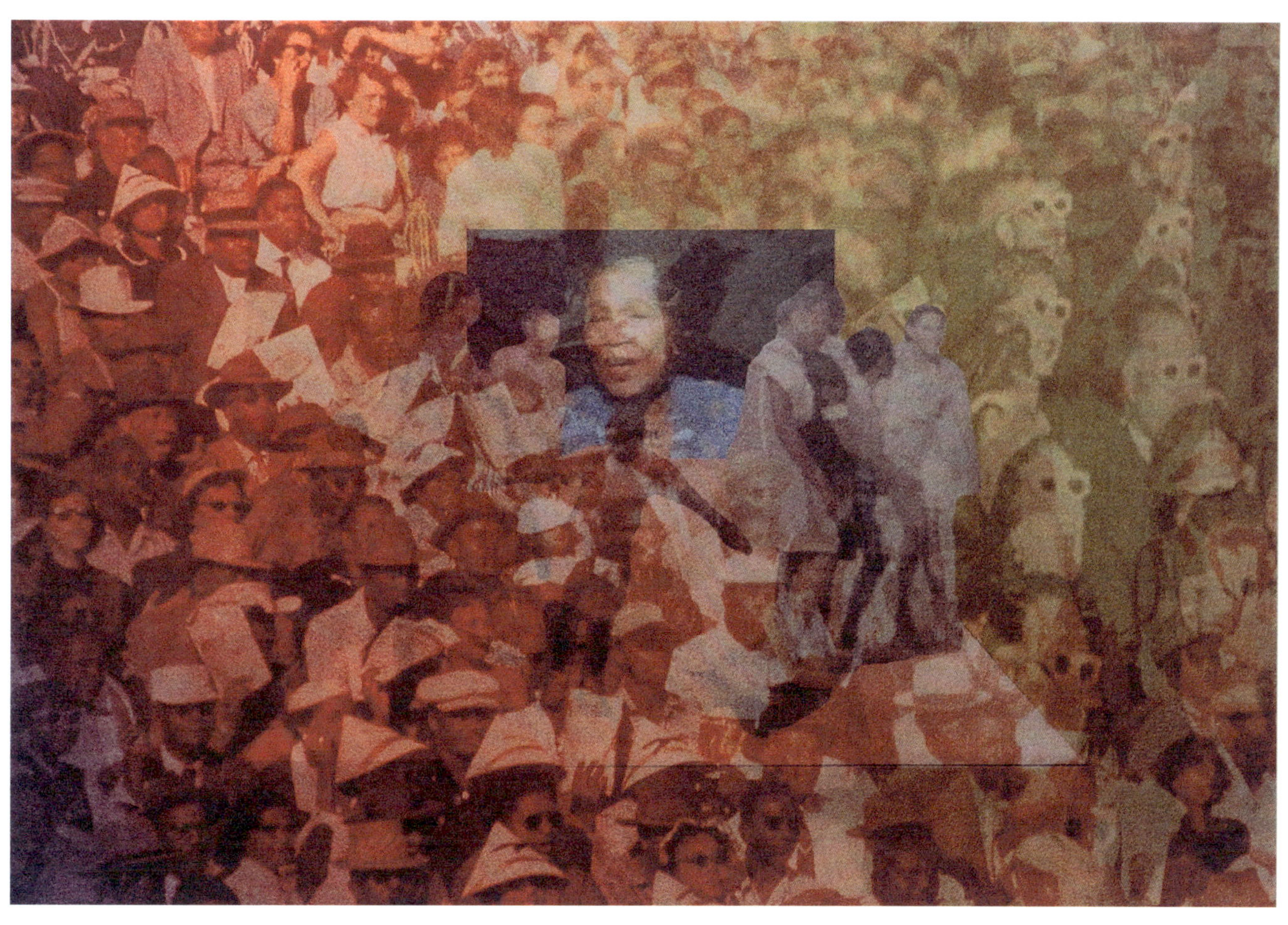

From the Joy of Seeing Them, to the Pain of Being Them II, 2023, lenticular print mounted on dibond

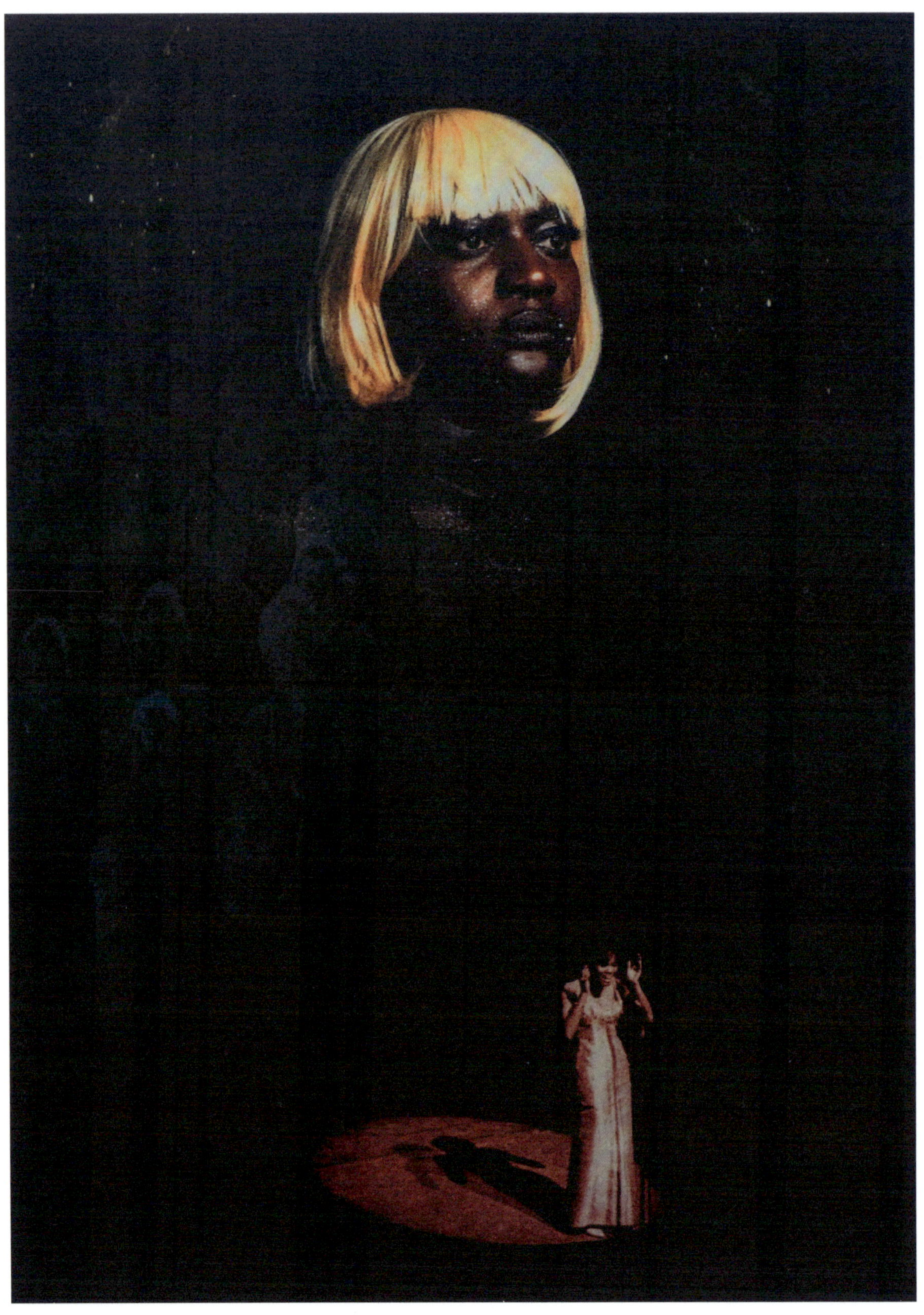

From the Joy of Seeing Them, to the Pain of Being Them, 2023, lenticular print mounted on dibond

From the Joy of Seeing Them, to the Pain of Being Them, 2023 (detail)

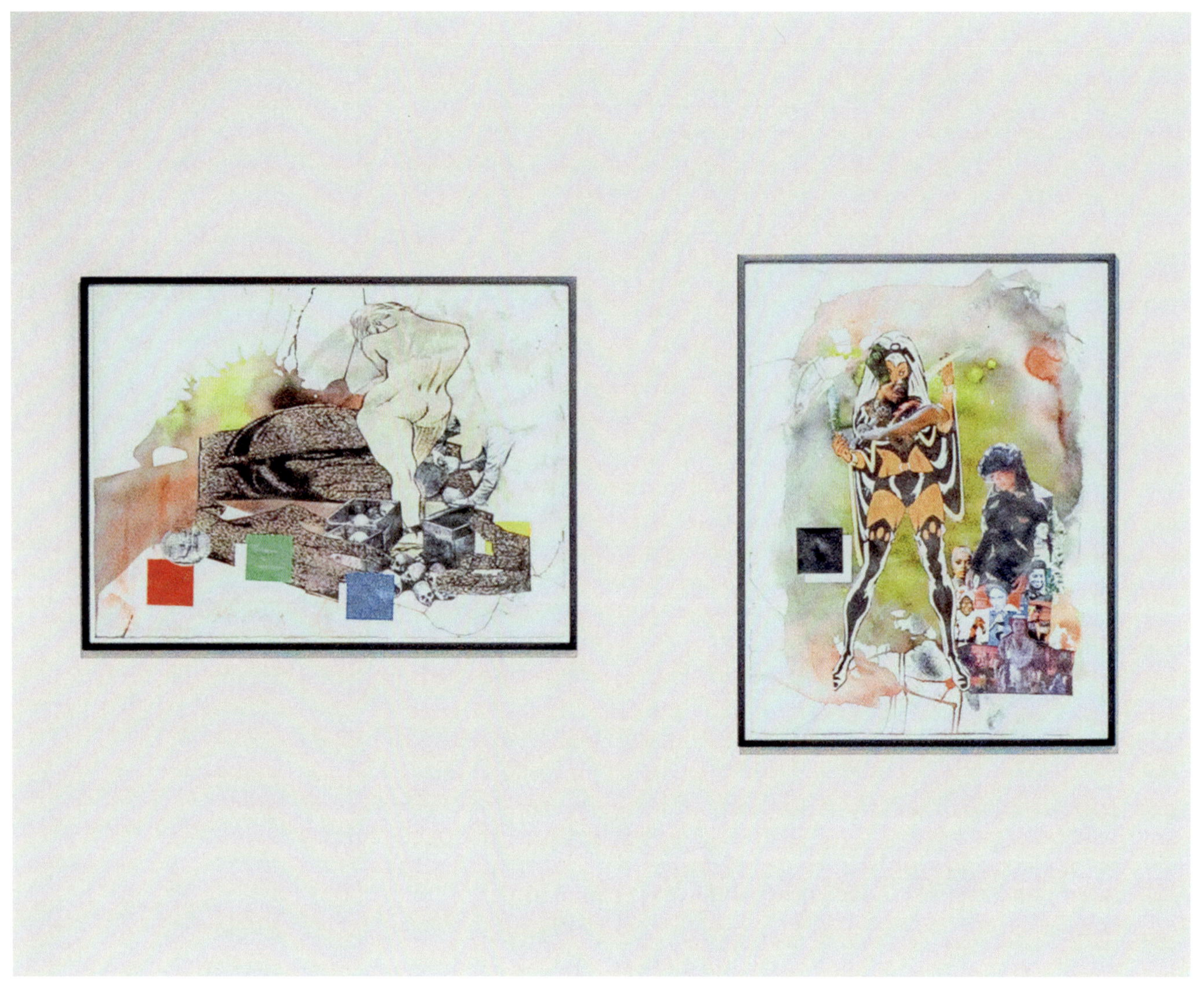

Pages 202–212: All works are from *gods and monsters that white people make up to kill us all*, 2024.
Full captions appear in the checklist on pages 273–282.

Left: *GHOUL: White Girl War Machine, Garrison and the Brute. [. . .]*, 2024, paper, collage, color aid, and adhesive on paper

Right: *FINAL GYAL: Native Wife: Queens of the Damned: Sapphire Mammy Jezebel. Crawl on me. Sink into me. Die for me. Living dead girl. Crawl on me. Sink into me. Die for me. Living dead girl. [. . .]*, 2024, paper, collage, color aid, and adhesive on paper

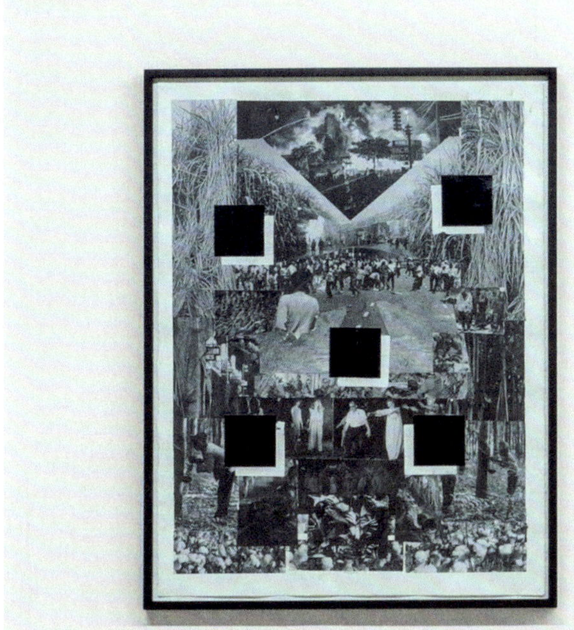

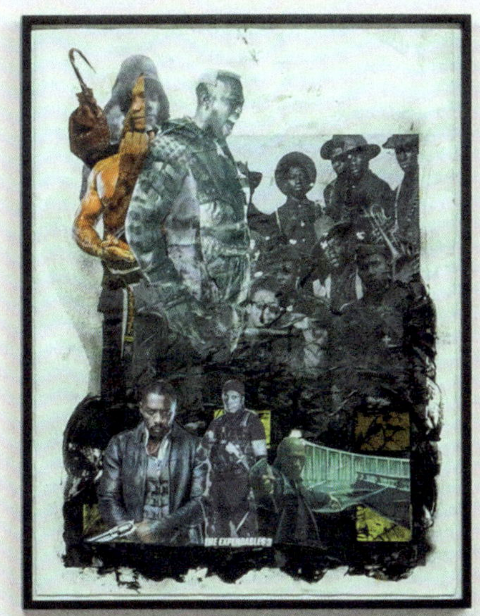

Left: *ZOMBIE (Sketch) Plantation Fantasies and Suburban Body Snatchers and the Power to Steal the Will of Others [. . .]*, 2024, paper, collage, color aid, and adhesive on paper

Right: *SOLDIER PSYCHO (Sketch) "This is your last chance. After this, there is no turning back. You take the blue pill—the story ends, you wake up in your bed and believe whatever you want to believe. [. . .]*, 2024, paper, collage, color aid, and adhesive on paper

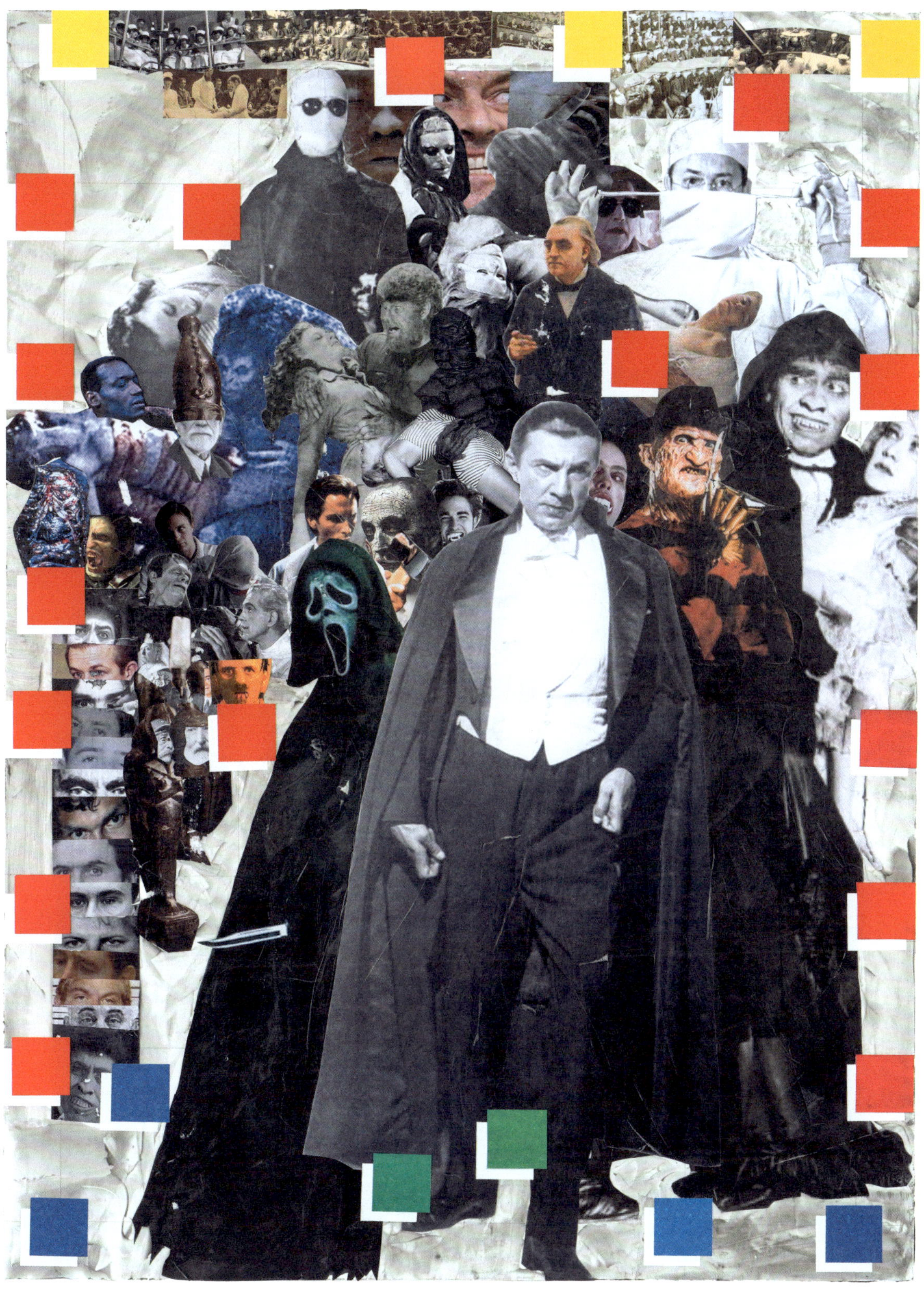

VAMPIRE: "I am Dracula. I bid you welcome. Listen to them. Children of the night. What music they make! The blood is the life, Mr. Renfield. I never drink . . . wine. There are far worse things awaiting man than death."[. . .], 2024, paper, collage, color aid, and adhesive on wood

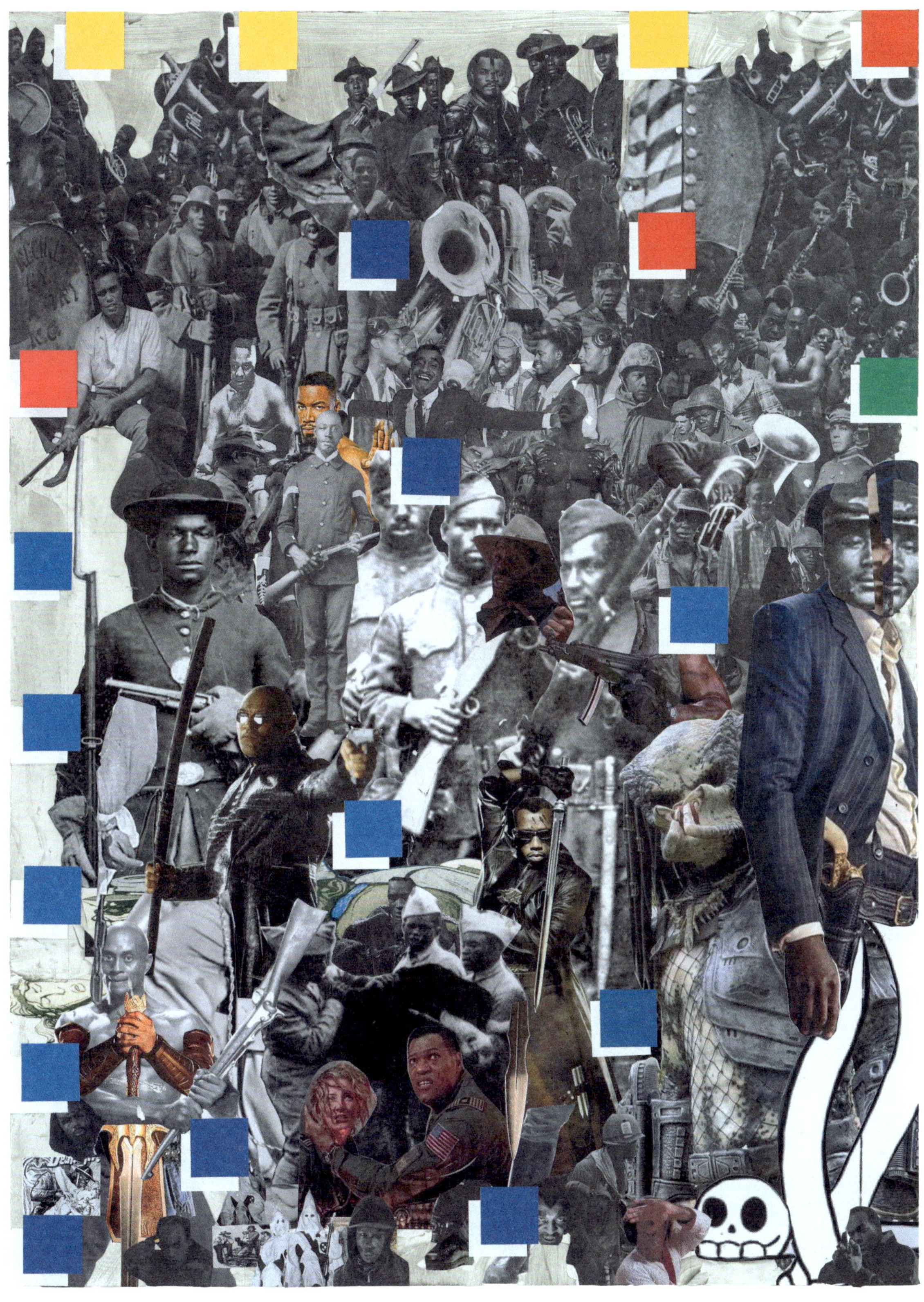

SOLDIER PSYCHO: "This is your last chance. After this, there is no turning back. You take the blue pill—the story ends, you wake up in your bed and believe whatever you want to believe. You take the red pill—you stay in Wonderland, and I show you how deep the rabbit hole goes" [...], 2024, paper, collage, color aid, and adhesive on wood

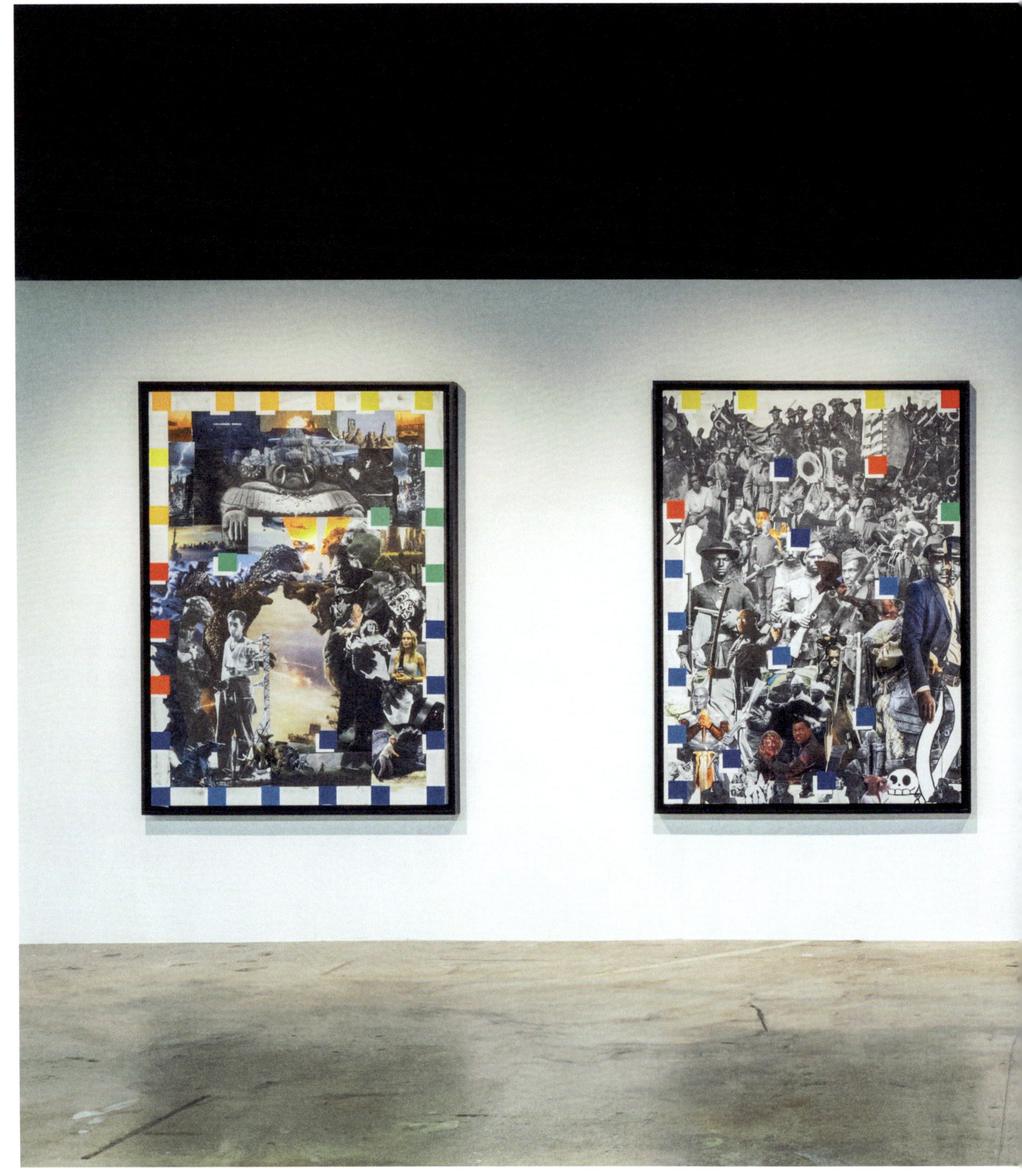

gods and monsters that white people make up to kill us all, 2024, installation view, *PANSORI: A Soundscape of the 21st Century*, 15th Gwangju Biennale, 2024

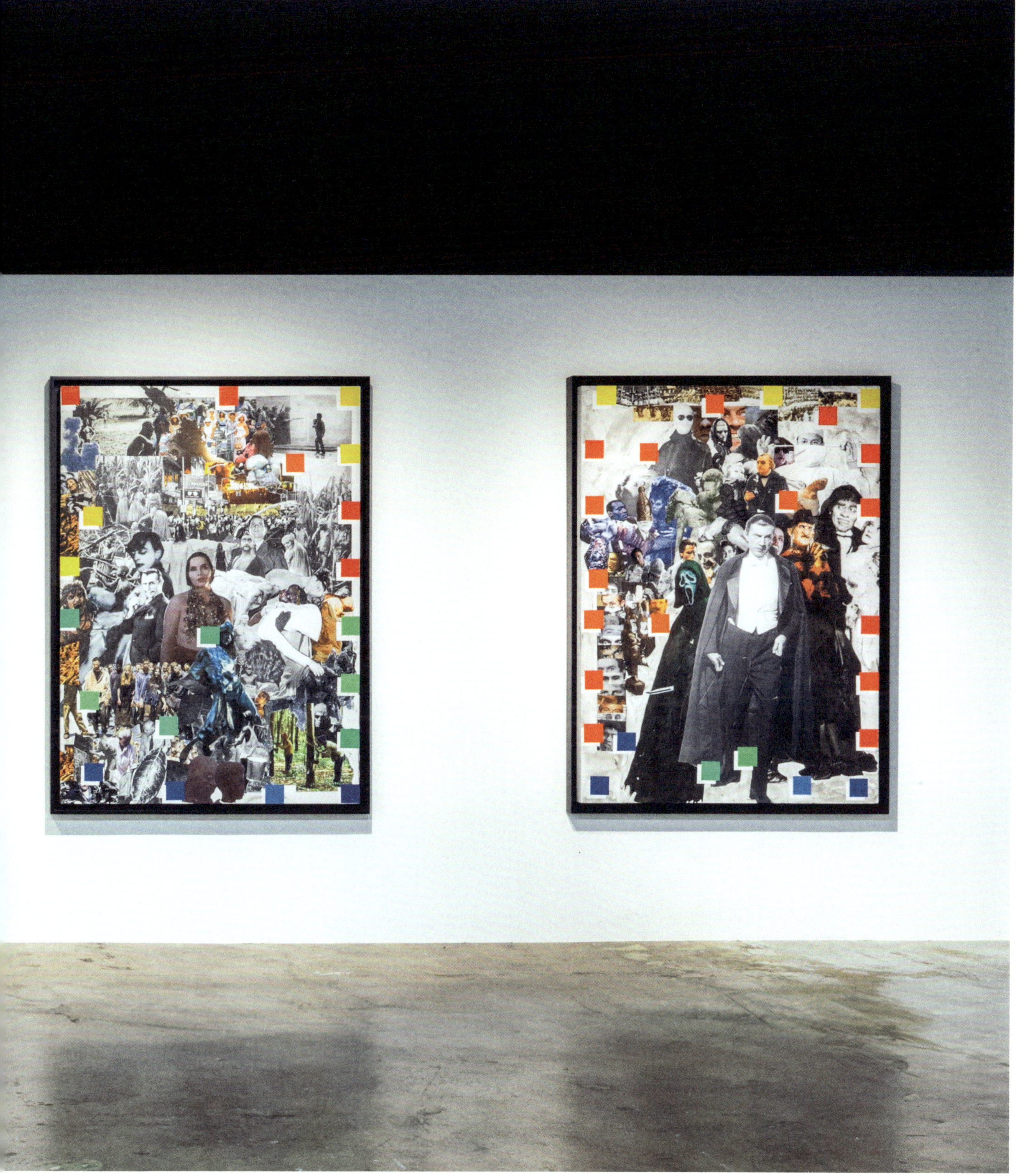

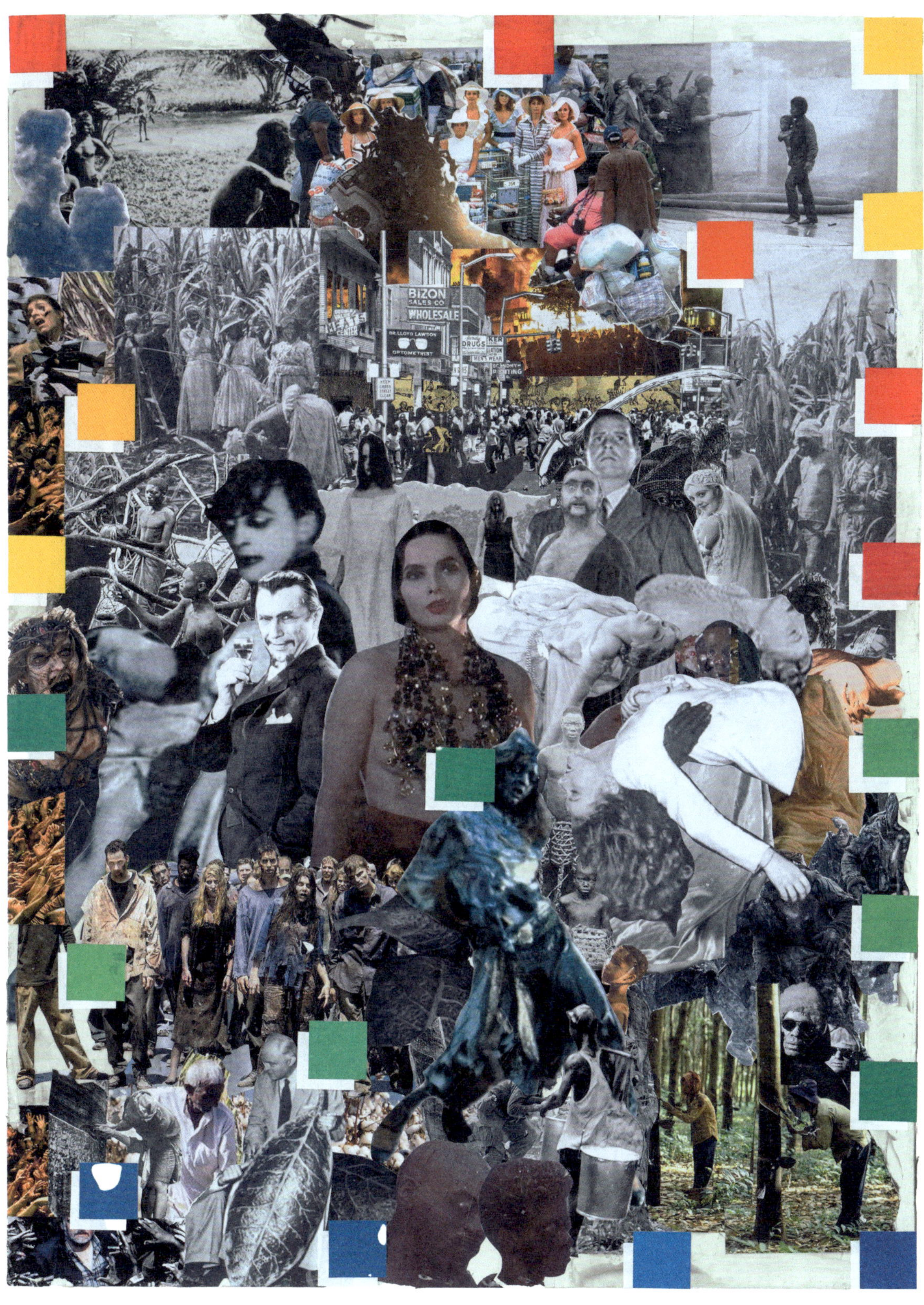

ZOMBIE: Somnambulists, Body Snatchers, Elixir Bearers, Wizards, Hypnotists, Poltergeists, Demon Masters, and Witch Covens all inhabit the shadowed realms of sugar, rubber, and cotton plantations, hidden deep within the ghettos of every outpost in the vast, dark expanse of the Imperial world. […], 2024, paper, collage, color aid, and adhesive on wood

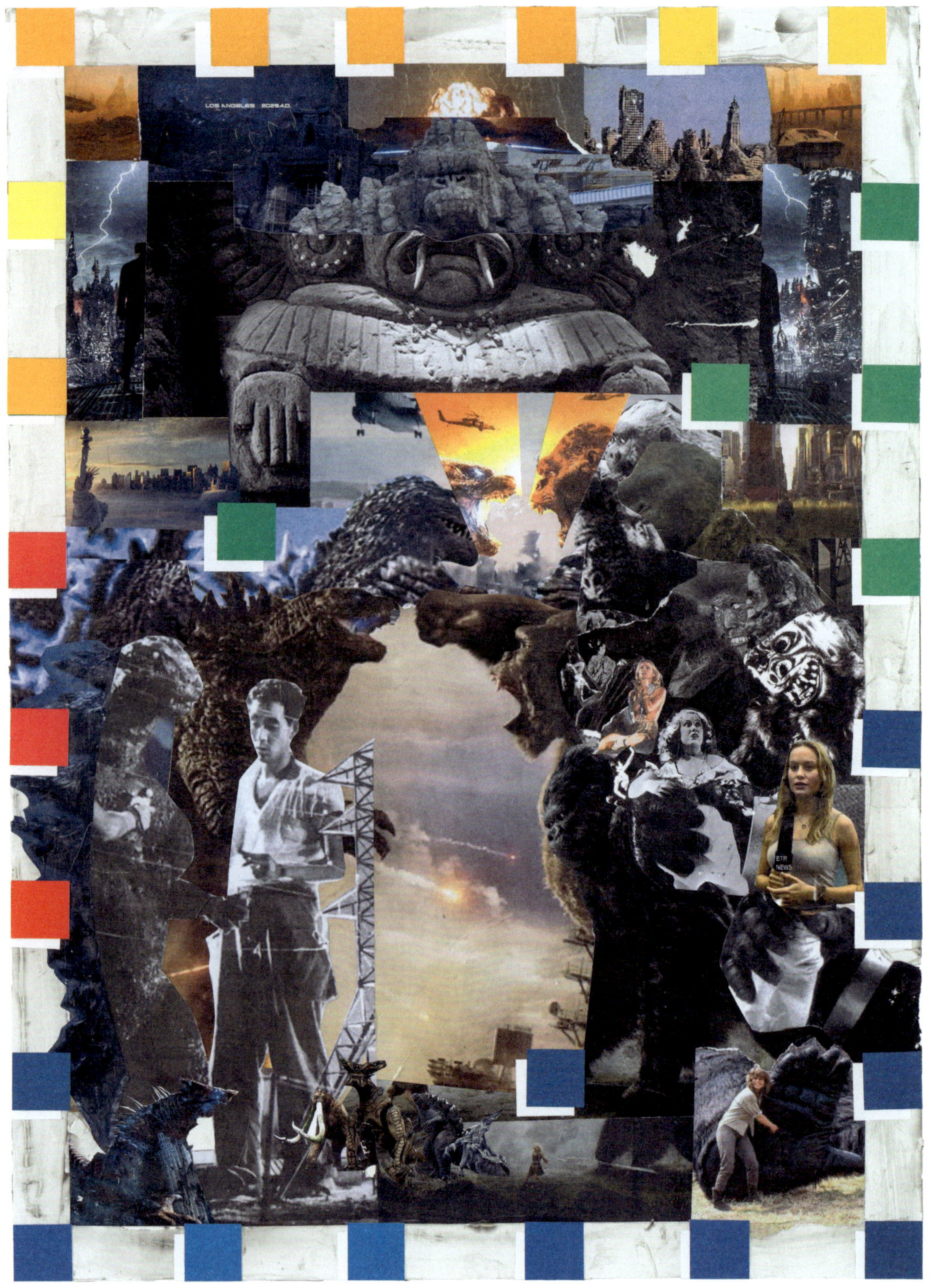

BEAST: "I am become Death, the destroyer of worlds. Oh no, it wasn't the airplanes. It was Beauty killed the Beast." "When Kong is put in chains and displayed in New York, the film evokes an unmistakable echo of the slave trade. Kong, in his brute strength and childlike emotions, is a cinematic symbol of the fear and fascination that black men elicited in white America. [...]", 2024, paper, collage, color aid, and adhesive on wood

A KANDIS WILLIAMS READER

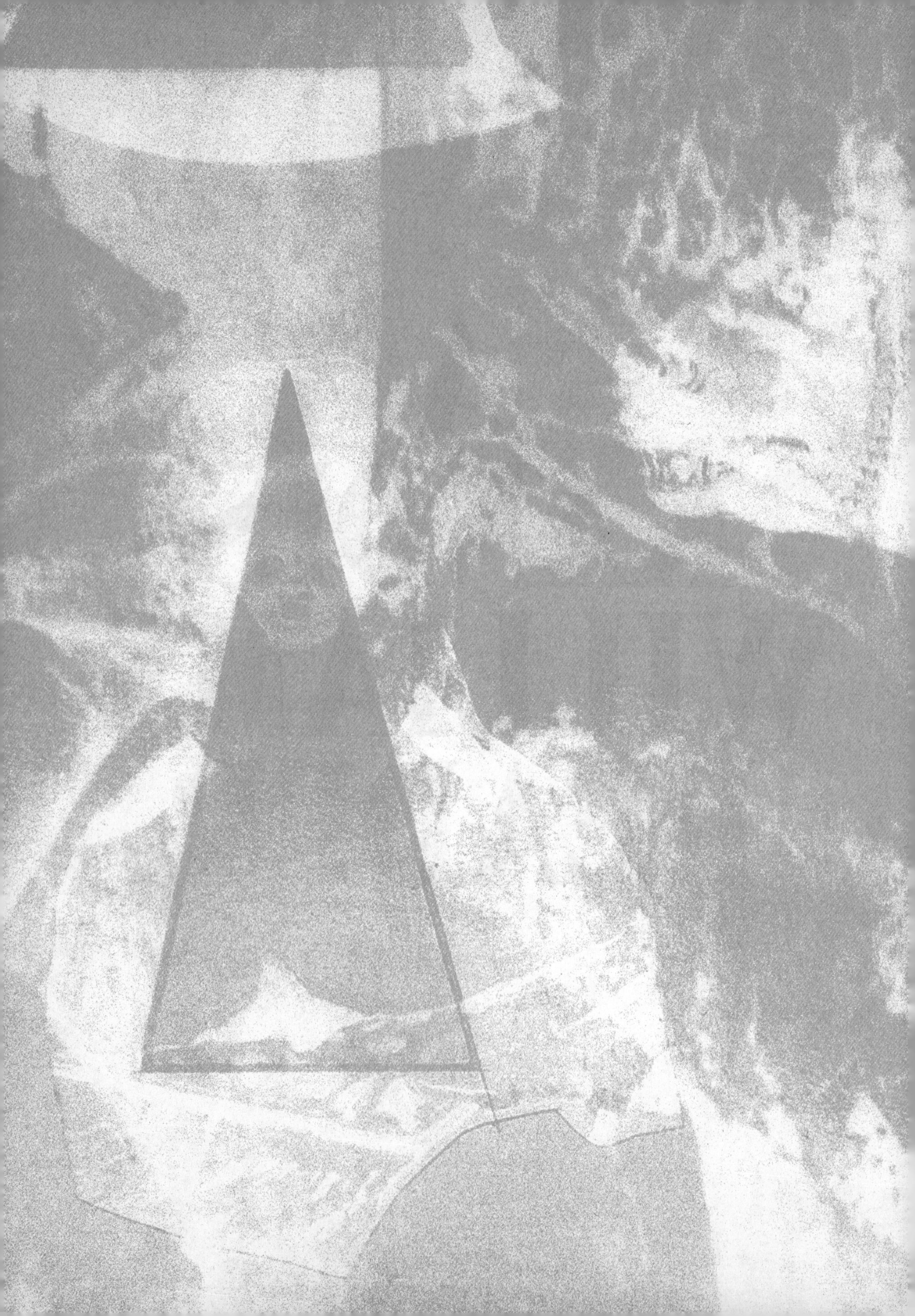

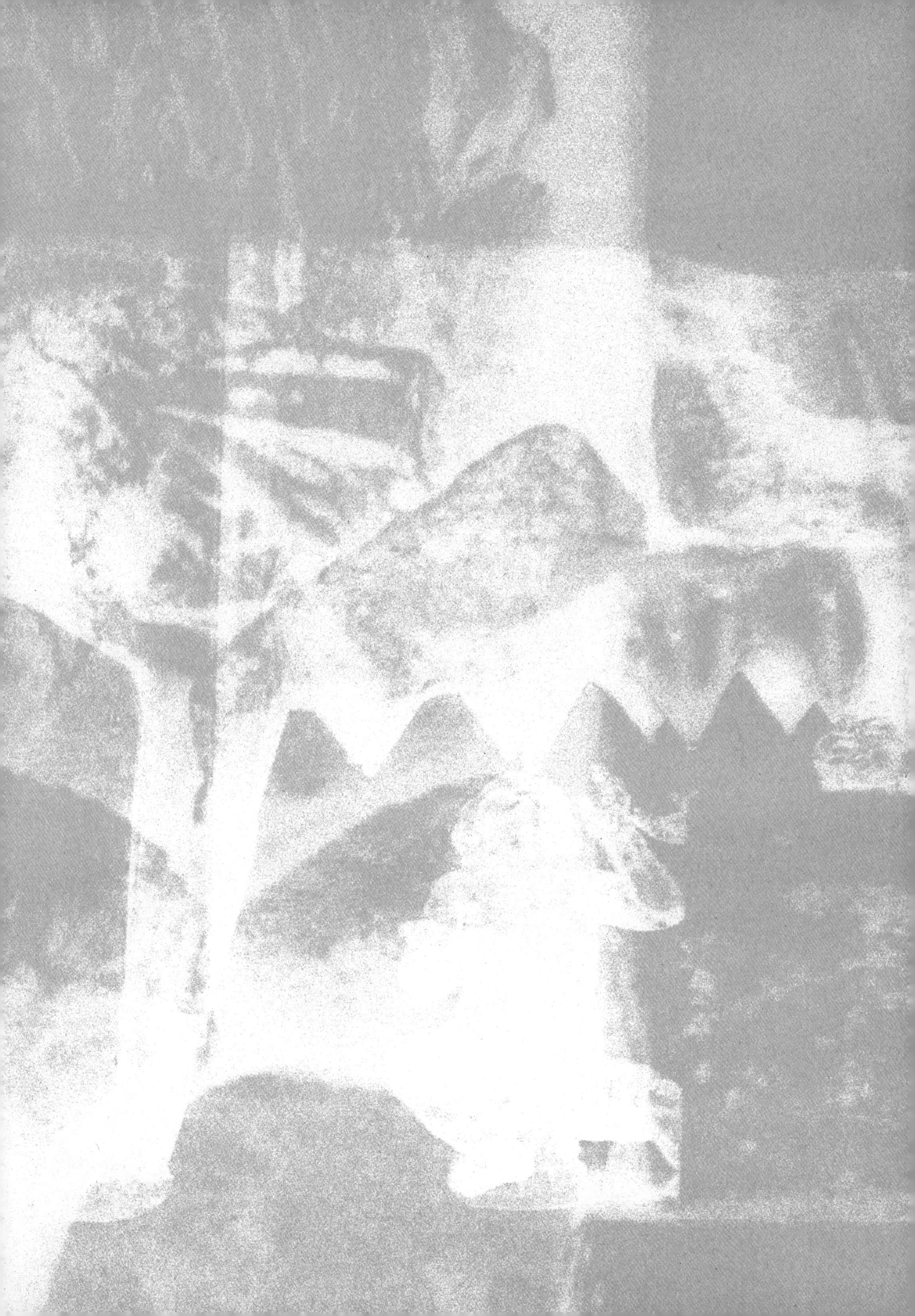

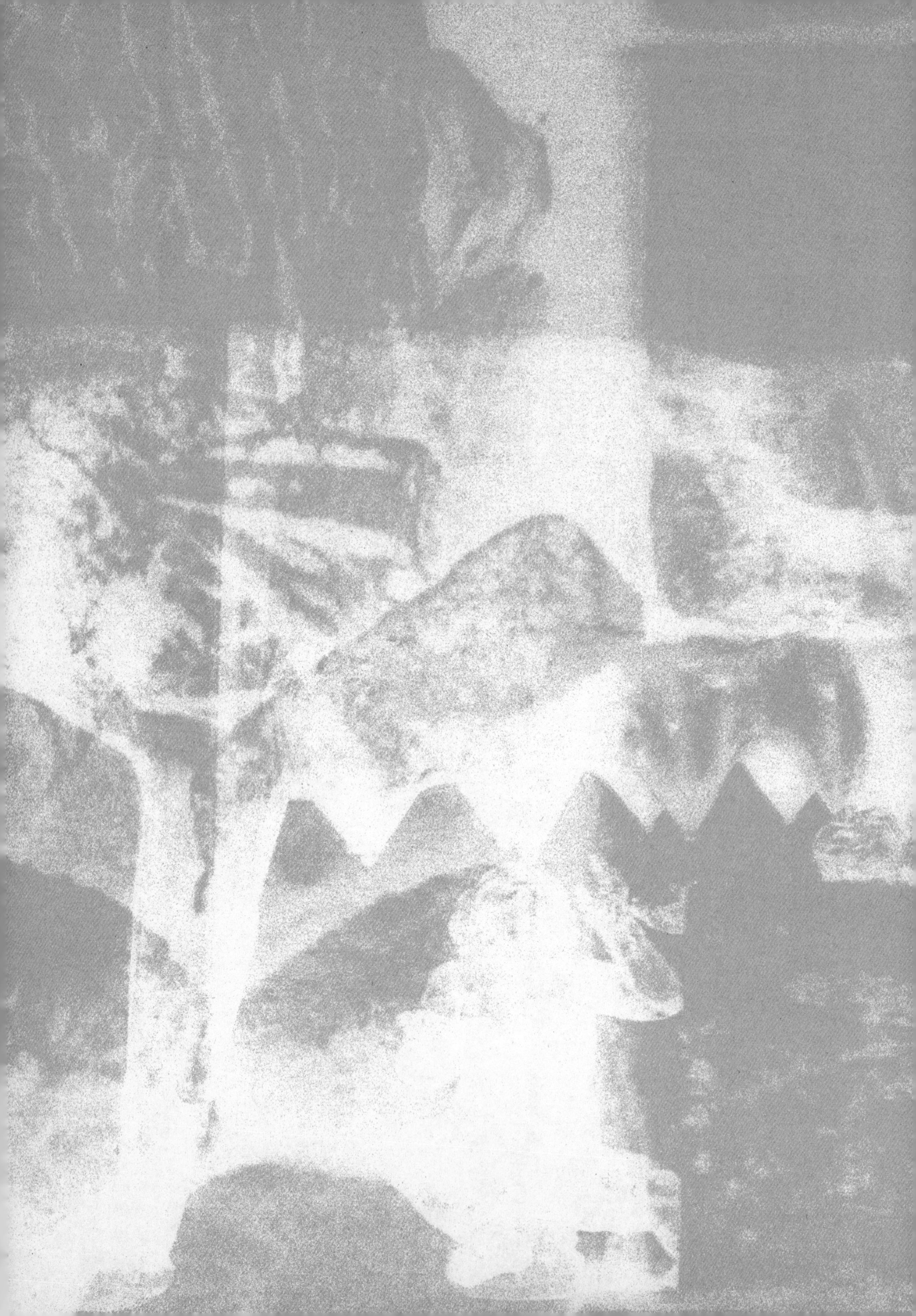

Following is a selection of four reprinted essays by scholars whose critical theories of race, gender, and power resonate deeply within Williams's practice. These essays serve as intellectual cornerstones, offering frameworks that have shaped her approach to art making as well as her wider interrogation of social and political structures, revealing the rich theoretical terrain that her work inhabits. As an artist committed to excavating the psychospiritual dimensions of Black life, Williams draws from a vast range of theoretical influences. The selected essays here collectively invite readers to consider the historical contexts, theoretical debates, and critical insights that have shaped and fueled Williams's aesthetic practice. —Taylor Jasper

CONTENTS

1 (LIFE) ÷ 0 (BLACKNESS) = ∞ − ∞ OR ∞ / ∞: ON MATTER BEYOND THE EQUATION OF VALUE

Denise Ferreira da Silva

1. A thing, affair, concern

2. That which constitutes or forms the basis of thought, speech, or action

3. In purely physical application

4. The substance, or substances collectively, of which something consists; constituent material, esp. of a particular kind. [rare]

Contrasted with form:

22. Philos.

> a) In Aristotelian and scholastic philosophy: that component of a thing which has bare existence but requires an essential determinant (form) to make it a thing of a determinate kind.
>
> b) In scholastic philosophy: the result of the first act of creation, i.e., substance without form. Obs
>
> c) In Kantian philosophy: the element in knowledge supplied by or derived from sensation, as distinct from that which is contributed a priori by the mind (the forms of intuition and the categories of the understanding).[1]

What if blackness referred to rare and obsolete definitions of *matter*: respectively, "substance . . . of which something consists" and "substance without form"? How would this affect the question of value? What would become of the economic value of *things* if they were read as expressions of our modern grammar and its defining logic of obliteration? Would this expose how the *object* (of exchange, appreciation, and knowledge)—that is, the economic, the artistic, and the scientific thing—cannot be imagined without presupposing an ethical (self-determining) thing, which is its very condition of existence and the determination of value in general?[2] Black Lives Matter, as both a

This essay first appeared in *e-flux journal*, no. 79 (February 2017).

Notes have been edited to conform to the present publication's style.

1—"Thing," n., *OED Online*, Oxford University Press.

2—A reminder to the speculative realists: wishing the subject out of existence by holding on to an independent object without attending to how one informs the other is not enough for announcing a whole new philosophical age. For an extended engagement with speculative realism, see Denise Ferreira da Silva, *Notes toward the End of Time* (London: Living Commons, 2017).

movement and a call to respond to everyday events of racial violence (the killing of unarmed black persons by police) that rehearse the ethical syntax that works through/as the liberal democratic state,[3] signals a political subject emerging in the scene of obliteration through a sentence without a (self-determined) subject.

What I do in this text is activate blackness's disruptive force, that is, its capacity to tear the veil of transparency (even if briefly) and disclose what lies at the limits of justice. With a thought experiment that I call the Equation of Value, designed to help the imagination break away from the enclosures of modern thought, this speculative exercise reaches for The Thing,[4] which is the referent of blackness, or that which in it is exposed as the excess that justifies otherwise untenable racial violence.[5]

When taken not as a category but as a referent of another mode of existing in the world, blackness returns The Thing at the limits of modern thought. Or, put differently, when deployed as method, blackness fractures the glassy walls of *universality* understood as *formal determination.* The violence inherent in the illusion of that value is both an effect and an actualization of self-determination, or autonomy. My itinerary is simple. It begins with considerations of the role of *determinacy*—formal determination articulated as a kind of efficient causation—in modern thought, and closes with a proof of the Equation of Value, intended to release that which in blackness has the capacity to disclose another horizon of existence, with its attendant accounts of existence.

"WITHOUT PROPERTIES"

In her 2014 installation *In Pursuit of Bling*, Otobong Nkanga worked with mica and other minerals that glitter-image colonial violence, thereby making it impossible not to *see* the hole in the Green Hill (the site of a German mining operation in Namibia)—especially when

3—Take, for instance, the increase in the number of homicides in Chicago last year [2016], which has been attributed to, among other things, the unwillingness of police officers to work in the city's black and brown neighborhoods. (See https://www.chicagotribune.com/2017/01/01/how-to-stop-guns-gangs-and-poverty-chicago-seeks-solutions-after-violent-2016/.) But, of course, the city's police officials are very quick to blame anti-police brutality mobilizations. (See https://www.chicagotribune.com/news/local/breaking/ct-two-shot-to-death-in-uptown-marks-first-homicide-of-2017-20170101-story.html.)

4—With this move to claim The Thing—which here refers to Hegel's formulation of it, as will be clear later in this text—I am proposing a radically immanent "metaphysical" point of departure inspired by the failures of quantum physics, which expose the fundamental indeterminacy of the reality beyond space-time, at the quantum level, that is the plenum. For elaboration of this argument, see Denise Ferreira da Silva, "Toward a Black Feminist Poethics: The Quest(ion) of Blackness toward the End of the World," *Black Scholar* 44, no. 2 (2014).

5—For an analysis of police brutality as the mode of deployment of racial violence characteristic of the liberal modern state, see Denise Ferreira da Silva, "No-bodies: Law, Raciality and Violence," *Griffith Law Review* 18, no. 2 (2009): 212–236.

I think about the minerals used in everything around me regardless of where they come from, precisely because they come from another "place of obscurity."[6] Listening to the artist's comments on these minerals, I wonder about the many ways in which her intention activates blackness's creative capacity, which at first manifests as a disruptive force. I find this in her distinction between what she terms "space of shine" and "places of obscurity," which comes through in images, artifacts, and movements—exhibitions and performances—and which exposes obvious but frequently obscured linkages between spaces of plenty and places of scarcity. Much like blacklight, Nkanga's intention seeps through *In Pursuit of Bling*, illuminating that which must remain obscure for the fantasy of freedom and equality to remain intact.[7]

In Pursuit of Bling, however, inhabits an artistic scene still framed by what the postcolonial literature scholar and critic David Lloyd calls "Western aesthetic culture," which not only produces the "disposition of the subject," as figured in Kant's disinterested "subject of judgement" or "the Subject without properties," but also provides the very condition of possibility for the notion of a "common or public" domain that holds the Kantian rendering of humanity as an ethical entity.[8] When describing *In Pursuit of Bling*, Nkanga notes that its chapters do several things, including to "look at the notion of power" (by which she means colonial and imperial power as well as capitalism) "through the notion of shine." Reading the work with her intention, I find that it does more than comment on power. For *In Pursuit of Bling*, like other works in her portfolio,[9] performs both as an item in the anticolonial arsenal and a site of confrontation; that is, it works for the exposure of how colonial violence remains active in the global present. In doing so, it punctures the presumed transparency of the subject of aesthetic culture, whose whole ethical framework rests on a formulation of universality held by our modern formalized syntax. For the most part, what I do here is try to emulate Nkanga's artistic intervention into Western aesthetic culture with an analytic formal artifact—that is, the proof of the Equation of Value—which might implode the basis of the ethical grammar that cannot but provide a negative answer for the never-asked question for which Black Lives Matter demands a different answer.

Hence, I do not engage with what Sylvia Wynter claims to be the core of racial subjugation, namely, the hierarchical division of the human

6—"Crumbling through Powdery Air," a lecture by Otobong Nkanga, Städelschule, Frankfurt, July 14, 2015. (Recording provided to the author by Clare Molloy.)

7—See Denise Ferreira da Silva, "Blacklight," in *Otobong Nkanga: Luster and Lucre*, ed. Clare Molloy, Philippe Pirotte, and Fabian Schöneich (Berlin: Sternberg Press, 2017).

8—David Lloyd, "Race under Representation," *Oxford Literary Review* 13, no. 1 (1991): 62–94; 64.

9—Such as, for instance, the exhibitions *Crumbling through Powdery Air*, Portikus, Frankfurt, September 2015; and *Comot Your Eyes Make I Borrow You Mine*, Kadist, Paris, June 2015.

between rational/irrational, or "selected/dysselected."[10] My critical move here is not about ideological unveiling (as in exposing how European Man "overrepresents" the human, thus disavowing all other modes of being human); nor does it attempt to delineate an outside space from which to expose that "other" side of the "color line" dividing white/European (human) from nonwhite/non-European (nonhuman). For I am not interested in a transcultural (transcendental or physiological or symbolic) human attribute that would be both the condition of possibility for what is activated in Western European being and all other modes of being, and that which has already been mapped by anthropology, cognitive science, or neurology. My attention to Nkanga's intention immediately takes me away from the usual analytical path. It takes me further in/down/through but beyond the observed divisions, beyond what the artist has already offered in the minerals which in her work expose the links between "places of shine"/"spaces of obscurity," after and against that which gives meaning to the "/" that signals it. More particularly, I am interested in the ethical indifference with which racial violence is met—an indifference signaled by how the obvious question is never (to be) asked because everyone presumes to know why it can only have a negative answer. For this reason, I move to expose how determinacy, which along with *separability* and *sequentiality* constitutes *the* triad sustaining modern thought, operates in the ethical syntax in which this indifference makes sense as a (common and public) moral stance.[11]

When considering the "Subject without properties" it is always helpful to recall its genealogy, in particular how it emerged in efforts to answer another question that very few thinkers explicitly formulated: How to describe the world in such a way as to make it possible to establish that the human mind can know the truth of things in it without the need for divine revelation? This genealogy usually opens with Francis Bacon and René Descartes as crucial players in assembling tools and scientific programs intended to ensure just that. What interests me in their attempts is the account of causality they compile through a selective appropriation of Aristotle's famous four causes, namely, material, formal, final, and efficient.[12]

Bacon and Descartes emphasize *efficient causality*—that is, the idea of cause and effect—in modern knowledge. Though each grabs on to efficient causality for different reasons—or, to put it better, in the effort to address different issues—both do so in the preambles to knowledge

10—Sylvia Wynter, "Unsettling the Coloniality of Being/Power/Truth/Freedom: Toward the Human, after Man, Its Overrepresentation—An Argument," *CR: The New Centennial Review* 3, no. 3 (2003): 257–337.

11—For an account of these pillars, see Denise Ferreira da Silva, "On Difference without Separability," in *Incerteza Viva: 32nd Bienal de São Paulo*, ed. Jochen Volz and Júlia Rebouças, exh. cat. (São Paulo: Fundação Bienal de São Paulo, 2016), 57–65.

12—For descriptions of the four causes, see Aristotle, *Metaphysics* (London: Penguin, 1998).

programs devised to break through the mold of medieval scholasticism held together by authority, syllogism, and an image of the world governed by Aristotle's final and formal causes. Like his contemporaries, Bacon postulated that scientific knowledge should deal with what was known as "secondary causes," through which the divine author performs his work in/as nature. In the *New Organon* (1620), Bacon, advancing an ambitious knowledge program intended to replace Aristotelian orthodoxy, claims that material and efficient causes are all that matter for understanding the book of "God's Work," i.e., for understanding nature. Drawing from pre-Socratic philosophers such as Democritus, Bacon describes the elements constituting the world as "corpuscles" (atoms), which carry in themselves the force—or what he calls "form"—imprinted on them by the divine author. Nevertheless, while celebrated for introducing the inductive and experimental methods into Western science, Bacon does not occupy the same position as Descartes, precisely because, in addition to providing an acceptable ground for the claim that the human mind alone can decipher the book of nature, Descartes successfully demonstrated that the mind itself was such a ground when he established its existence and essence as the *formal* (thinking) thing, or *res cogito*.

Not surprisingly, *formalization* is the most evident contribution Descartes made to modern knowledge. For Descartes locates efficient causality in the very movement of thought that establishes *I think, therefore I am* as the ultimate ground for ontological and epistemological statements.[13] He was not the first or the only one to make a case for replacing syllogistic logic with mathematical necessity; Galileo had done the same. Nevertheless, *effectivity*, or efficient causality, was central to his claim that the mind has direct access to truth because it is supported by how adequately its workings are captured by mathematical tools and reasoning. Effectivity also governs Descartes's investigations of nature. For instance, in "The Treatise on Light," Descartes, like Bacon and other philosophers of that era, privileges the investigation of nature from the point of view of the examination of what Galileo called "local motion," that is, the spatial dislocation of bodies:

> Someone else may if he wishes imagine the "form" of fire, the "quality" of heat, and the "action" of burning to be very different things in the wood. For my own part, I am afraid of going astray if I suppose there to be in the wood anything more than what I see must necessarily be there, so I am satisfied to confine myself to conceiving the motion of its parts. For you can posit "fire" and "heat" in the wood and make it burn as much as you please: but if you do not suppose in addition that some of its parts move or

13—This is accomplished through Descartes's famous thought experiment, his systematic doubt. See René Descartes, *Meditation on the First Philosophy: Philosophical Essays and Correspondence* (Indianapolis: Hackett Publishing, 2000), 97–141. How it does so is evident in the account of his method provided in "Rules for the Direction of the Mind," in Descartes, *Meditation on the First Philosophy*, 2–28.

are detached from their neighbors then I cannot imagine that it would undergo any alteration or change.[14]

In sum, the emergence of modern science can be described as a shift from a concern with forms of nature, which prevailed in scholastic thought, to an inquiry into the efficient causes of changes in the things of nature. For Descartes, as for Galileo and later for Newton, change (as motion in space and alteration) results from the operation of efficient causes, the effects of which can be mapped mathematically. Resting on the two onto-epistemological components of effectivity and necessity, the "Subject without properties" (i.e., the Cartesian cogito) began a trajectory that would extend beyond the confines of knowledge to become the ruler of modern economic, juridical, ethical, and aesthetic scenes.

THE ETHICAL SCENE OF VALUE

Negroes are enslaved by Europeans and sold to America. Bad as this may be, their lot in their own lands is even worse, since there a slavery quite as absolute exists; for it is the essential principle of slavery, that man has not yet attained a consciousness of his freedom, and consequently sinks down to a mere Thing—an object of no value.[15]

The call for Black Lives (to) Matter hides the question it answers: Why don't black lives matter? More precisely, it exposes how this question already contains the Kantian program and its equation of the universal and the formal—through articulating determinacy as efficient causation, or effectivity—which guides modern ethical, economic, and juridical formations. For, as a tool of modern knowledge, the category of blackness figures the operation of efficient and formal causes (that is, anatomic forms and organic processes) in the production of a racial subject destined to obliteration. Efficient and formal causes are conjoined in Kant's account of knowledge and the figuring of reality, which is putatively a philosophical presentation of Newton's natural philosophy. In it, the world becomes an effect, that is, the result of determination—of judgements or decisions reached by the pure intuitions and the categories of the understanding, that is, the tools available to the mind to access the Truth of the things of the world. This is so because, when he repeats Galileo's and Bacon's rejection of final and formal causes—in the famous statement that science is not interested in the Thing-in-itself (essence)—Kant defines the limits of knowledge as that which in things—now objects—is available to the senses (movements and alterations). Furthermore, repeating Descartes's assertion that the mind can only know with certainty that which is akin to it—that

14—René Descartes, "The Treatise on Light," in *The World and Other Writings* (Cambridge: Cambridge University Press, 2004), 6.

15—G. F. W. Hegel, *Lectures on the Philosophy of History* (Kitchener: Batoche Books, 2001), 113.

is, the abstract or the formal—Kant consolidates modern thought when he elevates the formal (as the pure or transcendental) to that moment that is before and beyond what is accessible to the senses. Only there, as Descartes had stated about a century before, is the mind comfortable dealing with the sort of objects—numbers and geometrical forms—which it can handle without reference to space-time. For only objects exhibiting such attributes can allow for the kinds of statements Kant considers proper to knowledge, that is, statements that add to what is known about something without drawing from experience. My objective in rehearsing this argument in this context is simply to highlight how, while formalization remains central to modern thought, effectivity constitutes the main descriptor of the world, as knowledge becomes interested in what happens (events, movements, and alteration). More importantly, effectivity refers both to the senses' *access* to the things of the world (being affected or moved by them) and to the mind's *capacity* to resolve the manifold into the basic tools (categories) that the understanding has available for the "higher" moments of cognition—that is, abstraction and reflection—as well as for the task of knowledge—that is, determination.

Among other things, in Kant's account of knowledge Descartes's formal thing (the cogito) not only knows itself (its existence and essence) without the aid of its body but also envelops Bacon's material and efficient causes, and takes the lead in the task of classifying and measuring nature. For instance, in his *Lectures on Logic* we find Kant employing the categories of the understanding in a description of Bacon's method for producing his tables; in this description, Kant subsumes Bacon's method into his own rendering of Descartes's "formal I" as a transcendental (a priori, pure, or formal) condition for knowledge.[16] Of course, the reference to Bacon's program is more evident in what is called Kant's "pre-critical" work. However, determination—that is, the attribution of one, and just one, predicate to a subject—remains central in his rendering of knowledge as a matter of judgement (that is, of decision), as well as in the very definition of the critical task, which privileges the exposure of grounds. In any event, as noted before, determination is crucial to Kant's notion of synthetic judgements a priori, as it is the term he uses for what Descartes called the "nexus" of consequences that the rational mind follows when attempting to establish something with certainty.[17] There is no question that determination is a task of the mind.[18]

16—Immanuel Kant, *Lectures on Logic* (Cambridge: Cambridge University Press, 1992), 82–98.

17—See, for instance, Kant's analogy for how synthetic judgements work: "x is therefore the determinable (object) that I think through the concept a, and b is its determination or the way in which it is determined. In mathematics, x is the construction of a, in experience it is the concretum, and with regard to an inherent representation or thought in general x is the function of thinking in general in the subject." Immanuel Kant, *Critique of Pure Reason* (Cambridge: Cambridge University Press, 1999), 51.

In sum, determinacy as deployed in Kant's knowledge (scientific) program remains the core of modern thought: it is presupposed in accounts of the juridical and ethical field of statements (such as the human-rights framework) which (a) presume a *universal* that operates as an a priori (formal) determining force (effectivity), and which (b) produce *objects* for which "Truth" refers to how they *relate* to something else—relationships mediated by abstract determinants (laws and rules) that can only be captured by the rational things' (including the human mind/soul) "principles of disposition."

With the consolidation of the Kantian knowledge program starting in the nineteenth century, knowing and all other activities of the mind are reduced to determinacy: namely, the assignation of *value* that refers to a universal (scale or grid), while the object of knowledge becomes a unity of formal qualities (properties, variables, etc.), that is, an effect of judgements that produce it through measurement (degree) and classification (position). Precisely this notion of effectivity lies at the core of the modern ethical program and accounts for how difference plays into it. For there too the assignation of value results not from direct comparison—the juxtaposition of two or more things—but from the operation of a universal (formal or transcendental) mediator—the universal unit of measurement or the universal basis for classification. That is, the assignation of value results from the operation of something which shares in the attributes that universal reason acquired in the late eighteenth century.

Let me briefly elaborate on this by situating blackness in the Kantian design of the modern ethical scene of value.[19] Here, as we know, the guiding ethical entity is humanity, which Kant describes as the sole existing thing possessing dignity, that is, possessing intrinsic value. Among existing things, humanity is highest in the figuring of determinacy because it alone shares in the determining powers of universal reason, since it alone has free will, or self-determination.[20] Though humanity, in Kant's formulation, already refers only to Europeans, the closing of humanity's ethical boundaries occurs in the nineteenth

18—"There is in the soul a principium of disposition as well as of affection. The appearances can have no other order and do not otherwise belong to the unity of the power of representation except insofar as they are amenable to the common principio of disposition. For all appearance with its thoroughgoing determination must still have unity in the mind, consequently be subjected to those conditions through which the unity of representations is possible. Only that which is requisite for the unity of representations belongs to the objective conditions. The unity of apprehension is necessarily connected with the unity of the intuition of space and time, for without this the latter would give no real representation. The principles of exposition must be determined on the one side through the laws of apprehension, on the other side through the unity of the power of understanding. They are the standard for observation and are not derived from perceptions, but are the ground of those in their entirety." Kant, *Critique of Pure Reason*, 53.

19—For a discussion of racial difference in regard to Kant's framing of aesthetics, see Lloyd, "Race under Representation."

20—Kant, *Critique of Pure Reason*.

century, both in Hegel's revision of the Kantian program and in the deployment by scientists of man and society of the tools of scientific reason to account for human difference. In Hegel's version, this happens in an ethical account that transforms World History into a scene of development (the self-actualization of universal reason), which culminates in the mental and social (juridical, economic, symbolic) configurations found in post-Enlightenment Europe.[21]

Both the scientific and ethical figurings of determinacy would enter into nineteenth-century scientific accounts of human difference, which produced the notions of racial and cultural difference. Both notions are manufactured in knowledge procedures that produce physical and social configurations as *effects* and *causes* of (explanations for) mental (moral and intellectual) differences. Further, these procedures deploy the European/white mind as the universal gauge, since it alone shares a key quality with universal reason (or with Hegel's "Spirit"), namely, self-determination. In this way, this earlier moment of racial knowledge yielded indexes of human difference—i.e., the naming of racial collectives such as the Negro, the Caucasian, the Oriental, and the Australian—that transformed economic differences resulting from conquest, colonization, settlement, and enslavement into presentations of (Hegel's self-actualizing) universal reason, identifying spatial and bodily configurations that, in their turn, produced the mental (intellectual and moral) forms that caused the differences in social configurations found in the European continent and its colonies.[22]

My point here is that the very arsenal designed to determine and to ascertain the truth of human difference already assumed Europeanness/whiteness as the universal measure, that is, as the bodily, mental, and societal actualization of universality. This has several consequences, the most relevant (to my argument here) being the occlusion of the latter as a term of comparison. More explicitly, economic differences resulting from hundreds of years of expropriating land and labor were attributed to racial and cultural difference. In racial knowledge, they become the effects of particular bodily arrangements, which are established as the causes for particular mental (moral and intellectual) traits, which are themselves expressed in the social configurations found across the globe. Put differently, both the anthropological and sociological versions of racial knowledge transform the consequences of hundreds of years of colonial expropriation into the effects of efficient causes (the laws of nature) as they operate through human forms (bodies and societies). In sum, as a category of racial difference, blackness *occludes* the total violence necessary

21—G. F. W. Hegel, *Hegel's Science of Logic* (Amherst: Humanity Books, 1969).

22—The argument in this and the following section is presented in Denise Ferreira da Silva, *Toward a Global Idea of Race* (Minneapolis: University of Minnesota Press, 2007).

for this expropriation, a violence that was authorized by modern juridical forms—namely, colonial domination (conquest, displacement, and settlement) and property (enslavement). Nevertheless, blackness—precisely because of how, as an object of knowledge, it occludes these juridical modalities—has the capacity to unsettle the ethical program governed by determinacy, through exposing the violence that the latter refigures.

THE EQUATION OF VALUE

To explore this potential of blackness to unsettle ethics, I will now tackle the unquestioned question reiterated by the disregard for lives lost in the streets of the US and in the Mediterranean Sea: Why don't black lives matter? To do this, I use that which grounds the modern knowledge program—mathematical reasoning—to devise a procedure that unleashes blackness to confront *life*. Using what I call the Equation of Value, I describe blackness's capacity to unravel modern thought without reproducing the violence housed in knowledge and in the scene of value. My proof of this equation is designed to sidestep the hegemony of the Kantian subject and to make it possible to expose the disruptive/creative capacity that blackness hosts/holds.

In the modern Western imagination, blackness has no value; it is nothing. As such, it marks an opposition that signals a negation, which does not refer to contradiction. For blackness refers to matter—as The Thing; it refers to that without form—it functions as a nullification of the whole signifying order that sustains value in both its economic and ethical scenes.[23]

The crux of this exercise is to provide an account of *opposition* that figures *nullification* instead of *contradiction*. This is crucial for distinguishing a radical engagement from a critical one—because the latter cannot but assume the Kantian forms when it seeks to expose their conditions of possibility.[24]

Let us first see how the figuring of opposition as contradiction would work in relation to black life. Life is the form; the positive position vis-à-vis life is figured as "1," and the negative position is figured as "-1":

i. positive life = 1
ii. negative life = -1

23—For an elaboration of this view of blackness as a Thing, see Ferreira da Silva, "Toward a Black Feminist Poethics."

24—This is the case with Hegel's and Marx's renderings of dialectics, in which negation (opposition) appears as contradiction. In both, the distinction is between opposed presentations of the same form: for instance, in Marx's account of capitalism, property (or the means of production) is the form, while the fundamental oppositional social entities are defined in terms of whether they have a positive or negative position in regards to it: respectively, having property (capitalists) or not having it (the proletariat).

If blackness occupies the place of negative life—that is, life that has negative value, that *does not matter*—then

iii. blackness = -1

Let me now figure the relationship between life (1) and blackness (-1) using basic mathematical procedures: addition, subtraction, multiplication, and division. Addition in this case becomes subtraction because of blackness's negative value:

a) 1 (life) + -1 (blackness) = 0

When simply combined with life, blackness brings about nullification (0); when added to the positive form of life, blackness *obliterates* it.

As discussed previously, value, because it is both an effect of determinacy (Kant's account of knowledge) and is equated with determinacy (Kantian and Hegelian ethical scenes), it is (a) *determinate*, resulting in relations marked by effectivity (efficient causation), that is, relations marked by power differences insofar as one element effectively acts upon another; and it is (b) *determinant* insofar as it is the *effective* element—that is, it is the form which is applied to matter (content).

To express the relation between blackness (0) and life (1) in terms of effectivity, I use multiplication (×) and division (÷):

b) 1 (life) × -1 (blackness) = -1
c) 1 (life) ÷ -1 (blackness) = -1

When blackness multiplies or divides life, it remains in its negative expression, as blackness (-1)—that is, as lack, as a symbol of an absence (of life).

My next move is to take blackness's power to annihilate life (a) and deploy it to multiply (×) life. If

iv. life = 1
v. blackness = 0

then we find that

d) 1 (life) × -1 (blackness) = -1
e) 1 (life) × 0 (blackness) = 0

The movement in both cases is unmistakably violent; it refigures dialectics. In (d), negativity (blackness) engulfs value, and in (e) it destroys it. Put differently, in (d), life without value—that is, blackness (-1)—disappears with life, and in (e), blackness as a figuring of the absence of form (blackness = 0) disappears with the form (life = 1) and releases *matter* itself (0).

Taking this a step further, it might be possible to move away from dialectics and its deployment of effectivity, which cannot but reproduce violence, by dividing life by blackness:

f) 1 (life) ÷ 0 (blackness) = ∞ − ∞ or ∞ / ∞

Instead of the sublation (d) or obliteration (e) of the form, this procedure has no result because it is impossible to divide something by zero. I have chosen ∞ − ∞ (infinity minus infinity) or ∞ / ∞ (infinity divided by infinity) to picture the result because it is undeterminable, it has no form: it is ∞ minus itself or ∞ divided by itself. It is neither life nor nonlife; it is content without form, or *materia prima*—that which has no value because it exists (as ∞) without form.

In equating blackness with ∞ and capturing the rare ("of which something consists") and the obsolete ("substance without form") meanings of matter, I claim a radical praxis of refusal to contain blackness in the dialectical form. Though Frantz Fanon's refusal of dialectics is the most celebrated, I find this refusal also in Cedric Robinson's tracing of the black radical tradition; in Hortense Spillers's figuring of the flesh as zero degree of signification; in Saidiya Hartman's refusal to rehearse racial violence as the moment of black subjectification; and in Fred Moten's descriptions of blackness in the scene of violence which refuse a simple reconciliation with the categories and premises of modern thought.[25] When blackness's oppositional power refers to matter—or, in Fanon's words, in the "night of the absolute"—it is possible to avoid the principle of contradiction and the accounts of self-determination it sustains; it is possible to avoid, that is, a return to Hegel (or Marx) via the shortcut of racial eschatology. What I hope this move against determinacy—the very notion presupposed in the question that Black Lives Matter sets out to challenge—makes possible is an appreciation of the urgency of bringing about its dissolution. For the work of blackness as a category of difference fits the Hegelian movement but has no emancipatory power because it functions as a signifier of violence which, when deployed successfully, justifies the otherwise unacceptable, such as the deaths of black persons due to state violence (in the US and in Europe) and capitalist expropriation (in Africa). That is, the category of blackness serves the ordered universe of determinacy and the violence and violations it authorizes. A guide to thinking, a method for study and unbounded sociality[26]—blackness as *matter* signals ∞, another world: namely, that which exists without time and out of space, in the plenum.

25—Frantz Fanon, *Black Skin, White Masks* (London: Pluto Press, 1986); Cedric Robinson, *Black Marxism* (London: Zed Press, 1983); Hortense Spillers, "Mama's Baby, Papa's Maybe: An American Grammar Book," *Diacritics* 17, no. 2 (1987): 65–81; Saidiya Hartman, *Scenes of Subjection* (Oxford: Oxford University Press, 1997); Fred Moten, *In the Break* (Minneapolis: University of Minnesota Press, 2003).

26—For black study, see Stefano Harney and Fred Moten, *The Undercommons* (Wivenhoe, England: Minor Compositions, 2013).

REFLECTIONS ON "WHITENESS AS PROPERTY"

Cheryl I. Harris

I. CHATTEL

Chattel (Black) is the fusion of race and property—embodied as always essential and forever disposable.

II. TIME

Hard time.

8 minutes and 46 seconds is an eternity. Centuries without a breath.

III. HOME

Home is not a haven. You can be shot eight times in your home, in your bed. Before anything. Before you can breathe.

IV. TERRA NULLIUS

A walk in the pandemic. Dappling sunlight through the leaves. A quiet street in early morning. The symphony of birds. The air as clear as the sky is blue. A bucolic scene that conjures security, tranquility, timelessness. It was always meant to be. But it is a mirage: the tableau was born in theft, and theft continues to sustain it. Through violence, the land and the people are transformed into property, into commodities, abstracted into investments, financial products, and debt instruments.[1] Protected by law, this property regime is reassured of its logic and projects a raceless façade.

V. THE WEIGHT

> *[H]istory is not the past. It is the present. We carry our history with us.... If we pretend otherwise ... we literally are criminals.*
>
> —James Baldwin, 1980[2]

This essay first appeared in *Harvard Law Review* 133, no. 9 (2020).

Notes have been edited to conform to the present publication's style.

1—Black bodies were cast as living currency around which were built valuation systems, insurance, financial products, banking institutions, and other forms of financialization central to the development of racial capitalism. See, e.g., Eric Williams, *Capitalism and Slavery* (1944) (discussing the constitutive role of new world slavery in developing industrial capitalism); Calvin Schermerhorn, *The Business of Slavery and the Rise of American Capitalism, 1815–1860* (2015), 2 ("North American capitalism developed in the context of an Atlantic system of exchange most recognizable perhaps in the transatlantic slave trade and the systems of indebtedness responsible for its contours"); Matthew Desmond, "In Order to Understand the Brutality of American Capitalism, You Have to Start on the Plantation," *New York Times Magazine*, August 14, 2019, https://www.nytimes.com/interactive/2019/08/14/magazine/slavery-capitalism.html (noting that "[t]o raise capital, state-chartered banks pooled debt generated by slave mortgages and repackaged it as bonds promising investors annual interest....—bonds ... [that found] buyers in Hamburg and Amsterdam, in Boston and Philadelphia").

2—James Baldwin, "Black English: A Dishonest Argument," in *The Cross of Redemption: Uncollected Writings* (2011), 154.

But it is not so: the racelessness of the façade is a myth. We know this because the incommensurable weight of the unreckoning is pressing down. The heft of history is too heavy to toss aside, to float away.

VI. PREEXISTING CONDITIONS

A rupture—a break in the façade—is erupting from intersecting pandemics, each reflecting intersecting systems of domination and extraction.[3] Power organizes hierarchies. Inequality is not the product of dysfunctional culture, or the biology—the "comorbidities"—of misbehaving, undisciplined bodies: rather, racial regimes construct and exploit vulnerabilities.[4] These are preexisting conditions, embodiments, material manifestations of exploitation. This is a feature of racial capitalism.[5]

VII. HERE AND THERE

The pandemic is global and universalizing. The pandemic is locally targeted and differentiated. Dissolving the notion of secure borders and the boundaries of property, the virus demonstrates the capacity to disrupt key presumptions, that threat can be reliably marked through phenotype and emanates only from specific racialized bodies. Like state-sanctioned racial terror, danger is free floating, ubiquitous, and hidden: it is at once anywhere and nowhere.

VIII. MAPS

Yet, systems of racial/spatial ordering persistently track the prevalence and lethality of the pandemic.[6] Zip codes do more than encode maps; they tell stories.[7] Black geographies,[8] Latinx spaces, "ghettos,"

3—Professor Kimberlé Crenshaw defines intersectionality as "an analytic sensibility, a way of thinking about identity and its relationship to power. Originally articulated on behalf of Black women, the term brought to light the invisibility of many constituents within groups that claim them as members but often fail to represent them." Kimberlé Crenshaw, "Why Intersectionality Can't Wait," *Washington Post*, September 24, 2015, https://www.washingtonpost.com/news/in-theory/wp/2015/09/24/why-intersectionality-cant-wait. Intersectionality critiqued the erasure of Black women's experience in antidiscrimination law and antiracist racist and feminist politics as exemplary of deficiencies of the traditional antidiscrimination paradigm:

> Underlying this conception of discrimination is a view that the wrong which antidiscrimination law addresses is the use of race or gender factors to interfere with decisions that would otherwise be fair or neutral. This process-based definition is not grounded in a bottom-up commitment to improve the substantive conditions for those who are victimized by the interplay of numerous factors. Instead, the dominant message of antidiscrimination law is that it will regulate only the limited extent to which race or sex interferes with the process of determining outcomes. This narrow objective is facilitated by the top-down strategy of using a singular "but for" analysis to ascertain the effects of race or sex.

Kimberlé Crenshaw, "Demarginalizing the Intersection of Race and Sex: A Black Feminist Critique of Antidiscrimination Doctrine, Feminist Theory and Antiracist Politics," *University of Chicago Legal Forum* 1989, no. 1, article 8 (1989): 139, 151 (using an intersectional analysis to assess how Black women are marginalized, not in service of marking particularity for its own sake, but to unmask how systems of power interact and operate to produce subordination).

4—Professor Ruth Wilson Gilmore defines racism as "the state-sanctioned and/or extralegal production and exploitation of group-differentiated vulnerability to premature death." Ruth Wilson Gilmore, *Golden Gulag: Prisons, Surplus, Crisis, and Opposition in Globalizing California* (2007), 247.

"barrios"—all places where "others" live—are structurally deprived of the means or opportunity to protect, to provide shelter (in place), their occupants always in fraught relation to place, to property, to rights. The places are erased, renamed, redeveloped, improved. Sometimes there are traces.[9]

5—Professor Cedric Robinson's seminal work *Black Marxism* considers "the encounter of Marxism and Black radicalism" to more carefully analyze the relationship between race and capitalism:

> The development, organization, and expansion of capitalist society pursued essentially racial directions, so too did social ideology. As a material force, then, it could be expected that racialism would inevitably permeate the social structures emergent from capitalism. I have used the term "racial capitalism" to refer to this development and to the subsequent structure as a historical agency.

Cedric J. Robinson, *Black Marxism* (2nd ed., 2000), 2.

6—See Andrea N. Polonijo, "How California's COVID-19 Surge Widens Health Inequalities for Black, Latino and Low-Income Residents," *The Conversation*, July 30, 2020, https://theconversation.com/as-covid-19-surges-in-california-black-latino-and-low-income-residents-face-higher-death-rates-why-health-inequality-is-widening-143243.

7—See Office of Inspector General, United States Postal Service, "The Untold Story of the ZIP Code" (2013), i, https://www.uspsoig.gov/sites/default/files/reports/2023-01/rarc-wp-13-006_0.pdf ("The code was originally intended to allow mail sorting methods to be automated but ended up creating unimagined socio-economic benefits as an organizing and enabling device. The ZIP Code became a social tool for organizing and displaying demographic information, a support structure for entire industries such as insurance and real estate, and even a representation of social identities").

8—Professor Katherine McKittrick describes Black geographies as follows: "These black geographies, while certainly not solely inhabited by black bodies, are classified as imperiled and dangerous, or spaces 'without'/spaces of exclusion, even as those who have *always* struggled against racial violence and containment populate them." Katherine McKittrick, "On Plantations, Prisons and a Black Sense of Place," *Social and Cultural Geography* 12, no. 8 (2011): 947, 951 (citations omitted).

9—See, e.g., Abby Phillip, "A Permanent Reminder of Wall Street's Hidden Slave Trading Past Is Coming Soon," *Washington Post*, April 15, 2015, https://www.washingtonpost.com/news/morning-mix/wp/2015/04/15/a-permanent-reminder-of-wall-streets-hidden-slave-trading-past-is-coming-soon. The African Burial Ground was unearthed when construction commenced in 1991 on a new federal office building. See National Park Service, African Burial Ground, "History and Culture," https://www.nps.gov/afbg/learn/historyculture/index.htm. As a predicate to building, federal law requires an archeological site review. In this case:

> Preliminary archaeological research excavation found intact human skeletal remains located 30 feet below the city's street level on Broadway. During survey work, the largest and most important archeological discovery was made: unearthing the "Negroes Burial Ground"—a six-acre burial ground containing upwards of 15,000 intact skeletal remains of enslaved and free Africans who lived and worked in colonial New York. The Burial Ground's rediscovery altered the understanding and scholarship surrounding enslavement and its contribution to constructing New York City. The Burial Ground dates from the middle 1630s to 1795. Currently, the Burial Ground is the nation's earliest and largest African burial ground rediscovered in the United States. ("History and Culture.")

More recently, the commemoration of the 1921 Tulsa Race Massacre highlighted the history of the Greenwood district, also called "Black Wall Street." See generally Tulsa Historical Society and Museum, *1921 Tulsa Race Massacre*, https://www.tulsahistory.org/exhibit/1921-tulsa-race-massacre. Following the arrest of a young Black man who had been on an elevator with a white woman, despite the absence of any evidence of wrongdoing, the media and rumor mill inflamed local white mobs, who then threatened to take him from official custody.

IX. MOURNING FOR WHITENESS

One of William Faulkner's most famous and controversial novels, *The Sound and the Fury*, took its title from Shakespeare's *Macbeth*.[10] Macbeth's soliloquy is a bitter lament, characterizing life as "but a walking shadow, a poor player/That struts and frets his hour upon the stage/ And then is heard no more: it is a tale/Told by an idiot, full of sound and fury,/Signifying nothing."[11] Faulkner's novel, told through the voices of multiple characters, relates the dissolution and unraveling of the Southern aristocratic Compson family over a period of thirty years at the early part of the twentieth century. The story recounts their loss of material privilege, family, integrity, sanity. But it is more: As the incomparable Toni Morrison also teaches, it is a tale about race, the declining value of whiteness, and the crisis that attends its diminution.[12] Morrison's essay, entitled "Mourning for Whiteness," written in the wake of Trump's election in 2016, describes the contemporary manifestation of Faulkner's tale in Trumptime.[13] She notes that while Black enslavement buttressed the meaning and value of whiteness, "in America today, post-civil-rights legislation, white people's conviction of their natural superiority is being lost. Rapidly lost. There are 'people of color' everywhere, threatening to erase this long-understood definition of America.... The threat is frightening."[14]

She continues:

> In order to limit the possibility of this untenable change and restore whiteness to its former status as a marker of national identity, a number of white Americans are sacrificing themselves.... So scary are the consequences of a collapse of white privilege that many Americans have flocked to a political platform that

Armed Black citizens surrounded the courthouse and temporarily thwarted the attack, retreating back to the Greenwood district when they came under fire. In the early hours of June 1, 1921, white mobs descended on Greenwood. Not only did the authorities not assist the residents; but they also deputized and armed a corps of all white men, many of whom were earlier part of the mob, to "restore order." Along with the state National Guard, these men violently removed and arrested Greenwood's Black residents, effectively leaving the area open to plunder and arson. Estimates are that between 150 and 300 Black men, women and children were killed by private and state-sanctioned violence. Nearly all the structures in the area were destroyed. No one was prosecuted for these crimes. For a definitive and powerful treatment of this history, see Alfred L. Brophy, *Reconstructing the Dreamland: The Tulsa Riot of 1921—Race, Reparations, and Reconciliation* (2002).

10—See William Shakespeare, *Macbeth*, act 5, scene 5, lines 2381–2385.

11—Shakespeare, *Macbeth*.

12—See Toni Morrison, "Mourning for Whiteness, Aftermath: Sixteen Writers on Trump's America," *New Yorker*, November 21, 2016, https://www.newyorker.com/magazine/2016/11/21/aftermath-sixteen-writers-on-trumps-america#anchor-morrison.

13—See Morrison, "Mourning for Whiteness."

14—Morrison.

> supports and translates violence against the defenseless as strength. These people are not so much angry as terrified, with the kind of terror that makes knees tremble.[15]

Morrison invokes another Faulkner novel, *Absalom, Absalom!*,[16] to illustrate the visceral nature of this fear and the racial terrorism it produces. In the novel, Quentin, a member of the Compson clan (who commits suicide in *The Sound and the Fury*), retells a story told to him of a fallen Southern white patriarch. The tragedy unfolds when the patriarch's son, Charles, learns that the person seeking to marry his sister is their long-lost half-brother. While troubled by this circumstance, Charles, the brother, reluctantly comes to accept the relationship, notwithstanding its incestuous character. However, when Charles later learns that the brother-fiancé is part Black, Charles kills him to prevent the marriage of his Black half-brother to their white sister. For Morrison, this story at the heart of the novel reflects the terror that accompanies the loss of whiteness. And, so she argues:

> William Faulkner understood this [terror] better than almost any other American writer. In Absalom, Absalom, incest is less of a taboo for an upper-class Southern family than acknowledging the one drop of black blood that would clearly soil the family line. Rather than lose its "whiteness" (once again), the family chooses murder.[17]

Morrison thus marks the 2016 election as reflective of a moment of white panic, a break, a breakdown, at once political, affective, and institutional. The outcome of the 2016 election is not history but a present anxiety—a reminder that indices of public disapproval do not portend transformation. How should one reckon with the fact that the misdeeds, malfeasance, and racist distemper of the Trump administration are well known, but, for a significant percentage of the (white) population, have not proved disqualifying?[18]

X. STARVATION WAGES

Whiteness does not confer immunity from disaster on all white bodies, however. Poor and working-class whites suffer greatly in all areas;

15—Morrison.

16—William Faulkner, *Absalom, Absalom!* (1934).

17—Morrison, "Mourning for Whiteness."

18—Recent polling data shows a clear majority of voters disapproving of Trump's presidency; see "Trump Job Approval," Gallup, https://news.gallup.com/poll/203207/trump-job-approval-weekly.aspx (showing 56 percent disapproval in tracking averages on July 23, 2020), and despite criticisms of his handling of the COVID-19 pandemic, he still is ahead of or tied with his presumptive opponent, former vice president Joe Biden, in several key states and appears to have a firm hold on approximately 40 percent of voters. See "General Election: Trump vs. Biden," Real Clear Polling, https://www.realclearpolitics.com/epolls/2020/president/us/general_election_trump_vs_biden-6247.html.

the gap between them and wealthier whites is profound, and, by all metrics, growing.[19] "White," "poor," and "sick" are words that can and do converge. Yet, whiteness mitigates risk through racial/spatial structures that sort probabilities and distribute access and opportunity. Thus, while Trump's exhumation of the promise to protect the suburbs[20] and "our way of life"[21] may seem hopelessly retrograde, the point is that the spatial allusion is readily legible as a racial geography of exclusion. Everyone knows what this means.[22] Everyone knows who is being hailed.

The relationship of the white working class to whiteness has long been debated. W. E. B. Du Bois described the consequence of racial segregation as a political and economic success, through which the often meager wages paid for white labor under capitalism are supplemented by "a public and psychological wage"[23]—the wages of whiteness. The notion of a public and psychological wage is not metaphoric

19—See, e.g., Rakesh Kochhar and Anthony Cilluffo, "Income Inequality in the U.S. Is Rising Most Rapidly among Asians," Pew Research Center, July 12, 2018, https://www.pewsocialtrends.org/2018/07/12/income-inequality-in-the-u-s-is-rising-most-rapidly-among-asians/ (discussing the rising inequality within different racial groups, including whites).

20—Annie Karni, Maggie Haberman, and Sydney Ember, "Trump Plays on Racist Fears of Terrorized Suburbs to Court White Voters," *New York Times*, July 29, 2020), https://www.nytimes.com/2020/07/29/us/politics/trump-suburbs-housing-white-voters.html.

21—President Donald J. Trump, "Remarks at the 2020 Salute to America," July 4, 2020 (transcript available at https://www.whitehouse.gov/briefings-statements/remarks-president-trump-2020-salute-america/ [https://perma.cc/3DB3-ZGRE]).

22—Sometimes, the racial meaning is clear. Justice Harlan's dissent in *Plessy v. Ferguson*, 163 U.S. 537 (1896), similarly rejected the state's argument that de jure segregation did not constitute unconstitutional discrimination under the Equal Protection Clause because it treated Blacks and whites equally through a rule of prohibition:

> It was said in argument that the statute of Louisiana does not discriminate against either race but prescribes a rule applicable alike to white and colored citizens. Everyone knows that the statute in question had its origin in the purpose, not so much to exclude white persons from railroad cars occupied by blacks, as to exclude colored people from coaches occupied by or assigned to white persons. (556 – 57, Harlan, J., dissenting)

23—As Du Bois put it:

> The political success of the doctrine of racial separation, which overthrew Reconstruction by uniting the planter and the poor white, was far exceeded by its astonishing economic results. The theory of laboring class unity rests upon the assumption that laborers will unite because of their opposition to exploitation by the capitalists. This would throw white and black labor into one class [But i]t must be remembered that the white group of laborers, while they received a low wage, were compensated in part by a sort of public and psychological wage. They were given public deference because they were white. They were admitted freely with all classes of white people to public functions, public parks, and the best schools. The police were drawn from their ranks, and the courts, dependent on their votes treated them with such leniency as to encourage lawlessness. Their vote selected public officials, and while this had small effect upon the economic situation, it had great effect on their personal treatment and the deference shown them.

W. E. Burghhardt Du Bois, *Black Reconstruction* (1935), 700–701.

or abstract. While not easily measurable in currency, white workers received a material advantage relative to the precarious conditions of Black life. In contrast to their Black counterparts, white workers enjoyed the ability to move through public space. Moreover, as Du Bois argued, white workers operated with the knowledge and expectation that the coercive apparatus of the state—police, the courts, the law—would represent and be responsive to white interests.

Although much has changed, the current iteration of racist populism is built on that belief. Despite evidence that this belief may be misguided or betrayed, the underlying institutional structures are built to reinforce it. Whiteness as property undergirds a white subjectivity that is induced to reject any sense of connection to Blackness. Instead, white subjectivity is constructed in antagonism to, and perceives itself as victim of, Blackness. As Professor Derrick Bell describes, the fact that the face at the bottom of the well is Black operates as racial reassurance for those outside the white elite.[24] Racial capitalism fosters a white coalition between elites and the majority of whites, who reside outside the charmed circle but tend to identify their race, rather than their class position, as the cause of their predicament.

The presumption had been that illuminating shared interests would create common ground across racial divides to support progressive, redistributive social policy. As the position of working-class people has eroded, particularly since the "Golden Age of Capitalism," the dire conditions have further eroded the advantages of whiteness. However, the argument for transformation has been undermined by racially encoded discourses of corruption, fraud, and undeservingness that have legitimated the hollowing out of an already partial and weak care infrastructure.[25] The neoliberal paradigm of public austerity and financialization are the presumed cure. Public goods and services are replaced by debt. The result is that some whites are dying of whiteness.[26]

XI. EXPECTATIONS

It is commonplace that the system of property in the United States is intimately tied to race. Beginning with Eric Williams' 1944 classic, *Capitalism and Slavery*,[27] generations of historians have marshaled evidence and retold the story that the foundations of modern society

24—See generally Derrick Bell, *Faces at the Bottom of the Well* (1992).

25—See generally Ian Haney López, *Dog Whistle Politics: How Coded Racial Appeals Have Reinvented Racism and Wrecked the Middle* (2014).

26—See Jonathan Metzl, *Dying of Whiteness: How the Politics of Racial Resentment Is Killing America's Heartland* (2019), 1–8 (describing how white racial resentment fueled opposition to policies such as gun control, expanded health care benefits, and state education funding that ultimately reduce life expectancy and well-being for whites).

27—See Williams, *Capitalism and Slavery.*

were built through slavery. While the framework of settler colonialism is of more recent vintage,[28] the insight that colonialism is a system of racialized domination and economic exploitation is an idea that goes back at least as far as Du Bois. Yet, these fundamental truths resist remembering.[29] The relationship between present forms of property and this history often is presented as unfortunate, but too remote in time to factor in any significant way into the present.

At one level this can be attributed to the perennial question of the contemporary relevance of historical events, but temporal remoteness may not be the only reason that the racial foundations of property remain so persistently obscure. These continuities are resisted through the assertion of expectations. Expectations and, specifically, settled expectations are inscribed and reinscribed through racial hierarchy and are recognized in law as property. Legality places the power of the state behind particular expectations and legitimates them, notwithstanding their violent racial origins. Legality has material and conceptual consequences: as signified in Jeremy Bentham's famous aphorism, expectations affirmed as property are not physical but metaphysical; a "mere conception in the mind,"[30] forming intrinsic value so that "our property becomes part of our being."[31] This intimate, affective tie is mutually constitutive of both property and "our being"—of subjectivity. And this subjectivity takes the concept of property deep into the heart of race and race deep into the heart of property.

Time and time again, the law elevates and ratifies (white) expectations with regard to property. Yet these determinations fail to liquidate the claims of the racially dispossessed.

XII. "I'LL TAKE THAT BOX OF REPARATIONS."

—Cassandra Wilson, from the song "Justice"[32]

Of necessity, asserted expectations of the dispossessed challenge and threaten to undo established expectations. Legality, reflecting

28—See Patrick Wolfe, "Settler Colonialism and the Elimination of the Native," *Journal of Genocide Research* 8, no. 4 (2006): 387, 388 (describing settler colonialism as a particular form of colonization in which settler colonizers rely on the logic of elimination in service of the construction of a new society on expropriated Indigenous land; settler colonists "come to stay" as "invasion is a structure not an event").

29—See Greg Grandin, "Capitalism and Slavery," *The Nation*, May 1, 2015, https://www.thenation.com/article/archive/capitalism-and-slavery/ (describing ever recurrent scholarly focus on the relationship between capitalism and slavery).

30—Jeremy Bentham, *Theory of Legislation*, trans. R. Hildreth (2nd ed., 1871), 112.

31—Bentham, *Theory of Legislation*, 115.

32—"Justice," on Cassandra Wilson, *Belly of the Sun*, Blue Note, 2002.

the enforcement of expectations as property, is tied to predictability, and protection of the value of future expectations, which presumably cannot be radically disturbed. Stability is a paramount value, claiming both moral and economic ground, outweighing other normative and justice concerns regarding racial dispossession.

But legal regimes cannot forestall crisis. Indeed, they may precipitate and fuel crisis. The denial of claims of redress, often expressed through the language of property as repayment for debts owed, has not foreclosed the demands for justice.[33] Indeed, these demands repeatedly erupt, grounded in the refusals of the dispossessed to accept the existing baseline and the racialized expectations on which they are based. The dominant consensus, cultivated by decades of colorblind racial ideology, has long asserted that the way forward to building support for change is to minimize the role of racial oppression. In fact, in demanding attention to the specifics of the conditions and precarity of Black life, in building, in organizing around the basic notion that Black lives matter, radical visions emerge that open up pathways to transformative change.[34]

33—Martin Luther King Jr. expressed the idea this way:

> One hundred years [after Emancipation] the Negro lives on a lonely island of poverty in the midst of a vast ocean of material prosperity....
>
> In a sense we've come to our nation's capital to cash a check. When the architects of our Republic wrote the magnificent words of the Constitution and the Declaration of Independence, they were signing a promissory note to which every American was to fall heir. This note was a promise that all men—yes, black men as well as white men—would be guaranteed the unalienable rights of life, liberty and the pursuit of happiness.... It is obvious today that America has defaulted on this promissory note.... Instead of honoring this sacred obligation, America has given the Negro people a bad check, a check which has come back marked "insufficient funds."
>
> But we refuse to believe that the bank of justice is bankrupt.... So we've come to cash this check—a check that will give us upon demand the riches of freedom and the security of justice.

Martin Luther King Jr., "I Have a Dream," speech delivered at the Lincoln Memorial, August 28, 1963 (transcript available at https://www.americanrhetoric.com/speeches/mlkihaveadream.htm).

34—The demands of the "Vision for Black Lives," developed through organizing coordinated by the Movement for Black Lives, represent the radical imagination that connects the struggle against the exploitation and destruction of Black life to transformation of the social and economic order. See "Vision for Black Lives," Movement for Black Lives, https://m4bl.org/policy-platforms/.

It is, as historian Robin D. G. Kelley described it, "a plan for ending structural racism, saving the planet, and transforming the entire nation, not just Black lives." Robin D. G. Kelley, "What Does Black Lives Matter Want?," *Boston Review*, August 17, 2016, http://bostonreview.net/books-ideas/robin-d-g-kelley-movement-black-lives-vision.

XIII. CODA

When you see something that is not right, you must say something. You must do something. Democracy is not a state. It is an act, and each generation must do its part to help build what we called* the *Beloved Community, a nation and world society at peace with itself. . . . Continue to build union between movements stretching across the globe because we must put away our willingness to profit from the exploitation of others.

—John Lewis, 2020[35]

35—John Lewis, "Together, You Can Redeem the Soul of Our Nation," *New York Times*, July 30, 2020, https://www.nytimes.com/2020/07/30/opinion/john-lewis-civil-rights-america.html.

INTERVENTIONS: THE DEVIANT AND DEFIANT ART OF BLACK WOMEN PORN DIRECTORS

Mireille Miller-Young

Vanessa Blue decided to become a porn director thanks to her grandparents. "My grandparents had a whole room dedicated to smut," she explained. "Smut and two Lazy Boys."[1] I had gone to visit Vanessa in her Woodland Hills condo to talk to the performer-turned-director and webmistress about her life and latest work.[2] She told me about how she grew up with porn in her home, so it was in no way a foreign concept to her. In fact, when she began to perform in the late 1990s, it was her grandparents in Nebraska who found out first. "I'm looking at this movie *Dirty Debutantes #61*, and that sure does look like you," she recalled her grandmother saying, hilariously exaggerating her aged voice on the phone. "After that first scene and everybody found out, I was like fuck it. I might as well finish what I started," Vanessa explained, shrugging her shoulders.

"But what exactly drove you to start making your own porn, not just acting in it?" I asked. "I always loved porn and I always wanted to make it and to be a part of it," Vanessa asserted. "I liked watching people be free and enjoy themselves, and I liked shooting it. I always wanted to be behind the camera.... [I thought] Let me see if I can become the director." For Vanessa, being confronted by her grandmother about working as a porn actress forced her to think about what she really wanted. Her family did not celebrate her work in the sex industry but they understood it. What her family really wanted was for her to control her labor, rather than be controlled by someone else. If the sex industry offered that opportunity, then she should take it. Her grandparents sternly told her: "We are not saying it is wrong that you do porn, it's not. Just don't let these people fuck you. Don't stay there getting fucked. Figure out a way to make money off of it if that's what you like."

After many stops and starts, Vanessa Blue took her grandparents' advice and taught herself filmmaking and web design. She built her own editing studio from her earnings as a porn actress, exotic dancer, phone sex worker, fetish model, dominatrix, and private escort. She has directed over twenty hardcore videos and dozens of

This essay first appeared in *The Feminist Porn Book: The Politics of Producing Pleasure*, ed. Tristan Taormino, Celine Parreñas Shimizu, Constance Penley, and Mireille Miller-Young (New York: Feminist Press at the City University of New York, 2013), 105–120.

Notes have been edited to conform to the present publication's style.

1—Vanessa Blue, personal interview with the author, August 13, 2008. All quotes from Vanessa are drawn from the same interview.

2—I refer to my research interlocutors by their first name rather than their last name only to create consistency between those who employ last names in their professional personas and those who do not.

digital short films, which are distributed by major companies like Adam and Eve, Hustler, and Evil Angel's Justin Slayer International. She also distributes them herself through her suite of members-only websites and privately owned video hosting sites like Clips4Sale.com. Though working to make a living outside of the corporate adult-entertainment industry's influence, she remains very much tied to it. Vanessa is a compelling example of the possibilities and limits of pornography as a space where Black women vie to gain greater control over their labor but are nonetheless cleaved to the industry's inexorable capitalistic apparatus.

For Vanessa, control doesn't just mean achieving independence from porn producers who make a great deal of money off of her work as a performer while also treating her as a disposable working body; it means being able to decide when, where, and how she wants to employ her labor. It means avoiding unethical directors and producers who create exploitative and unsafe work environments, and treat her with little care, interest, or respect. There is a less tangible aspect to gaining control over the means of production in porn work as well: authorship. To create the terms of one's own performance and to catalyze one's own fantasies into the sex scene—these dimensions of a more autonomous sexual labor allow Vanessa to see herself as much more empowered behind the camera.

Moving behind the camera, then, is a kind of mobility that allows sex workers greater agency to traverse the barriers placed around them in the porn business. By highlighting this maneuver we can reveal the material factors that tend to restrict and bind the movement of sex workers, as well as the material forces that might facilitate their ability to claim a role in the means of production.[3] Scholarship on feminist pornography, which is notably an emerging field based on an emergent genre and practice, tends to focus on pornographic media texts that are produced and consumed in ways that push against or subvert gender and sexual normativity; are designed by and for women, transgender or genderqueer and queer people; and that destabilize the established binary model of female objectification for male viewing pleasure. Yet this vibrant movement to make new and different kinds of porn imbued with feminist politics, which began in the 1980s and blossomed in the 2000s, is not separate from the marketplace or from the politics of sexual labor.

3—This aspect of my argument is informed by Jane Juffer's work on the domestication of and women's access and uses of multiple forms of pornography and erotica. However, she advocates for prioritizing "material transgression" and "material factors that restrict movement" across boundaries, for they allow "the ability of women to literally enter into the means of production, to step across the threshold of an adult video store, to access an online sex toy shop, to buy a volume of literary erotica" over the feminist sex-positive "valorization of individuals' subversive abilities to appropriate texts," whereas I see a dual focus on material and textual appropriation and constraint as productive for my purposes here. Jane Juffer, "There Is No Place Like Home: Further Developments on the Domestic Front," in *More Dirty Pictures: Gender, Pornography and Power*, ed. Pamela Church Gibson, 2nd ed. (London: British Film Institute, 2004), 56.

Feminist pornography is a for-profit enterprise that relies upon sex workers to manufacture its subversive fantasies and build its consumer base. And like mainstream (heterosexual) pornography, its structure, networks, and modes of representation are regulated and sanctioned by the State, dependent on access to new media technologies, and embedded in the flows of global capital. Though feminism seeks to dismantle structural and discursive exploitation and oppression of women and marginalized populations, our feminist praxis is not external to or untouched by hegemonic systems of domination. Theorizing a feminist pornography then means thinking about a dual process of transgression and restriction, for both representation and labor.

The maneuvers by sex workers like Vanessa Blue to re-appropriate their images for their own profit and politics are necessarily shaped by the stultifying power of race in pornography's structural and social relations. While all of porn's workers are subject to the disciplining force of racialized sexuality, even the idealized white female porn star, women of color are specifically devalued within a tiered system of racialized erotic capital.[4] Within this hierarchy Black bodies are some of the most degraded, and their degradation mobilizes the very fetishism driving their representations. According to one adult video director I overheard at the Adult Video News Adult Entertainment Expo, "Black chicks are fucking skanks."[5] Not only does Black-cast pornography tend to be organized around a view of Black sexual deviance and pathology—often a low-budget affair presenting pimps and players trolling the 'hood for hoes and hookers—but Black porn actors tend to be paid rates half to three quarters of what white actors earn. In this way, Black labor in porn mirrors the exploitation of Black labor in "legitimate" arenas like service sector blue and pinkcollar jobs where Black workers confront systemic inequality, prejudice, and occupational health risks. Hence, in order to understand the ways in which Black pornographers like Vanessa Blue come to self-authorship and to make critical feminist interventions in the porn industry—and what is at stake in this important move—we must take seriously the overwhelming restrictions placed on Black women's sexual agency as performers and producers of porn.

In vital ways, Black women pornographers take on material constraints to enact expansive, and even radical, views of Black sexuality against deeply fraught imaginings of Black being. They work to alter the terms by which Black women's bodies are represented as simultaneously desirable and undesirable objects. Desirable for

4—On erotic capital see Adam Green, "The Social Organization of Desire: The Sexual Fields Approach," *Sociological Theory* 26, no. 1 (2008): 25–50. On employing erotic capital to read hierarchies in the sex industry specifically, see Siobhan Brooks, *Unequal Desires: Race and Erotic Capital in the Stripping Industry* (Albany, NY: SUNY Press, 2010).

5—See my article "Putting Hypersexuality to Work: Black Women and Illicit Eroticism in Pornography," *Sexualities* 13, no. 2 (2010): 219–235.

their supposed difference, exoticism, and sexual potency, Black women are at the same time constructed as undesirable, as these very same constructions threaten governing notions of feminine sexuality, heteronormativity, and racial hierarchy. In an industry where excessive sexuality would seem to be an asset, Black women's presumed hypersexuality ironically only undermines their value in the desire industries.[6] Whether located in the mainstream heterosexual market of pornography or on its marginalized outer limits, the disabling discursive construction of Black female sexuality provides an inescapable text that Black women behind the camera must confront and grapple with as they strive to author a pornographic imaginarium of and for themselves.

Resulting from the new ease and affordability of making and distributing pornography with digital technology, increasing numbers of Black women performers such as Vanessa Blue, Diana DeVoe, and Damali XXXPlosive Dares are getting into the production side of the industry. Building on the legacy of earlier Black women who attempted to create a Black women's sex cinema from inside the business, like Angel Kelly in the late 1980s, their work makes visible how pornographic authorship requires a new dimension of sexual labor. Not only are they becoming filmmakers in the traditional sense, they must fulfill a variety of roles: director, producer, editor, screenwriter, cinematographer, public relations agent, casting agent, acting coach, mentor, and distributor, to name a few. They must make themselves experts in new media technologies, ecommerce, and social networking in order to create, promote, and sell their films. Hence, calling them filmmakers, or even producers, does not capture the range of labor, expertise, or creativity involved in what they do.

Pornography created by Black women attempts to expand their sexual representations, performances, and labor beyond the current limits of the pornography industry and the confines of pervading stereotypes.[7] Vanessa's *Taking Memphis*, Diana's *Desperate Blackwives* series, and Damali's *Maneater: The Prelude* all display an interest in creating more dynamic roles for Black actresses in porn. Their work helps us rethink pornography and feminist pornography as voluptuous sites for Black women's intervention, imagination, and activism. Vanessa Blue's film work explores power reversals and role play while Diana DeVoe's large body of work tends to play with class by presenting Black women as bored, conniving, upper-income housewives (just like the reality TV

6—"Desire industries" is drawn from Brooks, *Unequal Desires*.

7—On Black women's representations in mainstream pornography, see my book *A Taste for Brown Sugar: Black Women in Pornography* (Durham, NC: Duke University Press, 2014). See also the cutting-edge work of Jennifer Christine Nash, "The Black Body in Ecstasy: Reading Race, Reading Pornography" (PhD diss., Harvard University, 2009), and Ariane Cruz, "Berries Bittersweet: Visual Representations of Black Female Sexuality in Contemporary American Pornography" (PhD diss., University of California, Berkeley, 2010).

stars they parody), or as cute and stylish hip hop generationers that obviously counter the image of the abject, low-class "ghetto ho."

Damali Dares, who is just getting started as a filmmaker, explained to me how her own sense of feminism motivated her to direct, produce, and star in *Maneater: The Prelude*, a film about a sexy detective who uses her sexuality to catch men who cheat: "Some guys would say I'm a man hater and I'm not. I just hate ignorant people, guys, or other females who try to take advantage of people. I've always been an activist and I'm always standing up for the underdog. So [the idea for the film] kind of came from both me as a person and also wanting to do that superhero type, save the world, one female at a time. It was really about empowering females."[8] As Damali describes, she was sometimes construed as a "man hater" for being outspoken about inequality and injustice, particularly, as she related to me, against sexism, racism, and homophobia. It is notable then that she turned an established antifeminist attack, "man hater" into "man eater" for a film that went on to be nominated for a 2010 Feminist Porn Award. Casting herself as the detective heroine who catches "guys who victimize women," and as the cuckolded wife who becomes empowered by learning the truth of her husband's infidelity (she walks out on him in the climactic scene of confrontation), Damali sought to use the dual role to portray women in charge of their lives, and in the process showed a dynamic figuration of Black female agency—one that employs the good girl/bad girl binary and dismantles it.

Black women filmmakers who are not adult actors, such as Shine Louise Houston (*The Crash Pad*, *Superfreak*, *Champion*), Nenna Feelmore Joiner (*Tight Places: A Drop of Color*, *Hella Brown*), Abiola Abrams aka Venus Hottentot (*Afrodite Superstar*), and Tune (*Day Dreamin*), also constitute part of this new Black women's sex cinema. Shine's and Nenna's work, which has garnered significant attention from queer and transgender communities of color, draws on performers and representations traditionally excluded from both mainstream heterosexual and alternative lesbian porn. Their work, rather, emphasizes the sheer range of embodiments, attractions, acts, and desires possible between Black women, other women of color, white people, and genderqueer and transgender persons—figurations absent in most porn. This new school of Black women porn filmmakers creates visual texts that forcefully intervene in the existing landscape of pornographic media and that prioritize complex views of desire and relation over static notions of race and gender performance. It also upsets ideas about consumption and the notion that Black pornography can only ever be offered up for someone else's fantasy—the purported white male gaze. Although their work addresses and appeals to a wide audience, these filmmakers create images that necessarily address other Black women. As Black women making pornography from their own points

8—Damali XXXPlosive Dares, personal interview with author, March 24, 2010.

of view, they also show the diversity of viewpoints, positionalities, and gazes of Black women as spectators.

Yet Black women porn filmmakers—both performers-turned-directors and non-performers—face a number of constraints. In my research in Black women's representations and labors in pornography, I interviewed dozens of Black performers active in the business since the 1980s. These ethnographic interviews and encounters provided the critical insights—the voices of these women are vital sources of knowledge about what pornography means to and for Black women. When I began my fieldwork as a graduate student at New York University in 2002 there was no work being done on the topic, and there were no Black women working as directors. Presently there are far fewer Black women active in directing and producing their own videos or video series than Black men, who have benefited from the patronage of white men who own the major and minor production houses, and their work is not as well-financed. Unlike the predominantly white male directors, producers, and distributors who run the porn industry, or many of the white female directors who have innovated a veritable feminist pornography movement since the 1980s, Black women do not have the capital, privilege, or influence to truly compete in the multi-billion-dollar trade of porn. They either must rely on traditional "boy's club" networks for production or distribution, or invent new modes to produce or distribute their work directly to consumers, which tends to limit their sales. A reason they have to become so good at many facets of making and marketing porn is that they often lack the resources to do otherwise. As Vanessa Blue explains, for Black women sex workers, gaining access to the means of production often involves negotiating a set of barriers and exploitations that do not exist for others: "I see that there are no women of my skin tone [making porn], I see that there are very few white women doing it. But what's stopping us from doing it? The more I talked to people about it, the more I found out the truth. I had to fuck a few people to get some more information, and I did." As a woman of color in the sex industry, no one takes you seriously, Vanessa told me, and they are certainly not willing to invest in you without some personal gain.

The phenomenon of Black female porn makers must be evaluated in light of Black sex workers' continued attempts to survive and succeed against tremendous barriers. Black women performers-turned-directors face an added stigma that other Black women pornographers do not. Because they continue to perform in their own films they are implicated as sex workers in ways that Black women directors coming from film schools and other paths not related to the sex industry avoid. Directors like Vanessa Blue and Damali XXXPlosive Dares also maintain other kinds of ties to the sex business through their performer websites and exotic dancing. Thus producing porn is for them part of an overall strategy to extend their professional persona into a lucrative brand, one with many formats, audiences, and streams of income. Yet creating images constitutes an important intervention into porn's representational economy, which may be considered a kind of activism in addition to a savvy hustle.

Illicit eroticism[9] is my term for conceptualizing how Black women sex workers employ their mythic racialized hypersexuality in the sexual economy.[10] By utilizing a sexuality intertwined with notions of deviance and pathology, I argue that Black illicit erotic workers are positioned as sexual outlaws who convert forbidden and proscribed sexual desires, fantasies, and practices (including prostitution) into a form of defiant "play-labor."[11] I also want to assert that this paradigm for negotiating structural and discursive forces of sexualized racism might include an added vector of activist production. That is, illicit eroticism should also capture how Black sex workers advocate for more just conditions in the sexual economy or greater personal autonomy when it comes to one's sexual choices and labor. Hence, illicit erotic activism would include making porn that undermines, or re-imagines, the status quo of Black representational politics and organizes labor to improve conditions for sex workers. Illicit erotic activism can thus theorize the involvement, incorporation, and interventions of Black women in feminist pornography and as feminist pornographers.

Vanessa Blue welcomed me with a warm and mischievous smile. I followed her, barefoot and dressed in a colorful, flowing sundress, into her home office. Explaining that she was in the middle of some important edits for a new project, Vanessa sat down at her desk with a confident grace, like the conductor of an orchestra, eminently sure the various parts of the symphony will coalesce, forming a masterpiece. The room was cluttered with equipment, yet organized. On her desk a Mac laptop was open to the movie editing software Final Cut Pro; notes, technical books, hard drives, and DVDs occupied the rest of the desk surface. A high-definition digital video camera stood on a tripod at the center of the room aimed at a canopy bed swathed in red satin and covered in velvet pillows. This was where she shot many of her videos. As Vanessa said, she likes "watching people be free and enjoy themselves." She was drawn to the idea of creating a space and environment where performers could take pleasure in their performances. "I knew I wanted to get behind the camera," she told me, "and I wanted to control the scene so that either I could get to fuck the way I wanted to fuck or produce the scenes that I knew this industry was missing."

9—See Mireille Miller-Young, "The Hip Hop Honeys + Da Hustlaz: Black Sexualities in the New Hip Hop Pornography," *Meridians: Feminism, Race and Transnationalism* 8, no. 1 (2008): 261–292.

10—I use the term *sexual economy* drawn from the work of Adrienne Davis, "Don't Let Nobody Bother Yo' Principle: The Sexual Economy of American Slavery," in *Sister Circle: Black Women and Work*, ed. Sharon Harley and the Black Women and Work Collective (New Brunswick, NJ: Rutgers University Press, 2002), 103–127.

11—Robin D. G. Kelley, *Yo Mama's Dysfunktional: Fighting the Culture Wars in Urban America* (Boston: Beacon Press, 1997), 45–46.

"What is the porn industry missing?" I asked. "As a performer," Vanessa explained, "sitting on the set and watching the director leave the room and leave the cameraman to finish the scene, to direct and make those people fuck a certain way. . ." She shook her head in disgust. "I grew up with an appreciation for smut, and it broke my heart that smut was being made by people who really didn't care." Vanessa powerfully indicts the management of porn production, which has standardized the filming of sex scenes to the extent that actors often feel they are handled more as automatons than real people, and directed to have sex that is mechanical, perfunctory, and even unerotic. This kind of schema is thought necessary to provide the market with a constant stream of pornographic media options that satisfy every taste at the cheapest cost. It replicates exactly what sells and innovates only when other things sell better. This economy opens up the process to an uncaring and sometimes unethical regime for sex workers. "Fucking" the way she wanted would mean having more freedom to decide how sex should proceed; that the interaction would be more organic and dynamic, if not erotic. It meant *not* following the predictable porn formula, but following a new calculus from her own imagination. Vanessa Blue rejects the politics of disposability that turns porn's workers, like women of color working under the conditions of neoliberal capital around the world, into "a form of industrial waste" to be "discarded and replaced."[12]

"My fans will not want to hear this," she explained, "but when I was working, it was a means to an end, and the end was to direct." For Vanessa, acting was a way to transition from being a contracted worker in the uninspired milieu of gonzo porn, to being the creator of the image and the terms of sexual labor. Now Vanessa shoots films that she makes and she performs in roles that she designs. In the process of converting her labor from contracted to creative author, she presents Black women's sexuality in ways that highlight this drive for authorship and self-determination. She aspires to eschew the framework of the stereotyped Black sexuality dominant in most porn, yet much of her work remarks on Blackness in ways that show its inextricable connection to systems of power. Vanessa exposes how Black feminist porn must contend with race, as Black female sexuality is sutured to racial histories that inform our contemporary fantasies and sexual economies.

In her adult feature (full-length narrative) films, like *Dark Confessions*, *Taking Memphis*, and *Black Reign*, Vanessa emphasizes the sexual autonomy of the female characters. Employing tactics that serve to humanize the performers and the characters, her camera closes in on and lingers on the faces, offering an embodiment beyond the often fractured "tits and ass" styling of so much porn. Vanessa creates a

12—Melissa W. Wright, *Disposable Women and Other Myths of Global Capitalism* (New York: Routledge, 1997), 2.

space for Black eroticism and Black subjectivity, centering themes of intimacy, mischief, power dynamics, and role-play. The presentation of cross and interracial intimacy pushes against the notion that relationships between Black men and women, and Black women and white men, are inherently alienating and objectifying.

In *Dark Confessions*, Vanessa employs the trope of the confession to elicit testimonials from couples about their fantasies, and as the box cover advertises, the fantasy is in "revealing their darkest desires." Vanessa takes on the role of the confessor, sitting invisibly behind the camera as she draws out the sexual fantasies of five Black male-female couples in this film, which is distributed by Adam and Eve, and marketed for a heterosexual-couples audience. Each interview, filmed in a medium range black-and-white shot, presents the couple sitting closely, holding or leaning on one another. The professional porn actors portray a familiarity and intimacy that is not usually present in most Black-cast porn, where normally a series of sex acts are strung together with little plot, characterization, or opportunity for the actors to speak. Here the actors improvise from the outline of a script, yet their articulations are fluid as they play off one another to construct an image of a relationship that appears quite realistic. Vanessa probes them with questions: How did you meet? How's the sex? What's your fantasy? Like most reality-influenced genres, we, the spectator, become participants in this will to knowledge of sexual desire and invested in its actuation. Rather than re-produce regulatory regimes of power on the subject, the discourses of sex produced by the confessional in this film present Black performances of intimate disclosure and relation.[13]

The fantasy of the female character in the first couple (played by Nyomi Banxxx) is to be interrogated—she wants her partner (played by Sean Michaels) to act like an FBI agent, dapper and smooth in a suit, with "minty fresh breath." The scene has a film noir quality, a spare set with a spotlight projected on a mysterious-looking woman in a vintage 1940s hat and dress. The color is faded to almost black and white save for the red of her lips, and later, her panties. True to noir aesthetics, she's smoking a cigarette, and the smoke plumes around her in the chiaroscuro of light and shadow reflected on the wall, perhaps mirroring the shadowy, forbidden nature of her desire. The fantasy here is the play of power through aggression and submission, mystery and impending action. Sean's debonair FBI agent seduces Nyomi's evasive femme fatale—her smoking, turning away, eye rolling, and resistance to his caresses and kisses build up the tension. With striking tenderness he holds her by the shoulders and kisses her cheeks and neck softly, and then as she finally returns the kiss, they move into an intense sex scene on top of the Federal Bureau of Investigation desk.

13—On the confessional as site for the production of sexual truth, see Michel Foucault, *History of Sexuality, Volume 1*, trans. Robert Hurley (1978; New York: Pantheon Books, 1990).

This refreshing intimacy does not mean, however, that Vanessa Blue avoids hardcore representations of dominance and alienation. In fact, she confronts power head-on and plays with it, especially in short films made for her website FemmeDomX.com. Using S/M fetishism—particularly the fantasy of Black women dominating white men—she *queers* racial and gender hegemonies by exposing their very constructedness. By creating fantasies that explode assumptions about what constitutes proper pleasure and pain for the Black body, she suggests that social power is changeable and that racialized sexuality can be toyed with for her own ends.

"Kink" is an under-explored arena of Black sexual culture, and a technology of the self that is, if acknowledged in the public domain at all, seen as the epitome of deviant sexuality.[14] The performances in Femme Dom X video shorts are very different from the sensuality of the feature film *Dark Confessions*. They involve ropes, chains, whips, torches, clamps, gags, harnesses, and other tools associated with the historical, nonconsensual mutilation and punishment of the Black body, but that are used in this context to expose power as a terrain of (consensual) play in fantasy. Here, Black dominatrixes, Vanessa included, torture white and Black men by making them crawl, beg, and subject themselves to all manner of abuse, including by painting their faces with lipstick and otherwise emasculating them with taunting acts. Ever playful, Vanessa's EbonyTickle.com uses "tickle torture" to show how even—here, in the excruciating and taunting tickling of female performers tied to her bed—kink can be mediated in ways that create a permissible environment where Black women sexual outlaws can be seen to play with the ever dangerous position of subordination and powerlessness. With the performance of subjection as submissives in Ebony Tickle, or of merciless domination as dominatrixes in Femme Dom X, Black actresses in Vanessa's film work illuminate the significance of racialized kink fetishism as an important market in the pornography industry for Black women looking to capitalize on the sexual scripts available for them.

Vanessa Blue's illicit erotic activism is about the use of what may be generally understood as super deviant sexualities to empower Black women's sexual performances in pornography. For Vanessa, Black women's performances of submissiveness or domination can be enjoyable acts, and ones that might encourage Black women spectators to explore their own "darkest desires." And while her interest is not

14—Anne McClintock, "Maid to Order: Commercial Fetishism and Gender Power," *Social Text* 37 (Winter 1993): 87–116. There is a paucity of research on Black women or men and "kink" or BDSM, but a few popular articles and blog essays or interviews exist. See Daisy Hernandez, "Playing with Race," *Colorlines*, December 21, 2004, http://colorlines.com/archives/2004/12/playing_with_race.html; Anna North, "When Prejudice Is Sexy: Inside the Kinky World of Race-Play," Jezebel.com, March 14, 2012, http://jezebel.com/5868600/when-prejudice-is-sexy-inside-the-kinky-world-of-race+play; Andrea, "Inter-view with Perverted Negress," Racialicious.com, July 10, 2009, http://www.racialicious.com/2009/07/10/interview-with-the-perverted-negress/.

in presenting a narrative of racial progress, overthrowing patriarchy, or in making sexually emancipatory or pleasurable texts outside the marketplace, her intervention is, I argue, quite progressive. This work asks us to think about what we might learn from pornography's most marginalized: how our pleasure is indeed tied to historical realities of our pain. What does it mean that some of the most preferable work for Black sex workers in porn—since fetish work often does not require penetrative sex, but the performance of a dominant or submissive role in non-penetrative sex acts—is tied up with these brutal legacies of sexual expropriation and sexual myth? Could taking pleasure in the most deviant articulations of Black sexual deviance offer a radical tool to negotiate and transform how power acts on our bodies and communities? Black women's objectification in pornography has a long history, emerging from New World slavery as a pornographic, voyeuristic, sexual economy. Yet since the earliest photographic and film productions of sexually explicit material made for sale in a pornographic market of images, Black models and actresses could be seen to return the objectifying gaze, and gesture to their own subjective understandings as sex workers and as sexual subjects.[15] If Black women's sex cinema offers a new frontier to present the inextricable bind between sexual labor and sexual fantasy, the task is to explore it as a new kind of voice in pornography, one that is never divorced from the marketplace, but in fact, shines a light on the ways in which Black women's sexualities are intimately linked with the project of authorship against, and in line with, inexorable myth.

Unconcerned with delineating what constitutes a positive or negative representation of Black female sexuality, Vanessa Blue offers a view into how representations of Black women's sexuality remain caught up in confining, binary scripts. This relentless binary, which is problematic for all women but especially so for women of color whose sexualities have been deployed as a primary mechanism of colonization, expropriation, and genocide, exposes the impossibility of rendering an authentic view of Black women's sexualities in any media, let alone pornography. Black feminist pornography instead provides a space where Black women performers can try on roles and stage imaginaries against expectations of decorum and normativity. This presents a powerful image for Black women spectators, too. They might identify with the image and connect it to their own sexual identities or experiences. Although there is little research on Black women's consumption of pornography, knowing that a Black woman created these films might foster a sense that they are invited to view a very different kind of image.

Nonetheless, a large segment of Vanessa Blue's work is not directed toward Black women viewers, but instead white and Black men. As a sex worker whose film work is tied to her professional persona and

15—This is part of my argument in my larger work. See *A Taste for Brown Sugar*.

brand and who, in the absence of investment or opportunities to be hired to direct for major companies must launch her own "do-it-yourself" media—from short fetish videos to live webcam shows—she must necessarily address the primary market for Black-oriented pornography. Like Diana DeVoe and Damali XXXPlosive Dares, Vanessa and other Black women performers from the mainstream heterosexual porn industry make money by cultivating a white, Black, and brown male fan base. Their authorship is always tied to the need for savvy self-promotion. This fact means that their work differs sharply from Black women sex filmmakers who are not sex workers.

Abiola Abrams aka Venus Hottentot brought her background in film studies, art, and creative writing to her collaboration with pioneering feminist pornographer Candida Royalle for *Afrodite Superstar* (Femme Productions, 2007). Royalle's Femme Productions produced the film and guaranteed its audience would be women and couples interested in her quasi-softcore aesthetic. Coming to the film as an unknown entity in the mainstream or feminist porn world, Abrams was freer to use goddess imagery, a critique of hip hop's misogynist violence toward Black women, and Black feminist poetry throughout the film than if she had been a sex worker needing to assure fans would buy the film and keep her employed.[16] In fact, she went into the project not seeing it as pornography for the purposes of titillation and masturbation, but as a "sex film" which would offer a political statement about the richness and complexity of Black women's fantasy lives.[17] But her reliance on established porn actors to carry the film, such as India, Mr. Marcus, and Justin Long, as well as the inexperienced leading actress's performance (Simone Valentino), meant that the film would be marketed as a couples or woman-friendly porno even while it circulated as a feminist art statement of sorts. This fact underscores and expands upon Angela Carter's insistence that pornography "can never be art for art's sake. Honourably enough, it always has work to do."[18]

Black feminist and queer filmmakers coming from outside the industry produce for a different market and face a different set of expectations from their audiences than Black performers-turned-producers of porn. For the former, consumers are largely women and transgender and queer people looking to find authentic images of themselves and their sexual communities, representations lacking in most porn. This sense of authenticity is underscored by the fact that the sex workers employed for these films are part of these very same communities, often renowned performance artists and actors from the San Francisco Bay area, the queer porn San Fernando Valley. Both Shine Louise Houston and Nenna Joiner use queer people of color from their own circles of

16—Abiola Abrams, personal interview with author, April 10, 2009.

17—Abiola Abrams, personal interview with author, April 10, 2009.

18—Angela Carter, *The Sadeian Woman* (London: Virago Press, 1979), 12.

friends and collaborators in their films, and market, in part, to those same circles. Although the consumption of their work extends much farther afield, this community-based approach also presents a kind of political intervention. While Black performers-turned-directors employ filmmaking as a facet, albeit politically charged, of their strategic sexual labor, Black women filmmakers who are not performers do not engage illicit erotics in the same way. Rather than use their own sexualities for commoditized gains, they propel the sexualities of others to enact fantasies of their own design, fantasies that intervene in the narrowed landscape of possibilities for Black female sexuality under racial capitalism.

But that's not to say that these Black women auteurs do not deploy their own embodiments, and specifically the deviance attached to their Black female bodies, in the pornoscape. Shine Louis Houston, for instance, launches her body into her texts in unexpected and subversive ways. In *Superfreak* she appears as the ghost of notoriously naughty funk singer Rick James, whose 1981 hit "Super Freak" describes "a very kinky girl, the kind you don't take home to mother . . ." Inhabiting James' spirit, Shine brings to life a trickster figure bent on turning one character after another into a "superfreak." Using her own body to set in motion the pleasure inducing, orgiastic scene, Shine moves from cultural producer (whose role is to represent or depict sex) to sexual laborer (whose role is to trade/on sex) to sexual intellectual (whose role is to critique sex labor and sex representations, as I do) to superfreak (who performs all of the above). This schema, offered by L. H. Stallings in her radical theory of Black erotic rebellion called the "Politics of Hoin'" opens up ways of thinking about Black women pornographers as not so much divided by their interests in porn as united by a shared politics—porn as a site of possibility for Black women's own intervention and critique.[19]

What does it mean to be a superfreak? For Black women the politics of respectability has overwhelmed our ability to think of sex apart from the threat of harm to our womanhood and to our communities.[20] Through the prioritization of normative gender and sexual codes, behaviors, and relations we have sought to recuperate our *selves* from myths associated with Black sexual deviance, and the systemic violence attached to those myths. Pornography offers a site to see how

19—L. H. Stallings, "Superfreak: Black Female Masculinity Spectacle/Spectator in Lesbian Pornography," paper presented at Race, Sex, Power: New Movements in Black and Latina/o Sexualities, University of Illinois, Chicago, April 2008.

20—On the "politics of respectability," see the classic work by Evelyn Brooks Higginbotham, *Righteous Discontent: The Women's Movement in the Black Baptist Church, 1880–1920* (Cambridge, MA: Harvard University Press, 1993). Related to respectability politics is Black women's "culture of dissemblance"—their strategies of masking, avoiding, and resistance against racialized sexual stereotyping. See Darlene Clark Hine, "Rape and the Inner Lives of Black Women in the Middle West: Preliminary Thoughts on the Culture of Dissemblance," in *Words of Fire: An Anthology of African-American Feminist Thought*, ed. Beverly Guy-Sheftall (New York: New Press, 1995).

those myths attach to fantasies and to labor arrangements, but also, to make visible the pleasures taken in the queerness of deviance.[21] These pleasures are articulated by those who do sexual labor, those who depict sexual acts, those who offer intellectual critiques of them, and by those that do all of the above. In fact, these directors show the important overlaps between sex work and cultural production and cultural critique. Their body of work exposes the defiant sensibilities and subversive politics of Black feminist pornographies as they enact a charged eroticism that is full of voluptuous potential.[22]

This nascent cinema powerfully indicts the antiporn feminist viewpoint—if one is preoccupied by pornography's objectification of women one needs only to look to women's pornographic filmmaking to see how women might make use of objectification as a technology of feminism. Claiming subjectivity, critiquing representation, constructing new sexual languages, and aiming for new forms of economic survival and mobility, the many agents of feminist pornography are at the vanguard of the feminist movement. A movement stultified in its reformist program of (neo)liberal rights struggles, it routinely leaves out the critical sexual/cultural workers who are trying to offer a revolutionary paradigm of gender and sexual rights and relations while at the same time entering into the means of production. Black feminist pornographers are on the front lines of what I see as one of the most exciting directions in modern feminism—one that can make plain (and explicit) the inextricability of racialized genders and sexualities to any new modes of capital and methodologies of creative self-fashioning we feminists undertake. Just as Black feminists have challenged the mainstream feminist movement to be accountable to race, class, and nation as they act intersectionally and contingently with gender,[23] Black women bring a special insight to feminist pornography: one person's fantasy is another person's work, and the workers have fantasies of their own.

21—On deviance as a site of potential for Black (sexual) politics, see Cathy Cohen, "Deviance as Resistance: A New Research Agenda for the Study of Black Politics," *Du Bois Review: Social Science Research on Race* 1, no. 1 (2004): 27–45.

22—Here I am thinking of L. H. Stallings, *"Mutha" Is Half a Word: Intersections of Folklore, Vernacular, Myth, and Queerness in Black Female Culture* (Columbus: Ohio University Press, 2007).

23—On intersectionality, see Kimberlé Crenshaw, "Mapping the Margins: Intersectionality, Identity Politics, and Violence against Women of Color," *Stanford Law Review* 43, no. 6 (1991): 1241.

"AN IMPOSSIBLE FORM": THE ABSENCE THAT KEEPS ON GIVING

Mlondolozi Zondi

Perhaps absence is a gift.

—mayfield brooks, "The Artist Is Not Present"

God, dance is an impossible form.

—Ralph Lemon, *Geography: Art, Race, Exile*

There is a subject position whose formlessness is irreducible to an aesthetic choice aimed at corporeal dissolution or willful self-abnegation, but is rather a condition of (non)being produced through structural violence. Black aesthetic practices described as formless embrace a *de*form that already constitutes blackness, and not formlessness as a visual/performance motif, as is often the case in Western aesthetics' "epistemic turns and revolutions."[1] The "West," here, is not a specific geographical location; rather, as Édouard Glissant describes it, "It is a project, not a place."[2] The condition of "being without form,"[3] as Calvin Warren theorizes, marks historico-political maneuvers of violence that rendered corporeal integrity an impossibility for African-derived people.[4] Black corporeal/figural *form*'s equivalency to humanity or personhood can neither be presumed nor incontrovertibly substantiated. The figuration of "the black body" does not allow entry into the category of the human, and it is not a "body" in the same way that other bodies are bodies. Its emergence deranges the very meaning

This essay first appeared in *liquid blackness* 8, no. 1 (April 2024).

Notes have been edited to conform to the present publication's style.

1—For this distinction, see Tiffany Lethabo King, "Humans Involved: Lurking in the Lines of Posthumanist Flight," *Critical Ethnic Studies* 3, no. 1 (2017): 162.

2—Édouard Glissant, *Caribbean Discourse: Selected Essays* (Charlottesville: University Press of Virginia, 1992), 2.

3—Calvin L. Warren, *Ontological Terror: Blackness, Nihilism, and Emancipation* (Durham, NC: Duke University Press, 2018).

4—My use of "African derived" as opposed to "African-descended" and correlate terms is consistent with Frank B. Wilderson's use of the term to draw attention to slavery's violent capture of Africans. The transatlantic slave trade was not a movement of choice, exile, nor analogous to immigration. Not only does "African-derived" direct attention to this violent capture, but it implicitly critiques those rhetorical strategies which (un)intentionally sanitize slavery through sentimentality, obscuring the unquantifiable brutality of slavery's deformation of natal community. See Frank B. Wilderson III, "Grammar and Ghosts: The Performative Limits of African Freedom," *Theatre Survey* 50, no. 1 (2009): 119–125; *Orlando Patterson, Slavery and Social Death: A Comparative Study* (Cambridge, MA: Harvard University Press, 1982).

of what constitutes a body, since, as Thomas DeFrantz has argued, it comes before the law already as both its antithesis and condition of possibility.[5] In his study of Pablo Picasso's relationship to the African figure, Simon Gikandi also notes that "the black body represented the corporeal form out of order, even in nature, and hence already in defiance of the laws of proportion and symmetry."[6] Both authors describe a negation that grants coherence to the negative/positive polarity and the law. What do we do with this incommensurability between form and meaning? Black political thought and artistic practice have focused on wrestling with this voided subjectivity imposed from *outside*, either by suturing its fragmentation through "imitation of a form of being"[7] or inventing an African subject position that embraces the rupture of disintegrated form as a point of departure for the dissolution of the anti-black world. What African and African-derived thinkers and makers do with this *de*-form in black aesthetics has political stakes outlined in the following pages.

In this article, I consider African contemporary/experimental dance practices not only as invested in formal aesthetic in(ter)vention but as making those formal choices to draw attention to the scene of violence where blackness meets form. Black dance is pliably positioned, and this allows it *to be moved* in a manner that elicits both approval/applause and repulsion. Black dancers spectacularize the figuration that evidences the Negro's "natural" primitive status, the African's banishment from secure categorization within the human, while also remaining a sign of presumed magical creativity, a gift that keeps on giving.

In reaction to the ontological turn in black studies and its abstractionism, a consistent concern becomes how to understand the "actual body" outside of its theorization as absence in abstract discourse. The concern misreads black ontological negation, or what mayfield brooks frames as "absence," to be reducing "the body" to a purely discursive and dematerialized site. Such affirmative empiricism takes biology as a determinant for presence and presumes that same "presence" to indicate "the black body's" endowment with the capacities afforded to universal personhood. I maintain that the "materiality" of "the black body" is less a corroboration of its access to subjectivity than an indication of its vertiginous suspension in dissimulation and exorbitance, a

5—Thomas DeFrantz, "The Black Beat Made Visible: Hip Hop Dance and Body Power," in *Of the Presence of the Body: Essays on Dance and Performance Theory*, ed. André Lepecki (Middletown, CT: Wesleyan University Press, 2004), 71.

6—Simon Gikandi, "Picasso, Africa, and the Schemata of Difference," in *Beautiful Ugly: African and Diaspora Aesthetics*, ed. Sarah Nuttall (Durham, NC: Duke University Press, 2006), 40.

7—Jared Sexton, "On Black Negativity; or, The Affirmation of Nothing," interview by Daniel Colucciello Barber, *Society and Space*, September 18, 2017, https://www.societyandspace.org/articles/on-black-negativity-or-the-affirmation-of-nothing.

virtual orbit around negation and wealth.[8] This signals its unremitting openness to the whims of negrophobic and negrophilic violence regardless of the *form* or affective posture "the black body" takes.

The second part of this article will meditate on the above provocation in a non-comparative way alongside the choreographic interventions of Germaine Acogny (Senegal) and Faustin Linyekula (DRC), whose work not only contributes to formal dance innovation but questions the philosophical foundations of apprehending form. Both choreographers dissect the surfaces and depths of colonial violence, indicting the hands, weapons, pens, and utterances responsible for ongoing anti-black warfare that bleeds over to black intracommunal relationality. Acogny addresses the chasm in the black intracommunal inaugurated by the transatlantic slave trade, and in *Fagaala* (2005), she meditates on the 1990s genocide in Rwanda. Linyekula considers the "Africanist presences"[9] in European modernism, the sadist atrocities enacted at the command of Belgian King Leopold II in the Democratic Republic of the Congo/Zaire, as well as the long-term postindependence civil war in the country. Not only do they call attention to the formal aspects of this brutality, but they reveal (post)colonial terror's de-formation of language to explain these horrors. They move toward and against the common sense reductive conceptualization of the "black dancing body" as the quintessence of natural joie de vivre, facilitating an opportunity to more assiduously broach the manifold functions and aims of black dance as a mode of negotiating (epigenetic) memory; conveying or encrypting tactics of struggle through passing on gesture; inquiring about gravity, the laws of physics, and the mathematical meter; undermining logocentrism through open-ended improvisation; and tending to psychosomatic wounding contra the seriality of catharsis and its "telos of perfect closure."[10] African enslavement and colonial violence are sites par excellence for modern(ist) experimentation with "the black body." Such experimentation is irreducible to brutal enfleshment and domestication but extends to coerced jubilance that equally facilitates the annulment of African life. Elsewhere, I have drawn attention to Africa's position in Western aesthetics as a source of inspiration and extraction, framed as a space where contemporary artistic experimentation and conceptualization can never thrive or even occur.[11] In these instances, as Achille Mbembe posits:

8—Rizvana Bradley, "On Black Aesthesis," *Diacritics* 49, no. 4 (2021): 21–53; Fred Moten, *The Universal Machine* (Durham, NC: Duke University Press, 2018), 182–183.

9—Brenda Dixon Gottschild, *Digging the Africanist Presence in American Performance: Dance and Other Contexts* (Westport, CT: Greenwood, 1996).

10—Joseph Roach, *Cities of the Dead: Circum-Atlantic Performance* (New York: Columbia University Press, 1996), 33.

11—Mlondolozi Zondi, "Black Performance Theory," review of *Black Performance Theory*, ed. Thomas F. DeFrantz and Anita Gonzalez, *Text and Performance Quarterly* 37, no. 3–4 (2017): 278–281.

> Africa exists only as an absent object, an absence that those who try to decipher it [*sic*] only accentuate. . . . Thus, we must speak of Africa only as a chimera on which we all work blindly, a nightmare we produce and from which we make a living—and which we sometimes enjoy, but which somewhere deeply repels us, to the point that we may evince toward it the kind of disgust we feel on seeing a cadaver.[12]

If, from this perspective, Africanity is coterminous with absence, the void, the abyss, African performance—even that which is considered "cutting-edge"—cannot be incorporated with ease into general categories of contemporary experimental dance. My curiosity lies in what contributes to the unfathomableness of an experimental African practice in discourses of the avant-garde (broadly construed) as well as why the West needs Africa to signify perpetually for its own psychic and economic stability as a site of simultaneous absence and (resource) extraction, as well as aesthetic innovation. This is not an effort to join the ranks of the Western canon or exalt canonicity but to highlight contemporary African aesthetic contemplation on form and formlessness as contending with a "form of being" whose absence and exorbitance equally *gift* Western modernity/modernism its form.

ON ANARRANGEMENT

Choreography and colonialism share a defining attribute of order and arrangement. Choreography is more than "the art of making dances"; it is rather devised to instill obedience and domestication.[13] As an "apparatus of capture,"[14] choreography's historical development entailed turning dancing into writing/documentation through choreographic scores and treatises that share ontological properties with cartographies of colonial empire. If choreography domesticates movement into order and its objective is to implement and reproduce "whole systems of obedience,"[15] then colonialism, as V. Y. Mudimbe argues, basically means "organization, arrangement."[16] "Anarrangement,"[17] instead, attends to both blackness's relationship to form at the level of ontology, as well as at the level of black aesthetic operations that

12—Achille Mbembe, *On the Postcolony* (Berkeley: University of California Press, 2001), 241.

13—Susan Leigh Foster, *Choreographing Empathy: Kinesthesia in Performance* (London: Routledge, 2011), 40.

14—André Lepecki, "Choreography as Apparatus of Capture," *TDR: The Drama Review* 51, no. 2 (2007): 119–123.

15—André Lepecki, "Choreopolice and Choreopolitics; or, The Task of the Dancer," *TDR: The Drama Review* 57, no. 4 (2013): 16.

16—V. Y. Mudimbe, *The Invention of Africa: Gnosis, Philosophy, and the Order of Knowledge* (Bloomington: Indiana University Press, 1988), 1.

17—Fred Moten, *In the Break: The Aesthetics of the Black Radical Tradition* (Minneapolis: University of Minnesota Press, 2003), 1.

shun the mastery of Western techne. “Anarrangement” and “antichoreography”[18] are not about refurbishing mastery but rather the total destruction of mastery and the forms that sustain it. Literary theorist Houston Baker described this as the *deformation of mastery*, which is different from aspiring to mastery of form.[19] Taking this a step further, Rizvana Bradley and Denise Ferreira da Silva consider “both seriality and deformation not as formal deviations from the major paradigms of modernist art, but as aesthetic practices which enact the decomposition of the art historical canon, and of canonicity as such.”[20] Calvin Warren proposes anti-formalism since “antiblack violence depends on form to reproduce itself.”[21] Rather than clinging on to the mastery of form, I am curious about an anti-formalism that is not about rearrangement of the terms but about their total decomposition. “Anarrangement” as a black aesthetic operation is neither the arrangement nor rearrangement of the choreographic apparatus. The prefix *ana-* can also translate to “against” the choreographic and its defining aspirational mastery of form. These practices destroy form as a move away from the politics of reform.[22]

Dorothée Munyaneza, Faustin Linyekula, Ralph Lemon, Paul Maheke, Kettly Noël, Okwui Okpokwasili, Nadia Beugré, keyon gaskin, Nelisiwe Xaba, Dana Michel, mayfield brooks, Boyzie Cekwana, and Will Rawls are some of the black choreographers whose experimentations with form and concept test the potentialities of this formal decomposition. Their approaches to form, which sometimes diverge in content and political orientation, focus attention to the ways that the formlessness of black life is irreducible to an aesthetic motif. This occurs through either indifference to, or the breaking down of, canonical Western dance techniques to foreground black vernacular dance modes that have always been problematically conceived as incapable of perfect form. These are vernacular forms of dance that do not privilege rigid structure and develop in venues outside the theater. These practices of anarrangement move away from the proselytizing apparatuses of dance technique, asserting a black anti-choreographic stance that critiques representationalism and legibility (the tools of ethnographic knowledge-making that reinforce the idea of Africans

18—This deformation is what Rizvana Bradley calls the “anti-choreographic” or “anti-style.” Rizvana Bradley, “Black Cinematic Gesture and the Aesthetics of Contagion,” *TDR: The Drama Review* 62, no. 1 (2018): 19–21.

19—Houston A. Baker Jr., *Modernism and the Harlem Renaissance* (Chicago: University of Chicago Press, 1987), 49.

20—Rizvana Bradley and Denise Ferreira da Silva, “Four Theses on Aesthetics,” *e-flux Journal*, no. 120 (2021), https://www.e-flux.com/journal/120/416146/four-theses-on-aesthetics/.

21—Calvin Warren, “The Catastrophe: Black Feminist Poethics, (Anti) Form, and Mathematical Nihilism,” *Qui Parle: Critical Humanities and Social Sciences* 28, no. 2 (2019): 357.

22—Warren, “Catastrophe,” 369.

as knowable and affectable).[23] Here, sampling other styles of black movement is not an elevation of technique as such since, as Fred Moten and Stefano Harney note, "the black aesthetic is not about technique, is not a technique, though a fundamental element of the terror-driven anaesthetic disavowal of 'our terribleness' is the eclectic sampling of techniques of black performativity."[24] In that regard, the appeal to technique is the appeal to governance and order, and antithetical to an *itinerant drive* toward the abolishment of bondage. This appeal to order is also a possible trajectory, if not inevitable, for practices of anarrangement, making their radicality transient, specific to the moment, and susceptible to capture.

THE AVANT-GARDE

When Africans engage in nontraditional/nonfolkloric performance forms, those performances are presumed by critics such as Sharon Friedman as unoriginal, and African artists are perceived to be mimicking Euro-American artistic innovations.[25] This logic emanates from some of the West's self-aggrandizing narratives of periodization, which rehearse white artistic innovation as the origin point of modernism and postmodernism. Postmodernist performance is often chronicled as a soliloquy delivered by the West.[26] This is attributable to the avant-garde's "embedded[ness] in a theory of history . . . a particular geographical ideology, a geographical-racial or racist unconscious."[27] This suggests a connection between a Western-centric theory of history and what Moten is calling its racist unconscious. This theory of history and aesthetics cannot fathom modernism as emanating from any source other than itself. I am interested in thinking against the grain of solipsistic periodization to think (post) modernism and the "avant-garde" away from any geographical-racist originary tale and instead through a consideration of relations of domination emerging in the protracted time of the Middle Passage and colonialism. What is often rehearsed as the history of "postmodern performance" cannot be solely attributed to a Western tale that narrates figures such as Trisha Brown, Yvonne Rainer, Steve Paxton, Lucinda

23—Denise Ferreira da Silva, *Toward a Global Idea of Race* (Minneapolis: University of Minnesota Press, 2007).

24—Stefano Harney and Fred Moten, *The Undercommons: Fugitive Planning and Black Study* (Wivenhoe, UK: Minor Compositions, 2013), 48.

25—Sharon Friedman, "The Impact of the Tourist Gaze on the Voice of South African Contemporary Dance," in *Post-apartheid Dance: Many Bodies Many Voices Many Stories*, ed. Sharon Friedman (Newcastle upon Tyne, UK: Cambridge Scholars, 2012), 89–105. Friedman argues that African contemporary dancers are mimetic. Joseph Roach critiques this line of argumentation as the "relentless search for the purity of origins . . . a voyage not of discovery but of erasure." Roach, *Cities of the Dead*, 6.

26—Jay Pather, "A Response: African Contemporary Dance? Questioning Issues of a Performance Aesthetic for a Developing Continent," *Critical Arts: South-North Cultural and Media Studies* 20, no. 2 (2006): 9–15.

27—Moten, *In the Break*, 31.

Childs, and other white artists from the Judson Church experiments as sole progenitors, while the rest appear (if at all) to concurrently emblematize belated mimesis and Western innovation's atavistic anterior or maternal trace.

As a fractal condition instantiated by the trade in Africans as commodities, the black Atlantic is the gateway to modern culture.[28] Features and attributes of modern and postmodern culture such as citizenship, freedom, democracy, beauty, aesthetic value, breaks from tradition, and dissent from orthodox intellectual thought were instantiated upon, against, and by African enslaved "bodies"—sometimes as the "limit"[29] of those categories. Modern modalities of feeling/sensing/knowing, as well as tools of aesthetic judgment, cannot be separated from colonial exhibitions, human zoos, and the development of medical technologies. Nineteenth-century ethnological attractions in New York, London, Brussels, and other metropoles not only recruited continental Africans and other colonized Indigenous groups to perform but also recruited black Americans and other Diasporic Africans to "masquerade as African savages or wild men, . . . [and] pseudo-Zulus . . . when demand exceeded supply."[30] (Post)modernist genre categorizations are inextricably linked to modes of knowledge-making emerging from the long Enlightenment, such as natural science, botany, zoology, anthropology, and the philosophy of aesthetics. Our modern and postmodern aesthetic categories, tools of aesthetic judgment, and modalities of curating hierarchies of difference are entangled with taxonomy, anthropometry, craniometry, and other characteristics of eugenics.[31]

Thus, the avant-garde sensibility in postmodern performance is more than merely a form of Western intracommunal heterodoxy, where the "trailblazing young" dissent from the orthodoxies, laws, and conventions of the generations preceding them. When understood as and through historical relations of domination, the concept of the "avant-garde" also emerges as emanating from a deep craving for the different, strange, or deviant. This waywardness is often celebrated in postmodern performance periodization without situating the conditions of emergence for the craving, how and why it came to be, and which "bodies" became conduits for its intelligibility. It remains important to maintain skepticism

28—Krista Thompson, "A Sidelong Glance: The Practice of African Diaspora Art History in the United States," *Art Journal* 70, no. 3 (2011): 6–31.

29—Thompson, "Sidelong Glance," 21.

30—Bernth Lindfors, *Africans on Stage: Studies in Ethnological Show Business* (Bloomington: Indiana University Press, 1999), ix.

31—See Sylvia Wynter, "On How We Mistook the Map for the Territory and Re-imprisoned Ourselves in Our Unbearable Wrongness of Being, of Désêtre: Black Studies toward the Human Project," in *Not Only the Master's Tools: African-American Studies in Theory and Practice*, ed. Lewis R. Gordon and Jane Anna Gordon (Boulder, CO: Paradigm, 2006), 107–169.

regarding the West's self-preoccupied periodizations of the modern and the "avant-garde." This skepticism, rather than constraining us amid Eurocentric tales of white artistic rebels disgracing the Father/Norm, attunes us instead to modernism's "black *mater*nal/*mater*ial inheritances."[32] As Richard Iton contends, "We aspire to be modern, as if this were somehow a new position and as if blacks and nonwhites were not already clearly *and uncomfortably* modern, as if modernity were sustainable without the nigger and the fluid in/convenience that is blackness lying, albeit differently, both outside and inside its borders."[33] Reconfigured this way, the "avant-garde" is indebted to the enduring ruptures of colonialism, imperialism, and transatlantic slavery. The black avant-garde is not merely an add-on to, or mimicry of, already established norms and heresies within Western culture. If blacks are "already clearly and uncomfortably modern," then modernity/modernism is not a phenomenon that blacks either lack, aspire to, or mimic. Modernism is not a foreign garment that the African puts on in domesticated obedience. The modern and the African are oddly co-constitutive and entangled, meaning, as Steven Nelson and Huey Copeland argue, "any form of the modern is always already *blackened*, even if the fact is limited to the literal footnotes of the discipline."[34] Subversive white performances that have been immortalized as pioneering the "postmodern category" do so through a detachment from and/or appropriation of affects and characteristics of movement associated with blackness and indigeneity. This is a simultaneous embrace and disavowal of the long Enlightenment's ideas of beauty, (a)symmetry, and the sublime. The avant-garde sensibility is inseparable from a desire for the occlusionary identification constituted by "becoming minor," which is to say *becoming black*, since African subjectivity (and its aesthetic production) is the quintessence of radical dysaestheticness and dissymmetry in Western knowledge-making. The Western avant-garde aesthetic is realized through the simultaneous fetishization of the racialized atavistic, while erasing the historical relations of domination undergirding that same atavistic fetish. This erasure of historical conditions of emergence allows for the sensibility of the "new" and "cutting-edge"—which is a return to previously disavowed "barbaric" thought and action—to be propertied as white or non-black. What is considered "avant-garde" and categorized as "postmodernist," especially in dance, moves futuristically toward formerly repudiated content and form associated with "irrational" or chaotic blackness. Black performances concerned with reproducing the (*self* as) strange/deviant, no matter how pleasurable or counterhegemonic, are haunted by lingering anti-black onto-epistemes that produce(d) blackness

32—For a detailed reading of this material trace, see Moten, *In the Break*.

33—Richard Iton, *In Search of the Black Fantastic: Politics and Popular Culture in the Post–Civil Rights Era* (Oxford: Oxford University Press, 2008), 288.

34—Huey Copeland and Steven Nelson, *Black Modernisms in the Transatlantic World* (New Haven, CT: Yale University Press, 2023), 3.

as deviance par excellence rather than a consequence of deviant performative acts by black(ened) people. The African's formlessness, then, is construed as a "lack" that is accumulated to materialize white Western aesthetics of self-dissolution. It is the latter that enters discourse while the former is condemned to the space and function of primordial inspiration.

CHILDLESS MOTHER, MOTHERLESS CHILD, LOSE YOUR MOTHER

Dance scholar Joan Frosch's film titled *Movement (R)evolution Africa: A Story of an Art Form in Four Acts* (Joan Frosch and Alla Kovgan, 2007) documents a gathering of black choreographers from the African continent and the United States assembled in Florida to teach workshops, perform, and discuss the political and economic issues concerning contemporary Africanity in dance. The documentary is organized into four acts: "Mother Tongues," "(Re)invention," "Moments of Contact," and "Staging the (Un)imaginable." One of the central problems explored is the discords and continuities between traditional African dance and what, in the documentary, late Ivorian choreographer Béatrice Komve refers to as "Ç'est la nouvelle expression," a new expression.[35] The documentary presents a collaboration between black American choreographer Jawole Willa-Jo Zollar's Urban Bush Women and Senegalese choreographer Germaine Acogny's now-disbanded Compagnie Jant-Bi. A moment that stands out in footage of this collaboration is when Acogny and Jant-Bi performers sit on a dance studio floor observing a rehearsal by Urban Bush Women and begin tearing up. This tense moment is followed by the Jant-Bi company hugging the Urban Bush dancers. These tears are more than an outpouring of personal emotion or a window to interiority; rather, they augment the unmournable loss resulting from slavery's rupture of kinship, geography, and temporality. The tears are susceptible to a sentimental reading as signaling closure and redress, as an uncomplicated suture of a global African community. But they are also revealing an unspeakable realization that cannot be fully articulated with language and shows up as affect. By "affect," I am referring to the capacity to be touched or moved to tears in this case. Whatever potential for redress or reckoning of slavery's rupture lies in the work is quickly undone by Acogny's utterance of what she understands as African culpability in the trade, followed by a denial of said culpability. She states, "We are responsible for slavery, but I personally don't feel responsible . . . like the young Germans, like my husband who is German. He is not responsible; it was the others who did that."[36] The contradiction is further convoluted by analogizing African enslavement to a white German eschewing personal responsibility from the cruelties of the Holocaust in Europe. Fleshing out the problems of framing slavery in this manner deserves more careful

35—Komve, in *Movement (R)evolution Africa* (Frosch and Kovgan, 2007).

36—Acogny, in *Movement (R)evolution Africa*.

and lengthy engagement than possible in this essay. However, I want to highlight that the scene is instructive on how continental African attempts at reckoning with slavery that go beyond acknowledgment are sometimes limited by the void in language to explain this unsuturable injury. The scene documents a certain engagement with the ruptures of slavery, and the form this takes is a representation of fragmented signs and dense affects watered down by linguistic description and rationalization.

Acogny's momentous contribution to contemporary African dance is well documented and venerated in both academic scholarship and the professional dance industry.[37] As an effort to articulate her formidability and honor her contributions, academics and artists often refer to her as the "Mother of African Contemporary Dance."[38] As a choreographer and teacher trained in forms that include classical ballet, her defiance and selective borrowing of Western technique have been described as "enabl[ing] her to defy the colonizing project that the taxonomy had originally facilitated."[39] This relationship to Western technique is not an aversion to "technique" as such but a divestment from Western hegemony and domestication perfected through technique. The technique Acogny teaches at École des Sables in Senegal foregrounds indigenous African sensibilities and modes of knowing as opposed to mimicry of Western technique. École des Sables attracts dance students from around the world, many from the Global North. This introduces another set of problems regarding expectations of the technique to endow non-Africans with animism and vitality, as they come to Africa to be in touch with their primal instincts, sidestepping the rigor and invention contained in the Acogny technique.

Dance ethnographer Amy Swanson, who conducted research at the École, noticed that the school's survival rests on a certain strategic acquiescence to colonialist demands and appetites from non-Africans for a primitive Africa. For Swanson, "the Acogny Technique functions both as a saleable and consumable embodied practice that capitalizes on a growing global desire for contact with Africa and its cultural forms, just as it comprises a living, evolving vehicle of African identity affiliation."[40] The moniker "Mother of African Contemporary Dance"

37—See "Biennale Di Venezia: Germaine Acogny Awarded the Golden Lion of Dance 2021," Griot, February 18, 2021, https://griotmag.com/en/biennale-di-venezia-germaine-acogny-awarded-the-golden-lion-of-dance-2021/.

38—See Ananya Chatterjea, *Heat and Alterity in Contemporary Dance: South-South Choreographies* (Cham, Switzerland: Palgrave Macmillan, 2020), 134.

39—Susan Leigh Foster, "Muscle/Memories: How Germaine Acogny and Diane McIntyre Put Their Feet Down," in *Rhythms of the Afro-Atlantic World: Rituals and Remembrances*, ed. Mamadou Diouf and Ifeoma Kiddoe Nwankwo (Ann Arbor: University of Michigan Press, 2010), 125.

40—Amy Swanson, "Codifying African Dance: The Germaine Acogny Technique and Antinomies of Postcolonial Cultural Production," *Critical African Studies* 11, no. 1 (2019): 59.

assigned to Acogny is exploited by Global North participants in search of the figure and function of "Mama Africa." While this "capitalizing" might be less a naïve act of self-exoticization than a conscious survival tactic for the École, what gets obscured are the different desires among participants for seeking contact with Africans. White participants attending the school as a way of *playing in the dark*[41] is not conflatable with African American or Diasporic African participation as an attempt to assemble traces and shards of an irrecoverable *loss*. For dance theorist Jasmine Johnson, "non-black West African dance participants have sometimes treated the dance practice as a spaceship launching toward racial transcendence and sexual freedom."[42] She distinguishes this from African diasporic participation seeking community building in West African dance as well as its healing properties. Acogny states, "I know what Americans and especially African Americans (want), they want their traditional dances, they want their roots. But we can also invent a new dance."[43] Here, the discord lies in the African Diaspora seeking African dances preserved in their traditional form, while continental African dance-makers are stretching those dances beyond the logic of preservation and exposing them to processes of invention. Invention is already a defining feature of those "traditional dancers" as opposed to the preservationist impulse that characterizes Western technique. This is why Johnson calls for an attunement to West African dance that steers away from replicating systems of choreographic order and instead, "train[s] our eyes to look at what falls away, rather than what echoes" in contemporary African dance training.[44]

While Acogny's statement demonstrates the Global North's appetite for an Africa that signifies as alterity, a fertile ground for eternal extraction, the collaboration with Urban Bush Women moves appositionally to address what might be felt as the loss of native land and ancestral kin. It is a way to understand rather than swiftly mend the rupture. The African Diaspora's desire for "traditional dances" is also partly an attempt at achieving rootedness and groundedness in the wake of slavery's excision of natal ties. Black theorists such as Jared Sexton and Saidiya Hartman complicate this phantasy of groundedness, sparking curiosity about what can be invented and known in the act

41—See Toni Morrison, *Playing in the Dark: Whiteness and the Literary Imagination* (New York: Vintage Books, 1993).

42—Jasmine Elizabeth Johnson, "Casualties," *TDR: The Drama Review* 62, no. 1 (2018): 170.

43—Acogny, in *Movement (R)evolution Africa*. Acogny's shift away from "roots" and "the ground" to foreground invention circles right back to these tropes as she later states, "My technique is rooted in nature. It's important to put your roots in the ground." See Stefanie Jason, "Germaine Acogny: Dancing around Africa's Bodied Politics," *Mail and Guardian*, August 22, 2013, https://mg.co.za/article/2013-08-22-her-dance-reports-on-africas-bodied-politics/.

44—Johnson, "Casualties," 171.

of losing ground, of losing the *mother*/Mama Africa as (porno)trope. This separation, as they propose in psychoanalytical terms, would not be impetuous abandonment, but "a precondition for any relationship whatsoever."[45] It is a separation necessary for invention and the forging of politicized global black relations.

War can impact or inform both formal and stylistic choices in dance-making. In another dance piece shown in Frosch's documentary, titled *Fagaala* ("Genocide" in the Wolof language), co-choreographed by Acogny and Japanese choreographer Kota Yamazaki for Compagnie Jant-Bi, the cast of seven male dancers directs attention to the international community's silence and indifference to the 1990s genocide in Rwanda. Formally, they foreground movement motifs of fragmentation associated with falling, collision, slipping, and repetition, as well as the intensity of contractions and grotesque poses referencing Butoh (a performance form emerging in the wake of the United States' atomic bomb dropping in Hiroshima and Nagasaki). Rather than filling the silence with empirical facts, Acogny and Yamazaki gravitate toward the fictional by consulting Boubacar Boris Diop's novel titled *Murambi, the Book of Bones* (2000). They execute this exercise of creating a dance by leaning toward fiction because "through fiction we get to the real truth."[46] In *Fagaala*, the rendering of the genocide takes the form of "scream[ing] without screaming, speak[ing] without speaking" when language fails.[47] It is an impossible yet necessary lament for a loss that cannot be possessed as one's own. Acogny discusses encouraging the all-male cast to "get in touch with the feminine side . . . to feel what it's like to lose a child, feel the plight of women in war."[48] The feminine and the "mother" are recuperated here as a way of gendering not only the impulse for participation in war but drawing attention to the gendered erasure of some experiences of war. The "mother," then, in both *Fagaala* and the collaboration with Urban Bush Women, is invoked as a disavowed absence and recuperated presence.

When Congolese choreographer Faustin Linyekula was commissioned by the French Ballet de Lorraine in 2012 to reimagine the 1923 "negro-

45—Sexton, "On Black Negativity"; Saidiya V. Hartman, *Lose Your Mother: A Journey along the Atlantic Slave Route* (New York: Farrar, Straus and Giroux, 2007).

46—Acogny, in *Movement (R)evolution Africa*.

47—Acogny, in *Movement (R)evolution Africa*. In Mark Franko's inquiry about dance and the notion of the gift, he asks if dance, rather than giving back, can turn toward "rendering, rather than responding to disaster." Franko, "Given Movement: Dance and the Event," in *Of the Presence of the Body: Essays on Dance and Performance Theory*, ed. André Lepecki (Middletown, CT: Wesleyan University Press, 2004), 114.

48—Acogny, in *Movement (R)evolution Africa*.

49—Jean Börlin and Faustin Linyekula, *La création du monde*, 1923/2012. Performed by CCN Ballet de Lorraine, 2012. Video, Numeridanse TV, 3:21. https://www.numeridanse.tv/en/dance-videotheque/la-creation-du-monde-1923-2012.

cubist fantasy" ballet by Darius Milhaud titled *La création du monde*, Linyekula pointed out the African shadows that lurk in European classical and modern dance.[49] To mark this absence/"shadow," Djodjo Kazadi, the only black dancer in the cast, unleashed a desperate cry at the end of the performance. The ballet is based on Blaise Cendrars's account of an origin myth by the Fang people of Gabon. In his *Anthologie nègre* (1921), Cendrars masquerades as an expert on Fang mythology, obscuring that he lifted the published writings of French missionary ethnographer Henri Trilles. Klaus-Peter Köpping aptly refers to this chain of appropriations as "effacements" because they are "veritable forgeries through writing over and covering the sources."[50] Milhaud's *La création* perpetuates this effacement by relying on an appropriation manufactured by Cendrars as an original African myth. This becomes a replacement of the Fang myth with one that fails to acknowledge the names of the myth's creators. Linyekula reimagines these multiple effacements in *La création* by calling attention to the absented figures in European ballets. He writes, "All the dancers [in European white ballets] are negroes, all writers of the shadows! . . . It's time that finally I meet all these negroes who have filled the stages and wings down the ages."[51] He references European modernity to take it apart and reveal its foundational monstrosity, exposing the colonial violence that conditions European modernism/modernity. This illustrates the unavailability of the integrity of the body to the black dancer, and why contemporary experimental black dance practices eschew aesthetics of cultural/national pride.

Like most successful experimental African choreographers, Linyekula resided, trained, and presented work in Europe before returning to a war-torn DRC in 1997 and later forming Studios Kabako in 2001. Like Acogny, he meditates on war's capacity to not only exert influence on aesthetic deformation but also render the deformation of the physical form through mutilation. Instead of celebrating cultural heritage, he examines and works from an aspect of his heritage that he describes as an "abyss" and "a pile of ruins." He posits,

> Tell me Cendrars, how do you preserve the integrity of the body when you are just violence and stumps? And you, Senghor, what would have happened if the African national ballets had challenged the national body rather than celebrated it? All of it would have made a negro ballet, I think, a ballet of cruelty, of mutilations, of dishonest compromise, a ballet of shame. . . . And hurray for the losers! A rattling of tambourines with holes in them for the losers![52]

50—Klaus-Peter Köpping, "Performing 'Africa': Linyekula's Re-vision of *La création du monde* as Critical Pastiche," in *Moving (across) Borders: Performing Translation, Intervention, Participation*, ed. Gabriele Brandstetter and Holger Hartung (Bielefeld, Germany: Transcript, 2017), 56.

51—Faustin Linyekula and Kunstenfestivaldesarts, "La création du monde," Kunstenfestivaldesarts, July 2, 2020, https://kfda.be/en/festivals/2012-edition/programme/la-creation-du-monde/.

52—Linyekula and Kunstenfestivaldesarts, "La création du monde."

Deformation of the body, rather than merely referring to a stylistic device, points to his dance-making approach that emphasizes the "holes," "stumps," and "mutilations" in/of the body on multiple scales, from the individual to the national body. In the DRC, any discussion of the deformation of the body cannot circumvent King Leopold of Belgium's genocidal investment in the country. Leopold is responsible for murdering an estimated ten million Congolese in addition to forced labor and using techniques of bodily mutilation to force productivity in rubber plantations. Leopold's regime capitalized on the cruel taste-making properties of the aesthetic by simulating the severed hands of Congolese people in the form of chocolate to be sold and consumed by Belgians. Severed African limbs satiated culinary pleasures and invigorated Belgium's "culture of taste."[53] The "black" and the "aesthetic" are fundamentally antagonistic dance partners.

Black dance facilitates attunement to the above, to the forgotten and effaced shadows and ghosts appearing only as unreliable flickers in the moment of performance. Instead of rushing to rationalize them or enforce coherent form and meaning upon them, there exists another itinerary to forgo *remaining* through methods and regimes that seek to arrange that madness into intelligible order, that sanitize the fissures of colonial violence and its afterlives with an uncomplicated fiction of a national body politic. Through the ruminations of Acogny and Linyekula, we glean, at times against their authorial intentions, contemporary black dance's insistence to *remain* in the entropic field as an impossible form, a rendering of absence while negotiating capture, arrangement, formalization, cooptation, and effacement. Returning to Johnson's "spaceship" metaphor, these dance-makers' anarrangement remains susceptible to cooptation and extraction, or get rewarded as an effort to defang their anticolonial impulse, even while turning coloniality on its head. As Athi Joja contends, "black people's anarrangement of Western aesthetic form cannot escape blackness,"[54] which has not been extricated from what must be extracted, tamed, and possessed. Any antichoreographic gesture "escaping the colonial script" is also available to be possessed. Black dance, in moments, is a scream without a voice, a disarticulation without language, frustrating routine protocols of signification and interpretation. While it is often understood as the balm soothing the enduring colonial wound, black dance is also the *evidence* and recording of the wounding, and it exposes the prematurity, insufficiency, and cruelty of the "balm."

53—See Simon Gikandi, *Slavery and the Culture of Taste* (Princeton, NJ: Princeton University Press, 2011).

54—Athi Joja, personal communication with the author, July 19, 2023.

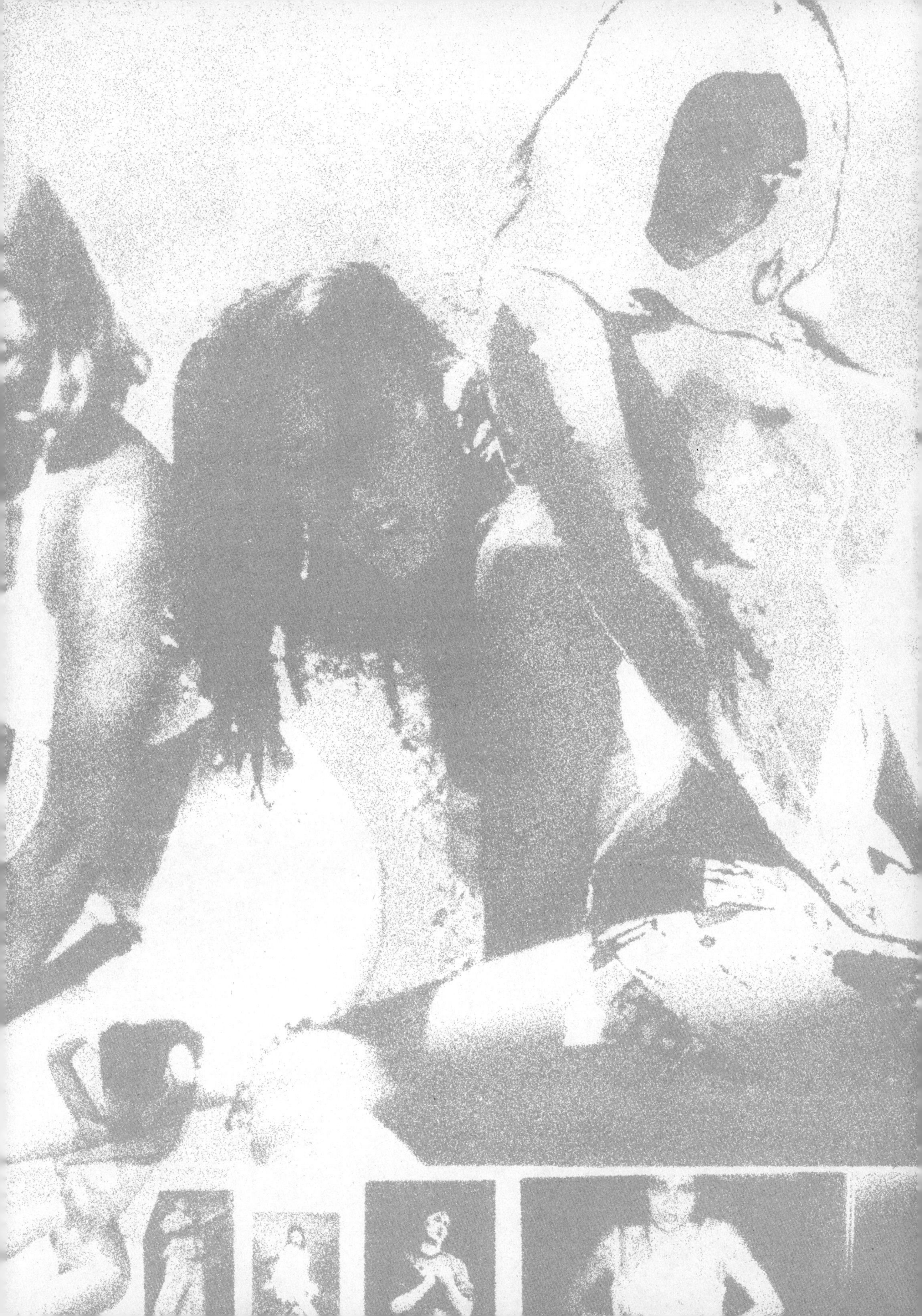

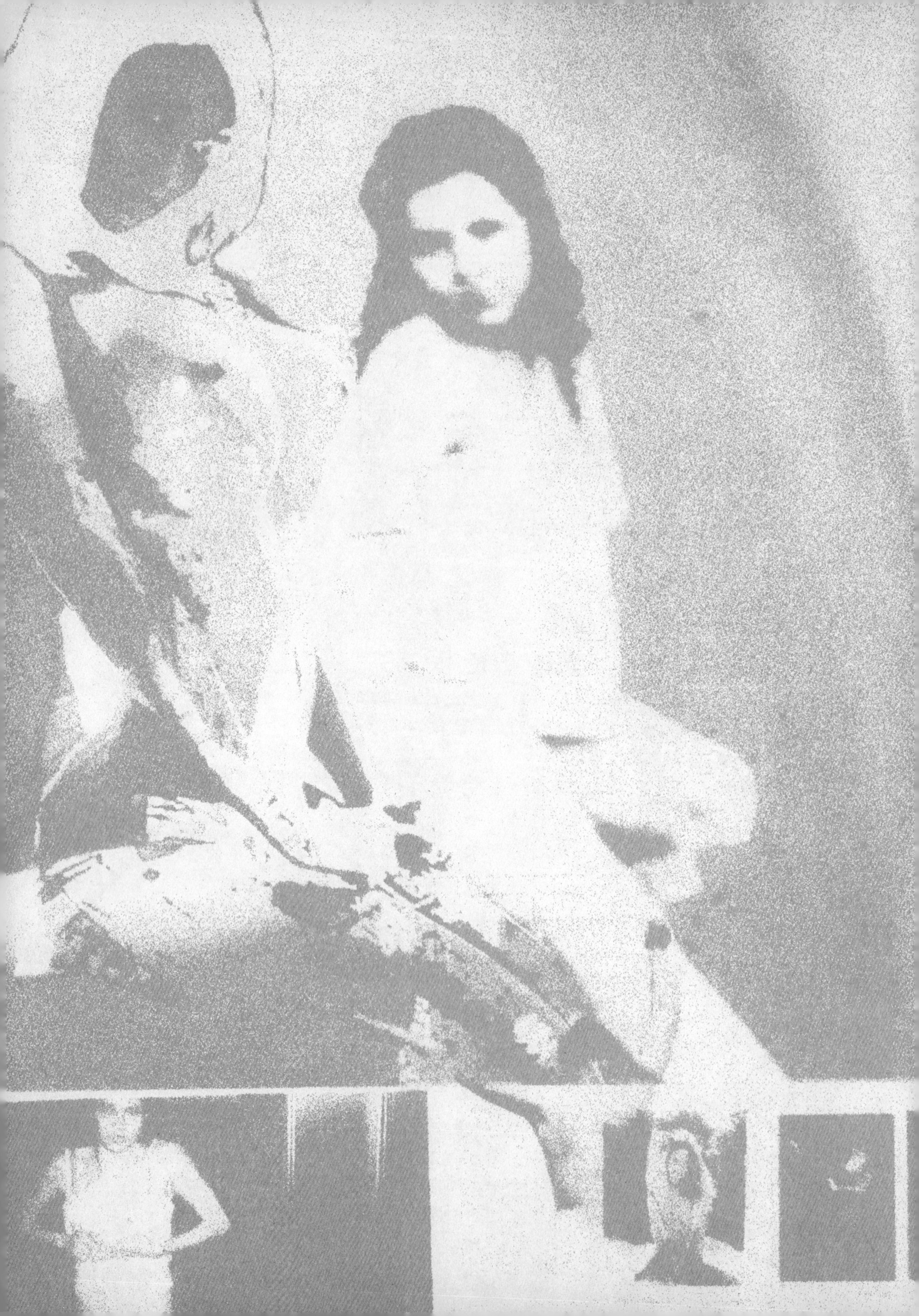

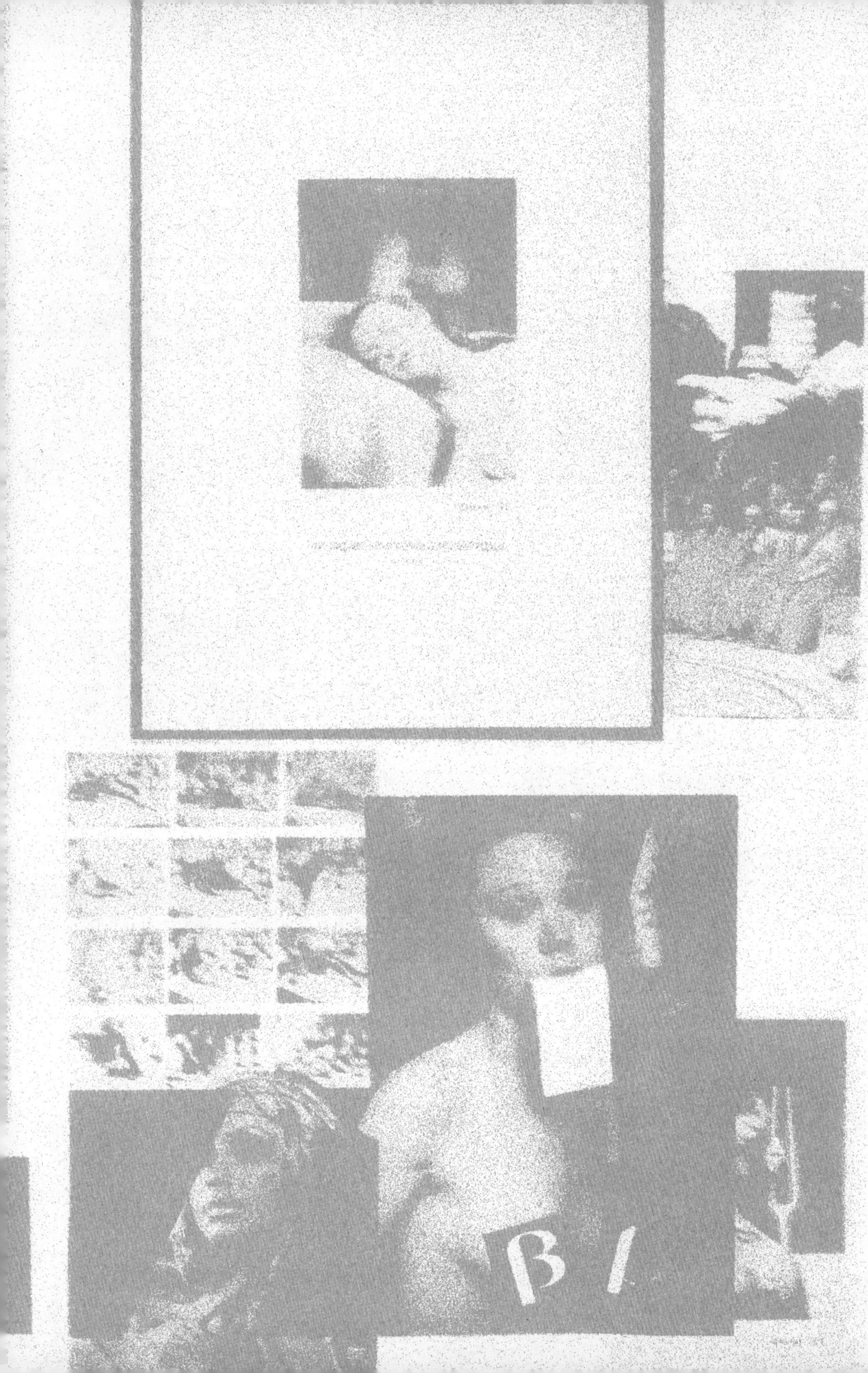

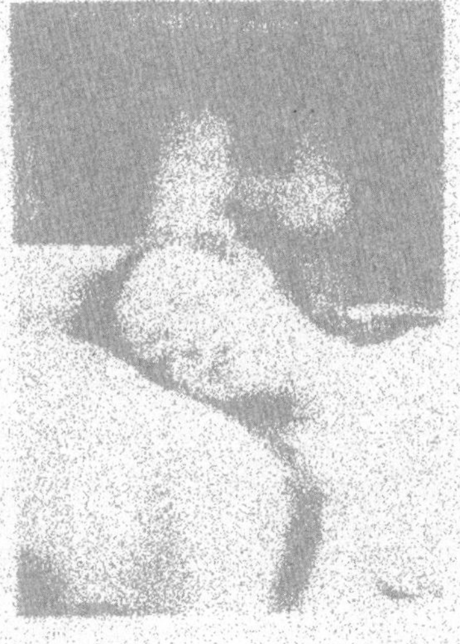

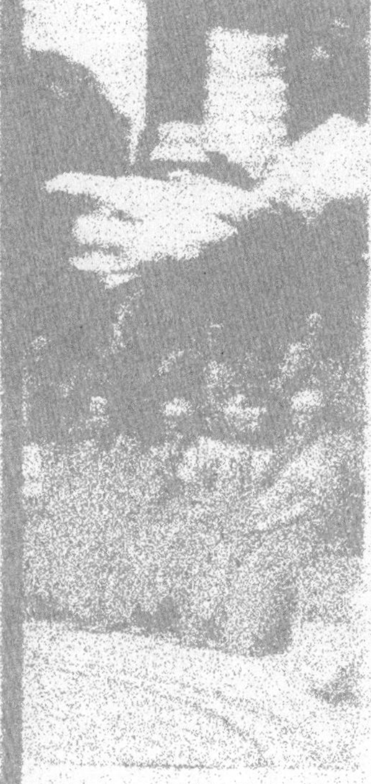

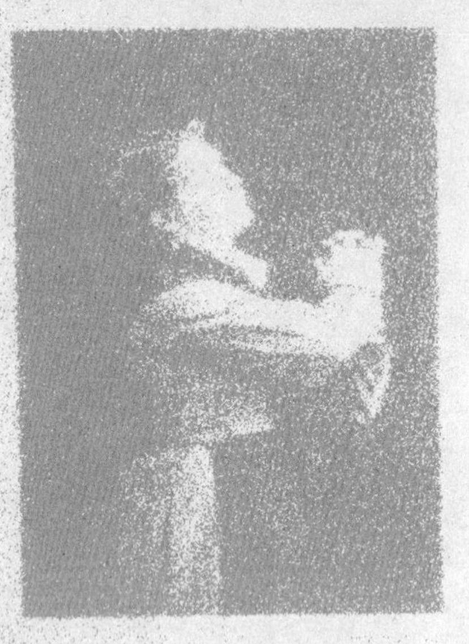

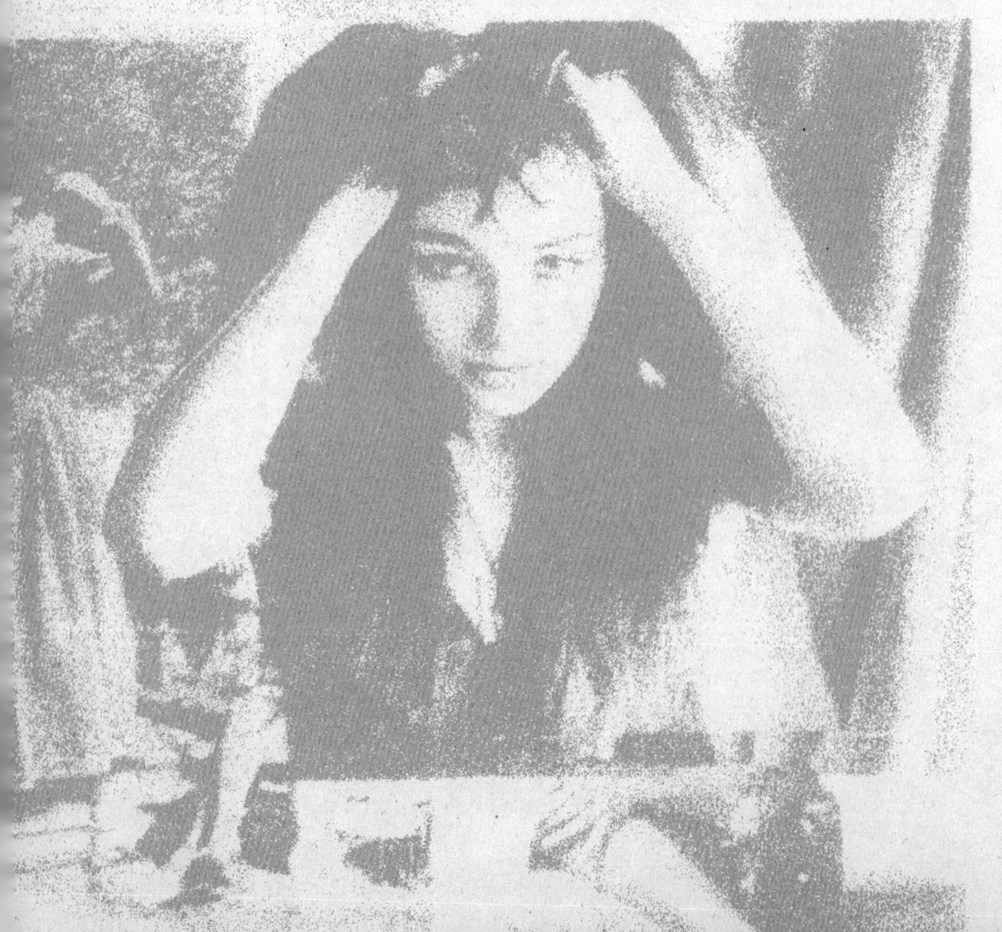

The following works are listed chronologically and then alphabetically within the same year. Captions for works illustrated in the plates but not included in the exhibition are listed after the works in the exhibition and follow the same ordering method.

All works are by Kandis Williams (US, b. 1985).

Cervical Smile, 2016
vinyl adhesive on plexiglass
90 × 48 in.
(228.6 × 121.9 cm)
Courtesy the artist; Heidi, Berlin; and Galerie Hubert Winter, Vienna

Eurydice, 2017–2021
two-channel HD video installation (color, sound)
dimensions variable
20:37 min.
Courtesy the artist; Heidi, Berlin; and Galerie Hubert Winter, Vienna

Mothers and sisters seem here to have been revealed as the true love objects of these men. The words of the incest taboo have written "the water is wide, and they cannot get across." We now also have a way of understanding why "good" women have to be husband-less, why they have to be pale as death. It is their very suffering, their attitude of sacrifice, the traces of self denial on their faces, that give them their deathlike beauty. Why? Because the sons/brothers want it that way. They may produce one Red outrage after another as pretexts, but it's clear enough that they are the ones who want to see the "mask" on these women. The mothers/sisters are called upon to demonstrate that they, too, are consumed by suffering because they are unable to fall into the tender embrace of the sons/brothers. This is the only embrace that the sons/ brothers believe the women really want. In short, it is the sons' merciless jealousy that has the husbands killed off (by the "Reds") and makes martyred angels of the mothers and sisters, 2017
vinyl adhesive on plexiglass
75 × 46 in. (190.5 × 116.8 cm)
Courtesy the artist; Heidi, Berlin; and Galerie Hubert Winter, Vienna

Acheron Death Mask II, 2018
sticker on mirror glass
48 × 48 in. (121.9 × 121.9 cm)
Courtesy the artist; Heidi, Berlin; and Galerie Hubert Winter, Vienna

The Bathers of Acheron, 2018
paper, collage, and plexiglass
10 ½ × 8 in. (26.7 × 20.3 cm)
Collection of Roxane Gay and Debbie Millman

Cave before Cocytus, 2018
sticker on mirror glass
24 × 24 in. (61 × 61 cm)
Courtesy the artist; Heidi, Berlin; and Galerie Hubert Winter, Vienna

Collapse, Turn 'Round, 2018
paper and collage
10 ½ × 10 ½ in. (26.7 × 26.7 cm)
Courtesy the artist; Heidi, Berlin; and Galerie Hubert Winter, Vienna

Her and love are the same, 2018
paper, collage, and plexiglass
42 ¼ × 31 ¾ in. (107.3 × 80.6 cm)
Courtesy the artist; Heidi, Berlin; and Galerie Hubert Winter, Vienna

Iconic, the Face of, Death Mask I, 2018
paper, collage, and plexiglass
24 ¾ × 39 in. (62.9 × 99.1 cm)
Courtesy the artist; Heidi, Berlin; and Galerie Hubert Winter, Vienna

Landscape and RFD, 2018
sticker, collage, and plexiglass
21 × 21 in. (53.3 × 53.3 cm)
Courtesy the artist; Heidi, Berlin; and Galerie Hubert Winter, Vienna

The Mother the Son and the Holy Spirit, 2018
printed plastic and plexiglass
47 × 31 ½ in. (119.4 × 80 cm)
Courtesy the artist; Heidi, Berlin; and Galerie Hubert Winter, Vienna

Styxx, 2018
paper, collage, and plexiglass
7 ⅞ × 6 ½ in. (20 × 16.5 cm)
Private collection

Modernity is not merely a compromise between novel forms of commercially driven social organization and this archaic cultural pattern of patrilineal exogamy, but more fundamentally, a deepening of the compromise already integral to any exogamy that is able to remain patrilineal, 2019
acrylic and dye on canvas and board
48 × 48 in. (121.9 × 121.9 cm)
Collection Davida Nemerov

Annexation Tango, 2020
single-channel video (color, sound)
dimensions variable
10:19 min.
Courtesy the artist; Heidi, Berlin; and Galerie Hubert Winter, Vienna

Belladonna Atropos. On the one hand, the plant appears to withdraw from a human economy of desire and hovers at the limits of our affective identification. But it also produces profound effects on us, including setting in motion our imagination. This oscillation is not only a defining characteristic of vegetality but functions as a key trait of speculative literature, giving this genre a power and agency that is inherently linked to the vibrancy of plant matter. can all the tight pussy gals step forward?, 2020
toner, ink, and acrylic medium on paper
76 × 51 in. (193 × 129.5 cm)
Hammer Museum, Los Angeles
Purchased through the Board of Advisors Acquisition Fund

Calesita in monstera, fan palm, and fern arranged from Tango, Tarantella and Jitterbug, 2020
sublimation prints on cotton paper, copper wire, plastic, and vase
52 × 32 × 20 in.
(132.1 × 81.3 × 50.8 cm)
Private collection

Candombe Africano via Jitterbug to Virginia Georgia Mississippi, 2020
sublimation prints on cotton paper, copper wire, plastic, sumi ink, and vase
62 × 27 × 25 in.
(157.5 × 68.6 × 63.5 cm)
Courtesy the artist; Heidi, Berlin; and Galerie Hubert Winter, Vienna

Exotica, 2020
collage on artificial plant, fabric grow bag with moss, and vase
14 × 21 × 15 in.
(35.6 × 53.3 × 38.1 cm)
Courtesy the artist; Heidi, Berlin; and Galerie Hubert Winter, Vienna

Exotica, 2020
collage on artificial plant, fabric grow bag with moss, and vase
15 × 26 × 22 in.
(38.1 × 66 × 55.9 cm)
Courtesy the artist; Heidi, Berlin; and Galerie Hubert Winter, Vienna

Exotica, 2020
collage on artificial plant, fabric grow bag with moss, and vase
10 ½ × 14 × 10 in.
(26.7 × 35.6 × 25.4 cm)
Courtesy the artist; Heidi, Berlin; and Galerie Hubert Winter, Vienna

Exotica, 2020
collage on artificial plant, fabric grow bag with moss, and vase
25 × 12 × 7 in.
(63.5 × 30.5 × 17.8 cm)
Courtesy the artist; Heidi, Berlin; and Galerie Hubert Winter, Vienna

Exotica, 2020
collage on artificial plant, fabric grow bag with moss, and vase
17 × 9 × 8 in.
(43.2 × 22.9 × 20.3 cm)
Courtesy the artist; Heidi, Berlin; and Galerie Hubert Winter, Vienna

Exotica, 2020
collage on artificial plant, fabric grow bag with moss, and vase
15 × 15 × 14 in.
(38.1 × 38.1 × 35.6 cm)
Courtesy the artist; Heidi, Berlin; and Galerie Hubert Winter, Vienna

Exotica, 2020
collage on artificial plant, fabric grow bag with moss, and vase
13 × 10 × 8 in.
(33 × 25.4 × 20.3 cm)
Courtesy the artist; Heidi, Berlin; and Galerie Hubert Winter, Vienna

Exotica, 2020
collage on artificial plant, fabric grow bag with moss, and vase
14 × 18 × 15 in.
(35.6 × 45.7 × 38.1 cm)
Courtesy the artist; Heidi, Berlin; and Galerie Hubert Winter, Vienna

Malandro Mississippi CHAIN GANG Monstera adansonii, 2020
sublimation prints on cotton paper, copper wire, plastic, moss, and vase
18 × 16 × 15 in.
(45.7 × 40.6 × 38.1 cm)
Courtesy the artist; Heidi, Berlin; and Galerie Hubert Winter, Vienna

Nay, but tell me, am I not unlucky indeed, / To arise from the earth and be only a weed? / Ever since I came out of my dark little seed, / I have tried to live rightly, but still am a--weed! / To be torn by the roots and destroyed, this my meed, / And despised by the gardener, for being--a weed. / Ah! but why was I born, when man longs to be freed / Of a thing so obnoxious and bad as a--weed? / Now, the cause of myself and my brothers I plead, / Say, can any good come of my being a--weed? / Imagine smoking weed in the streets without cops harassin' / Imagine going to court with no trial / Lifestyle cruising blue behind my waters / No welfare supporters, more conscious of the way we raise our daughters / Days are shorter, nights are colder / Feeling like life is over, these snakes strike like a cobra / The world's hot my son got not / Evidently, it's elementary, they want us all gone eventually / Troopin' out of state for a plate, knowledge / If coke was cooked without the garbage we'd all have the top dollars / Imagine everybody flashin', fashion / Designer clothes, lacing your click up with diamond vogues / Your people holdin' dough, no parole / No rubbers, go in raw imagine, law with no undercovers / Just some thoughts..., 2020
xerox collage and ink on watercolor
76 × 51 in. (193 × 129.5 cm)
Michael Sherman, Los Angeles

They go from a fence, or a closed place for slaves, to a dancing gathering of Africans in Latin America; from the beating of drums to the place where they danced to the sound of drums, even to the Hispanic-Arab-African dance they call tango andaluz. Kizomba, Semba, Sea Kelp and Hanging Amaranthus arrangement, 2020
sublimation prints on cotton paper, copper wire, plastic, and vase
32 × 22 × 19 in.
(81.3 × 55.9 × 48.3 cm)
Private collection

Toxic Exotica, 2020
sublimation prints on cotton paper, copper wire, and plastic
39 × 166 × 6 in.
(99.1 × 421.6 × 15.2 cm)
Courtesy the artist; Heidi, Berlin; and Galerie Hubert Winter, Vienna

Transpositions, Sketch, Giant Tea Leaf and Money Plant, 2020
collage on paper
36 × 24 in. (91.4 × 61 cm)
Courtesy the artist; Heidi, Berlin; and Galerie Hubert Winter, Vienna

Transposition, Sketch, Monstera and Tumblr issued Tango, 2020
collage on paper
36 × 24 in. (91.4 × 61 cm)
Courtesy the artist; Heidi, Berlin; and Galerie Hubert Winter, Vienna

We have spared no expense. scope, scalpel, axe, drill. The Sort of Thing You Should Not Admit: violent death, turns out to be puzzlingly complex and if you have a problem figuring out whether you're for me or, then you ain't black., 2020
ink and cut-and-pasted printed paper on paper
73 × 51 in. (185.4 × 129.5 cm)
The Museum of Modern Art, New York
Fund for the Twenty-First Century, 2021

Atomic Karen, 2021
xerox collage and ink on watercolor paper
90 × 55 ¾ in.
(228.6 × 141.6 cm)
The Museum of Contemporary Art, Los Angeles
Purchase with funds provided by the Acquisition and Collection Committee and the Emerging Art Fund

Bitter Arrangement VI: Interactions of Color / ABCs of color, transjective cognition, 2021
aerosol spray and plastic
40 × 40 × 5 in.
(101.6 × 101.6 × 12.7 cm)
Private collection

Bolshoi to Harlem: Diaghilev to Dunham, certainly fictions—caste, stereotype, gender, and race—are a primary means of production, 2021
xerox collage and ink on paper
66 × 52 in. (167.6 × 132.1 cm)
Private collection

Genes, not Genius: Another aspect of the colonial educational and cultural patterns which needs investigation was expressed not only by hostility to African culture but by paternalism and by praise of negative and static social features. There were many colonialists who wished to preserve in perpetuity everything that was African, if it appeared quaint or intriguing to them, 2021
collage on artificial plant, fabric grow bag with moss, acrylic paint, and plastic
95 × 48 × 33 in.
(241.3 × 121.9 × 83.8 cm)
Courtesy the artist; Heidi, Berlin; and Galerie Hubert Winter, Vienna

Genes, not Genius: For jazz is orgasm, it is the music of orgasm, good orgasm and bad, and so it spoke across a nation, it had the communication of art even where it was watered, perverted, corrupted, and almost killed, it spoke in no matter what laundered popular way of instantaneous existential states to which some whites could respond, it was indeed a communication by art because it said, "I feel this, and now you do too." Virtuosity is bound to colorism, tokenism, trophyism, and the ruptures of interraciality on legacies of rape and social distortion of dark skin, reverse colorism is not real. The importance of dance in courtship and social gatherings is probably older than its use as recreation and entertainment, 2021
collage on artificial plant, fabric grow bag with moss, acrylic paint, and plastic
92 × 40 × 20 in.
(233.7 × 101.6 × 50.8 cm)
Courtesy the artist; Heidi, Berlin; and Galerie Hubert Winter, Vienna

Genes, not Genius: The overlying purpose is to address how the social production of biologically determinist racial scripts—which extend from a biocentric conception of the human—can be dislodged by bringing studies of blackness in/and science into conversation with autopoiesis, black Atlantic livingness, weights and measures, and poetry. A biocentric conception of the human, it should be noted up front, refers to the law-like order of knowledge that posits a Darwinian narrative of the human—that we are purely biological and bioevolutionary beings—as universal; elegance is elimination, 2021
collage on artificial plant, fabric grow bag with moss, acrylic paint, and plastic
92 × 41 × 18 in.
(233.7 × 104.1 × 45.7 cm)
Courtesy the artist; Heidi, Berlin; and Galerie Hubert Winter, Vienna

A Lift and a Kick conflated, 2021
xerox collage and ink on paper
66 × 52 in. (167.6 × 132.1 cm)
Courtesy the artist; Heidi, Berlin; and Galerie Hubert Winter, Vienna

Triadic Ballet, 2021
variable-channel video (color, sound)
dimensions variable
running time variable
Walker Art Center
Gift of the Pohlad Family, with additional funds from the T. B. Walker Acquisition Fund, 2024
Triadic Ensemble: stacked erasures, Russes de Monte Carlo, Harlem Dance, Wigman and Duncan, 2021
xerox collage and ink on paper
66 × 52 in. (167.6 × 132.1 cm)
Private collection

Visage, uses of portrait and mask from rulers to icons through Primitivism and phenotypical hierarchy, 2021
xerox collage and ink on paper
66 × 52 in. (167.6 × 132.1 cm)
Courtesy the artist; Heidi, Berlin; and Galerie Hubert Winter, Vienna

Death of A, 2022
four-channel HD video installation (color, sound)
dimensions variable
26:51 min.
Hammer Museum, Los Angeles
Purchased with fund provided by Susan and Larry Marx

From the Joy of Seeing Them, to the Pain of Being Them, 2023
lenticular print mounted on dibond
edition of 3 + 2 APs
46 ⅞ × 33 ⅛ in. (119 × 84 cm)
Courtesy the artist; Heidi, Berlin; and Galerie Hubert Winter, Vienna

From the Joy of Seeing Them, to the Pain of Being Them II, 2023
lenticular print mounted on dibond
edition of 3 + 2 APs
33 ⅛ × 46 ⅞ in. (84 × 119 cm)
Courtesy the artist; Heidi, Berlin; and Galerie Hubert Winter, Vienna

Going Thru It/Working Girl Color Theory/A Monologue – Thy Hand Belinda, 2023
two-channel video (color, sound) and four-channel analog slide projections
dimensions variable
36:10 min.
Courtesy Heidi, Berlin

Medusa, 2023
single-channel video (color, sound)
dimensions variable
34:10 min.
Courtesy Heidi, Berlin

BEAST: "I am become Death, the destroyer of worlds. Oh no, it wasn't the airplanes. It was Beauty killed the Beast." "When Kong is put in chains and displayed in New York, the film evokes an unmistakable echo of the slave trade. Kong, in his brute strength and childlike emotions, is a cinematic symbol of the fear and fascination that black men elicited in white America." (Bogle) "The arrogance of man is thinking nature is in our control and not the other way around." Johnson was more than just a champion in the ring; he was a symbol of defiance against the racial order of the time. His very existence challenged the prevailing stereotypes of black inferiority and submissiveness. Hollywood, however, often reduced his complex persona into a mere caricature, focusing on his relationships with white women and his supposed brutishness, thereby reinforcing the racial fears of white America. (Bogle) The imagination responsible for its enactment dwells in another dimension where geography can be specified beyond regional areas, portfolios, markets, and other fixed entities serving the interests of a dominant minority. Afro Asia persists as an imprecise category of analysis because it is but the shadow of a world whose disclosure would make all too clear the meagerness of what presently qualifies for 'world' status" (Kee) "This is Tokyo. Once a city of six million people. What has happened here was caused by a force which up until a few days ago was entirely beyond the scope of man's imagination. Tokyo, a smoldering memorial to the unknown, an unknown which at this very moment still prevails and could at any time lash out with its terrible destruction anywhere else in the world. There were once men who believed that this world belonged to them. But this night, Tokyo lies crushed and silent under the dark, menacing shadow of… Godzilla." from *gods and monsters that white people make up to kill us all*, 2024
paper, collage, color aid, and adhesive on wood
66 × 47 in. (167.6 × 119.4 cm)
Courtesy the artist; Heidi, Berlin; and Galerie Hubert Winter, Vienna

FINAL GYAL: Native Wife: Queens of the Damned: Sapphire Mammy Jezebel. Crawl on me. Sink into me. Die for me. Living dead girl. Crawl on me. Sink into me. Die for me. Living dead girl (Zombie, 2009). W. J. T. Mitchell points out that she is a "doubled figure of slavery, of both sexual and racial servitude," which is here made to appear "in the natural colors of power and sublimity." Burke, Mitchell claims, here confuses "sensory, aesthetic signals" with "the 'natural' orders of gender, social class, and symbolic modes." As such an incongruous mixture, it may be added, she becomes the point at which Burke's analysis breaks and is then sublime because she represents a point of contradiction, a lack of intelligibility, in Burke's aesthetic discourse itself. The black female continued to provoke speculations such as these, and not simply about her aesthetic qualities but also about the relationship between her "look," her anatomy, and her sexuality. Nineteenth-century images of the black female produced in Europe and Britain emphasized her grotesque nature as well as her (pathological) lasciviousness; the black female is represented, in both physical form and alleged desire, as a monstrous creature. As such, she becomes the site for another form of the sublime, one which draws upon the lure of her abjection, and the thrill which is not contained within the polite society of the sexes imagined by Burke. True to his wish to classify the effects of objects as beautiful or sublime, however, she also serves as a stereotype of difference, a collecting pool for all that is imagined as excessive to the ideology of Burke's aesthetic (Armstrong, 1996). More amazing examples of 'The Black Wife Effect': The viral trend that shows white men getting a much-needed glow up (online article, 2024). Mariya Savinova (Russia): "Just look at her!" Elisa Cusma (Italy): "These kinds of people should not run with us. For me, she's not a woman. …" (remarks made Olympic games 2024) A White Sci-Fi author once stated that blacks were unnecessary because aliens were already present." (Butler), from *gods and monsters that white people make up to kill us all*, 2024
paper, collage, color aid, and adhesive on paper
24 1/16 × 18 in. (61 × 45.7 cm)
Courtesy the artist; Heidi, Berlin; and Galerie Hubert Winter, Vienna

GHOUL: White Girl War Machine, Garrison and the Brute. White girl, for the white girl, they get all excited. Got enough in here to get us all indicted. Call up your girls, yeah they all invited. All I really need is your undivided. Undivided, undivided. All I really need is your undivided. Undivided, undivided. All I really need is your undivided (Scott, 2020). In the use of the brute in military propaganda and in popular monster forms, the virgin sacrifice elevates to mythological proportions, in psychopathic harmony, it shields collective punishment and corpses economies in the light of virtuous self- preservation at all costs. The brute virgin collapses into social fabric at the level of ultimate silence and democratization of shame and exile. As a white Double Consciousness pivots around its acceptance and misrecognition of the necropolitical real, we see it cleave to several primal images; the brute and the virgin as a sacrificial form can sub-symbolically identify two asymmetries between white double consciousness and the double consciousness of racially dominated peoples: the access asymmetry and the escape asymmetry. The sacrificial white woman with the devalue of the stained marked by the beast left flesh as a site of urgent reproductive terror on the one hand, and a site of illicit erotic currency, a hyper-patriarchal satisfaction of fetish fears, its asymmetries elide the spatial, interpersonal, and psychic barriers to remaking whiteness in a society in which the preservation of whiteness is structurally dominant (Hawkins Davis, 2024). "This association of France with the 'black atrocities' was reflected on all levels of the campaign. Popular media made out that France's desire for revenge was the source of the atrocities on the Rhine, and representatives of different organizations mobilized against 'the violation of the German woman by France.' They argued together with government agencies that the French appointed 'Negroes as rulers' in order to humiliate Germany. The critique of the use of colonial troops always targeted the French nation too. Large parts of the German press attributed the responsibility for the black crimes to France and used the 'Black Shame' to chain the French to the 'stake of world history' (Schandpfahl der Weltgeschichte). Campaigners saw 'the entire white world' standing against France" (Wigger, 2017), from gods and monsters that white people make up to kill us all, 2024
paper, collage, color aid, and adhesive on paper
18 × 24 in. (45.7 × 61 cm)
Courtesy the artist; Heidi, Berlin; and Galerie Hubert Winter, Vienna

SOLDIER PSYCHO: "This is your last chance. After this, there is no turning back. You take the blue pill—the story ends, you wake up in your bed and believe whatever you want to believe. You take the red pill—you stay in Wonderland, and I show you how deep the rabbit hole goes" (Morpheus, 1999). "The aesthetics of settler imperial failure contained in the transpacific cultural works I analyze allows us to think through the relationship between settler colonialism and military empire in this way: settler colonialism is at once military empire's proving ground, obscured condition of possibility, and imbricated partner in violence. The United States as the literal testing ground for bio-political tactics and technologies that are geopolitically and militarily projected abroad has produced and continues to produce Native American displacement and dispossession, and that geopolitical and military projection abroad in Asia and the Pacific in turn produces Asian migration and Indigenous Pacific Islander displacement and dispossession" (Kim, 2018, p. 16). "Ghosts are cosmological strangers in social classification, as noted previously, but their phenomenal (or 'social') existence, by definition, is inseparable from a particular history of death. The category of ghosts is a product of the interplay between cultural concepts and historical reality: the spirits of the dead fall into this category through a crisis in the social organization of commemoration and the historical events that cause this crisis" (Gordon). "That is, interracial intimacies move the politics of the public sphere to the erotics of the private sphere through the tropes of race, gender, and heterosexuality that come to displace the broader politics at work within these particular bodies . . . describes as 'masculinities in the contact zone'" (Rowe)., from gods and monsters that white people make up to kill us all, 2024
paper, collage, color aid, and adhesive on wood
66 × 47 in. (167.6 × 119.4 cm)
Courtesy the artist; Heidi, Berlin; and Galerie Hubert Winter, Vienna

SOLDIER PSYCHO (Sketch) This is your last chance. After this, there is no turning back. You take the blue pill—the story ends, you wake up in your bed and believe whatever you want to believe. You take the red pill—you stay in Wonderland, and I show you how deep the rabbit hole goes (Morpheus, 1999). When the legislature convened for its first session in 1913, the Democrats signaled their victory by immediately offering several bills against the Negro. Jack Johnson, champion a few years before, was then in the high tide of his prosperity. He was already married to a white woman, and it seems that in his theatrical engagements which followed after his victory, he was accompanied by another white woman who had fallen under his spell. Seeing their chance to get even, racially prejudiced persons brought a charge against him under the Mann Act. He was accused of transporting the woman in the case into the

different states where he gave shows. Instead, Mr. Johnson chose to open a saloon to cater to the worst passions of both races. When he was not on the road, he spent most of his time there, entertaining the wildest of the underworld of both sexes and especially of the white race (Wells, 1970). Marshall: This name was introduced to Britain about the time of the Norman Invasion of 1066, and is derived from 'marechal' (horse servant, or groom). Historic reliance on the horse ensured that its use soon became widespread in Britain and therefore Scottish ancestry should not be assumed on evidence of name alone. Like Steward or Constable, the post became a position of great dignity and eventually gave rise to the title Earl Marischal. This elevated position did not spawn the proliferation of the name, for most were of more humble degree who took the name of their trade when surnames became the vogue. "I saw this black guy with a beautiful spirit walking with a bop," Joanie Mitchell told writer Angela LaGreca. "As he went by me, he turned around and said, 'Ummm mmm, looking good sister, lookin' good!' Well I just felt so good after he said that. It was as if this spirit went into me. So I started walking like him. I bought a black wig, I bought sideburns, a moustache. I bought some pancake make-up. I was like, 'I'm goin' as him!'" (Hall, 2008), from gods and monsters that white people make up to kill us all, 2024
paper, collage, color aid, and adhesive on paper
24 × 18 in. (61 × 45.7 cm)
Courtesy the artist; Heidi, Berlin; and Galerie Hubert Winter, Vienna

*VAMPIRE: "I am Dracula. I bid you welcome. Listen to them. Children of the night. What music they make! The blood is the life, Mr. Renfield. I never drink . . . wine. There are far worse things awaiting man than death. (Lugosi 1931). The discovery by a boy that his genitals are the chief site of his sexual sensations gives rise to the castration complex, which exerts a determining influence on the formation of his sexual character. The boy fears that his penis will be removed as punishment for his forbidden sexual desires. This fear leads to the development of the Oedipus complex, and the resulting anxiety plays a crucial role in the formation of the superego." (Freud 1938) The virginal brides file past his tomb/Strewn with time's dead flowers/Bereft in deathly bloom/ Alone in a darkened room/ The count (bauhaus 1982) "I want my opera house!" (Kinski 1982) Lucifer's sin is what thinkers in the Middle Ages called "cupiditas."*1 For Dante, the sins that spring from that root are the most extreme "sins of the wolf," the spiritual condition of having an inner black hole so deep within oneself that no amount of power or money can ever fill it. For those suffering the mortal malady called cupiditas, whatever exists outside of one's self has worth only as it can be exploited by, or taken into one's self. In Dante's Hell those guilty of that sin are in the ninth circle, frozen in the Lake of Ice. Having cared for nothing but self in life, they are encased in icy Self for eternity. By making people focus only on oneself in this way, Satan and his followers turn their eyes away from the harmony of love that unites all living creatures. (Zimbardo, 2008),* from *gods and monsters that white people make up to kill us all,* 2024
paper, collage, color aid, and adhesive on wood
66 × 47 in. (167.6 × 119.4 cm)
Courtesy the artist; Heidi, Berlin; and Galerie Hubert Winter, Vienna

ZOMBIE (Sketch) Plantation Fantasies and Suburban Body Snatchers and the Power to Steal the Will of Others You're working on a new film now, about a Harvard graduate student who goes down to Haiti and uncovers what he thinks is the biological secret behind zombies. Um, so you were shooting on location in Haiti. And I don't, can't think of many films that have been shot there. There's been a lot of political upheaval there lately. Did that affect the making of the film at all? Wade Davis was a Harvard ethnobotanist, and he was commissioned by a large pharmaceutical company in a rather secret expedition to go to Haiti and find the botanical reason behind the creation of zombies. I personally met one, a 17-year-old zombie, quote, unquote, by the name of Rosemary. What they are, as it turned out after extensive research, is people that have been poisoned by a very subtle, very powerful neurotoxin that gives them all appearances of death. Their heartbeat, their respiration, and all other vital signs go down to the point where they cannot be determined by a typical rural doctor. The person is buried, and in the middle of the night is still alive, still fully conscious, although showing no signs of life, is dug back up, further poisoned, beaten, and quite often sold into slavery in Haiti for their work in the cane fields. All part of a tribal system of judgment. It's their form of capital punishment within voodoo. So, rather than thinking of zombies, think of somebody who's been poisoned by a neurotoxin and appeared to be dead, but was not, and has died, then returned to the living as a brain-damaged person with all of their volitional centers destroyed. That is what a zombie truly is. And this movie is about that actual factual process. The process existed for centuries and then was distorted by Duvalier, Papadoc Duvalier, and used as a tool of political oppression. If you spoke out too harshly against his government, you would be dragged from your house in the middle of the night and made into a zombie. Some of the most beautiful and gracious people I've ever met, taken individually, they're wonderful, marvelous people. Within a group of more than six

or eight, they can very quickly develop a sense of outrage and wanting to tear the house down because they've been oppressed so severely and most recently released from this. So, when we were dealing with large crowds and we had some scenes dealing with 4,000 people, we ended up in very dangerous situations. We ended up once having to evacuate our crew into a missionary compound in a small village far removed from any help. Were you perceived as the exploiter, as the filmmaker there? Not at first. I mean, we went in with all attempts to say we are bringing work and jobs and everything else. The people have been deprived for so long that any show of money whatsoever becomes what they perceive as the beginning of the gold mine opening up. We're hoping to open it next January on Martin Luther King's birthday (Wes Craven and Terry Gross, 1987)., from *gods and monsters that white people make to kill us all*, 2024
paper, collage, color aid, and adhesive on paper
24 × 18 in. (61 × 45.7 cm)
Courtesy the artist; Heidi, Berlin; and Galerie Hubert Winter, Vienna

ZOMBIE: Somnambulists, Body Snatchers, Elixir Bearers, Wizards, Hypnotists, Poltergeists, Demon Masters, and Witch Covens all inhabit the shadowed realms of sugar, rubber, and cotton plantations, hidden deep within the ghettos of every outpost in the vast, dark expanse of the Imperial world. "But if the commodity-form is not, presently, use-value, and even if it is not actually present, it affects in advance the use-value of the wooden table. It affects and bereaves it in advance, like the ghost it will become, but this is precisely where haunting begins. And its time, and the untimeliness of its present, of its being 'out of joint'. To haunt does not mean to be present, and it is necessary to introduce haunting into the very construction of a concept. Of every concept, beginning with the concepts of being and time. That is what we would be calling here a hauntology. Ontology opposes it only in a movement of exorcism. Ontology is a conjuration" (Derrida, p. 202), from *gods and monsters that white people make up to kill us all*, 2024
paper, collage, color aid, and adhesive on wood
66 × 47 in. (167.6 × 119.4 cm)
Courtesy the artist; Heidi, Berlin; and Galerie Hubert Winter, Vienna

ILLUSTRATED WORKS NOT IN THE EXHIBITION

Child M/other 1, 2013
acrylic paint and collage on canvas
11 11⁄16 × 8 ¼ in. (29.7 × 21 cm)
Private collection

Child M/other 3, 2013
acrylic paint and collage on canvas
11 11⁄16 × 8 ¼ in. (29.7 × 21 cm)
Private collection

Mother sister sister anchor arrangement, 2013
xerox, charcoal, and acrylic on paper
55 × 31 in. (139.7 × 78.7 cm)
Private collection

Pedestal, 2013
collage print on paper
50 × 40 ½ in. (126.8 × 102.8 cm)
Courtesy the artist; Heidi, Berlin; and Galerie Hubert Winter, Vienna

to be gazed at endlessly by the mother is a primary narcissistic demand, 2013
acrylic paint and collage on canvas
11 11⁄16 × 8 ¼ in. (29.7 × 21 cm)
Private collection

Demeter Persephone Downtown LA, 2014
mixed media on paper
43 × 46 ¼ in. (109.2 × 117.5 cm)
Courtesy the artist; Heidi, Berlin; and Galerie Hubert Winter, Vienna

The Endless Gaze, 2014
mixed media on paper
40 ¾ × 38 ¾ in. (103.5 × 98.4 cm)
Courtesy the artist; Heidi, Berlin; and Galerie Hubert Winter, Vienna

kid sister, 2014
mixed media on paper
44 × 49 in. (111.8 × 124.5 cm)
Courtesy the artist; Heidi, Berlin; and Galerie Hubert Winter, Vienna

M/other 4, 2015
acrylic paint and collage on canvas
8 ¼ × 11 11⁄16 in. (21 × 29.7 cm)
Private collection

Songye Shield, 2015
acrylic paint, ink, and collage on panel
55 ⅛ × 63 ⅛ in. (140 × 160.3 cm)
Courtesy the artist; Heidi, Berlin; and Galerie Hubert Winter, Vienna

Study, 2015
mixed media on board
70 ⅞ × 59 in. (180 × 149.9 cm)
Courtesy the artist; Heidi, Berlin; and Galerie Hubert Winter, Vienna

Study, 2015
acrylic paint, ink, and collage on canvas
31 ¾ × 37 ½ in. (80.6 × 95.3 cm)
Courtesy the artist; Heidi, Berlin; and Galerie Hubert Winter, Vienna

Study, 2015
acrylic paint, ink, and collage on canvas
49 ⅛ × 35 ⅜ in. (124.8 × 89.9 cm)
Courtesy the artist; Heidi, Berlin; and Galerie Hubert Winter, Vienna

Study, 2015
acrylic paint, ink, and collage on canvas
27 ½ × 19 ¾ in. (69.9 × 50.2 cm)
Courtesy the artist; Heidi, Berlin; and Galerie Hubert Winter, Vienna

Study for Liza Jane (Unborn Daughter), 2015
acrylic paint, ink, and collage on paper
58 × 55 in. (147.3 × 139.7 cm)
Courtesy the artist; Heidi, Berlin; and Galerie Hubert Winter, Vienna

Study for Liza Jane (Unborn Daughter), 2015
collage on paper
30 5⁄16 × 42 1⁄8 in. (77 × 107 cm)
Courtesy the artist; Heidi, Berlin; and Galerie Hubert Winter, Vienna

Study for Liza Jane (Unborn Daughter), 2015
mixed media on board
70 7⁄8 × 59 in. (180 × 149.9 cm)
Courtesy the artist; Heidi, Berlin; and Galerie Hubert Winter, Vienna

Esophagus Pin-Up, 2016
vinyl adhesive on plexiglass
48 × 90 in. (121.9 × 228.6 cm)
Courtesy the artist; Heidi, Berlin; and Galerie Hubert Winter, Vienna

Venus is a Sacrificial Form, 2016
vinyl, phototransfer, and acrylic paint on canvas
76 × 44 in. (193 × 111.8 cm)
Courtesy the artist; Heidi, Berlin; and Galerie Hubert Winter, Vienna

The Midnight Snack, Well-a, whosonever told it, that he told a- He told a dirty lie, babe. Well-a, whosonever told it, that he told a- He told a dirty lie, well-a. Well-a, whosonever told it, that he told a- He told a dirty lie, babe. Well the eagle on the dollar-quarter, He gonna rise and fly, well-a. He gonna rise and fly, sugar. He gonna rise and fly, well-a. Well the eagle on the dollar-quarter, He gonna rise and fly, well-a (Chorus) Sung by "22", Little Red, Tangle Eye, and Hard Hair, accompanied by double cutting axes, 2017
vinyl adhesive on mirror
10 × 9 3⁄4 in. (25.4 × 24.8 cm)
Private collection

the set-up Out of the blackest part of my soul, across the zebra striping of my mind, surges this desire to be suddenly white. I wish to be acknowledged not as black but as white. Now—and this is a form of recognition that Hegel had not envisaged—who but a white woman can do this for me? By loving me she proves that I am worthy of white love. I am loved like a white man. I am a white man. Her love takes me onto the noble road that leads to total realization. . . . I marry white culture, white beauty, white whiteness. When my restless hands caress those white breasts, they grasp white civilization and dignity and make them mine., 2017
vinyl adhesive on mirror
32 × 23 3⁄8 in. (81.3 × 59.4 cm)
Private collection

Snow, if sign value and exchange value (sign form and commodity form) really are implicated, by reason of their logical form, in the framework of a general political economy, we can claim no affinity of the same order linking symbolic exchange and use value; quite the contrary, because the former implies the transgression of the latter, the latter the reduction of the former, 2017
vinyl adhesive on mirror
48 × 31 7⁄8 in. (122 × 81 cm)
Private collection

'We are too much in the habit of looking at falsehood in its darkest associations. . . That indignation which we profess to feel at deceit absolute, is indeed only at deceit malicious. We resent calumny, hypocrisy, and treachery because they harm us, not because they are untrue.' ruskin, 2017
vinyl adhesive on mirror
8 × 15 in. (20.3 × 38.1 cm)
Private collection

Crowd on the marshes of Lethe, 2018
sticker and plastic
16 × 13 1⁄2 in. (40.6 × 34.3 cm)
Private collection

co-response-ability with/for the unknown Other, 2019
xerox collage and ink on paper, framed
42 × 52 1⁄4 in. (106.7 × 132.6 cm)
Courtesy the artist; Heidi, Berlin; and Galerie Hubert Winter, Vienna

In an events-without-witness era, 2019
xerox collage and ink on paper, framed
36 × 46 1⁄4 in. (91.4 × 117.5 cm)
Courtesy the artist; Heidi, Berlin; and Galerie Hubert Winter, Vienna

Primitive accumulation: Kant, Marx, Albers, Jackson, 2019
acrylic and dye on canvas and board
48 × 48 in. (121.9 × 121.9 cm)
Private collection

transformed relations-without-relating, 2019
xerox collage and ink on paper
43 13⁄16 × 35 3⁄4 in. (111.3 × 90.8 cm)
Private collection

When the chief passes by, the dancers have 'to die': they throw themselves down, hiding their faces with their hands. Crafted during the Johnson, Nixon and Reagan admin-is-trations, the current federal "starve the beast" movement is designed to reestablish numerous forms of domination by comprehensively trans-forming key ins-titutions within the national and international political economy, that is, 'deevolution' at home and 'neoliberalism' abroad, 2019
ink, dye, and collage on canvas
36 × 46 1⁄4 in. (91.4 × 117.5 cm)
Courtesy the artist; Heidi, Berlin; and Galerie Hubert Winter, Vienna

After birth all diligence is transferred to the calves; then the farmers brand them with their mark and the name of their breed And set aside those to rear to perpetuate their kind, to keep as sacred for the altar, or to cultivate

earth and turn over the uneven field breaking its clods. the rest of the cattle pasture on green grasses, but train those that you'll prepare for work and service on the farm when they are still calves and set them on the path to dociling with their youthful spirits are willing, while their lives are tractable. some few women are born free, and some amid insult and scarlet letter achieve freedom [sic] with that freedom they are buying an untrammeled independence and dear as is the price they pay for it, it will in the end be worth every taunt and groan., 2020
sublimation prints on cotton paper, copper wire, plastic, and vase
64 × 32 × 25 in.
(162.6 × 81.3 × 63.5 cm)
Private collection

Because the forest is so densely grown with thistles and thorns, I had to send my slaves ahead of me with axes to hack out an opening for me to uncover specimens. Feet don't fail me now Take me to the finish line. Oh, my heart, it breaks every step that I take, But I'm hoping at the gates, they'll tell me that you're mine., 2020
xerox collage and ink on watercolor paper
47 × 51 in. (119.4 × 129.5 cm)
Mohn Family Trust Collection

Convict leasing "depended upon the heritage of slavery and the allure of industrial capitalism," the combination of which produced a modern system in which capitalist development was forged through structures of antiblack racism and terror. Dandelion and Devil's Ivy arrangement-line, color, mass: death life and surveillance., 2020
sublimation prints on cotton paper, copper wire, plastic, sumi ink, and vase
33 × 21 × 18 in.
(83.3 × 53.3 × 45.7 cm)
Private collection

Exotica, 2020
sublimation prints on cotton paper, copper wire, plastic, and vase
63 × 23 × 20 in.
(160 × 58.4 × 50.8 cm)
Courtesy the artist; Heidi, Berlin; and Galerie Hubert Winter, Vienna

Exotica, 2020
sublimation prints on cotton paper, copper wire, plastic, and vase
60 × 30 × 20 in.
(152.4 × 76.2 × 50.8 cm)
Courtesy the artist; Heidi, Berlin; and Galerie Hubert Winter, Vienna

Exotica, 2020
sublimation prints on cotton paper, copper wire, plastic, sumi ink, and vase
33 × 23 ½ × 22 in.
(83.8 × 59.7 × 55.9 cm)
Courtesy the artist; Heidi, Berlin; and Galerie Hubert Winter, Vienna

Otto Preminger's Carmen Jones-October 28th 1954, Brown v. Board of Education-May 17th 1954, 2020
sublimation prints on cotton paper, copper wire, plastic, and vase
66 × 30 × 22 in.
(167.6 × 76.2 × 55.9 cm)
Private collection

Sea Kelp and Weeping Willow Bouquet, 2020
sublimation prints on cotton paper, copper wire, plastic, and vase
57 × 24 × 23 in.
(144.8 × 61 × 58.4 cm)
Private collection

Transposition, Sketch, Swiss Monstera Candombe potted roots, 2020
collage on paper
36 × 24 in. (91.4 × 61 cm)
Private collection

Bitter Arrangement IV: Overseers, Aerial, apprehension and authorization, 2021
aerosol spray and plastic
40 × 40 × 5 in.
(101.6 × 101.6 × 12.7 cm)
Private collection

Bitter Arrangement V: Descending, subjectivization with/in/out compassion, 2021
aerosol spray and plastic
40 × 40 × 5 in.
(101.6 × 101.6 × 12.7 cm)
Private collection

Black Box, 4 points: Ausdruckstanz and Körperkultur holds Orientalism, Primitivism, Islamophobia, and Anti-Indigenous Ideologies, 2021
xerox collage and ink on paper
41 ½ × 29 ½ in.
(105.4 × 74.9 cm)
Mohn Family Trust Collection

Black Box, 4 points: Greco Biblical Impulse—Clytemnestra, Eurydice, Princes, Queens, and Holofernes, 2021
xerox collage and ink on paper
41 ½ × 29 ½ in. (105.4 × 74.9 cm)
Mohn Family Trust Collection

Black Box, 4 points: Horton, Ailey, McKayle contractions and expansions of drama from vernacular—arms outstretched and entangle, 2021
xerox collage and ink on paper
41 ½ × 29 ½ in. (105.4 × 74.9 cm)
Mohn Family Trust Collection

Black Box, 4 points: Wading in water, Archipelago, Myth, Revelations—B. Gottschild principle—muffled lines and ruptures—hyper-interpretation of Africanist presence(s), 2021
xerox collage and ink on paper
41 ½ × 29 ½ in. (105.4 × 74.9 cm)
Mohn Family Trust Collection

"Britannica" now: choreography, the art of creating and arranging dances. The word derives from the Greek for "dance" and for "write." In the 17th and 18th centuries, it did indeed mean the written record of dances. In the 19th and 20th centuries, however, the meaning shifted, inaccurately but universally, while the written record came to be known as dance notation. In biological taxonomy, race is an informal rank in the taxonomic hierarchy for which various definitions exist. Sometimes it is

used to denote a level below that of subspecies, while at other times it is used as a synonym for subspecies. A race is a grouping of humans based on shared physical or social qualities into categories generally viewed as distinct by society.[1] The term was first used to refer to speakers of a common language and then to denote national affiliations. By the 17th century the term began to refer to physical (phenotypical) traits. Modern science regards race as a social construct, an identity which is assigned based on rules made by society.[2] While partially based on physical similarities within groups, race does not have an inherent physical or biological meaning. [1][3][4] Dance notation, the recording of dance movement through the use of written symbols. Dance notation is to dance what musical notation is to music and what the written word is to drama. In dance, notation is the translation of four-dimensional movement (time being the fourth dimension) into signs written on two-dimensional paper. A fifth "dimension"—dynamics, or the quality, texture, and phrasing of movement—should also be considered an integral part of notation, although in most systems it is not, 2021
artificial plant, fabric grow bag with moss, acrylic paint, and plastic
106 × 33 × 25 in.
(269.2 × 83.8 × 63.5 cm)
Private collection

Hyper-interpretation—to be seated—figures sexualized and anonymized at rest, en largesse to stereotyping distribution, 2021
xerox collage and ink on paper
64 × 47 in. (162.6 × 120.1 cm)
Private collection, Maryland

Notes for Stage, Cult, and Popular Entertainment according to place, person, genre, speech, music, and dance, 2021
xerox collage and ink on paper
48 × 48 in. (121.9 × 121.9 cm)
Antonia Ax:son Johnson Family Collection

On the contrary, a legend gradually formed, which was neither investigated nor questioned. The legend covered the past with a blanket of oblivion: there had been no modern dance, it seems, under the Nazis, just a bit of ballet at the most. Modern German Dance, the so-called Ausdruckstanz, Expressive Dance, it was claimed, belonged to the great tradition of the artistic avantgarde in the early 20th century and hence was by definition progressive. Each instance of its performance according to how well it manifests the intention and the detail of the choreography, might then be thought to have a form outside of performance and that form pre-exists any written documents. Writing about and on behalf of black artists, Locke refused the responsibilities and limits of politics in artwork in favor of "expression." He argued that the purpose of black artwork was not to correct white supremacist misrepresentations of black life or history or to "demonstrate" that black people were, in fact, worthy of social and political inclusion. (That he took for granted, just as he should have.) Rather, Locke thought that (black) artwork should be "expressive of" "Negro life," in all its variety and vitality. Expressiveness was for Locke the mark of the most successful modern art, 2021
collage on artificial plant, fabric grow bag with moss, acrylic paint, and plastic
98 × 42 × 36 in.
(248.9 × 106.7 × 91.4 cm)
Collection of Suzanne McFayden

Where copyright law grants protection to "original works of authorship fixed in a tangible medium of expression," white mainstream culture has historically dismissed African American artistic forms like the blues and jazz as the product of "natural" expression rather than original authorship, that is, as "genes, not genius"—B. Gottschild / the term "vernacular" dancers to refer to those performers who appeared primarily in social clubs, nightclubs, and vaudeville stages, rather than on the high-art concert stage. That modern artists collaborated with Nazism reveals an important aspect of modernism, uncovers the bizarre bureaucracy which controlled culture, and tells the histories of great figures who became enthusiastic Nazis and lied about it later, 2021
collage on artificial plant, fabric grow bag with moss, acrylic paint, and plastic
109 × 40 × 18 in.
(276.9 × 101.6 × 45.7 cm)
Collection of Pamela Thomas-Graham

LENDERS

Galerie Hubert Winter, Vienna
Roxane Gay and Debbie Millman
Hammer Museum, Los Angeles
Heidi, Berlin
The Museum of Contemporary Art, Los Angeles
The Museum of Modern Art, New York
Davida Nemerov
Private collections
Michael Sherman
Kandis Williams

CONTRIBUTORS

Artist and philosopher DENISE FERREIRA DA SILVA is Samuel Rudin Professor in the Humanities and co-director of the Critical Racial & Anti-Colonial Study Co-Laboratory at New York University, and adjunct professor at the Monash University School of Art, Architecture, and Design (Australia). Her artistic and academic works reflect and speculate on themes and questions crucial to contemporary philosophy, aesthetics, political theory, Black thought, feminist thought, and historical materialism. She is the author of *Toward a Global Idea of Race* (2007), *A Divida Impagavel* (2019), and *Unpayable Debt* (2022), and co-editor (with Paula Chakravartty) of *Race, Empire, and the Crisis of the Subprime* (2013). Her artwork includes the films *Serpent Rain* (2016), *4 Waters-Deep Implicancy* (2018), *Soot Breath/Corpus Infinitum* (2020), and *Ancestral Claims/Ancestral Clouds* (2023), in collaboration with Arjuna Neuman; and the relational artistic practices Poethical Readings, Sensing Salon, and Reading with Echo, in collaboration with Valentina Desideri. Her writings have appeared in art spaces such as *Canadian Art*, *Texte zur Kunst*, and *e-flux*.

CHERYL I. HARRIS is Rosalinde and Arthur Gilbert Foundation Chair in Civil Rights and Civil Liberties at UCLA School of Law. A founding faculty member of the Critical Race Studies Program, Harris is the author of the acclaimed essay "Whiteness as Property" (*Harvard Law Review*). Her scholarship focuses on race and property and the Black freedom struggle in shaping American law. An award-winning teacher, she has lectured and been a part of convenings across the globe in Europe, South Africa, Australia, New Zealand, Zimbabwe, and Israel/Palestine. A longstanding member of the National Conference of Black Lawyers, Harris has been a part of human rights delegations reporting on conditions in areas such as Northern Ireland and Haiti. She has played a key role in organizing racial justice campaigns on issues ranging from educational equity to reparative justice. Currently, she is revising Derrick Bell's seminal textbook *Race, Racism and American Law* and working on a project on race, property, and debt.

TAYLOR JASPER is Susan and Rob White Assistant Curator, Visual Arts, at the Walker Art Center. She helped organize *This Must Be the Place: Inside the Walker's Collection* (2024) and the museum's presentation of *Sadie Barnette: The New Eagle Creek Saloon* (2024), and is co-curating (with Jenny Gheith) *Suzanne Jackson: What Is Love* (2026), a major retrospective charting the career of the painter, dancer, poet, teacher, and scenic designer. Previously, she was curatorial associate, visual arts, at the Momentary in Bentonville, Arkansas, where her projects included *Olalekan Jeyifous: All you touch you change. All you change, changes you* (2020) and *Neka King: To Enter Recorded History* (2021–2022), and curatorial research assistant at the Virginia Museum of Fine Arts, where she was an integral part of the curatorial and editorial teams for *The Dirty South: Contemporary Art, Material Culture, and the Sonic Impulse* (2021).

MIREILLE MILLER-YOUNG is associate professor of feminist studies at the University of California, Santa Barbara. Her research has been supported by the W. E. B. Du Bois Advancing Equity through Research Fellowship at Harvard University, the Institute for Cultural Inquiry in Berlin, and the Woodrow Wilson National Fellowship Foundation. Her award-winning book *A Taste for Brown Sugar: Black Women in Pornography* (2014) innovated academic and public discussions on race, porn, and sex work. She was coeditor of *The Feminist Porn Book: The Politics of Producing Pleasure* (2013) and lead coeditor of *Black Sexual Economies: Race and Sex in a Culture of Capital* (2019). Publishing in numerous anthologies and news outlets including *Coming Out Like a Porn Star*, *New York Times*, *Washington Post*, and *$pread*, a sex worker magazine, Miller-Young is currently working on the Black Erotic Archive, a multimodal archival initiative to recover, preserve, and share Black erotic media history.

DENISE RYNER is a writer and curator working in Toronto and Philadelphia, where she is Andrea B. Laporte Curator at the Institute of Contemporary Art, University of Pennsylvania. Recent independently curated projects include *Sediment: The Archive as a Fragmentary Base* (2023–2024) at Concordia University's Leonard & Bina Ellen Art Gallery, Montreal, and the Art Museum at the University of Toronto; and *Ceremony: Burial of an Undead World* (2022), co-curated with Anselm Franke, Elisa Giuliano, Claire Tancons, and Zairong Xiang at Haus der Kulturen der Welt, Berlin. Until 2022 she was director/curator at Or Gallery, Vancouver, British Columbia. She has published critical essays and reviews in *CMagazine*, *Blackflash*, and *Canadian Art* as well as in numerous exhibition catalogues, and was co-editor of *Canadian Art*'s "Chroma" issue (Fall 2020).

MLONDOLOZI ZONDI is an artist and assistant professor of comparative literature at the University of Southern California. Zondi's work is forthcoming or has been published in *TDR: The Drama Review*, *ASAP Journal*, *liquid blackness*, *Contemporary Literature*, *Text and Performance Quarterly*, *Mortality*, *Canadian Journal of African Studies*, *Safundi*, *Performance Philosophy*, *Espace Art Actuel*, and *Propter Nos*.

WALKER ART CENTER BOARD OF TRUSTEES 2024–2025

WALKER ART CENTER STAFF

Ruweyda Ahmed
Rahma Ajaraam
Hannah Allen
Matthew Allen
Aslı Altay
Jacob Andrews
Kristen Andring
Justin Ayd
Maneli Aygani

Nick Barker
Finley Barnes
Lydia Barnes
Doug Benidt
Carol Bessler
Kyle Bilz
Philip Bither
Andrew Bogard
Chase Brenke
Scott Browning
Gabriela Bruner
Roman Buck
Caroline Byrd

Alex Callais
Alexa Carter
Mary Ceruti
Kennedy Christensen
Felice Clark
Robert Cosgrove
Naomi Crocker
Kevin Curran
Doc Czypinski

Janine DeFeo
Liz del Toro
Pablo de Ocampo
Ava Deshazer
David Dick
Andrea Dowd
Donna Dralle
Lilly Drew
Megan Dunn

Judy Earl
Barbara Economon
Sierra Ikwe Edwards
Ryan Ellingson
Spencer Emmanuel
Brandon Eng
Siri Engberg
Nazlı Ercan
Darren Erickson
Hannah Erickson

Catt Fear
Roman Feldhahn
Georgia Feldman
Makenzie Flom
Robert Frank
William "Billy" Gustavo Franklin

Richard Gangelhoff
Sophia Gayle
Teejah Gilfillian
Deborah Girdwood
Matthew Goldencrown
Hannah Goldfarb
Nathan Gould
Ricky Graham
John Greenwald
Jon Grippen
Rosario Güiraldes

Anna Haglin
Jessica Hakala
Peter Hannah
Christopher Harrison
Wyatt Heatherington Tilka
Camille Hempel
Kam Herndon
Kensie Herrick
Grover Hogan
Brian Huddleston
Henriette Huldisch
Amanda Hunt

Aimee Ilkka
Hania Imdad
Tasia Islam

Sam Jamison
Jihea Jang
Taylor Jasper
Eden Johnson
Pamela Johnson
Stephanie Johnson
Jason Jones
Rachel Joyce
Leif Jurgensen

Jonathan Karen
Morgan Kavanagh
Sophie Keiser
Kate Kelley
Alex Kermes
Joe King
Jon Kirchhofer
Christa Kootz
Aili Kotnik
Courtney Kowalke
Svea Krisetya
Sebastian Kulow

Charles LaBerge
Sarah Lampen
Muriel Lang
Sydney Larson
Megan Leafblad
Jordan Lerner
Michael Lind
John Lindell
Doug Livesay
Cuba Lopeztegui
Kaya Lovestrand
John Lyon

Elizabeth MacNally
Julie Magnuson
Jaidyn Martin
Michelle Maser
Dita Masters
Becca Mayo
Kirk McCall
Erin McNeil
Kyle Meerkins
Lena Menefee-Cook
Cortney Mentzos
Deborah Meyer
Aloe Miller
Cheryl Miller
Laura Moran
Kaya Morris
Jeff Morrison
Chelsea Moskal
Michael Muenchow
Diane Mullen
Peter Murphy

Kayla Nordlund
Nastja Nykaza

Sherisa Oie
Mark Owens

Shivani Pargal
Keith Parker
YunYun Patten
Tim Piotrowski
Michelle Poss
Matthew Prediger
Barthollomew Presby
Sarah Purgett
Pavel Pyś

Laurel Rand-Lewis
Sophia Reed
Evan Reiter
Wallace Rice
Jennifer Riestenberg Pepin
Aaron Robinson
Jessica Rolland
Mark Rusch
Aster Ryan

Crystal Sander
Genevieve Satre
Tracy Schultz
Joel Schwarz
Morgan Seemann
Jeffrey Sherman
Gordon Silva
Tammy Smith-Foyt
Diana Soderholm
Ashley Solem
Robert Somers
Marla Stack
Christopher Stevens
Shayne Stockberger
Glen Straight
Summer Stuedell

Kim Hollingsworth Taylor
Francine Teah

Patricia Ledesma Villon
Jesstine Voeltz
Julie Voigt
Jill Vuchetich

Kazjmire Wagner
Kova Walker-Lečić
Leia Wambach
Lydia Wilkie
La'Kayla Williams
Fletcher Wolfe

Ivonne Yañez
Molly Yang
Jake Yuzna

Minna Zhou

All works by Kandis Williams are © Kandis Williams.
The following credits are listed by page number.

JASPER, A METHOD

22, 26, 31, 34–35
Courtesy the artist

25
Courtesy the artist; Galerie Hubert Winter, Vienna; and Heidi, Berlin. Photo: Simon Veres

28
Courtesy The Museum of Contemporary Art, Los Angeles. Photo: Jeff Mclane

32–33
Courtesy the artist. Photo: Inna Svyatsky

RYNER, RETREAT AND RECLAIM

41
Courtesy Institute of Contemporary Art at Virginia Commonwealth University. Photo: David Hale

43
Courtesy Read & Co. Classics

44
Courtesy Night Gallery, Los Angeles. Photo: Nik Massey

46, 50–52
Courtesy the artist

48
Public domain

49
Public domain, via Wikimedia Commons

PLATES

57, 59–60, 64, 67, 71–72, 74, 77, 80–83, 85–87, 90–99, 101, 103–105, 108, 111–113, 115, 117 120–121, 124–125, 138–143, 156–161, 171, 175, 184–189
Courtesy the artist

61, 63, 107, 136–137, 182–183
Courtesy the artist. Photo: Nik Massey

65, 68, 78, 89, 109, 116, 123, 147 (top), 190–193
Courtesy the artist and Heidi, Berlin

69, 73, 75, 79
Courtesy the artist. Photo: Ruben Diaz

119, 134–135
Courtesy the artist and Heidi, Berlin. Photo: Nik Massey

122
Courtesy the artist and Heidi, Berlin. Photo: Joshua White

126
Courtesy Hammer Museum, Los Angeles.

129
Courtesy The Museum of Modern Art. Image © The Museum of Modern Art / Licensed by SCALA / Art Resource, NY

131, 133
Courtesy the artist. Photo: Marten Elder

144–146, 147 (left, right, bottom), 148–153
Courtesy the artist. Photo: Paul Salveson

155
Courtesy The Museum of Contemporary Art, Los Angeles. Photo: Jeff Mclane

163, 165–167, 169, 172–173, 177, 178 (left), 179–180
Courtesy the artist and 52 Walker, New York. Photo: Kerry McFate

178 (right), 181
Courtesy the artist; 52 Walker, New York; and Heidi, Berlin. Photo: Kerry McFate

194–197
Courtesy the artist and Heidi, Berlin. Photo: Marjorie Brunet Plaza

199–201
Courtesy the artist and Heidi, Berlin. Photo: Mizuki Tachibana

202–203, 208–209
Courtesy the artist and Heidi, Berlin. Photo: STUDIO POSSIBLE ZONE

205, 207, 211–212
Courtesy the artist. Photo: Inna Svyatsky

DISPLAY IMAGES

4, 287
Courtesy the artist and Heidi, Berlin

13–16
Courtesy the artist. Photo: Ruben Diaz

53–56, 269–272
Courtesy the artist

213–215
Courtesy the artist and Heidi, Berlin. Photo: Nik Massey

Cover and flaps
Courtesy the artist

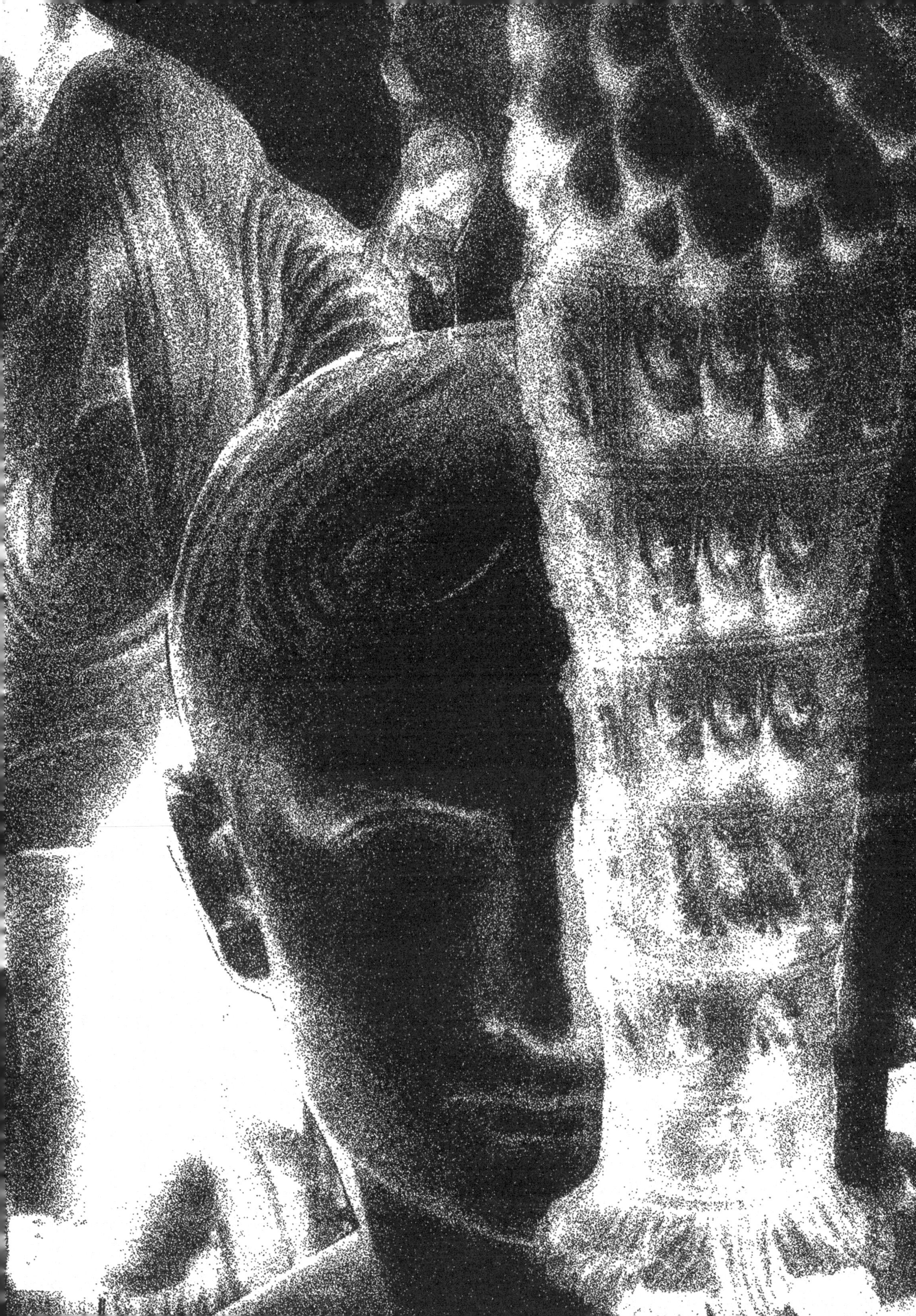

Published on the occasion of the exhibition *Kandis Williams: A Surface*, curated by Taylor Jasper, Susan and Rob White Assistant Curator, Visual Arts, with Laurel Rand-Lewis, curatorial fellow, and organized by the Walker Art Center, Minneapolis.

Walker Art Center, Minneapolis
April 24–August 24, 2025

Kandis Williams: A Surface is organized by the Walker Art Center, with support from the Edward R. Bazinet Charitable Foundation and the Pohlad Family. The exhibition catalogue is supported by Rosina Lee Yue and a grant from the Andrew W. Mellon Foundation in support of Walker Art Center publications.

Available through D.A.P./ Distributed Art Publishers
75 Broad Street, Suite 630, New York, NY 10004
www.artbook.com

ISBN: 9781935963332

Library of Congress Cataloging-in-Publication Data

Names: Jasper, Taylor, editor. | Rand-Lewis, Laurel, editor. | Walker Art Center, organizer, host institution.
Title: Kandis Williams : a surface / curated by Taylor Jasper with Laurel Rand-Lewis.
Description: First edition. | Minneapolis : Walker Art Center, [2025] | Includes bibliographical references. | Summary: "Published in conjunction with the exhibition Kandis Williams: A Surface, this first museum survey offers an in-depth exploration of the artist's versatile practice spanning collage, sculpture, film, performance, writing, pedagogy, and publishing. Williams's multidisciplinary practice leverages the experience of the body alongside personal and communal histories to explore and challenge notions of race, nationalism, authority, and eroticism, among other subjects. Williams is also the founder and editor of Cassandra Press, a publishing and educational platform that produces and distributes Black scholarship"-- Provided by publisher.
Identifiers: LCCN 2024046658 | ISBN 9781935963332 (softcover)
Subjects: LCSH: Williams, Kandis, 1985---Exhibitions.
Classification: LCC NX512.W54 A4 2025 | DDC 709.2--dc23/eng/20241023
LC record available at https://lccn.loc.gov/2024046658

Head of Design, Content, and Communications
Aslı Altay

Director of Design
Mark Owens

Publications Manager
Jake Yuzna

Designer
Nazlı Ercan

Editor
Michelle Piranio

Image Specialist
Sebastiaan Hanekroot, Colour & Books

Proofreader
Dianne Woo

Printed by
die Keure, Belgium

Typefaces
Hawthorn, Feijoa, ABC Marfa
Paperstocks
Muken Lynx, Holmen Book, Sirio

Cover
Kandis Williams, *The Midnight Snack, Well-a, whosonever told it, that he told a- He told a dirty lie, babe. Well-a, whosonever told it, that he told a- He told a dirty lie, well-a. Well-a, whosonever told it, that he told a- He told a dirty lie, babe. Well the eagle on the dollar-quarter, He gonna rise and fly, well-a. He gonna rise and fly, sugar. He gonna rise and fly, well-a. Well the eagle on the dollar-quarter, He gonna rise and fly, well-a (Chorus) Sung by "22", Little Red, Tangle Eye, and Hard Hair, accompanied by double cutting axes*, 2017